Zolar's
Encyclopedia of
ANCIENT
and
FORBIDDEN
KNOWLEDGE

Zolar's
Encyclopedia of
ANCIENT
and
FORBIDDEN
KNOWLEDGE

PRENTICE HALL PRESS • NEW YORK

Published in 1986 by Prentice Hall Press
A Division of Simon & Schuster, Inc.
Gulf + Western Building
One Gulf + Western Plaza
New York, NY 10023

Previously published by Arco Publishing, Inc.

PRENTICE HALL PRESS is a trademark of
Simon & Schuster, Inc.

Zolar.
    Zolar's encyclopedia of ancient and forbidden knowledge.

    Previously published as: The encyclopedia of ancient and
forbidden knowledge.
    1. Occult sciences.   I. Title.   II. Title: Encyclopedia
of ancient and forbidden knowledge.
BF1411.Z64   1984   133   83-15812
ISBN 0-668-05894-3 (Paper Edition)

Manufactured in the United States of America

10   9   8   7   6   5   4   3   2   1

First Prentice Hall Press Edition

DEDICATION

I dedicate this book to those Ancient Wise Men whose diligent application to the Science of the Heavens made this work possible.

All modern research is based upon their findings. Much of my present work has been taken from old out-of-print manuscripts, whose authors have long since passed on. Their written words will herein be preserved for posterity.

Permit me to say, no grander or more soul-enobling theme has ever been presented to the human intellect than the philosophy and language of the Heavens. It opens to our inspection an endless volume of sublime grandeur. Whoever watches fair Venus in her march, with nothing save the philosophy of distance, time, and motion to observe, will find a deep satisfaction — beyond the mundane considerations of the materialistic life.

Unto him who reads the language of the Heavens, and catches the inspiration of her loftier melodies, there is a positive charm and enchantment, which makes every Star a divinity and lights all space with prophetic wisdom.

It is the Wise Man who rules his Stars, and the fool who blindly obeys them.

The Heavenly bodies predispose and influence, but they do not compel.

> Man's wisdom is in no way subjugated, and is no one's slave; it has not renounced or surrendered its freedom.
>
> Therefore the stars must obey man and be subject to him, and not he to the stars.
>
> Even if he is a child of Saturn and if Saturn has overshadowed his birth, he can master Saturn and become a child of the sun.

Paracelsus
Astronomia Magna 1537

There's not a pulse beat in the human frame which
Is not governed by the Heavens above us.
The blood, in all its ebb and flow,
Is swayed by them as certainly as
Are the restless tides of the salt sea
By the resplendent Moon; and at thy birth,
Thy Mother's eyes gazed not more stead-fastly on thee
Than did the Stars that rule thy destiny.

ZOLAR

PREFACE

Most people spend 90% of their time doing what other people want them to do instead of what they want to do themselves. Most people, perhaps you, are haunted by self-destructive feelings they don't understand. These are feelings which may frighten and depress you, for example: the constant fear that other people are somehow better; the fear that you are now, and will always remain, a second-class citizen in life; or the crushing realization that you always feel poor no matter how much money you earn, and always feel inadequate no matter how great your accomplishments.

Because of two crippling pressures — the constant attempts of other people to exploit you and your own self-destructive feelings of inferiority — you spend your life in an emotional prison instead of a palace. You allow yourself to be surrounded by enemies instead of friends. You accomplish only a fraction of what you are really able to accomplish. You find yourself constantly driven away from the real enjoyments, the real achievements, the real meaning, of your life.

Learn to control your destiny. Study the Ancient sciences, for this knowledge will guide you through the present age of anxiety and depression.

The very first step for the reader into the hidden pathway of nature's mysteries is the face-to-face confrontation with a starting fact — the fact that all his preconceptions, all his education, all his accumulated materialistic wisdom, are unable to account for the simple phenomena which transpire and transcend the action and interaction of life forces on the planet on which he lives.

As a chemist, he may pursue the discrete discontinuities of force until they are lost within the realms of the imponderable. "The great unknown," or "the aching void," as it is christened amid the groans of scientific travail, swallows him. But he can get no further.

As a physicist, he may decompose light and sound into what he thinks are their component parts and, with scientific accuracy, dissect before your very eyes these truths as a surgeon would his anatomical subject. No sooner is that point reached than the shy molecules and timid vibrations become alarmed at man's daring presumption, and fly into the realm of the infinite and occult unknown. There in the aching void they sport in delight, safe from man's vulgar intrusion.

The realm of the unknown imponderables is the Universal, an infinite ocean of something, yet nothing, which Science created in her frantic endeavor to account for the material phenomena of the real world. For a time, she was infinitely pleased with her own peculiar offspring, which has now become a restless phantom, a grim, unlovely spectre, which haunts the laboratories of its parent night and day, until at last Science has become frightened at her own child. Now Science tries in vain to slay that ghost of her own creation, but she dares not enter the void she has called into existence, and there pursue and recapture the truant atoms and timid vibrations of this sublunary sphere we call Earth. But much is missing!

Therefore, at the very outset of man's pilgrimage through these vast and "scientifically unknown" regions, the reader had best unload all the heavy and useless baggage of educated opinion and scientific dogmas which he may carry. If he does not, he will find himself top-heavy, and will either capsize or be buried amid the debris of conflicting opinion.

The only equipment which man has found useful, and which will repay the cost of transportation, is an unbiased, open mind, logical reasoning, genuine common sense, and a calm, reflective brain. Anything else on the voyage into the unknown upon which we are now about to embark is simply useless, costly deadweight, hence, so far as modern science is concerned, the less the reader has, the better. If he can use his scientific acquirements merely as aids and crutches in climbing the spiritual steps of Occultism and if he will find Science an auxiliary force, the Science is no longer a sacred cow, but a functional tool.

But this is an exceedingly rare gift, and one seldom found. It also has a delusive snare, because nine out of every ten people cheat themselves into the belief that they possess such an ability; whereas, in reality they are woefully deficient. It is always a safe course to mistrust the absolute in all opinions and reasoning.

Before starting out on such a mighty and important undertaking, we must draw serious attention to the major obstacle of the voyage — the one which will be the most difficult to surmount. This hidden rock, upon which so many profound students of the Occult become shipwrecked, is the failure to realize the duality of Truth. The Truth of appearances. The Truth of realities. The former is relative; the latter is absolute!

If we possess half of anything, we know by the laws of

common sense and logical reasoning that there must be another half somewhere. No subtle twist of metaphysical sophistry can cheat us into the belief that we possess the whole. We know and see that we have just exactly half, and no more.

Futhermore, when we look at any known thing, we know that for it to possess the attributes of a thing it must possess three dimensions — length, breadth, and thickness. This being so, we also know it has, broadly speaking, two sides — an outside and an inside. The outside is not the same as the inside, any more than the boiler is the steam which drives the engine.

This logical process of reasoning is the only chart which has so far been prepared for the Occult explorer. It is vague and probably unsatisfactory; yet, when it is used in conjunction with man's conscious intuition (the only true compass to guide man in his winding, uneven pathway upon the shores of the Infinite), one never need fear being lost or failing in his endeavors to know the Truth.

In order to carry the same line of reasoning a little further, let us take a type of architecture, the Gothic, for example and examine a well-known specimen of this structural conception. The mind will say, "What a beautiful building; how imposing and grand; what a triumph of man's mechanical skill!"

So it appears, and upon the plane of visual appearance, so it really is. Consequently, it is a truth for the time. But when examined in the light of Occult Science, we find this visual truth is only relative. It is only a truth on the external, transitory plane of material phenomena. We see, that in addition to being the result of man's trained mechanical ability, it is the external form of his mental ideal. It is the phenomenal outcome of man's creative attributes.

When we look at this solid building from the earth's plane, we only see the outside of an object having length, breadth, and thickness. We know there must be an inside, but we must enter the interior plane before we can see it. Therein we shall find the building as it exists within the subjective world of its architect. The solid stone edifice will crumble to decay and fall; in the end not one material particle will remain to indicate the place whereon it stood. Hence, the building was not real; it was only a passing appearance assumed by matter under the moulding forces of man's mechanical ability. When the forces which gave it shape and form became polarized by the restless oceans of planetary magnetism, it dissolved and finally vanished "like the baseless fabric of a dream."

Even though the external structure of stone and mortar was lost within the realms of "the great unknown," the idea which created it was eternal. It was a spiritual reality. Therefore, the idea was the absolute truth, reality, yet the actual nonreality of stone appeared to be the real.

It is these delusive appearances which created the confusion regarding the exact meaning of the terms "Spirit" and "Matter." Science refers all she cannot grapple with to some undiscovered forces of Matter, whereas Theology refers them to the Spirit. Both are right, and both are wrong!

As we explore the territory belonging to both Spirit and Matter during the progress of our journey, we will state that Spirit and Matter, as we know them, are but the duality of expression of the one great Deific principle. The duality is due to a difference in polarity. Spirit and Matter are a unity under two modes of action. This duality can be comprehended in its true relationship when viewed from both planes and realized by the true science of correspondence. Science is but a material system of symbolism from which we regulate our conceptions of all things.

Plato said that ideas rule the world. And Plato was right; for, before the devine ideal was evolved from within the divine sensorium, the Universe was not. The result of the divine ideal was the creation of a pure symbolic form.

Just as symbols are the product of ideas, so in their turn, ideas are the symbols of thought. Thought itself is but the symbolic response of the Self to the pulsating throb of the radiant Soul. Beyond this we cannot penetrate, even in our most exalted conceptions. Thus, all serious study and medition as to the nature and existence of God is unprofitable, and cannot bring the reader any substantial return either in this world or the next. The infinite can never be comprehended by the finite. We must rest satisfied with the certain knowledge that we can, by one grand chain of sequences, trace the transmission of thoughts, ideas, and symbolic forms to their divine source.

The angelic world is but a prototype or symbolic expression of the divine sphere of the Infinite. The celestial world is but a reflection of the angelic. The spiritual world is the prototype and the symbolic outcome of the celestial heavens. The Astral is the reflection of the spiritual sphere. And lastly, the material is but the concrete shadow of the Astral Kingdoms.

Now the reader can preceive how we, in our present state, are a long way down on the scale of creative life. But if we exist, we know by the laws of our being that we can and shall sind our way back through this valley of the shadow. We can leave this plane of inverted images and delusive appearances for the bright realms of our former state. There in those spheres of pure angelic life we can exist with the everliving reality of all the infinitude of apparent realities.

CONTENTS

THE OLDEST SCIENCE IN THE WORLD
page 1

BOOK 1
Ancient and Forbidden Knowledge

BOOK 11
The Art
of Prophecy

Zolar's
Encyclopedia of
ANCIENT
and
FORBIDDEN
KNOWLEDGE

The Oldest Science
in the World

Before we can discuss what is the oldest science in the world, we must arrive at some conclusion as to the definition of science. What exactly is science? Buckets and buckets of ink have been used in defining the word, but they all boil down to the statement: Science is knowledge arrived at by the scientific method. Even more buckets of ink have been used in trying to define scientific method. The essential of the method may easily be described. They are a series of steps, the first of which is direct observation.

Of course, what the scientist observes is often the result of deliberately contrived experimentation. Contrived in some cases, as it were, to reveal what the scientist wants to see. After such a scientist has made a whole string of direct observations, he goes into a huddle with himself, pulls his beard, scratches his head, or perhaps contemplates his navel. From all of this he forms an hypothesis or an explanation of some kind for the things he designed the observations and experiments to reveal. This hypothesis is a guess — an educated guess, perhaps, but still a guess.

The next step is a simple one. The scientist says to himself, "I know my idea is right, and if I do some more experiments I will be able to prove it." The final step, then, for this scientist, is to do the new experiment. If the experiment proves his guess, everything is fine. But if it doesn't — which is often the case — he uses Finagle's Laws and introduces a constant into the mathematics or a fudge factor into the experiment. Frequently, merely fudging a little doesn't really prove the original hypothesis, so he takes one other step and draws on the truly mystical realm of mathematics — the art of juggling figures. Now the hypothesis is substantiated, and it can be called a theory. The theory is nothing, then, but a well-tested guess.

Yet such scientists have overwhelming confidence in their own ability, and thus make no attempts to teach the limitations of science. In fact, they rarely recognize the limitations. But there are limits to science.

Let us consider the question: Can science disprove ghosts? Many students of modern science would agree that science has found no evidence, nor reason to suspect evidence, of spirits. Such things are only superstitions. But ghosts and spirits *can* appear when the psychological conditions are exactly right. Perhaps one of the very necessary conditions for the appearance of any ghost is the absence of a modern scientist. What then? Science would and could investigate ghost after ghost but no evidence of ghosts would be found. And ghosts would continue to appear when the cynical scientists weren't looking.

This is a very simple case, yet it illustrates the true impossibility of disproving things by the scientific method. Perhaps this is the case in the current investigation into flying saucers. The Air Force and the scientists seem much more interested in disproving their existence than they are in proving it.

Not many years ago any claim about unknown forces from outside our world affecting the lives and behavior of human beings would have thrown scientists into an uproar. To accept such a concept would have been to acknowledge a belief in Astrology. To the cynical scientist, believing in Astrology is like believing in ghosts or witchcraft.

Paradoxically, scientists consider Sir Isaac Newton one of the greatest of all scientists. They conveniently forget that

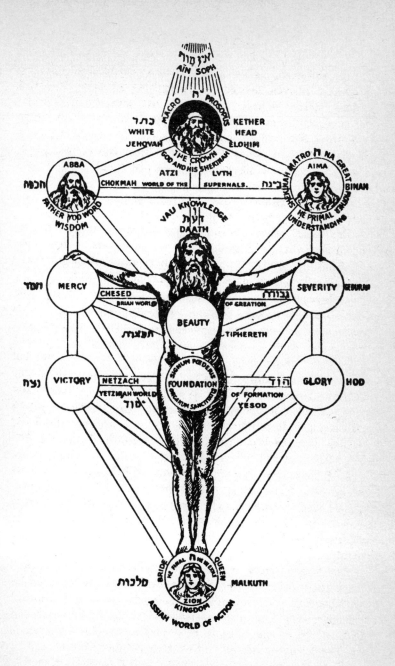

THE SACRED TREE OF THE SEPHIROTH

Newton chose Astrology as his life's work! It was with great reluctance that he took up the study of astronomy. He accused his colleagues of thinking too materialistically. He also accused them of neglecting the real cause of events. When fellow members of the Royal Society — true-blue scientists — asked Newton why he believed in Astrology, he replied, "I do not believe in a universe of accidents and, after all, I have studied the subject and you haven't."

Other notable men who firmly believed in Astrology were Chaucer, Dante, Shakespeare, Cromwell, Copernicus, Kepler, Plato, and Bacon. The great Nostradamus based all his predictions on Astrology.

Astrology is the oldest science in the world. It had its origins in the worship of the moon. Through the long nights before any history books were written, generations upon generations of savages sat and contemplated the wondrous and orderly procession of the seasons and the shining stars in the heavens. Man soon gave them names, and the names were those of the animal spirits he worshipped.

In Mesopotamia, archaeologists have unearthed clay tablets recording astrological events which are over sixty centuries old. Five thousand years ago the astrologer-priests predicted the flooding of the rivers by watching the starry heavens. The Assyrian priests discovered the Zodiac and its twelve divisions. They even learned to calculate the irregular paths of the major planets and predicted eclipses.

In the early days, Astrology was a bloody, religious faith. It was reserved for the king and rich, powerful citizens. When a major event occurred in the heavens, a ritual murder frequently occurred. Such murders rivaled the blood baths of the Aztecs.

Yet Astrologers of the ancient world were the Wise Men who were the earliest mathematicians and who arranged the first calendars. These same Astrologers were the founding fathers of the first universities, and they built the world's first skyscrapers in order to observe the stars in the heavens.

The ancients discovered that each planet controlled the health of certain parts of the body, and they thought certain food plants grew best when planted during the full moon.

Charlemagne, William the Conqueror, and the Crusaders required the sanction of the stars. War, peace, treaties, coronations, marriages, operations — all these required a special horoscope. The poisoning Borgias cast horoscopes before giving arsenic to their enemies. Until just before the Spanish-American War, medicine depended on Astrology. Herbs, plants, and elixirs were all more potent when gathered or manufactured during the proper phase of the moon.

During the late nineteenth century and the early years of the twentieth century, prior to World War I, Astrology fell into disrepute. The centuries of opposition by religion, philosophy, and science drove it underground. Einstein's works were the vogue!

In World War II the "royal art" played an odd role in the management of this great war. Hitler had a battery of Astrologers and planned his campaigns on the basis of their horoscopes. There was nothing for Roosevelt and Churchill to do but to employ a special supersecret Astrologer to tell them what the German Astrologers were telling Adolph Hitler.

Even so, the cynical scientific opinion was that Astrology was nothing more than a form of witchcraft or mysticism. At best, it was accepted only as a pseudo science. Today, however, the climate is rapidly changing. There is evidence emerging which shows even the cynics that what goes on in the heavens may have cause-effect connections with all of us here on earth.

The great Swiss psychiatrist, Carl G. Jung, was intrigued by Astrology. Astrologers have always known that by comparing the horoscopes of married couples, or couples about to be married, they can determine actual or future harmony or disharmony. Jung began using horoscopes to examine the planetary aspects in the charts of 483 married couples (966 persons). He used a large group of single couples who hadn't met as his control group. His remarkable conclusion was: "The statistical material shows that a practical as well as a theoretically improbable chance combination occurred which coincides in the most remarkable way with traditional Astrological expectations. That such a coincidence should occur at all is so improbable and so incredible that nobody could have dared predict anything like it. It really does look as if the statistical material had been manipulated and arranged so as to give the appearance of a positive result."

Even though the cynical scientists are becoming interested in Astrology again, they are still reluctant to acknowledge their interest. A few, though, do speak out. Frank Brown, a biologist at Northwestern University, has demonstrated that oysters sense the position of the moon and regulate their activities by it. Ordinarily oysters open and close their shells in phase with the ocean tides. Doctor Brown wanted to see what oysters would do if there were no tides. He hauled some out of the sea off New Haven, Connecticut, shipped them to Evanston, Illinois, and put them indoors in a tank of seawater at an even temperature under a steady, dim light. For two weeks they continued to open and close their shells in phase with the tides at their old ocean home.

Abruptly they changed their rhythm. Their shell-opening cycle slipped into phase with the tides which would have existed in Chicago had there been an ocean covering Illinois. His hypothesis was that it is not the ebb and flow of tidal water, but the position of the moon itself which governs the oysters' behavior. The mystery now is, What is the force from the moon which causes this?

It is a statistical fact that the birthdays of geniuses, of criminals, of the mentally deranged, tend to be grouped in seasons; for example, persons born in March tend to outlive those born in the summer months, and geniuses are born more frequently in the spring. Physiologists explain these statistics by talking about seasonal variations in maternal nutrition during the pregnancy or seasonal changes in the endocrine activity of the mother, exposing the fetus to differing hormonal environments.

It is well established that the earth's atmosphere contains an electric current composed of ascending negative ions and descending positive ions. This field varies with the seasons and Zodiac and could conceivably influence maternal metabolism during gestation.

Business cycles were for many years believed to coincide with sunspot intensity. One explanation was that sunspots cause magnetic and ionic storms which alter the ionic equilibrium of the atmosphere. If the proportion of positive ions increases, it would cause headaches and malaise, thus depressing morale and causing a slump in business activity.

A meteorologist of the Radio Corporation of America once investigated the effect of various planets on electric storms in the ionosphere and developed formulae which were very similar to those used by Astrologers in their calculations of the influence of planets on personalities. Although no scientist has yet determined the physiologic or psychologic effects of ionic storms on the individual, the problem remains open.

German seismologist Rudolf Tomascheck found that strong earthquakes usually occur when Uranus is within fifteen degrees of the meridian. Two of the world's worst tremors took place when Uranus was in a very specific aspect in relation to several other planets. It is highly possible that changes in the interplanetary gravitational field might produce a "tide" within the earth's molten core. This "tide" would place a heavier stress on a surface fault and thus earthquakes would occur.

The "Third Eye" or pineal gland, which was Descartes' site of the soul, is now considered a "clock" for the onset of puberty. It is definitely affected by the planets and the seasons.

Throughout the history of time, man has always wanted to know and understand the world in which he lives. It has been the custom to treat many of man's attempts at knowledge of nature as folly and superstition, or as pure nonsense. Currently it is the custom when teaching the history of science to state, "True science started with Thales." But man has always asked questions about the universe in which he lives. It is far too easy, and really immature, for the modern scientist to dismiss ancient knowledge and science as crude contrived superstition. It takes knowledge and experience to compare and judge ideas and beliefs which arise from a different mode of life than that of the world today.

The world has affected man in many ways, and has always left strong emotional imprints upon his mind. Fire, flood, crop failure, disease, defeat, and misfortune directly affected man's fate and well-being. Such things as comets, eclipses, and the stars were observed carefully and studied. These phenomena impressed man, and he believed they were vital to his life and welfare. Theories and hypotheses were devised for the coordination and interpretation of the sensory data collected. Early man developed these theories and hypotheses to the best of his ability and not because of fear or superstition. Many such theories failed to survive when time, ideas, values, tools, and basic assumptions changed with man's ever upward progress. New theories were found more acceptable and replaced the old. The old theories, however, were not acts of childishness or idiocy. In reality, these old theories were modified, expanded, and changed gradually over the years to form the new concepts.

The Astrological outlook was a set of hypotheses which filled a vacancy in the mind of early man. This outlook has outlasted any purely emotional or prejudiced beliefs. In spite of its repeatedly being challenged and attacked by materialistic and fatalistic tenets the Astrological outlook remains important today.

Astrology found its support among the most learned as well as among the common people, and this is why it has endured for nearly six millennia. It was deep within the womb of Astrology that Astronomy was nurtured, and there has never been any competition or conflict between the two. They were very closely connected and inseparable for many centuries.

From natural Astrology came the calendar and the ability of man to predict the movements of the sun, moon, and various planets. Natural Astrology advanced through the ages and in time was able to predict eclipses of the sun and moon and the appearance of comets. Judicial or mundane Astrology was studied as a method of predicting and foretelling the future. Not only was it studied to determine the character and fate of various individual men, but it was also studied to predict plagues, wars, earthquakes, and other natural and historical events. It is this branch of ancient Astrology which is the Astrology of today. It was, and is, thought by many of the cynical to be a pseudo science, and is jumbled together with palmistry, numerology, and magic.

Yet, Astrology is defined as the study of the sun, moon, planets, and stars. It is disappointing that the modern scientist has not examined this age old science with the modern methods and tools of present day technology, to prove, or disprove, the effect of the heavenly bodies upon the affairs and well-being of mankind.

Alchemy has faired better throughout recorded history; it is readily accepted as the forerunner of modern chemistry. The modern chemist has even succeeded in the principal purposes of medieval Alchemy. It is now possible to change base metals into gold and silver. Pharmacological chemistry is now approaching the other great goal of Alchemy by seeking substances which will cure the physical and mental ailments of man. Modern pharmacy has enabled mankind to live longer and healthier lives. The medieval Alchemist was unable to do either, but he made the basic chemical discoveries which led to modern day molecular and atomic chemistry.

Most modern day chemists are willing to credit the medieval Alchemist with scientific achievement. The alchemical workshops even resembled the modern chemical experimental laboratory. But the original four Greek elements of earth, air, fire, and water have now been expanded into well over a hundred.

	DRY	WET
COLD	Earth	Water
HOT	Fire	Air

Empedocles taught that everything was formed of these four elements mixed in different proportions by attractive and repulsive tendencies. The four elements were themselves formed by the attractions or repulsions of two pairs of contrasting qualities or cosmic forces.

Alchemy contained many highly theoretical components which were derived from the abstract philosophers, such as Empedocles, Plato, and Aristotle. Yet, the immediate observed events, the sight of compound changing color, vapor turning to metal, or water turning to air — these were undeniable facts. These were also subject to the Alchemist's control, for he could repeat them at will.

Neither Astrology nor Alechmy was ever an obstacle to progress. Progress always requires change — change in ideas and change in beliefs. Yet, all change is not a forward progress. A change of ideas or change of beliefs can result in extreme scepticism and regression.

Science should be viewed as an aspect of human behavior and founded on a cultural matrix. True knowledge comes from deep human understanding — an understanding which is sympathetic and not critical. Such should be one's approach to the study of Astrology and the Occult. Both have been with us since before the coming of a written history; they have survived thousands of years and will continue to survive for many more.

Man is ever seeking ways to control his fate and destiny. Man is ever asking questions about his Universe. No question should ever be considered foolish, superstitious, or stupid if it concerns where and whence man came, where man goest, or why is man.

BOOK I

The lure of the unknown and the lure of hidden things have long intrigued the human mind. Along with such skills as throwing rocks and fashioning flintstone spearheads, primitive man developed more subtle crafts, such as foretelling the weather by the ways the birds flew or the winds blew. From those beginnings came modern sciences like ballistics and meteorology; and the same applies in many other instances.

Two factors were present in most primitive sciences: the Psychic and the Occult. The practitioner of a craft possessed a special faculty not given to ordinary mortals, enabling him to gain unique results and issue reliable forecasts. He backed this up by knowledge of secret subjects which he was pledged not to reveal. This combination of psychic power and occult learning has persisted into modern times. Skilled artists regard their work as "inspired" and rely on "trade secrets" for results. So the pattern is similar, even though many things that once created awe and wonderment are now explained by modern science. The cycle may now be bringing us to new wonders, perhaps including some revivals from the past.

The Kabbalah is a metaphysical system by which the elect shall know God and the Universe. It will raise him above common knowledge and make him understand the profound meaning and the plan of creation. These secrets are immanent in Holy Writ, yet not grasped by he who understands the texts literally. The Old Testament is a book of symbols; its narrations are the mantle in which are clothed sublime revelations.

These simple accounts are not the whole truth. If this were so, Writ could not be called the Book of Books; if the wise men of today would meet and compose collectively a similar book, it would without doubt be more coherent, less obscure and less shocking.

The Hebrew letters in which the sacred texts are written are not just signs invented by man for the recording of things, events and thoughts. Letters and numbers are reservoirs of divine power.

1

The Kabbalah

When man cannot understand nature, and insofar as he cannot understand it at any point, he is confronted with an actual vacuum, and into this he projects himself. What is sought in Alchemy or the Hermetic Books or the Memphite Theology, or in fads like flying saucers, is the basic spiritual pattern of the human mind in symbolic garb, as it presents itself in the individual and behind that, in the enduring structures of the human organism.

As the speculative constructions of religion fall away as explanations of "reality," they assume the character of symbolic masks of the states of the Soul. If they persist in the practices of a cult, we say they have been etherealized. It is precisely their irrationality which keeps this dogma and ritual alive. If they can be reduced to "commonsense" explanations or denials they soon die away. Only the mysteries survive, because they correspond to the processes of man's internal life — outward visible signs of inner spiritual realities.

Kabbalism dates back into the most obscure past of Judaism. What are the distinguishing ideas of Kabbalism? It is first of all a theory of emanations (degenerative monism, philosophically). The inscrutable Godhead fills and contains the Universe. To become active and creative, God emanated ten *sephiroth* or intelligences. A special prominence is given to one of these emanations, which functions as a female principal in the Deity. This is the final emanation, Malkuth the Queen, the physical manifestation of Deity in the Universe. She is thought of as a divine woman — the Bride of God.

Finally, the "innermost secrets" of the Kabbalah are what are *Occult* in all occultism, erotic mysticism, and a group of practices of the sort we call yoga. For the Kabbalist the ultimate sacrament is the sexual act, carefully organized and sustained as the most perfect mystical trance. Over the marriage bed hovers the *Shekinah*. Kabbalism also includes a group of divinatory and magical practices, manipulations of the alphabet, magic spells, and rites. All of these elements go back to very early days. It is these beginnings which shed most light on scholarly Kabbalism and go far to illuminate the real, the abiding, spiritual meaning. By and large the special details of Kabbalism are what is Occult in occultism everywhere; most of the world's religions can be reinterpreted in these terms, which give Kabbalism its fascination and its substance.

Kabbalism is probably the only religious movement of the Gnostic type to come full circle — to create mysteries and explain them, to hide secrets and discover them, and come at last back to the greater mystery from which it started, with deeper insights and wider knowledge. Insight and knowledge of what? In the last analysis, of the human soul, of man within himself, united with another in marriage, united with his fellows in love.

In modern times there have been all sorts of rationalizing, philosophizing, psychologizing movements which have in fact accomplished similar ends. These are either eccentric indiviuals or modern sophisticated cults. No matter who wrote or gathered and edited the tracts of the *Zohar*, it shows all the signs of being perfectly natural.

The Kabbalah, playing as it does such an important part in the unveiling of the Scriptures, must be understood by those who wish to enter into the details and comprehend fully the methods used by Kabbalists. Hence, the first and most important question to be answered is, what is the Kabbalah?

It is easy to give an explanation of the meaning of the word itself, for its root is *Kbl,* which means "to receive;" hence, the Kabbalah is the "received" doctrine. It is the esoteric side of the scriptures of the doctrine of the heart, in contradistinction to the doctrine of the eye — the inner Truth as opposed to the outer form.

There is, however, no Book of the Kabbalah, no manuscript called "The Kabbalah;" but many manuscripts and books were written based upon the Kabbalistic knowledge, and these different works are known collectively as the Kabbalah. They are, however, merely opinions and statements embodying the ideas of the Hidden Wisdom. These have been taught to companies of students by the teachers of the Secret Doctrine even though they were seldom written down.

We have to remember, however, when entering upon a study of the Kabbalah, that it is to be viewed in three ways: historically, as regards the documents, etc.; in reference to the Kabbalistic methods of teaching and unveiling the mysteries hidden in the Scriptures; and finally, as the Kabbalah, the Wisdom itself, or Spirit, Soul, and Body. Everything in the whole Universe must of necessity be threefold, as will be proved later. The Kabbalah is no exception.

It is well to remember these distinctions and to realize the difference between the Kabbalistic wisdom, the means of production, and the product or appearance. The Kabbalah, then, viewed from this point of view, is not a book as so often thought, just as the Occult teaching, the Secret Doctrine, is not a book, even though *The Secret Doctrine* happens to be the name of a book containing many of its teachings.

What, then, is the Kabbalah, and whence does it

originate? These questions have puzzled the minds of many scholars in the past and still continue to puzzle many in the present, especially those who endeavor to fix and tabulate the Ancient Wisdom. They are those who do not look beyond the surface.

Hitherto nothing definite has been settled as to the origin of the Kabbalah. As regards the documentary evidence, there are few historical facts of an exact kind upon which the intellectual writers could fall back; hence, many have been driven into the realm of surmise and opinion.

One declares, repeating the information given in a very old manuscript, that this wisdom was given by God himself to a company of angels. Esoterically speaking, he may be correct, if he thinks of an Avatar in the place of a personal God, and of Masters instead of Angels. Another declares the Kabbalah, or rather that part of it comprised under the title *Zohar,* is the work of Simeon ben Yochai, who lived at the time of the destruction of the second Hebrew Temple. Others declare it is a modern invention and the work of Moses de Leon.

All seem to forget that the Kabbalah itself, being the expression of Cosmic Truth, can have had no actual beginning, but must be as eternal as Truth itself!

It is reasonable to suppose, and many other Occultists who have an excellent knowledge of the past declare, that there were always some great ones upon earth with a knowledge of the Secret Wisdom or Kabbalah. There were, indeed, always men who knew of these doctrines, and they were continually giving them out to the world in different lands at different epochs as required — sometimes in one form and at other times in another, but ever it was the same Truth. Veiled in the teachings of the Kabbalah or the vehicle for the Divine Wisdom, it is eternal, for it is the means of manifesting the knowledge stored up in the memory of Nature.

This Aether of space is a veritable picture gallery, or rather a kinematograph which, when wound up by the initiated seer, shows picture after picture of the Past. These pictures are the true memory of Nature impressed upon Aether of Akasha, just as human memory of the past is impressed upon the matter of man's brain. If the one statement is found to be reasonable then the other is not a whit less so.

In this sense, the Kabbalah had no beginning except as the world itself had a beginning, and man himself had a beginning, for the Divine Wisdom is Eternal in the Heavens.

But there must have been a time when the wisdom was first promulgated, when these Kabbalistic doctrines were first given out to students. True, but then we have to consider our knowledge of history does not take us far enough back into the time stream. Wherever we look, apart from the ordinary historical records, we find this inner teaching has existed.

We see it hidden in the ancient writings of South America, in the temples and on the stones and monuments of Egypt, in sacred writings the world over, in Sanskrit, in Greek, in Latin, and in Chinese. It is found in any sacred writing which is truly sacred, one which is capable of teaching Truth to man.

In the Vedas it looms large; it is to be found upon the papyri of the Priests of Egypt, on the stones of Assyria and Babylon, in the writings of the ancient Persians and Sassanians, and in all countries and in all climes. In Peru and in other parts of America, in China, in Japan, and throughout Asia, Africa, Europe, and Australia, everywhere traces of this great ancient wisdom are found.

It is, however, sufficient to know that the Kabbalistic works date back considerably. The date can be placed to the doctrines of the ancient Egyptians, and it may be said that in the opinion of many students, the Kabbalistic teachings were undoubtedly of Egyptian and Chaldaic origin as far as the Jews were concerned.

The Book of *Zohar* is said to have originated with Rabbi Simeon ben Yochai. The Book of *Zohar* is said by its compiler to have been discovered in a cavern where it had lain for many years; it is not an unlikely tale. It is quite reasonable to suppose Moses de Leon did find some old manuscripts written by the disciples of Rabbi Simeon in the second century. He could have edited them, rearranged their teachings, and added some of his own wisdom — of which he had an abundance. However, this does not dispose of the fact that the Kabbalah itself is of infinitely greater antiquity even if a few of its doctrines may have been written down in the second century. Hence, the student is reminded that the study of Kabbalah is not exclusively a Jewish work, but the work of ancient students of the Occult, whose ideas are beyond the reach of sectarian differences.

The history of books is not important after all; it is "The Thing-in-Itself" which matters to the truth seeker. Let us, then, leave these dates and data, for the history of the Kabbalah has not yet been, nor ever will be, written by any scholar whose knowledge is in his head only.

The ancient races preserved the remembrance of a primitive book, written in hieroglyphs by Sages of the earliest epoch of our world. It was simplified and vulgarized in later days, and its symbols furnished letters to the art of writing, characters to the Word, and the signs to all true philosophy.

This book was attributed by the Hebrews to Enoch, seventh master of the world after Adam; by the Egyptians to Hermes; and by the Greeks to Cadmus, the mysterious builder of the Holy City. This book was the symbolical summary of all primitive tradition, called subsequently Kabbalah, meaning "reception."

The tradition in question rests on the one dogma of Magic: "The visible is for us the proportional measure of the invisible." Now the ancients, observing that equilibrium is the universal law in physics and follows the apparent opposition of two forces, argued from physical to metaphysical equilibrium. They maintained that in the First Living and Active Cause there must be recognized two properties which are necessary one to another. These were stability and motion, necessity and liberty, rational order and volitional autonomy, justice and love, whence also severity and mercy. And these two attributes were personified, so to speak, by the Kabbalistic Jews.

According to the Kabbalah, this is the groundwork of all

religions and all sciences — triple triangle and a circle. The notion of this triad was explained by the balance multiplied by itself in the domains of the ideal. From it came the realization of this conception in symbolic forms. The ancients attached the first notion of this simple and impressive theology to the idea of numbers and qualified the figure of the first decade in the following manner:

1. The Crown, the equilibrating power *(Kether)*.
2. Wisdom, equilibrated in its unchangeable order by the initiative of intelligence *(Chokmah).*
3. Active Intelligence, equilibrated by Wisdom *(Binah)*.
4. Mercy, which is Wisdom in its secondary conception, ever benevolent because it is strong *(Chesed)*.
5. Severity, necessitated by Wisdom itself, and by good will. To permit evil is to hinder good *(Geburah)*.
6. Beauty, the luminous conception of equilibrium in forms, intermediary between the Crown and the Kingdom, the mediating principle between Creator and Creation, or a sublime conception of poetry and its sovereign priesthood *(Tifereth)*.
7. Victory, the eternal triumph of intelligence and justice *(Nesah)*.
8. Eternity, the conquests achieved by mind over matter, active over passive, life over death *(Hod)*.
9. Foundation, the basis of all belief and all truth, the *Absolute* in philosophy *(Yesod)*.
10. The Kingdom, the Universe, the entire Creation, the work and mirror of God, the proof of all supreme reason, the formal consequence which compels us to have recourse to virtual premises, the enigma which has God for its answer. Supreme and Absolute Reason *(Malkuth)*.

Here is the religious and Kabbalistic key of the Tarot, formulated in technical verses after the mode of the ancient and wise lawgivers.

1. A Conscious, Active Cause in all we see,
2. And number proves the living unity.
3. No bound hath He who doth the whole contain
4. But, all preceding, fills life's vast domain.
5. Sole worthy worship, He, the only Lord,

6. Doth His true doctrine to clean hearts accord.
7. But since faith's works a single pontiff need,
8. One law have we, and at one altar plead;
9. Eternal God for aye their base upholds.
10. Heaven and man's day alike His rule enfolds.
11. In mercy rich, in retribution strong,
12. His people's King He will upraise ere long.
13. The tomb gives entrance to the promised land, Death only ends; life's vistas still expand.
14. Good angels all things temper and assuage,
15. While evil spirits burst with wrath and rage.
16. God doth the lightning rule, the flame subdue.
17. His word controls both Vesper and her drew.
18. He makes the moon our watchman through the night,
19. When dust to dust returns, His breath can call,
20. Life from the tomb which is the fate of all.
21. His crown illuminates the mercy seat,
22. And glorifies the cherubs at His feet.
23. These doctrines sacred, pure and steadfast shine;
24. And thus we close our number's scale divine.

Four suits present the Name of every name.
THE FOUR ACES
Four brilliant beams adorn His crown of flame.
THE FOUR TWOS
Four rivers ever from His wisdom flow.
THE FOUR THREES
Four proofs of His intelligence we know.
THE FOUR FOURS
Four benefactions from His mercy come.
THE FOUR FIVES
Four times four sins avenged His justice sum.
THE FOUR SIXES
Four rays unclouded make His beauty known.
THE FOUR SEVENS
Four times His conquest shall in song be shown.
THE FOUR EIGHTS
Four times He triumphs on the timeless plane.
THE FOUR NINES
Foundations four His great white throne maintain.

THE FOUR TENS
One fourfold kingdom owns His endless sway,
As from His crown there streams a fourfold ray.

By this simple arrangment the Kabbalistic meaning of each card is shown. We can thus understand how the ancient pontiffs proceeded to make the oracle speak. The chance dealing of the Tarot deck invariably produced a fresh Kabbalistic meaning, exactly true in its combinations, which alone were fortuitous. Seeing that the faith of the ancients attributed nothing to chance, they read the answers of Providence in the oracles of the Tarot.

As to the Court Cards, a final couplet will suffice to explain them:

KING, QUEEN, KNIGHT, PAGE
The married pair, the youth, the child, the race;
Thy path by these to Unity retrace.

The Kabbalist's task is to unriddle this hidden meaning through methods handed down by tradition. The verities thus gathered are in accord with the principles established by the founders. But who were these founders? History and legend disagree on this point. In Kabbalistic writings we read God Himself revealed the Kabbalah to mankind in Biblical times.

Adam received a Kabbalistic book from the angel Raziel; and through this wisdom he was enabled to overcome the grief of his fall and to regain dignity. The Book of Raziel was handed down to Solomon, who by its power subdued earth and hell. The book *Yetzirah* is attributed to Abraham; but the prevalent Jewish opinion is that on Sinai, Moses received the key of how to interpret mystically the Scriptures.

A cosmogony based upon letters existed in Israel 150 years before our Christian era. It is also likely that the Hebrew priesthood heeded oral traditions, as did the priests of other nations. Empirical lore lived beside the Scriptures, for Esdras refers to the revelation made to Moses by God: "These words thou shalt declare and these thou shalt hide . . ." (Exodus II, 14:5-6).

Remnants of so venerable an age are evident in the numerous works of the Kabbalah. Many of its ideas are latent in the apocalyptic texts written in the first and second century of our era. Yet the origin of a well-defined Kabbalistic doctrine must be placed in eternity.

How strange the destiny of the Jews, those scapegoats, martyrs and saviours of the world. A people full of vitality, a bold and hardy people, which persecutors have failed to destroy, for they have not yet accomplished their mission.

The monarchs of science are the priests of truth, and their sovereignty is hidden from the common multitude. The kings of science are men who know truth, and the truth has made them free. If you hold by anything in this world more than reason, truth, and justice; if your will be uncertain and vacillating; if logic alarms you; if the naked truth makes you blush; if you are hurt when your errors are found, do not read this. At the same time, do not claim it as a pack of dangerous lies.

The Astrologer avails himself of a force which he knows; the sorcerer seeks to misuse one he does not understand. The Astrologer is the sovereign pontiff of Nature; the sorcerer is her profaner.

To know. To dare. To will. To keep silent!

Man becomes king of the beasts only by subduing or taming them, otherwise he would be their victim. The world is a field of battle. Liberty struggles with inertia by its opposition of active and vital force.

Dictators are millstones. If you cannot be the miller, you must be the grain. He alone can possess the pleasure of love who has conquered the love of pleasure. To be able to forbear is to be strong. To yield to the forces of nature is to follow the stream of negative life and to be the slave of minor causes. To resist and subdue nature is to make for one's self a personal and imperishable life.

To succeed in performing something we must know what is proposed, or at least we must have faith in someone who does know. The intelligence and will of man are instruments of incalculable power and capacity. Intelligence and will possess an instrument of faculty which is imperfectly known, the omnipotence of which belongs to the domain of Astrology.

Supreme intelligence is of necessity reasonable. God may only be an hypothesis, but he is an hypothesis imposed by good sense on true human reason. Necessity, liberty, and reason — these are the great supreme Triad. Fatality, will, and power — such is the divine Triad.

Fatality is the inevitable sequence of causes and effects in their determined order. Will is the directing faculty of intelligent forces for the conciliation of freedom with the necessity of life. Power is the wise application of will which enlists fatality in the accomplishment of the desires. The forces of nature are at the disposal of those who know how to control them.

Sexual physical love is ever an illusion, for it is the result of an imaginary mirage. Rivalry often creates success, since we work harder at that which resists us.

Faith (aspiration towards the infinitive), the noble self-reliance sustained by confidence in all virtues (the faith which in weak natures may degenerate into pride) is represented by the Sun. Hope, the enemy of avarice, is represented by the Moon. Charity, in opposition to luxury, is represented by Venus. Strength, superior to wrath, is represented by Mars. Prudence, hostile to idleness, is represented by Mercury. Temperance, as opposed by gluttony, is represented by Saturn. Justice, in opposition to envy, is represented by Jupiter. Such are the symbols borrowed by Astrology from the ancient Hellenic cults.

In the Kabbalah of the Hebrews, the Sun represents the angel of light; the Moon, the angel of aspirations and dreams; Mars, the destroying angel; Venus, the angel of loves; Mercury, the angel of progress; Jupiter, the angel of power; and Saturn, the angel of the wilderness. Infancy is dedicated to the Sun, Childhood to the Moon, Youth to Mars and Venus, Manhood to Mercury, Maturity to Jupiter, and Old Age to Saturn.

The seven colors of the prism, and the seven musical

notes, correspond also to the seven planets of the ancients —
they are the seven chords of the human lyre.

KABBALISTIC WISDOM

Thoughts untranslated into speech are lost to humanity.
Words uncomfirmed by acts are only idle words. Thoughts
formulated into speech and confirmed by acts constitute a
good work or a crime. Hence, in either vice or virtue, there is
no utterance for which we are not responsible. Above all else,
there are no indifferent acts. Curses and blessings invariably
produce their consequences. Every action, whatever its
nature, whether inspired by love or hate, has its effects
analogous to its motives and its extent and its direction.

Unpopularity may be a proof of integrity and courage,
but never of policy or prudence. The closer the bonds which
unite two persons, the more terrible the consequences of
hatred between them. To pardon is never a crime, but to
curse is always a danger and an evil.

Reason has been given to all men, but all do not know
how to make use of it. It is a science to be acquired. Liberty
is offered to all, but not all men are free. It is a right that
must be earned. We attain nothing without more than one
effort. The destiny of man is to be enriched by his own
earning. Afterwards he is to have the glory and pleasure of
dispensing it.

MODES OF INTERPRETATION

The different methods are as follows:

1. The key to the Scriptures is in the meaning of the Hebrew
   letters themselves (see Appendix), in addition to their meaning
   collectively. Each letter has many meanings according to the
   plane of manifestation from the human and man's
   surroundings to the Cosmic and its surroundings. It is
   sufficient to say that they constitute a veritable mine of great
   wisdom and are collectively the true key to the Scriptures.

2. Each of the Hebrew letters has in common with the letters of
   many other languages, notably the Greek, a numerical value.
   These values are often written down in place of the letters of a
   word which they represent. This then constitutes the

numerical value of that word. From this method, wonderful teachings can be derived, especially with the aid of one who has had experience in Kabbalistic studies. It is called *Gntria* or *Gematria* (a synonym for the Greek word *Grammeteia)*, which means literally "the amounting to." Words of similar values are used to explain the deep truths hidden in the combinations of letters which are called words.

3. The third method is called *Temura*, which means "to change," and is called "permutation" by Christian Kabbalists. This is an anagrammatical method in which the letters of a word are changed about in order to form another word, or at times reversed, as the case may be; in this way many mysteries are brought to light.

4. *Notariquon* is a method in which the initials of words are taken to form other words. The simplest example is of the *Chochmah Nestirah*, which means the "hidden wisdom." The answer is shown us by the teacher who points to its initial letters from the word *Ngh* and *Chn*, the former referring to Rest *(Pralaya)* and the latter to Grace. Yet both are symbols showing the result of a study of the hidden wisdom or *Chochmah Nestirah*. Such study is supposed to bring grace, lead to rest, and to the ultimate perfection of man. In a sense this is the human condition of *Pralaya*, the condition of Heaven upon Earth. The true meaning of *Notariquon* is simply "quick writing" or "shorthand."

5. Finally, there are the "Four Ways" — the four ways of interpreting the Sacred Scriptures.

There is no special authority for these statements, but they are well known and accepted by Kabbalistic students, having been handed down from father to son, throughout the ages. The four ways of reading the Sacred Scriptures according to Kabbalists, as mentioned in the Book of the Zohar, are:

First, the *Psht*, or *Pshat*, is the plain or simple literal rendering of the superficial knowledge which anyone may read. The second method is called *Rmz*, or *Ramaz*, literally, "a hint," and is intended for students who are developing their intellect and who do not wish to be taught by those who see only the literal meaning. The third, *Drsh*, or *Darash*, is the inferential method of reading, in which the eye of intuition (the eye of the Spirit) is opened. Then man transcends far above the lower mind and far beyond the intellectual reasoning of the brain consciousness, as is well known to all

Occult students. Finally, there is the fourth, and most important method, called *Sud*, or *Sod*, literally, "secret." This method is taught by initiates to their beloved disciples only. They are careful to whom they divulge this, the deepest of mysteries, knowing that "Those who hunt what the Gods hide have trouble for their pay."

The four ways of reading the Sacred Scriptures correspond to the Four Initiations of Life — the lessons which man has to learn whilst passing through the experiences of the physical, emotional, mental, and higher planes. These experiences have to be gained chiefly while in the dense physical body. The man who has mastered all these four ways and who has passed the initiations of Earth, Water, Air, and Fire rises above them and becomes a Pure One *(Tahar)*.

It is curious to note that the same teachings are in the Sanskrit, for in that wonderful language the word *Tahar* or *Arhat* means a "Perfected One," *Mahatma-a,* or Master.

A Master is one who has passed these four initiations, but this does not mean that he has merely learned to read the Sacred Scriptures as written upon paper. There are other scriptures, the scriptures formed in the hearts of men, as well as in the Mind of God. Those who would be perfect have to learn to read these "Sacred Scriptures" in the four manners corresponding to *Pshar, Ramaz, Darash,* and *Sud.*

This then is the goal set before us; this is the Law: "Be Perfect, even as the Father in Heaven is perfect." By conquering all the worlds, by experiencing all things, by reading the Sacred Books, whether in the hearts of men, or whether in the records of man or nature, we rise above the necessity for earthly lessons and become free from our bonds, perfect masters of the arts and crafts. Thus viewing life, the Kabbalist attains to Paradise. The secret is hidden in the four words *Pshat, Ramaz, Darash* and *Sud* — the initials of which yield *Prds* (Paradise).

What is Paradise? Is it a beautiful Garden of Eden, or a materialistic heaven? Paradise or Nirvana is a state of consciousness, a condition, in which man becomes all that there is and in which he feels himself to be at one with all that exists. He is at one with God and man and henceforth has no further lessons to learn upon earth. He has attained the Goal set before humanity. He may then pass on to higher realms and enter a new order of beings. He may remain to help in the great work on earth — to uplift and benefit his younger brothers.

All this is hidden in the words *Pshat, Ramaz, Darash,* and *Sud.* As man progresses through the different experiences of life and passes the initiations represented by these four words (the Four Ways), he extracts from each the essence of spirit and adds it to his store of experience.

NUMERICAL VALUATION

In ancient times, the world was not overburdened with literature as it is now, when millions of books which all treat the same unimportant material matters are produced in such ghastly numbers. In those days, man depended more upon personal teachings, and when ready received his just reward from his teacher.

The method of teaching was the Kabbalistic one of using the sacred scrolls, upon which were written glyphs and symbols. Upon this foundation man built a solid structure of knowledge. The teachings related to the Macrocosmos, the large world or the Universe, and to the Microcosmos, the reflection of the larger world to the small one called Man. From these teachings, hidden in these glyphs and symbols, a universal science is obtained — a science which treats of the Becoming of the Universe, of flux and efflux, of *Manvantara* and *Pralaya,* from the generation of the "Gods" to the perfection of Man.

One of the methods used to unravel the mysteries hidden in these sacred writings or scrolls is that of *Temura* or permutation, the anagrammatical method of changing the position of the letters and forming a word to create a new word which then explains the original. A striking example of this method, is the following:

The writers on Alchemy speak of a mysterious

substance to which no name is given. It is said to be the cheapest thing in the world and costs nothing, yet it cannot be bought, but is actually given "for nothing" to all who are entitled to it. What is this mysterious thing? The Kabbalist answer is, "It is Grace."

The Hebrew word *Mchn, Mechein,* meaning literally "from grace," has six permutations of great significance: *Mchn,* "from grace;" *Mnch,* "from the one who rests"; *Chmn,* meaning "rich oil"; *Nchm,* "to comfort"; *Nmch,* "to obliterate"; and finally, *Chnm,* "for nothing." In these permutations there is hidden a teaching of the deepest significance.

He who has passed through the fires of life and seen the emptiness of carnal things, of things transitory — those things which at the utmost last but for a lifetime — he who has reached this stage becomes *Mnch,* the one who rests from action. He has discovered after bitter lessons, after repeated trials and tests, that all mundane things are useful only because of the lessons which they teach the Soul.

Having thus learned from long experience that nothing in the world of man may bind him, he becomes *Mnch.* He goes out into the world a disciple doing the work of his Master, doing his Master's will, seeking to bring anew to earth the mighty truths so long hidden from a materialistic world. Whatever storm there may be without, however much it may pour with hailstones, however fearful the lightning and thunder in the world of man, he stands calmly by, ready to serve those who are sent to him. He has learned from the Silence and becomes *Mnch.*

Thus he acquires Grace, *Mchn,* — that grace which is his due through resting from effort, whilst ever in the midst of the fight. This Grace, of *Mchn,* is like unto "rich oil," which is *Chmn,* pouring down upon him, anointing him and opening up a wider field of consciousness to him. It tells of perfect unity and *at-one-ment.* This plane or condition of being is known in the East as the Buddhic, and is spoken of in the West as Cosmic Consciousness. Entering into this condition of Buddhic consciousness through the anointing, all his doubts and fears are dispelled. Never again can he complain that there is no purpose in life, nevermore will he rail at the gods for the faults of man, for now he *knows,* he realizes and understands the *reason.* He sees the Purpose shining even in the darkest night of misery. Thus knowing much he is enabled to forgive all, and sets his feet firmly upon the path of Attainment.

Henceforth, as he looks around him and studies the Sacred Scriptures written in the hearts of men, he sees nothing evil, except in a relative sense. There are only lessons to be learned and a *something* beyond all forms which is Real and Everlasting. Nothing which is human is evil in his sight, nothing that is human is wrong; there is no sin but what he might have committed, no stage but what he himself has passed in his upward climb. Knowing the effect of these lessons upon himself, he realizes all is for the best. God, in truth, is indeed in his Heaven, and all is right with the world.

This then is the meaning of the Alchemists when they assert that the sacred fire cannot be bought but is to be had "for nothing." This nothing is a very precious "something," for it is Grace, without which no man can safely be entrusted with the Grand Secret.

We may read the lessons contained in these *Temuras* in a shorter way as follows:

The Grace of God is like unto *rich oil* pouring out from the Heavens, coming "to comfort" the "one who rests" from strife and serving "to obliterate" all evil, so that *nothing* is left but the Perfected One, the *Tahar* or *Arhat.*

All love emotions are expansive; all emotions of hatred are restrictive. Hope and faith are of the nature of love and expand the Soul; but fear and doubt and despair are of the nature of hate and contract our Souls, thus making us feel uneasy and unhappy. The snake stands for contraction, for tightness and indrawing; when men fight and quarrel with one another, they always resemble more or less the old snake, each drawing to his side, anxious for self-preservation. Freedom from the snake's anguish can only be had by ceasing from the snake's ways and learning to obey the law of love, the first dictate of which is self-sacrifice.

There is no death; there is no destruction. All is but change and transformation — first the caterpillar, then the chrysalis, then the beautiful butterfly. Likewise, first physical man, then the mighty mind, and at last a noble Soul.

The scientific mind of this age requires a logical and well-reasoned foundation for every statement which claims its attention. Credence is given to naught but the senses and their testimony. Even in the realms of psychology and metaphysical research, the scientific mind clings to this rule and demands compliance with its own conditions.

Naturally the Pilgrim on the Path to the Masters finds himself at a loss to reconcile the man of science. His cold, calculating mind and relentlessly exacting methods forget a manner of procedure. This is nothing else but the faith of a little child. Fortunately this does not sound as ridiculous now as it would have fifty years ago. A great number of men, distinguished for their learning and sound knowledge, are no longer strangers to the spirit and things spiritual.

To the ordinary mind, even of cultured people, thought is identified with Self, and any mental movement within them is looked upon as the guidance of the Self. This is why they get angry when their wills are thwarted and their desires opposed. Taking their mind to be themselves, their spirit rushes out against the supposed enemy who dared to frustrate what the mind had planned.

The disciple, distinguishing between the eternal and evanescent, and knowing the mind to be as unreal as the lower manifestations which he has already conquered, cannot by any possible chance get angry or wish ill to his opponents. No matter whether his grievance be real or fancied, the knower of truth is far above the mind and its complications and has actually nothing to lose or gain. There may arise an exceptional occasion when for the sake of "younger souls" and their evolution, a defense will be made by an Occultist against slander.

Those who transcend the personality and the passions completely find the consciousness of the Higher Self. Those who have won the victory and scaled the heights return to testify to the Light — the brightness of which has left its reflection upon their faces. We can see their shining auras and their glorified countenances, for they, without ceasing to be children of the earth, have become citizens of the celestial realms. They are now the twice-born sons and daughters of the Father of Lights, whose limitless splendor must remain a mystery to the world at large to the end of time.

The ultimate end of science is to explain the facts of nature. How does science accomplish this? By generalization and deduction, which means the placing of the newly discovered fact or the newly revealed truth at the side of facts already known and truths already familiar to man. But in the nature of things, science must stop somewhere. The latest fact still requires a further generalization in order to account for its own origin. Scientific methods lead to metaphysics.

The basis of all scientific research is the trinity of time, space, and matter, which are themselves mental conceptions. Now seeing that these fundamental conceptions of time and space, which form the warp and woof, are essentially spiritual notions, it naturally follows the subject aware of these must be above and independent of them.

Prior to this stage, man can never think of anything except as it is, was, or will be. Likewise we can never think of anything which does not occupy any space at all or which is devoid of all matter whatever. But the Atomic consciousness needs no such support to substantiate the operation of its interior sight. It works on the formless plane, and its experiences are so far removed from our earthly ones that any terms we may use for their description must be inadequate.

However, the imperfection of the instrument does not detract from the excellence of the master. The insufficiency of temporary channels does not lessen the fullness of the eternal fountain. The shortness of our sight and the narrowness of our horizon leave untouched the limitlessness of the Divine Wisdom.

These truths were known to all initiates of ancient times. They are now being revived and proclaimed anew to a doubting world. They are all founded upon the same principle on which the Cosmos itself is founded — Love. But while being rooted and grounded in the very nature of things, and identical with the Self in all creatures, they are meant to be revealed to the few only, the majority of the race being insufficiently prepared for them.

Love, the motive power of all that lives and breathes, must be the guiding star of every disciple who has entered and is making progress upon the Path. It is not only his safety valve at every step of the way, but serves also to fathom the depths of the water surrounding him during his voyage to the other shore. The storms and the winds threatening his Individual Life may often be of such vehemence that constant reliance and steadily increasing faith in the powers above are needed.

Only faith, hope, and love can save the disciple from destruction. His enemies are many and mighty; their number and their power keep increasing as he nears his goal. His only chance of escape is to hide himself in the bosom whither naught that is evil can follow him — the bosom of the Eternal Father and Mother.

To the doubting world this may still be fancy and childish talk, but we can wait patiently until the doubters grow in knowledge and increase their insight. In the course of time, these truths will become common knowledge and no more doubted or wondered at than is present day science.

The Alchemists, who will forever remain our philosophers, friends, and guides in these matters, knew long ago that the whole Universe is one homogeneous whole and that we, being members of the whole, serve our ends best by living for others. Sacrifice, therefore, is the highest form of life, and self-renunciation, the highest form of self-realization. The proofs in favor of such a conclusion are so numerous and so substantial as to amount to nothing less than a mathematical demonstration.

2

The Realm of Spirit

It is Nature which teaches all things; she receives of the pure spirit that instructs her. Everything coming from the light of Nature must be learned, except for the image of potentiality. Man is given creativity and potentiality, for he possesses life and spirit.

The Kabbalah is actually an intensified development of the teachings of an earlier oriental mystical trend, and centers around two basic problems: (1) How to reconcile the relation of Spirit, the most exalted and most spiritual Being, to the gross materialistic world. (2) How could such a Spiritual Being create a material world, and from where did the earthen matter come? The solution to these problems is best expressed by one word, Mediation, which means there are mediators between Spirit and the material world by means of which the true relations are carried out. The mediators have been identified differently in past ages as angels, as powers of God embodied in the letters of the alphabet, or as occult allegorical powers called *sephiroth*.

The true essence of Spirit and God, according to the Kabbalah, is unknown. We only know pure Spirit is unlimited and infinite. It is accordingly denominated in the *En Sof* (Endless) and it must, however, reveal itself to the world and to the mind of man. To review, there are ten manifestations of power and media of Spirit called *sephiroth*. These are: *Kether* (Crown), *Chokmah* (Wisdom), and *Binah* (Love and Understanding), forming the first triad, which relates to pure being; *Chesed* (Kindness), *Geburah* (Power), and *Tifereth* (Beauty and Glory), which are the moral qualities; *Nesah* (Victory), *Hod* (Spendor), and *Yesod* (Foundation), representing the world of nature; and *Malkuth* (Leadership), which harmonizes the nine active principles and acts as the medium between the *sephiroth* and other links in the great chain of being and existence. The *sephiroth* are the instruments by means of which Spirit created the world and through which it is manifest to the world.

Pure Spirit, per se, is then a diffusive, nonatomic, uncreated, formless, self-existent being. It is silent, motionless, unconscious, and possesses in its sublime purity only one attribute expressible in human language. This is absolute and unconditioned potentiality or creativity.

Such is the realm of Spirit, which for the sake of linguistic convenience, was termed by the Occultist "the realm of unmanifested being." We do not have to deal with the first emanation of this inconceivable state. Yet the Kabbalah contains many long and elaborate treatises upon the various emanations of all ten *sephiroth*. These are, for the most part, written in such an allegorical style as to be useless to most Western readers. Even the Oriental mind finds them somewhat unsatisfactory, and in many respects totally misleading.

The first emanation or manifestation from this realm of formless being and power claims the reader's closest attention. It forms the key note of the entire divine anthem of creation. This emanation, called by Kabbalists *Kether* (the Crown), when stripped of its allegorical and mystical veil, is the simple and naked activity of pure motion.

Thus, we see the first action of the unconscious mind is thought, and thought implies a vibration or motion. At the very moment the Deific mind vibrates with thought, there springs forth from the infinite womb of Divinity the duality of all future greatness. This duality is the Kabbalistical twins *(Hokmah* and *Binah)* of Love and Wisdom. In turn, they mean the attributes attraction and repulsion, of pure force and pure motion. They are male and female, coequal and coeternal, and express themselves as activity and repose.

No matter how recondite or abtruse our speculations may be, when the orbit of our metaphysical mediation is complete, we find ourselves face-to-face once again with our original starting point. This is the infinite triad of Love, Wisdom, and Crown. In other words, this triad is the one primal force of pure being containing unlimited potentialities within itself.

With this divine trinity we, as investigators of nature's occult mysteries, must rest contented. We console ourselves, whenever necessary, with the certain knowledge that the nearer we appear to approach the great white throne of the Infinite, the farther the divine center recedes from us.

If this were not so, there could be no eternity for the atoms of differentiated life. Consequently, the immortality of the Soul would be an empty dream or a mere figment, hatched by some evil and infernal power within the overheated imagination of poor deluded mankind.

Before going any further, the reader should commit to memory the following doctrines. These are taught by the Occult initiates of all True wisdom. They are doctrines to us in our present mortal state, since we cannot demonstrate them externally by any known form of scientific experiment.

1. The whole Universe is filled with the pure, motionless, formless spirit of creative and pure Divinity.
2. The Universe is boundless and unlimited, a circle whose circumference is everywhere and whose center is nowhere. The Universe is a duality and consists of the manifest and the nonmanifest.
3. The life principle emanates from the pure vortices of the central spiritual Sun of the manifest Universe. From this mighty, inconceivable center of life emanate spiritual rays which are scintillating with activity.

The vast, motionless void, the awful universe of silent, formless spirit now becomes alive with an infinite number of subordinate universes. The rays at various points in space are brought into focus. At these points or foci are formed the centers of smaller universes. An example of this great process may be seen upon our material plane by observing how primary suns throw off a series of secondary suns. These secondary suns then throw off the planets. The planets now become the parents of the moons.

The science of correspondence states, "As it is above, so it is below."

Remember well these basic doctrines.

The divine purpose of all creation is the differentiation of the unconscious formless one. The grand outcome of this great purpose is the ultimation of intelligencies. Then separate minds reflect the idea of the universal mind, and conscious, individualized mentalities possess immortal souls capable of eternal progression. They are differentiated life atoms which become of themselves secondary factors and the arbitrators of the destinies of manifold worlds.

The processes of creation are a duality of Involution and Evolution. The one is inseparable from the other. Paradoxical as it may appear to the uninitiated, it is a devine truth that the Evolution and ultimation of spiritual life is accomplished only by a strict process of Involution. It is from the without to the within, or from the infinitely great to the infinitely small.

To better understand this mystery we must use a series of symbols. Accordingly, we conceive the divine focus of the primal essence to be the spiritual center of a universe. This ray constitutes a triune from which emanates the pure white light of the formless one. This center constitutes a realm of *sephiroth,* a sun-sphere of living potentialities — pure divine beings infinitely beyond the highest archangelhood. As such, we conceive of it as floating, as if it were a speck in the infinite ocean of divine love, surrounded by the effulgent brightness of the nameless Crown.

This divine sphere is completely passive in such a stage. Nirvana reigns upon and with the blissful radiance of its motionless bosom. But the time approaches when its great mission in the scheme of creation must begin. The moment arrives, and as the first creative pulsation of thought in the whole sphere of motionless, formless, soft light flashes forth, it is sparkling with living spiritual energy. Now, behold what a change has taken place!

The soft, white light has ceased and in its place there goes forth in every conceivable direction the mighty oceans of force — each ocean differing in its velocity, color, and potentiality. The passive has now become active, the motionless has commenced to move, and the void of space is transversed upon the wings of light.

The Sun has become refracted, and a portion of the Infinite Light is decomposed into its original unlimited attributes. This is related in the mystical allegorical language of the Kabbalah as the evolution of seven active *sephiroth* from the first trinity of Love, Wisdom, and Crown.

It is these seven active *sephiroth* which constitute the seven principles of nature. They form seven points or subcenters around their divine parent center, the spiritual sun. These are the seven states of angelic life from whose divine spiritual matrix issue all the life atoms of their created universe.

When the dawn of any universe commences, the pure formless essence is indrawn, before being involved by the Deific will of the angelic hierarchies. It is indrawn from the realms of unmanifested into the sun-sphere of creative life. By this contact it immediately undergoes a great change. It is formless no longer, but atomic, and endowed with the attribute or state of polarity.

This polarity evolves a sort of partnership and equally divides the formless substance into two basic parts. Each part is a necessary attendant upon the other in manifested existence. One is positive, the other negative. The positive ray is that which constitutes the living spiritual fire of all things.

Its atoms are infinitely fine. The negative ray is ever tending toward a state of rest or inertia. Its atoms are coarse and loose when compared with those of the positive ray.

It is the substance formed by the negative ray which constitutes every species of what is called matter. It forms all, from the inconceivably fine etherealized substance which composes the forms of the divine archangels of the sun, down to the coarse mineral veins of dense heavy metal.

Therefore, when speaking broadly of spirit and matter, the terms are perfectly meaningless in an occult sense. That which we call spirit is not pure spirit, but only the positive or acting attribute of that which we term matter. Hence, matter is so far unreal; it is only an appearance produced by the negative ray, and this appearance is the result of polarity or of more motion. One is straight and penetrating, the other is round and enfolding.

With this necessary digression we resume our discussion. From the seven angelic states mentioned before, spiritual involution commences. Each one of the seven spheres is a reflection of one of the seven refracted principles which constitute the divine mind. From this reflection springs forth angelic races, second only in mental power and potentiality to their parents. Then, in turn, there are produced still lower celestial states — each state of sphere corresponding in nature, color, and attributes to the sphere from which it was born or reflected. Though each state in the descending scale is similar by correspondence, it becomes less in size and more material. The spiritual potencies of its angelic races are weaker and less active, because they are more and more involved with matter as they descend the scale.

Thus does involution proceed; involving state after state, and sphere after sphere, forming a series of circles whose line of motion or descent is not in the plane of its orbit. Thus the form becomes as a spiral until the lowest point is reached. Beyond this point motion is impossible, and the infinitely great has become the infinitely small. This is the great polarizing point from which the material world is reflected. It is the lowest possible spiritual state of life, which formed the first ethereal race of human beings upon our planet. Thus it ushered into existence the famous Golden Age of mythological celebrity.

There are thus two schools for man. The school of the earth, which teaches earthly things, has as its schoolmistress Nature, and is indeed Nature herself, inculcates knowledge of itself and of those things which are in it. Then there is the other school — that from above. There the teacher is Deific spirit. It teaches us in the reborn body, not in the old body; and in this reborn man, it teaches heavenly wisdom.

What is there in us, mortals, which has not come to us from the *sephiroth?* Whatever teaches us the eternal also teaches us the perishable, for both spring from the realm of spirit.

There are many who deem man and his power to be the highest good. There are men who consider the *Malkuth* to be the highest good, or hold the highest good to be their fellow men who do them a good turn, give them gifts, or help them. But in this they are mistaken. For is there not the triad Love, Wisdom, and Crown above the emperor? Is there not someone who gives to the man, who in turn gives you what you need? Is not this someone more? We may rise as high as we can, in search of the highest good, but all this remains within the earthly sphere; that which is eternal is above all this.

If he who has the power is just in himself, the power must so subjgate him so that he is sadder than those under him. For power comes from Spirit and bears the human burdens that derive from it. It follows that to each is given the spirit he desires: to one the spirit of wisdom, to another the spirit of science, to a third the spirit of faith, to a fourth the spirit of healing, to a fifth the spirit of power, to a sixth the spirit of prophecy, to a seventh the spirit of tongues. Thus God gives diverse things through Spirit, and not just one, but many hundreds, so man may know how marvelous is the Spirit from which all things come.

Each is twofold: on the one hand there is the knowledge we learn from men, on the other hand the knowledge we learn from the Spirit. The making of glass is not an art for him who has learned it from someone else. But he who was the first to invent it of himself deserves to be praised as an artist, for in him we feel the action of Spirit. But in him who can do only what he has learned from others, the presence of Spirit cannot be felt. Man can do none of this by his own strength; all his wisdom, his reason, and everything that is in him cannot discover the new, let alone fully develop its properties. Those who learned from the first teachers learned directly from others, but they too lived by the Spirit. For it was put into those men, and it has thus come down from the first to the most recent man. And thus the Spirit triumphs on earth among men.

3
The Origin of
Physical Life

The Involution of Spirit and the reactive Evolution of Matter are based upon absolute laws, which man may realize. One form disappears only to give place to another more perfect form; this is a fact observed throughout nature. Those who possess the attributes of Soul-light in a sufficiently developed state can perceive the hidden potentialities latent within the outward form. This being so, we know previous to this natural evolution, which we distinguish all around us, there must have been a process of involution. During this process, these latent potentialities became involved with the external matter.

From nothing, nothing can be produced; it is therefore only the blind and unreasoning who follow such an illogical creed as the one thus summarized:

> *From nothing we came, and whatever our station,*
> *To nothing we owe an immense obligation.*
> *Whatever we do, or whatever we learn,*
> *In time we shall all into nothing return.*

To the cold, heartless supporter of this annihilating

system of nothingness — one who flaunts his superficially learned authority under the name of Agnosticism — we reply with the realized consciousness of a deathless, progressive immortality:

> *From an infinite source midst realms of light,*
> *An offspring from Nature, my soul stood its flight,*
> *To gain amid matter, with its trials and pain,*
> *The knowledge to carry it homeward again.*

The immutable laws of nature may be traced backward into the eras of sun formation, or carried forward beyond the present into the equally dim vista of the eternal future. Those who can see and realize for themselves the planes of both cause and effect will understand. To be able to do this we must attain the soul state of equilibrium where both realms unite. Then there is neither cause nor effect, but the two are one.

THE CELESTIAL STATE

This state contains the mystery of those inconceivable laws by the operation of which the Self becomes an acting entity. It suffices to say that this is a state of celestial life wherein the purely embryonic center in the divine arc of progressive being is located. This is the point where the diffusive intelligence of the infinite spirit becomes differentiated and atomic. The Divine Self of the human Soul is absolutely atomic. It is as eternal and immortal as the infinite. Though atomic, it is only so as a purely spiritual conception, a point of radiant light, totally free from matter, and incapable of uniting itself except by means of reflection.

The twin souls, male and female, or heavenly Isis and Osiris, are the two halves. They are the masculine and feminine attributes of the Divine Self. They have alternate cycles of activity and repose. During the cycle of their fruitful activity, the two respond with intense vibrations to the divine song of creation. This creates an influx of the formless, motionless spirit into the celestial sensorium, and the whole sphere becomes radiant with the scintillations of spiritual harmony. Obeying the creative impulse, these streams of spiritual force flow along to the convergent poles from the various centers of the sphere. Each force from the male is met and balanced by that of the female. The contact produces, by the exact equilibrium of the masculine and feminine natures, the living external sparks of immortal life.

In the process of time, these pure twin souls, unconsciously obeying the internal impulse, become attracted towards matter. Up till now, they were pure and innocent, knowing neither good nor evil. Thus the Divine Self, which is incapable of descent into matter, projects the two souls into the vortex of cosmic evolution, where they become separated and ultimately incarnated within the minerals of a planet. This is the lowest point in the arc. In this state, these souls constitute the hidden fire and spirit of matter and are its latent force.

THE MINERAL STATE

The souls have arrived at the mineral state, and we now must ascertain the origin of its motor or its life. We know within the mineral lies concealed the potencies of an immortal being.

Chemical force is death — balanced, still, and motionless. Spiral motion is the motion type of life. It is the true motion of life. It is a spiritual screw, and with all the mechanical advantages of a screw, it penetrates the universe of matter. The spiral varies in magnitude from the infinite to the infinitesimal. The lesser forces are but an infinite fraction less than the greater forces. The spiral may be almost infinite in its sweep of curve, and will require almost an eternity to reach its culminating point. Or with the greater the diversity in power, the curve will become less, until we have the infinitesimally small spiral which will culminate almost instantly. Between these two extremes we have every phenomenon of life, from that of the tiniest insect to the great cosmic life of an Astral Universe.

THE VEGETABLE STATE

Motion is the life of matter; but we must now seek for a still higher form, the immediate product of matter. Having asserted that the spiral is the motion of life, we will be substantiated in our assertion by the vegetable kingdom. As external evidence, then, let us call to our aid the phyllotaxy of plants. On the stems of plants the leaves are placed so a line wound around the stem, and touching the petiole of each life, would be a spiral. Where the leaves are in two rows, the space between two opposite leaves is just half a circle or half the circumference of the stem. Where there are three rows, it is one-third the circumference, and so on. The facts are demonstrated by botanical science, and not only confirm our assertion, but also show that vital force is subject to measurement.

In order to understand how the vegetable evolves from the mineral, the spiral motion of life must be held in view. Also, the various changes of atomic polarity must be clearly understood. For instance, the atoms of oxygen and hydrogen by combination produce a substance (water) which is the direct polar opposite of their original flammable states. From this change of polarity we have clouds, oceans, and rivers. Now when the vapor from these waters is drawn upward by the heat of the sun, a small fraction becomes decomposed into the gaseous state. Although decomposed, the atoms are actually the same after combining into the substance known as water as they were when uncombined. They have only a different angle of motion. Before, they rotated in a circle; they now ascend and revolve in the form of a spiral. In this ascension they attract or are attracted by the atoms of carbonic acid gas. Instantly a violent rotation among the various atoms is produced and they combine. Another transformation has taken place; a new thing has been produced as a molecule or germ of physical life.

Under the control of a central atom of fire, the predominating forces of oxygen and carbon unite, and this union produces another change of polarity. They become attracted to earth. The water or moisture receives them, and a species of vegetable slime is the natural result. When this vegetable product has served its purpose and decays, its liberated atoms arise in their spiral motion. In turn, they become attracted to, or themselves attract, some of the atoms in the air with which they have a natural affinity.

The same process of polarization is repeated, with some slightly different vibration, and a still higher germ of life is evolved. The lowest form of the lichen may result. From the liberated atoms of this life, spring forth still higher and higher types of the same family until the climax is attained. Then, by a higher and more ethereal attraction, the polarized units bring forth the next higher form of life. Thus, as the ages roll on, from this original form issues all species, classes, and families of vegetation. From these evolve, through the medium of water, a still higher round in the gamut of being, animal life, and finally Man.

INCARNATION AND REINCARNATION

Probably no truth has been more completely inverted by the ignorant and concealed by the learned than reincarnation. In every age it has been thought necessary by the priesthood to overawe the uneducated masses by some species of pious jugglery. The popular theory of reincarnation, as understood and taught today, is a typical example of truth perverted. By reincarnation we mean the doctrine of the rebirth of the human soul in various human forms and personalities, in different ages, upon the same planet.

In every bundle of theological chaff there is, undoubtedly, a grain of genuine truth. We must bear in mind that the doctrine of human reincarnation is not a doctrine of Occultism. It is a theological doctrine of Oriental sacerdotal systems, formulated by the priesthood either to conceal the real truth, or to account for what they themselves could not understand. Up to a point, its teachings are those of truth itself, but beyond this point the doctrine of rebirth becomes one of the greatest delusions with which the mystical student must deal.

To those who are upon the plane of appearances, it possesses an almost irresistible attraction, since it appears to account, in a most rational and philosophical manner, for the wide differences manifested in the mental, social, and moral conditions of humanity. Upon the external material plane, it seems to settle the question of good and evil. It seems to harmonize all our inequalities with what seems divine justice. All these delusive appearances, however, are but empty shadows of the phenomenal world. They can only deceive those who are upon the external plane and who have obtained their knowledge of Occultism from the writings of others, accepting such teachings without verifying them for themselves.

There are two methods of verification: one, the actual experiences of the Soul; the other, the response of the Soul to the thoughts and ideas we derive from an author's work. But, unfortunately, this latter kind of verification is subject to serious drawbacks. A mediumistic nature will respond to error because of the more potent thought of the writer. If we are oversensitive, we may be superficial enough to respond to an erroneous idea through pure emotional sentiment.

These drawbacks have been seized by the Inversive Brethren to enable them to fasten this reawakening of the Karma and reincarnation delusion upon the sensitive minds and mediumistic natures of the human race. The most finely spun ideals of "the higher life" have been, and are continuing to be, presented by a host of sentimental, spiritually sick mystical writers to explain "the glorious mysteries" of nature and "the secret doctrine" of all religious philosophies. Yet they themselves, in real truth, know very little, apart from the mediumistic ideas which are projected towards them by the Inversive Magic. The whole is merely a metaphysical delusion cast over their mentalities by means of a magnetic glamor.

It seems very strange that these followers of "the path" which leads to physical reincarnation can be so blind as to imagine that this earth is the only place within the infinite Universe whereon divine justice may be satisfied, and due punishment meted out to the evil doer. The life beyond is far more real, far more earnest, and much more conscious than this life on earth. Surely, then, the Soul can work out its redemption better there than here. Surely, the Soul ought to have the privilege granted of being conscious of what it is suffering for. This is not the case according to the fallacies of esoteric Buddhism. Alas! The spiritually blind are blind indeed.

In the descent of life into external conditions, we must not omit the fact that in its descent the monad has passed through every state in the soul world. It passed through the four realms of the Astral Kingdom, and lastly, it reappeared upon the external plane at the lowest point possible. From this point we see it enter successively the mineral, vegetable, and animal life of the planet. In obedience to the higher and more interior laws of its own especial round, the divine attributes are ever seeking to unfold their involved potentialities.

No sooner is one form dispensed with, or its capabilities exhausted, than a new and still higher form is brought into being — each in its turn becoming more complex in its structure and diversified in its functions. Thus we see the atom of life commencing at the mineral in the external material world. The grand spiral of evolutionary life is carried forward slowly, imperceptibly, but always progressively. There is no form too simple, no organism too complete, for the inconceivably marvelous adaptability of the human Soul in its divine struggle of progressive life.

Yet, throughout the entire cycle of necessity, the character of its genius, the degree of its spiritual emanation, and the state of life to which it originally belonged, are perfectly preserved with exactitude. These states correspond, in a general sense, to the four ancient elements Fire, Earth, Air, and Water.

Yet, as a matter of purification alone, each atom must pass through all these states on its upward journey. Before the human monad can possibly attain the climax of its material evolution (the grand terminus of its earthly incarnations), it must also pass through certain phases of existence upon each planet; and its microcosmic nature in the embodied man bears a mathematical correspondence to these phases. Thus, between the mineral and man there is a perfect scale of life. No one form is parallel with another in the grand chain of cosmic being. Even the insects count, as the links, as progressive states in the Great Chain of Being.

In the whole of this great chain are seven worlds through which the soul migrates. No matter at what point or planet the Soul commences its toilsome cosmic journey, the seventh planet is always the end of its material orbit. This is the sphere wherein it attains the human form divine. In no case does the soul monad commence as a mineral and attain the animal or human upon the same planet. It becomes latent on each alternate orb.

For example, the mineral atoms on this earth will undergo a purely impersonal cycle upon Venus, which is their next sphere, and then become incarnated within the vegetable upon the next planet. The mineral atoms of the planet Mars, when they reach this planet, are purely impersonal beings and do not incarnate here as objective forms. They pass their cycle in the Astral spaces and then enter material conditions again upon Venus.

Thus the soul monad has four objective states, and three subjective. The objective states are one, three, five, and seven, or the mineral, vegetable, animal, and man. The three subjective states are two, four, and six, or the negative states of its embryonic being. After the soul attains the objective human form or seventh state, the next is beyond material matter. "Once and only once," saith the law. After this, Nature shuts the door behind her. Eternal progression is the anthem of all creative life.

When we apply these basic laws to external material life, we can gauge the Soul's past history with an accuracy which is truly marvelous. Thus, for instance, the truly martial individual belongs to the state of life known in Occult phraseology as Fiery. Those peculiar and especial attributes were "rounded out" upon the planet known as Mars. The fiery characteristics of an atom belonging to a state of life corresponding to the fiery triplicity were evolved through various organic forms during its cycle of incarnation upon the planet of Mars.

On the other hand, a Saturnine individual during his sojourn upon the Martial plane was only a little attracted to the Martial forms of existence. In fact, the soul monad, at that stage of its journey, passed through a kind of impersonal coma instead of an active evolutionary life. This happened because there was but only little affinity between itself and the planet. Consequently, the planet did not have sufficient attractive power to project the impersonal soul into the more outward forms of organic being.

The same may be said of each planetary characteristic. Their latent or active expression in the embodied individual reveals to the initiated mind the whole of the Soul's past history of its impersonal planetary life. A careful study of this will do much to explain the true and deeper mysteries of Astrology. The positions of the planets at a person's birth do not make him what he is; they only harmonize with his Soul's conditions.

During the process of the Soul's involution, the human monad is not incarnated in any form. The Soul descends into earthly conditions down the subjective arc of the spiral and reascends upon the objective. Rebirth commences when the objective mineral state is reached. The process of the monad's descent through the various realms is a gradual polarization of its Deific powers. This is caused by its contact with the gradually externalizing conditions of the downward arc of the cycle. At each step, the Soul becomes more and more involved within the material.

The sphere of the reincarnation — embracing the birth of an external form, its transient life and death, and the Soul's rebirth in a higher and more perfect form of life — is all between the Mineral and Man. Between these two planes, the Soul must pass through countless forms and phases. It is an absolute truth that man lives on many planets before he reaches this one. Myriad worlds swarm in space where the

Soul, in its rudimental states, performs various pilgrimages, until its cyclic progress enables it to reach our magnificently organized planet. Here its glorious function is to confer self-consciousness upon man. At this point, and this point alone, does it become a part of man. At every other step of the wild cosmic journey, it is but an embryonic being, a fleeting, temporary shape, an impersonal creature, from which a part of the imprisoned Soul shines forth. It is a rudimental form with rudimental functions, ever living, dying, and sustaining a brief spiritual existence only to be reborn again. Thus it sustains the successive round of births and deaths.

With each change, new organs and new functions are acquired and utilized by the gradually expanding Soul as a means of its further development. We see it in the spark of the flint. As we watch the revolving sparks of the mineral soul, we can see it burst forth in the sunlight in the garb of the lichen. It guards the snow-white purity of the lotus and animates the aromatic glory of the rose. It is the butterfly springing from the chrysalid shell, and the nightingale singing in the grove.

> From stage to stage it evolves
> New births and new deaths,
> Anon to die, but sure to live again,
> Ever striving and revolving upon the whirling,
> Toilsome, dreadful, rugged path,
> Until it awakes for the last time on earth,
> Awakes once more a material shape,
> A thing of dust,
> A creature of flesh and blood,
> But now a Man.

The grand, self-conscious stage — humanity — is attained, and the climax of earthly incarnation is now reached. Never again will it enter the material matrix or suffer the pains of past material reincarnations. Henceforth its rebirths are in the realm of pure spirit.

Those who hold the strangely illogical Oriental doctrine

of a multiplicity of human births have certainly never evolved a lucid state of Soul Consciousness within themselves. Had they done so, their theory of reincarnation (held by a vast number of talented men and women, well versed in wordly wisdom) would not have received the slightest recognition.

An external education is comparatively worthless as a means of obtaining a true knowledge of nature. Remember that though the acorn becomes the oak, and the cocoanut, the palm, the oak, though giving birth to myriad others, never again becomes an acorn, nor the palm, the juicy nut. So it is with man! When once the Soul becomes incarnated in the human, and thus attains the consciousness of external life, man becomes a *Self*-responsible being, accountable for his actions.

This accountability constitutes his earth Karma, and the reward or punishment is consciously and divinely administered. The Soul is not ignorantly ushered into the world, completely unconscious of its past load of Karma. Such a means of redemption, instead of being divine, would be void of justice. It would be diabolic!

When human laws punish the criminal, he is conscious of the misdeed for which he is suffering. If this were not so, the punishment would be unjust. For this reason we do not punish irresponsible children, or insane men.

It is useless, however, to deal any further with such a transcendent delusion. We will only say that all the so-called reawakenings of latent memories by which certain people profess to remember certain past lives are explained (in fact are only really explainable) by the simple laws of affinity and form.

Each race of human beings is immortal in itself; so likewise is each period. The first-period generation never becomes the second, but those belonging to the first become the parents or originators of the second. Each period generation constitutes a great planetary family, which contains within itself races, subraces, and still lesser groups of human souls. Each state is formed by the laws of its affinity, or a trinity of laws.

At the expiration of one period generation, the polar day of evolution is brought to a close. The life wave leaves the shores of the planet. The second round or period of humanity does not commence until the human life wave, having gone round the whole planetary chain reaches the planet again. This is a period considerably over fifteen million years.

This is the exact length of a polar day or the period of the earth's poles making one complete revolution in the heavens. This then is the exact duration of the life wave upon our planet; hence, man is similar to the acorn and the oak. The embryonic, impersonal Soul becomes man, just as the acorn becomes the oak. And as the oak gives birth to innumerable acorns or embryonic oaks, so does man, in his turn, become the means of giving spiritual birth to innumerable souls. There is a correspondence between the two.

From what has been said, one will perceive that each period generation of humanity becomes more numerous than the one before. The expanded material knowledge of each succeeding period generation makes it possible for our earth to sustain a greater number of humans upon its given surface.

All things originate as the objective outcome of the divine and subjective idea or the human Self. This is the offspring of celestial harmony, a differentiated atom of diffusive formless spirit. Through it the activities of paternal souls are representative of the love, wisdom, intelligence, and truth within the sun-sphere of all creative life.

Reincarnation within progressive material forms is not only for the purpose of evolving and energizing the latent powers of the human Soul. If this were true, and man alone was the sole object of development, it would constitute the basis of absolute selfishness. But as there is no selfishness in the creative design, we can assert that such human exclusiveness is only an appearance. When we penetrate below this plane of appearances, we find a countless realm of beings — equally as immortal as man — going through their cyclic rounds, obeying the same universal laws as ourselves.

These realms constitute the steppingstones for external humanity in its journey towards the Infinite. The organisms of humanity, in their turn, form the evolutionary spheres or material means by which these realms pass through their cycles of progressive life. If we make use of certain planes for our Soul's advancement, it only follows as a matter of reactionary law or justice that we should render an equivalent service in return. Thus we have the importance of a True Knowledge of our hidden or Hermetic constitution.

Man, as we behold him by means of the physical senses, appears to us a wonderful specimen of mechanical skill and architectural beauty. Each organic part is exquisitely formed and is in perfect unison, as is each part with the whole. There is little wonder that the human organism was taken as the finite type of the unknown infinite. If this is true upon the external plane, it is infinitely more so upon the internal plane. There, bone, flesh, blood, and hair, the externals of the outward body, are seen to be nothing but the crystallizations of an ethereal force. They are held together by the mental being; yet are not held together as a matter of necessity or for the sake of their own especial evolutions, but simply as the natural outcome of their ethereal activities.

In order to present a clear and definite picture of what Man really is, we will list his Hermetic constitution:

1. A Physical Form fourfold in its composition, consisting in a general sense of bones, blood, flesh, and hair. This form as a whole is composed of a finite number of separate organic cells, each cell constituting a minute system of its own, which in its turn was formed by the crystallization of imponderable forces around a living Spirit.

2. An Electrovital Body, seemingly composed of pale phosphorescent light, enclosing a glittering skeleton framework of electric fire. This is the electromagnetic form, inseparable from the physical body during life, and dependent upon the active presence of the physical for its continued existence. The pale phosphorescent light presents a perfect outline portrait of the physical body, while the fiery skeleton shows the interior electronervous system of

the living organism. The branches of the nerve system, spreading out in every direction from the great trunk lines of spinal cord and brain, present to the trained spiritual sight an infinitude of fine pencil rays of light darting in straight lines with inconceivable rapidity toward every point of the compass.

3.   An Astral Form, so called because it is composed of the magnetic light evolved by the planet. This Astral light differs in quality and degree upon every orb in the Universe since it is generated from the universal ether of space. It may be called the ether under a change of form and capacity. It is the soul of the material planet, and consequently the cause of the planet's external phenomena. To give a better idea of this almost unknown Astral light, we will use an illustration. We say that water is salt, brackish, bitter, sulphuric, sweet, or fresh. This is exactly the case with the Astral fluid. It differs upon every Star. It is this difference which constitutes the strikingly different qualities of each planetary influence.

This Astral Form presents a perfect image of the external personality, even to style and condition of the clothing worn at the time. This form is easily separable from the physical organism and constitutes the true or real personality. By personality we mean the Persona, or the appearance assumed by the Soul during its sojourn within the material vortices of planes of cosmic force. This form is under the direct control of the mental being animating it and under suitable conditions can be made to assume temporarily any image or form within the grasp of the dominating mind. When the Astral double is absent from the physical body, the body, if awake, performs in a purely automatic or mechanical manner. It is also susceptible to the pain and injury which may befall the absent double. The Astral is also very susceptible to magical operations. Probably nine-tenths of all black magic injuries are performed by means of or upon this Astral ethereal form.

4.   The Animal Soul, or the portion of the animating entity incarnated within the microcosm. This constitutes the lower arc of its universe. This animal soul is formless in regard to its separate expression, and can be traced only in the lower lines and shadings of the human countenance. It is the seat of all the selfish desires. These desires are in

themselves lower than the human sphere, but are still evolving upward through it from the animal. Their activities are strictly confined to the Astral and material planes.

5.   The Spiritual Body is a finely etherealized organism which in the majority of the present generation is either latent or embryonic. It is the Soul's expression of the heavenly raiment of the purified man.

6.   The Divine Soul, or the section of the entity incarnated within the microcosm which constitutes the higher arc of its universe. This Soul, like the lower one, is formless as to its separate expression; yet it can be traced in the higher lines of the human countenance. It is the seat of the good, unselfish, and noble aspirations. All those actions which spring forth spontaneously to aid the weak, the suffering, and the afflicted, which are disassociated from any interested motives of Self, come from it.

7.   The Pure Spirit entity itself is called the Divine Self. This is the divine atom of life, the central controlling spiritual Sun of the microcosm. It is never incarnated within the form until the seventh state or perfect manhood is attained.

The above are the divisions of the human constitution, as viewed from without and within. Upon the surface this division will not appear to differ very materially from the septenary formula of the Buddhist cult. But, in reality, there is the difference which exists between cause and effect.

The Buddhists say that it is the evolution of this principle which gives the power of understanding and that without this we should be upon the plane of the animal and act from mere instinct. When this principle is active, man becomes noble, human, and capable of understanding. Instead of being a creature of instinct only, man becomes a reasonable being.

We question the whole of such teachings. For instance, a man may be the intellectual giant of his age, so far as mere mental capacity is concerned, and yet be the most selfish, unjust, and immoral of all men. History teems with such examples! At the same time, some of nature's noblest souls have been those whose intellectual abilities have been below the average.

"This fifth principle," we are told by the Buddhists, "is the highest principle of the animals." But Hermetic initiates deny this as true. They assert that this "principle" is no principle at all, but merely a form. In real fact, there are only three principles in an active state — animal, human, and Deific. The remaining four are merely forms or reactions. It is the action and reaction of these principles which produce every class of mental phenomena in existence — be it vegetable sensitivity, animal instinct, human reason, or Deific perception. Those three active principles form the three primary colors of the Soul's spectrum, while the remaining forms are simply complementary reactions.

We must now briefly sketch the Hermetic constitution and present the fourfold teaching of the Western initiates. Man consists of three duads which stand as Refraction and Reflection of one another.

Man as he appears to the outward sight is very different from the being within. He contains a universe of life within his organism; myriad spirit atoms are evolving through him. They are as independent of him, in reality, as man is of the planet which gave him birth. The truly human being is the most interior core or spiritual soul. The whole of the lower nature and the external organism are only the various realms of being which the human monad has conquered and subjected to its imperial rule during its cyclic journey. We should say, the externals are the reflections of those elemental states moulded more or less rudely by the human soul after its own divine form. The millions of separate entities within the human sphere are no more the *real* man than the forty million inhabitants of France were Napoleon, who ruled them with his imperial will.

A few words are necessary regarding the Will and the Reason. Will is universal; it is as impossible to point out where it begins or where it ends as it is to separate the colors of the rainbow. The power of the Will upon the external plane depends upon the strength of the electrovital constitution. Upon the Spiritual plane, it depends upon the activity of the spiritual constitution. Within the Astral plane, the potent will must have both of these activities well developed to be successful. The true form of psychic training, then, is to evolve that which is most latent so as to bring about an equilibrium. In the great majority of cases it is the Spiritual which requires training.

Considering the Will is a universal power, it naturally follows that the strength of our Will must depend upon the capacity we possess for absorbing and reprojecting the power. In fact, man's Will is only limited by his capacity to absorb the Universal Will. This Will is not a principle; it is only an active result. It is transcendental matter in rapid motion. Everything utilizes some portion of this Universal Will in its own peculiar way.

Manas, or Mind, is simple only mental capacity, and like the Will is not a principle, but a result. Intellect is the offspring of innumerable and constantly changing causes or combinations of force never repeated; consequently, no two people are exactly alike. The seat or mainspring of reason, intellect, understanding, and mind is the consciousness. Whether it will be good or evil depends upon the respective activities of the animal and divine Souls. The higher the Soul evolves, the more spiritual the understanding becomes, until perfect rapport with the Divine Spirit is attained. This is the true *at-one-ment*. Man is made perfect.

KARMA

"Karma is the law of consequences – of merit and demerit," say the Buddhists. "It is the force which moulds our phyical destiny in this world and regulates our period of misery or happiness in the world to come." We are also told, "Karma is the cold, inflexible justice which metes out to each individual the exact same measure of good and evil at his next physical rebirth that he measured to his fellow men in this." This Karma at death remains somewhere down upon the Astral planes of the planet, like an avenging demon, waiting anxiously for the period of Devachanic happiness to come to an end. Then it will reproject the poor unfortunate Soul once more into the magnetic vortices of material incarnation. There, with its load of bad Karma hanging like a millstone round its neck, it will in all probability generate a still greater load of this theological dogma. Consequently, at each rebirth, it will sink deeper and deeper, unless the Spiritual Self can bring it to some consciousness of its fearfully sinful state. How this transpires is not satisfactorily explained.

If the human Soul only received punishment for the sins and wrongs it inflicted upon others during a previous life, the Soul when it first became incarnated must have started on its human journey without any Karma to suffer for. One is naturally led to ask, "How did it first begin to commit sin?" We are distinctly told that what we now suffer at the hands of others is only a just repayment for our own past sins. If we had no past sins, we should be perfectly free from trouble. We are distinctly taught that the first or preadamite men, those of the Golden Age, were perfect. How did this abominable Karma get a start in the world? This question must be fully explained.

We have a general idea of the Karma of Theosophical Buddhism. Before discussing the origin of this Oriental delusion, we will present the Hermetic doctrine of Karma.

1. Karma is not an active principle; but, on the contrary, it is a crystallized force. It is the picture gallery or cosmic play of Nature.

2. Karma constitutes the scenery, essence, and mental imagery of a person's total past existence.

3. The Karmic spheres of an individual's existence exists as Astral life currents along which the soul traveled and which become crystallized forms. These are expressive of the actions and motives which prompted them. Therefore, our past Karma constitutes the Soul's past history in the Astral light. It can be deciphered by the properly trained Lucid, and even by some mediumistic clairvoyants.

4. Karma is the offspring of everything, or everything that possesses pictorial records of its past evolutions. It is by means of this Karma that the psychometric sensitive can read the unwritten past. Without Karma, the powers of

Psychometry would be totally useless. However, they can only deal with small Karmas. On a grander scale, the Karma of moons, planets, suns, and systems exists. Races of men, species of animals, and classes of plants also evolve special racial Karmas which constitute their Astral world.

5. The harmonies and discords of Cosmic evolution generate their special Karma just as thoughts and emotions do.

6. Karma is absolutely confined to the realms of the Astral light, and consequently is always subjective. Karma can only exist as long as the Soul which generates it is attached to the same planet. When the Soul leaves the planet, the Karma disintegrates. A Soul cannot carry its Karma around the Universe with it, since Astral light differs in quality and degree upon each orb.

7. When the Soul enters the spiritual states of the Soul world (which the Buddhists term *Devachan)*, the power of its earthly Karma can never reattract it to earth. Its influence over the Soul is lost forever. The lower can never control the higher! To assert that the past fossilized Karma can reattract the soul from the realms of spiritual happiness and reproject it into the mire of earth is to exalt matter to the throne of a Diety. This degrades pure Spirit to the level of a passive brute substance.

From the above seven statements, Hermetic initiates assert that Karma is not the primary law of consequences and destiny. It is not an active principle always at work readjusting Nature's ridiculous mistakes. Nature has never yet made a mistake!

On the contrary, Karma is a result — the subjective outcome of innumerable laws and forces — and in this life it is utterly powerless to effect either good or evil. But, upon the interior plane, upon or within the Astral sphere of the disembodied Soul world, this Karma becomes the Book of Life from which all our actions in this material life are judged. At death we are surrounded by and compelled to exist within our own Karma. We are forced by the laws of magnetic affinity to work out our own redemption, ever face-to-face with the grim idols of our earthly past. The foul, unlovely pictures of every unclean imagination will haunt us, and set our very Souls aflame with the consciousness of every injustice and wrong we committed.

The only redeeming feature will be the good Karma, the kind unselfish thoughts and noble aspirations we have evolved. All our true, unselfish love for our fellow creatures will spring up like flowers at our feet, and help to aid and brighten our path upward and onward through the spheres of purification and purgatory. At last we shall enter the sphere of immortal life, where those whom we have loved below may be waiting to greet us.

We have asserted that Karma is utterly powerless to effect either good or evil so far as the material destiny is concerned. While this is true within certain limits, seeing Karma is but the Astral record of the past, yet this statement requires more explanation. It is not the actions we commit which can, in themselves, bring happiness, misery, benefit, or misfortune. It is the effect which our actions have upon others that really produces immediate material results. The precise effect which any action will have will depend entirely upon the peculiar mental states surrounding us at the time.

For instance, in one age it may be considered a meritorious action to roast a poor, helpless medium under the name of witch; but at another period in history, such an action may be followed by an indignant spirit of public resentment. Then a terrible penalty will be imposed by the law of the state to satisfy the public sense of justice. The praiseworthy actions of one age become the criminal ones of another. We see that the results of any action upon the material plane depend upon the physical, moral, mental, cultural, and spiritual development of mankind. This is not the case, however, within the Astral Soul world. There, absolute justice is the universal law. The mighty hero of a thousand fights, who dies surrounded by all the pomp and vanity of public worship, comes face-to-face with the fearful reality that he is a bloodstained murderer. As such, he must work out his own salvation amid trial and suffering.

His purgatorial state will depend upon his motives and the consciousness of his earthly actions. If he was a true patriot, who fought simply for the love and liberty of his country against cruel oppression, his conscience will deal lightly with him. But if love of fame and martial glory were his chief motives, and constituted the greater part of his Karma, then the worst will happen to him.

In the Hermetic definitions of Karma, the Soul when working out its past iniquities is perfectly conscious of its task. It knows the true why and wherefore of its suffering. It also has the certain hope of final emancipation, however, not until, as the parable says, "thou hast paid the uttermost farthing." This is the truth and justice of nature's laws revealed.

But in the definition of Buddhism, the justice is absolutely wanting. In their outrageous scheme of esoteric philosophy, the millions of Souls upon the earth are perfectly ignorant of what they are suffering for. They are ushered into the world for the purpose of undergoing the fiery torments of their old, fossilized Karma. They are completely ignorant of the facts. How can the average mortal work off his bad Karma when he does not know he has any? How can he work when he does not know what he is working and suffering for?

If we cruelly abuse a dog when it is full-grown for some offense or other committed when a puppy, it would be considered outrageous cruelty. The dog would be perfectly ignorant of what the punishment was for. The same may be said of inflicting punishment upon the material man for some forgotten offense of his infancy. Remember, no punishment is just when the one punished is ignorant of the cause. Punishment under such circumstances not only ceases to be just, but becomes a diabolical injustice. Since the common justice of human nature condemns this, how much more severe must be the condemnation of that justice which is Divine!

If human suffering is not the result of previous Karma, you may ask, what is the real cause of so much misery in the world? Human suffering is the result of innumerable laws, which in their action and reaction produce discord at intervals in the scale of human development. For all practical purposes they may be classed as primary and secondary. The primary cause is racial evolution. Each round and each race of the round requires different external conditions in order to evolve its chief attributes. Each period generation becomes the special means by which a certain one of the Soul's attributes is rounded out.

Let us explain. The first or primal race was that of the Golden Age. They were a purely ethereal race of beings and cannot be strictly classified with humanity; nor were they really incarnated in gross matter. For this reason, their penetrative power was very small. Thus, though highly spiritual, they were correspondingly simple. They lived an ideal life amid semispiritual surroundings.

The second race, that of the Silver Age, penetrated deeper into matter than their forefathers of the Golden Age. Their bodies consequently became more dense and material. Toward the termination of this race, and at the beginning of the third or Copper Age, the equator of our arc was reached on the descending scale. Here it was that the first murmurings of a mental storm began to manifest themselves. Emigrations and partings took place between what were previously a united people, and consequently, separate national interests began to evolve. When our earth reached the equinoctial points of the year, storms and tempest resulted. It is the same with the progress of man around the cycle of the higher planes. With the copper race, a still further descent took place and a still greater increase of self-interest was evolved. Kings ascended thrones and sacerdotal systems were formulated. The strong began to assert their greater forces. The weak gradually sank into subjection.

A still further descent occurred, and we came to the fourth race, the bottom rung on the cyclic ladder, fittingly known as the Iron Age. This was the turning point of the seven races, wherein the Soul attains its greatest penetrating power. Spirit can descend no lower! Kings and their priestly counsellors became true despots. The masses became helpless and oppressed. Next comes a higher cycle of evolution. The fifth race, beginning at the end of the fourth, reaches up to the equinoctial line of the mental arc on the ascending scale. Consequently another stormy period commences. All is strife and turmoil. It is the struggle of the oppressed against the oppressor. It is not the gentle mental storm of the Silver Equinox. A spirit period of light preceded that era. It is the storm of war and bloodshed — of a fierce democracy battling for the rights of man against usurped authority. It happened because the Iron Age of oppression preceded it.

We are at the present time passing through this fearful equinoctial period. The fifth race is coming to a close. Already forerunners of the sixth race are among the people, aiding in the spread of the glorious truth. No wonder, then, the signs of the times are so significant. A real interest in mental and spiritual science is rapidly reawakening within the minds of humanity.

The secondary causes are man's ignorance and his animal nature. Man makes the conditions which are necessary for his progress by alternately struggling with and yielding to his basic animal desires. Yet, Nature, the experience the Soul gains thereby, and material incarnation might be dispensed with. The state of suffering depends upon the race, but the effects of that suffering are in exact fulfillment of Nature's requirements.

Might-causes produce might-effects. This law is absolute! Every spiritual atom of life is the direct result of a cause. These atoms differ in power and potency, as the Stars differ in their magnitude. Nature's aim is not equality. In spite of the apparent fact that all forces are ever striving for equilibrium, her grand goal is diversity.

Nature's end, then, is the very opposite of equality; for the grand ultimate aim of every force is the production of variety. The only real difference in any of her infinite number of parts is that of polarity. The only difference between the Hottentot and the intellectual genius of modern civilized society is their Souls' respective polarity. It is simply a question of personal opinion as to which of the two is the best and wisest.

The civilized shams and personal adornments of society

may more than counterbalance the crude decorations of the savage. The false theology and cant of orthodox religion, combined with the many erroneous theories of so-called science, may more than make up for barbarian ignorance. Many savages are more learned in the real laws of nature than are our college professors. But be that as it may, the savage will be the gainer in most cases. He will not have false dogmatic opinions to unlearn and forget, nor the morality of our populous centers.

The external differences between the two are only in appearances, evolved chiefly by our own thoroughly biased and artificial education. Another factor in these secondary causes of human suffering is the human Will. This is Man's capacity for utilizing the great will-force of the cosmos. Ignorance alone limits human possibilities, for it is Man's place in nature to sway the mighty pendulum of force between the higher and the lower states of life. The supermundane and submundane realms of being are his mission, which consists in evolving the attributes of the Soul. If suffering is necessary to enable Man to accomplish this, then he will suffer.

But the causes and consequences be what they may in this life, what the soul suffers from discord it will be justly compensated for by the sum total of the results when the cycle of its purification is over. Then the past can be measured at its true worth.

We have presented, as concisely as possible, the Hermetic explanation of Karma, and have shown that it is not the all-ruling force Buddhism would make it.

We will now expose this Oriental delusion and reveal its priestly origin. We must carefully bear in mind a few all-important facts regarding the esoteric philosophy of the dreamy Orient. The basic truths of all religion, especially those relating to the Soul, its nature, incarnations, and Karma, were rigidly concealed from the people by a jealous Oriental priesthood. In the place of truth, fiction was substituted. The real truth was veiled, and the appearances of truth taught instead. In order to obtain absolute power, it became necessary to formulate a dogma. Their high priest, the pontiff or hierophant, as he was called, was made a direct incarnation of the Deity or a reincarnation of that Being.

In the process of time, the priests themselves became corrupt and worldly; consequently, their spiritual perception sank into mental reflection. They not only lost the secrets of their religion and mythology, which were never committed to writing, but also became the dupes of their own theology. They accepted their formulated husks as Divine Truth.

The history of the rise and fall of nations, and the research of all genuine Occultists, will support the above. In fact, *Isis Unveiled* teems with facts corroborating our statements. Hermetic initiates assert emphatically that both doctrines, reincarnation and Karma, are nothing more than the theological dogmas of an interested sacerdotal system.

The teachings based upon these doctrines by the Buddhists and other religious systems are false. The real facts of reincarnation and Karma were originally concealed and then forgotten in the lapse of time. It is very easy indeed to prove that the accepted theories of the Theosophical Buddhists are nothing but the popular external dogmas taught to the ignorant masses of ten thousand years ago.

The oldest records we possess prove human reincarnation and Karma were the popular doctrines of the masses; consequently, they were only appearances. They were untrue because the real truth was always concealed from the general public. This doctrine of Karma is one of the most interesting features of all Buddhist philosophy. There has been no secret about it at any time. Certainly, this is exactly what all true Hermetic initiates claim. It is a dogma of the Buddhist church, and was never concealed because it was not worth concealing.

On the contrary, it was always taught to the suffering masses, groaning beneath despotic rule. It was exceedingly potent as a means of making the people submit quietly to the authority of the Church and the tyranny of the King. The masses were taught to believe that by submitting to the yoke, they were thus working off previous bad Karma. This was a very convenient doctrine, we must all admit.

The chief Hierophant of Buddhism and the Tibetan adepts is the Taley Lama of Lhassa. Every Lama is subject to the grand Taley Lama, the Buddhist Pope of Tibet, who holds his residence at Lhassa and is said to be a reincarnation of Buddha. Buddhists would have us really believe Buddha continues to incarnate and reincarnate age after age. We can only say that no Soul who has passed through the trials of material incarnation and the fires of Spiritual purification would submit to continually exist and re-exist within a material organism. Thus it would endure from age to age — the hell of a Grand Lama's life. The formulae, ceremonies, and usages of a religious potentate are indeed a hell to the pure in heart.

The false assertions that with very high adepts and other exalted souls these things are different, that Nature's laws are either reversed or transcended, are told as facts. To this we say that such statements are false!

Nature is no respecter of persons, and neither Buddha nor any other Soul can continue to reincarnate from age to age. The most such a dominant mind may do would be to obsess and mould an unborn fetus to suit its purposes. Then, by virtue of such obsession, partially inhabit the material body. Under these circumstances the physical body is but the helpless machine of a dominant foreign mind. We scarcely need say that no purified Soul would sink to such a plane of existence.

4

The Mysteries of Sex

Four things play a part in conception and birth: body, imagination, form, and influence. The "body" as ordained in the beginning must become a *body* and nothing else. For it is a law of Nature that the oak tree must arise from an oak; the same is true of the body of man. From the *imagination,* and its objects, the child receives its reason. And just as Heaven infuses the child with its motion — its good and evil qualities — sometimes strongly, sometimes weakly, so the imagination of man has a course and makes the child's reason turn to higher or lower things. The third thing, the *form,* compels the child to look like the one from whom it descends. And finally, it is the *influence* that determines the health or sickness of the body. For in the same way as a strong architect erects good and solid buildings, and a weak one, weak buildings, so it is in the conception of a child.

It has been well said, "Man is most ignorant of those things which are most manifest." In some departments of nature this is true, and probably in no other "manifested" department of man's being is this truth more strikingly apparent than in his sexual nature. He is aware that animal nature is divided into two great classes, male and female, but he knows almost nothing of the spiritual principles which underlie this physical expression of sex.

Man is fully aware that the union of the two organisms is necessary for the purpose of procreation, but he is fearfully ignorant of those interior processes which produce the actual germs of life. He is acquainted with the fact that in the lower strata of animated existence bisexual organisms are the general rule and that occasionally this bisexual nature becomes manifested among men, as seen in the hermaphrodite.

But he is quite at a loss to account for such "monstrous" productions. Hence it may be truly said, "Man is most ignorant of those things which are most manifest." Therefore, in order to enable the reader to clearly grasp the various connecting links in the mystical ramifications of sex, to see their perfect harmony, and to understand their relation to each other, we will first speak of the origin of sex. Secondly, we will describe as clearly as possible its nature and functions. Thirdly, we will point out the relation of the sexes to each other. Lastly, we will present a brief application of the whole as it relates to man and the Universe.

The infinite ocean of formless spirit within its latent bosom contains all that is, or ever can be. Therefore, it contains all the elements of sex in their primal state. When the first pulsations of thought which evolved "the divine idea" became manifest, Nature arrayed herself under two modes of motion, action and reaction. The in-breathing and the out-breathing of this divine thought thus instituted the first spiritual attributes of sex in the earliest dawn of creation.

Each function which we may designate as the inspiration and respiration of the universal life current became differentiated for all eternity as the primary fundamental principle of Manifested Being. The Kabbalistical initiates of the past ages formulated this same biune spirit as Love and Wisdom.

Love, as the negative or feminine ray, is content and ever seeks to enfold. Wisdom as the positive, masculine ray is restless and always in pursuit. The feminine forces are ever striving to encircle the atom and the masculine forces to propel it forward in a straight line. From this dual action of spiritual potentialities is born the Spiral or the motion of life and the symbol of eternal progression.

We cannot attempt any explanation of how the first forms of sexual life became ultimated, nor of the why and wherefore of this celestial existence. It is enough for us that we are enabled by the laws of correspondence to trace the origin of sex to the shores of the great fountain of all existence and to proclaim the central Self from which all manifested selves derive their being. In order that we may comprehend somewhat the mysteries of sex as we see them manifested in humanity, we must descend from these inconceivable heights of celestial glory. We must seek for the links of this continuous chain within the highest states of life approachable by the embodied human Soul. Only in these states can we obtain any definite idea of the interior significance of sex and its mighty importance as a factor in the immortality of human Soul. The first link of this celestial chain lies concealed within the bosom of the Unknown. What the succeeding links may contain we cannot tell, but they will bear a correspondence to the former, making due allowance for the difference of the time element. Therefore, since we can only guess as to the origin of sex, we will consider its correlatives.

It must be self-evident that the Self contains within itself all the primary elements of sex, but in a latent condition. These attributes have not been subjected to the requisite conditions for their evolution. In this state, then, there is neither love nor wisdom manifested within the Self. It cannot know happiness when it is ignorant of the opposite. It cannot form any conception of rest when weariness is unknown. There can be no real love for the Self when it has never experienced the various contrary conditions by which love is known and distinguished. The wisdom of the Self in this state is equally latent, since it possesses no means of arriving at a true knowledge of its surroundings.

In this state we behold the spiritual atom in its primal condition. The various series of states through which this divine Self must penetrate in order to evolve its Soul sphere are the means by which the internal potentialities of sex must be awakened. When this transpires the divine Self becomes pregnant with the dual forms of its own organic life and the twin Souls are born (the male and female elements of its being).

These are represented in *Genesis* as Adam and Eve, knowing neither good nor evil. This book is a beautiful description of the embryonic human Souls. These twin souls are the absolute expression of the masculine and feminine rays of which absolute atomic Self is composed. The masculine ray contains a portion of Self forces and the feminine ray must likewise contain a portion of the positive qualities. These souls, therefore, contain a portion of each other. They constitute the Sun and Moon of the Self's creation.

When they once become differentiated, they are as eternal and immortal as the Self which called them into existence. They can be neither absorbed nor annihilated by time or eternity. They constitute the divine idea of a deific parent, and as such they become the divine expression of love and wisdom upon earth.

There is a particular sense in which it is held that the union here below between husband and wife is the work of the Self, and here arises the sanctity and necessity of that act which is implied by the word union. Man is formed below on the model of that which is above. It follows he who, in Zoharic terminology, suffers his fount to fail and produces no fruits here, whether because he will not take a wife, whether his wife is barren, or whether he abides with her in a way that is against nature, commits an irreparable crime.

Man shall participate in the world to come because he has entered during this life into the joy of living honorably with his wife. The reason is that Soul as well as body shares in the Self by which children are engendered. This is the eroticism which characterizes the *ZOHAR,* according to some commentators.

This is the consequence respecting the fruit of marriages, but there is also a consequence within the measures of the union itself, so it is raised from the physical into a spiritual degree. The fulfillment, the raising of the heart and mind on the part of the Lover and Beloved, to the most Holy Shekinah, the glory which cohabits and indwells, during the external act.

This is true also on the reverse side of the process, so two spirits are melted together and are interchanged constantly between body and body. The sexes are then interchanged in a sense. In the indistinguishable state which arises, the male is with the female neither male nor female, they are both or either. So is man affirmed to be composed of the world above, which is male, and of the female world below.

Now according to the *ZOHAR* those words in the "Song of Solomon": "Thy breasts are better than wine," refer to wine which provokes joy and desire; and seeing all things are formed above according to a pattern which is reproduced faithfully below, it is held to follow when desire awakens beneath it awakens also on high.

We see, therefore, that the nature of sex is to give perfect expression to the two grand attributes love and wisdom. To attain this end, the divine Soul of the absolute Self becomes differentiated as the male and female consciousness of self. It is in perfect expression of the positive and negative forces of its being. Once this differentiation is completed they exist as the Divine Idea of the microcosm and constitute its universe. This being so, each portion of the dual Soul maintains forever the perfect symbol of its internal qualities and always gives expression, in its outward form, to the symbol of Nature.

The functions of the Soul are to awaken and round out those qualities and attributes which are latent within. As we have seen there are two sets of Soul qualities, one the necessary outcome of the other. Now we see the harmony and the philosophy of the twin forms of life. Both male and female possess the necessary positive qualities for the perfect subjugation of material forces.

Hence it is that, when the souls are projected on their journey into matter, they travel upon divergent lines. These lines form two sides of an equilateral triangle with matter as a base, while the apex indicates the central Self or point of projection. The return journey between the mineral and man forms another triangle. This marks off the objective and subjective arcs of the Soul's evolution. When both arcs are combined they represent the mystical seal of King Solomon, the double triangle or six pointed star. This completes two acts in the grand drama of life.

The closing tableau in the first represents the stationary forces of the crystal; in the second the external conditions of human life. The third and last act in the human arc briefly reviews the whole of the previous two. This evolves another six pointed star which represents the higher and lower planes of manifestation. But in its grand outlines, it is also a spiritual trine whose closing tableau represents the reunion of the twin Souls symbolized by the celestial marriage of the Lamb.

Thus we have the one divine Monad or Self to begin with, and in the course of its expression and its gradual evolution of its sexual attributes, we see it slowly transform into a trinity. This trinity, in the subcycles of its evolution, forms the three triangles, which constitute the symbol of its forces. These are three times expressed upon the three subcycles of its journey which are the subjective arc or the cycle of unconsciousness, the objective arc or the cycle of intelligence, and the ethereal arc or the cycle of Soul consciousness.

The results of our present studies show the origin of sex begins with the Self; the nature of sex is the manifestation of its spirit; and its functions are the spiral motion of its evolutionary forces which awaken and round out its latent possibilities.

Male and female exist in nature as the representative expressions of love and wisdom. Their functions correspond exactly with their sex, and in actual life, it may be truly said that woman is ever the center of love. Her thoughts and desires constitute the index of her mission on earth. In her we hold the gentle, yielding, loving nature which softens and harmonizes man's positive spirit of aggression.

In her delicate nature we see the lovely center of maternal care and affection. She is the weaker portion of the dual Soul upon the physical plane, but her physical weakness constitutes the great center of her spiritual strength. As the weaker sex, we should naturally think her true place was one of subjection to man. But on the contrary, her more delicate forces become her most potent weapon. Instead of being the subject, she ascends to the throne of the conqueror. Man becomes a pliable medium in her hands, and is led as a willing captive by her subtle power and resources.

The principle is that the male must be always attached to the female for the Self ever to be with him. All holiness might be practiced, the Secret Doctrine might be studied by night and by day, and the illuminations might overflow the intellectual part; but failing fulfillment of this counsel a man is not on the way which leads into true life. He is in that condition which is not good for man to be — alone — like Adam in the Garden.

But those who have the precept at heart and are therefore complete men, by their union with women on earth, remind us in one particular of many Sons of Israel and students of the Doctrine. They are travellers in search of wisdom; and they are also men of affairs, workers in the vineyard of this world as well as in the Astral Garden.

The general definition of love is a vivifying spirit which permeates all the world. It is a bond uniting the entire universe. But the proper definition of perfect love of man and woman is the concurrence of the loving with the beloved so the beloved shall be transformed into the lover. When such love is equal between the partakers it is described as the conversion of the one into the other being.

Below such human love in apotheosis there is not only that which subsists among mere animals, but in the hypothetical first matter, in the elements and in the heavenly bodies, which are drawn one to the other and move in regular order by the harmonious impulse and interaction of a reciprocal affection.

Hereof is the form and the spirit, and this Book of Love and its mysteries moves forward to deeper things, when the knowledge of Self is presented under a transcendentalized sexual aspect. The mind must be content to know according to the measure of its possibility and not excellence. This does not consist in the act which leads to love, nor in the love which succeeds such knowledge, but in the copulation of the most interior and united divine knowledge. This is the sovereign perfection of the created intellect, the last act and happy end in which it finds itself rather divine than human. Such copulative felicity cannot be continuous, however, during our present life, because our intellect is here joined to the matter of our fragile body.

In man we behold the positive, aggressive law of Creation and that portion of the Soul which becomes the restless explorer of nature, seeking for wisdom, man's will is electric, penetrating and disruptive. The will of woman is magnetic, attractive, and formative. Hence they express the polar opposites of nature's creative forces.

MAN AND WOMAN

The twin Souls are related to each other primarily as brother and sister, and finally as man and wife. In this latter state, their true meeting place is the plane of embodied humanity. But during the present cycle very few of these spiritual unions take place. But whenever the two halves of the same divine Self do meet, love is the natural consequence. This is not the physical sensation produced by the animal magnetism of their sexual natures, but it is the deep silent emotions of the Soul. It is the responsive vibrations of their internal natures toward each other and the blissful silence of two Souls in perfect rapport wherein neither careth to speak.

Spiritual love is the outcome of their divine relationship, and should never be set aside nor crushed by any worldly considerations. On the contrary, wherever possible, these pure intuitions of the Soul should be obeyed. They cannot deceive nor lead one astray, because the Soul never makes a mistake when claiming its own. Should circumstances in life or any other material consideration prevent their rightful union, the fact they have actually met will constitute an invisible connection, a spiritual rapport. With this between them, no earthly power or device can break the bonds, and deep down within the secret chambers of the self the image of the loved one will be treasured. Its continual presence will poison and corrode everything which pertains toward an ephemeral affection for another.

If a female should marry under these circumstances, and become the mother of children, it will often transpire that the actual germs of spiritual life will be transmitted by this absent Soul. The external husband provides only the purely physical conditions for the manifestations of the offspring. The rejected soul mate, the spiritual bridegroom is the real father, and very often the child born will resemble the image of its true Soul parent.

The spirit of a pregnant woman is so strong it can influence the seed and change the fruit in her womb in many directions. Her inner stars act powerfully and vigorously upon the fruit; its nature is thereby deeply and solidly shaped and forged, for the child in the mother's womb is exposed to the mother's influence. It is entrusted to the hand and will of its mother as the clay is entrusted to the hand of the potter, who creates and forms out of it what he wants and what he pleases.

God does not want man or woman to be like a tree which always grows the same fruit. He made each one different from the other. God left man free to propagate his kind; according to his will, he may beget a child, transmit his seed, or not. God planted the seed in all its reality and specificity deep in the imagination of man. If a man has the will, the desire arises in his imagination, and the desire generates the seed.

But man himself cannot kindle the desire, it must be fanned by an object. When a man sees a woman, she is the object; it depends only upon him whether he wants to fasten to it or not.

He himself must decide whether to let it act on him or not, whether to follow his intelligence or not. God has entrusted the seed to man's reflective reason because the reflective reason encompasses both his intelligence and the object that inflames his fantasy.

It is the same with woman. When she sees a man, he becomes her object, and her imagination begins to dwell on him. She does this by virtue of the ability bestowed upon her. It is in her power to feel desire or not. If she yields, she becomes rich in seeds; if not, she has neither seed nor urge. Thus the seed is left to the free decision of man, and the decision depends upon man's will. He can do as he wishes.

Since this free decision exists, it lies with both, with man and with woman. As they determine by their will, so will it happen.

Thus the most important of the relations of the sexes toward each other pertains to their sexual intercourse. Untold misery, suffering, and crime are born into the world through the sensual depravity of mankind. A man and wife should harmonize both in physical temperament and in magnetic polarity. No marriage should be thought of where these essential points are wanting. Neither wealth, fame, nor worldly position can compensate for their lack.

Discordant unions are the harbingers of sorrow, crime, and disease. Sexual union between inharmonious souls evolves the seeds of every species of wickedness and sexual disorder. It may not become readily apparent, but these seeds exist within the spaces of human life ready to spring into concrete form under the favorable conditions of discordance.

The purely martial man will prove a continual curse to the cold-natured saturnine woman, and vice versa. This may not be the fault of the man or woman. It is the discordant polarities of their astral constitutions. The same will hold good between natures of earthy triplicity and those born under the airy. Hence a true knowledge of the science of the stars is necessary for the production of conjugal harmony between the sexes.

Just as there is love between animals, female with male, so also among men love is often of the animal kind. This love has its usefulness, and its rewards; but it remains animal, it does not endure, and it reflects only the reason and aspiration of material man. It does not know higher goals.

It is because of this animal love that people can be friendly or hostile, well or ill disposed toward one another, exactly like animals are fierce and angry, envious and hostile toward one another. Just as dogs and cats hate each other, so nations fall into conflicts. All this is rooted in the animal nature.

When dogs bark and snap at one another, it is because of envy or greed, because each of them wants to have everything for himself, wants to devour everything himself and begrudges everything to the other. This is the way of beasts. In this respect, man is the child of dogs. He, too, is burdened with envy and disloyalty, with a violent disposition, and each man grudges the other.

When a man and a woman who belong to each other and were destined for each other by the stars come together, no adultery will take place, because they form one being. But if these two do not come together, there is no steadfast love; their love sways like a reed in the wind. When a man courts many women, he has not found the proper wife to complement him; similarly a woman who carries on amorous intrigues with other men has not found the proper husband.

It remains for us to apply the logical outcome of the principles of sex as they affect man, the universe, and the immortality of the Soul.

As we view the outward forms of man and woman we cannot fail to observe the perfect harmony between the external appearance and the internal cause. Their organisms are the concrete image of the principles concealed within. It would be the extreme height of absurdity for us to believe a materialized form bears no correspondence to the forces which created it. The form cannot exist without an internal cause, and the internal cause is powerless to produce any external form except the reflected image of itself and its functions.

Under these circumstances it must be evident every male organism is the absolute outcome of masculine forces, and every female organism the product of the feminine qualities. Therefore, a male soul cannot be born into the world under the cover of a female form. Neither can a female soul be ushered upon the planes of humanity imprisoned within the masculine body. These are nature's facts, which ought to be apparent to every thinking mind.

The human form applies to man as the material culmination of nature's sexual expression. Upon this plane she can go no further, for beyond this limit we step within the spaces of the ether. There nature continues her wonderful expression of sex in strict harmony with the laws of correspondence to the planes below. While dealing with the forms assumed by man we must notice those vital secretions which form the physical conditions for reproduction.

The seminal fluids are the most ethereal of all physical secretions and contain the very quintessence of human nature. The sexual organism exists as a factor in procreation; therefore, the sexual organs have their proper functions and use or they would not be present. To suddenly and completely suppress their natural functions would do a great deal of physical and spiritual harm. The reaction of them will create violent discord within the ethereal constitution.

To obey the laws of nature is the only safe and sure road to the spiritual evolution of the senses of the soul; and one of these laws is the rightful union of the sexes.

God ordained that marriage be sacred, but He did not prescribe the number of wives, neither a high nor a low one. He commanded: "Thou shalt be faithful to thy marriage vow and thou shalt not break it."

Why then issue laws about morality, virtues, chastity, and so forth? No one but God can give commandments that are permanent and immutable. For human laws must be adapted to the needs of the times, and accordingly can be abrogated and replaced by others.

When we regard the mystical ramifications of sex as represented in the universal creation of suns, stars, moons and planets, we see the same principles at work, even to their shape and the form of their orbit. The suns are masculine and represent the cosmic male spirit. The planets are feminine and consequently become the fruitful wombs of progressive life. The moons are neither one nor the other, for they are the conflicting offsprings of the disturbing forces within the sun and its planets. They are the lowest organic expression of planetary life, and as such represent the state of the hermaphrodite. Both in man and in the universe the potentialities of sex swing the mighty pendulum of thought and motion.

The grand object which the divine Self seeks to realize in the evolution of the human soul is the complete differentiation of its latent attributes. The soul, therefore, must become the expression of both its qualities and must express the true nature of the spirit. Thus male and female evolution is the outcome.

Each soul rounds out and completes its own section of the self, and in doing this it becomes individualized as a complete expression of one ray of the divine idea. It has a perfect identity with its source. Both male and female complete the whole and are related to each other as Osiris and Isis. Their individuality, in the form of their spiritual identity, is forever preserved. There they are united as well, and their separate consciousness becomes an attribute of their glorious immortality. Without sex there cannot be eternal life. To absorb or destroy these principles in the human organism brings about a divorce between the man and his divinity. Thus it robs the conscious humanity of its deathless immortality of soul.

5

The Soul

First, we must speak of the Soul. If it were possible for a duad to exist in which there was a distinction without a difference we should say such a combination was a perfect "Soul and Spirit." But since such a duad is not in existence, we must try to express both the distinction and the difference in other ways. In regard to Soul and Spirit, the one is not perceptible without the presence of the other.

The terms Soul and Spirit have become interblended in hopeless confusion, and it seems almost impossible to unravel the tangled skeins of the various definitions. We will try to present a clear, comprehensive outline of the two and show them as they really are when viewed in the light of spiritual illumination.

The Soul is not the Spirit, but it is that by which the Spirit is known. It is by the Soul that we understand the nature and power of the Spirit. When we come to define the Soul, we are compelled to use illustrations. The spiritual Self is an atom of divinity, a scintillating atomic point evolved from the Divine Soul. Now, while this is quite true as regards the Self, when we desire to define the Soul we must consider them as the cause and effect of spiritual evolution.

The Soul is formless and intangible, and constitutes the attributes of the Divine Spirit. We can only conceive and know of the Soul by learning the powers or attributes of the Spirit. When we have learned them, we shall possess a clear conception of the Soul and its real nature. In order to better understand, let us illustrate. Take a ray of light! What do we know concerning it? Nothing, except by its action upon something else. This action we term the attributes of light. In themselves the attributes of light are formless, but they may easily be rendered visible, either by their colors when refracted by the prism, or by their effects when concentrated upon material objects. Here we have what may be correctly termed the soul of a ray of light.

Another example as illustrative and expressive of the idea is the organism of man. Man possesses five external senses: seeing, feeling, hearing, tasting, and smelling. In reality, he has seven senses which may be used externally, but the two higher senses are still in embryo so far as present mankind is concerned. The sixth or coming race will evolve the sixth sense; the seventh race, the seventh sense; and then mankind will be physically perfect. But these two higher senses do not interfere with our illustration, so we will only consider man as he is, and be content with five senses.

All our knowledge at present concerning external phenomena must come through the mediumship of one or more of these five senses. The organs through which the functions of the senses become manifest are visible, but the senses themselves are invisible and formless. We know them only as attributes of the body; while the mind, which is perfectly and absolutely dependent upon the senses for information, represents the spiritual Self in its relation to the Soul.

The reader will observe from what is stated, the Soul itself is formless and intangible, and can only be defined as the attribute of Spirit. The one cannot exist without the other. There is the same difference between these two as there is between a ray of light and its action. The same distinction also holds as exists between the body and its physical senses. Without the one we cannot know the other, and vice versa.

A very large percentage of the readers of mystical literature imagine the human Soul is some kind of a spiritual organism — similar in many respects to the body — and the means whereby the Divine Spirit manifests itself. But this idea is radically erroneous. The spiritual body is the result or outcome of the Soul's action, but is not the Soul itself. It is an attribute of the Soul, just as the Soul is an attribute of the Divine Self.

Having attempted to define the Soul as distinct and yet inseparable from the Spirit, we will give some ideas about its attributes. In this connection it will greatly aid us if we first point out the differences between the Soul and the body, and also the correspondences between the two.

The physical body is evolved by a reflex action of the interior Soul during the process of its evolving. The medium between the two is the astral form. It is from the latter the body receives its form and force. The spiritual organism protects itself from the external plane by evolving an astral raiment. This raiment, or astral body, crystallizes a more or less distorted reflection of the spiritual form around itself. Thus it produces what is known as the human form divine, upon the external plane. This physical organism is constituted and evolved so as to render the most perfect expression (in unison) of the physical senses. No one sense is in excess in a perfectly sound human organism; while the lower animals generally have some extreme expression of one particular sense.

This human body, through the mediumship of the brain, which is the sounding board of the senses, communicates with the external world of the various elements. The result is form, sound, color, flavor, and odor. Our senses constitute the only source of our external consciousness. The intellectual state is based and dependent (while on earth) upon the continuance of the physical senses.

The sum total of human knowledge along some special lines, when tabulated and classified, is thus reduced to a system and called science. We are now able to see and appreciate the relation of the physical senses to the physical body, and grasp their importance to the still remoter mind which utilizes the knowledge gained.

The attributes of the Spirit, which we term the Soul, bear a correspondence to the physical senses of the body. That is, the Soul bears exactly the same relation to the Spirit as the physical senses to the human brain. Thus we have the senses which are Spiritual. The former are simply a reflection of the latter. The senses of the body and the senses of the Soul are the sides of the same attribute, one is the internal and the other is the external.

The intelligence, the mind, is back of the senses and utilizes and tabulates the impressions it received of the outer world. This world is one place the mind is itself powerless to penetrate. The mind is something above and beyond the senses, even though it is absolutely dependent upon them. It is the same with the Soul, and the Spirit.

All knowledge from without or within the universe of external life is received by means of the Soul, but at the back of this Soul there rests the eternal scintillating atom of Deity above and beyond any human conception. There it rests in serenity and peace, tabulating and utilizing all the knowledge and experience which the Soul in its various cycles is continually receiving and sending to it.

"As it is below so it is above." This law should ever be remembered. It is man's universal but infallible guide, and anything conflicting with it can be rejected as completely erroneous.

The seven senses below correspond to the seven senses above, and the results obtained in each case are the same but upon two different planes. These results may be fully expressed by the word "perception." Absolute perception implies absolute consciousness. Unlimited absolute perception, therefore, is the goal toward which the universe of manifested being is headed.

It is the climax of evolution. Progressive life is eternal. Thus we have a demonstration of the immortality of the Spirit and consequently the immortality of the Soul.

We have now arrived at the method of the Soul's enfoldment. Of this we can only speak in general terms. There are certain fundamental laws applicable to all. But, to be successful, something more is requisite. It is necessary for each Soul to follow a system especially adapted to its special state. Each person must find out for himself the special development required of him, unless he can come into contact with others capable of reading his Soul's requirements correctly and thus give him the necessary information.

There is a trinity of laws to be observed:

1. Physical harmony in one's surroundings.
2. Spiritual purity and complete isolation from impure currents of thought.
3. Evolve the states from within and the without will take care of itself.

These are the methods of the soul's unfoldment. Purity is the great touchstone, and as Jesus has truly observed, "Blessed are the pure in heart for they shall see God."

How many can follow out such a code? Not one in a million! The answer comes across the spiritual spaces of ether, and the saddening thought that such is indeed the truth compels us to offer a few words of friendly advice.

To be pure in body, a pure diet must be eaten. The highest form of food possible to man must constitute his physical sustenance. The products of the earth are plenty; they are simple but sufficient and not artificial.

If we cannot be perfect, then let us be the next thing to it. One should be as perfect as one's surroundings render possible. Learn to say "I will" and "I will not," and when you have said it see your assertion is sacredly maintained.

Let us remember the material life of man is only one second of his greater existence. It is one of the most unprofitable things in the world to be selfish. Selfishness is the road to the deepest hells of the Soul world.

Lastly, if these things are followed with an earnest loving spirit, rest assured the blossoms of the Soul will expand into full-grown flowers. For the labor and self-denial expended, we shall reap the spiritual rewards which will repay us ten thousandfold. Remember the words of the wise Proclus:

"Know the Divinity which is within you that you may know the Divine One, of which your Soul is a ray."

The triumph of the human Soul over the forces of matter is termed "adeptship." We do not refer to the attaining of immortality; the vast majority of mankind inherit immortality as the result of their humanity. This immortality is not completely assured until they have passed through the sixth state of the soul world.

We refer to those rare human beings, so organized as to be able to evolve the sixth and seventh states. They attain to the powers and blessings of their immortality while yet outwardly upon the human plane of existence.

The literary world has been flooded with descriptions and explanations of adeptship. Definitions have been given of the various degrees and grades of this exalted state. But so far the vague generalities of such expounders of any state higher than they themselves possess have failed completely. No human being can describe adeptship except the adept himself, or one who is his accepted neophyte. He is the future successor to the adept, who has passed the third initiation, and is in perfect magnetic rapport with the Master. He will succeed to the Master's place when that Master ascends to a still higher sphere of spiritual life and powers.

In order to present the subject as clearly as possible, we will consider first, the various grades of adeptship; second, the nature and functions of adeptship; and third, how adeptship is attainable by a neophyte.

Since the Grand Master is not an inhabitant of this earth, but has His throne and His Kingdom in the Spiritual, it is necessary that there be someone on earth to guide mankind and show it the way through the straits of life. There is no angel, no spirit on earth, to lead men; to man alone this task has fallen.

Therefore, it is not surprising many false paths are entered upon, and it is of great importance that man should recognize his shepherd and know who he is, lest a wolf be taken for a shepherd and mislead man by donning sheep's clothing, while concealing the devil within him. For each of the two paths — the narrow one through life and the broad one in the astral plane — has its own shepherd, and each of these shepherds reveals and shows us his way. But it is so hard to distinguish who is the shepherd, that it is almost impossible to tell the true Master from the false one.

In the first place, there are three distinct grades of this exalted state of adeptship (Master), each grade containing within itself three separate states of degrees of life and power. In the whole there are nine states of wisdom. These three principle grades may be designated as the Natural, the Spiritual, and the Celestial states of the Soul's progressive evolutions.

The first (the most external) relates to the world of physical phenomena, and deals exclusively with the elemental spheres of the planet and the Astromagnetic currents which control them.

The powers of the adept of this grade extend from the elemental zones of matter in the world of effects, up to the astromagnetic spheres in the realm of cause. "Beyond this Astral world they become powerless. Hence their highest achievements are within the realms of external magical phenomena."

The second grade constitutes the interior or Spiritual state of the first grade, relates to the realm of the Spirit and deals exclusively with the spiritual and ethereal forces of the planet. The adepts of this grade are the translated Souls of those who have graduated through the various degrees of the first. As such, they fulfill the duties of Master or Teacher to those who are still studying in the outer degrees of Spiritual life.

Their power extends from the magnetic zones of the Astral world up to the Astral world and up to the ethereal and Spiritual spheres of disembodied humanity. Beyond these states of Spiritual life, they cannot penetrate, hence their highest achievements are within spheres of disembodied existence.

Yet occupying as they do the interior degree of life, they are able to combat the hells, on the one hand, and to sustain the Heavens, on the other. These Spiritual adepts cannot descend to earth and manifest their power externally, without the aid of a properly trained instrument whose odylic sphere they may temporarily occupy. Their chief means of communication with the external world are the adepts of the first grade, through whom they transmit such portions of Spiritual truth as the world needs.

The third grade constitutes the internal of Celestial state of the second, and is the highest degree of Spiritual life the embodied human mind can comprehend. It relates to the higher states of the purified Souls. It is above and beyond what we know as human. Of its deific powers and potentialities we cannot speak. They are beyond the grasp of all external material life.

At this point, it is of the utmost importance the reader should clearly grasp the relation of these three grades to each other, in order to form a correct idea of the nature and functions of adeptship.

The first grade and the three degrees included within it embrace all the possibilities of humanity under the external conditions of the present cycle. The various Astral spaces which mark off the limits of these human possibilities constitute the boundary line of Nature drawn by the finger of Deity between the two worlds of human life (the Natural and Spiritual). When the external life mission of an adept of the first grade is fulfilled, a process analogous to physical dissolution occurs and the physical atoms which constitute the organism are liberated and the exalted Soul enters upon a higher state of evolution and life. Thus it becomes the

Spiritual man or an adept of the second grade. The second grade is thus a continuation of the first, but upon a higher and more interior plane. The scene of the Soul's activity is transferred from the Astral and magnetic spheres to the realm of Spirit.

This state holds the grand key of life and death, wherein all the greater mysteries of external life are concealed. It also stands midway between the man and the Deity, and thus is the equipoise between the human and the Divine.

There are seven states from the lowest grade of the human being on the external planes of matter up to the highest grade, or the perfect man. Also in the realm of Spiritual humanity, there are seven states from the perfect man up to the Deity. The vast importance of this grade of life, or Spiritual adeptship, is shown by the fact it is upon the boundaries of the sixth and seventh state of this grade the two halves of the Divine Soul become permanently and eternally united. The twin souls, male and female, then constitute the complete of the Divine Self.

The Deity has given man shepherds to lead him and show him the way in study and work. But the shepherds cannot of themselves gain such leadership and guidance, but only when inspired by the Deity. Man must be guided in a divine, and not in a human manner. Therefore the purified souls have ordained and appointed man's shepherds, and taught and instructed them as to what to teach and tell the people, in order that their will be obeyed.

One of the greatest gifts that the Deity bestows upon us is to provide us always with men who lead us and teach us and guide us in things eternal.

This is the true task of the pious teachers on earth, who take their instruction from the Master and who speak and lead. But not only are they deeply enlightened and speak important words, a marvel to all men; they also possess a mighty power on earth, which has been bestowed on them.

In discussing the nature and function of adeptship, we can deal only with the first grade, or adeptship of the external degree. It is impossible for the student to fully comprehend the powers of the second until he himself has attained the first. Therefore, to avoid misconception, let it be distinctly understood the whole of what follows pertains exclusively to that state of adeptship whose members live, move, and have their being and launch forth their powers, either upon the external planes of physical life, or else within the spheres of the Astral world immediately interior to it.

Since the adept is the perfect man, it is evidently necessary to understand what is the nature of his perfection. In the Occult sense of the term, man is a composite being possessing a seven fold constitution, and possessing seven cyclic states of existence, or the progressive states of evolution upon the physical plane. The perfect man, therefore, is he who evolves in full his composite being and attains unto the seven states while still existing in eternal physical world.

While on the other hand, the ordinary human being is compelled to attain perfection within the purgatorial states of purification of the Soul world. Ignorance and selfishness, or else the jarring discords produced by the combination of the two, force the great majority of mankind out of the central line of progressive evolution.

At the present time mankind has evolved but five physical senses. The perfect composite man, however, possesses not only seven physical senses, but also seven Soul senses, related to each other as follows:

PHYSICAL SENSES	SOUL SENSES
1. Touch	1. The power to psychometrize.
2. Taste	2. The power to absorb and enjoy the finer essence of life wave.
3. Smell	3. The power to distinguish the spiritual aromas of nature.
4. Sight	4. The lucid state called clairvoyance.

5. Hearing	5. The ability to perceive the ethereal vibrations termed clairaudience.
6. Intuition	6. The capacity to receive true inspirations.
7. Thought transference	7. The power to converse with spiritual intelligence at will.

When the human Soul has attained unto these seven states, his divine right to rule follows as a natural sequence. The powers of the will increase as the attributes of the Soul expand. Therefore it is perfectly useless to preach so much about cultivating the will, since this is accomplished by evolving the Soul qualities or senses.

The magical powers of the adept which enable him to partially control the elements and to produce various kinds of physical phenomena at will, are not the outcome of any terrific will force.

They are the mild expressions of a firm but gentle Soul in the process of evolving forms in the Spiritual imagery of thought. There is nothing "tremendous," nothing of "fearful intensity," about it, for the slightest tremor of the purified Soul when consciously placed in rapport with the Astral light will produce surprising results. The higher the plane from which the embodied adept projects his thought desire the more extensive and potential the phenomena will be in the sublunary world of effects.

Such then, is adeptship. Such are the glorious possibilities attainable by the human race when the Spiritual attributes of their being are allowed to grow and expand in the atmosphere of a pure and unselfish life. It is a state which may well be regarded as the climax of our Earth's possibilities upon her outward plane. A victory the human race may justly feel proud of, would be the grand triumph of the Soul over the forces of matter.

Man, too, can be presumptuous or not; therein he is like the devil when the devil was still an angel. And what befell the devil may also befall the men who are like him. Therefore we should be like the angels and not like the devil; for to this end we were born and sent into the world.

To what end does man live on earth, if not to become versed in the works of Spirit and to learn how all things have their source in Spirit.

We will explain, as far as permissible, "the modus operandi" by which adeptship is actually attained. But it will be necessary to consider who may and who may not possess the necessary qualifications, since the adept is, of a truth, like the poet, "born and not made." The adept is born a kind of his kind. He is a Spiritual and mental giant of his race, and cannot be made without possessing these qualities in a very highly developed state from his birth.

External life is too short and the antagonistic forces to be overcome are too great, during the present cycle, for the adept to come out of the rudimentary forces and embryonic Soul qualities of the average mortal. It has been stated by one who claims the honor of adeptship: "The adept is the rare efflorescence of an age."

This is, however, only figuratively correct as in truth there are several such adepts in each race during the course of a single generation. Each family of mankind ultimately produces the adept of its line, and then becomes exhausted for that cycle.

In the centuries past, the alchemists were the adepts. They approached the Soul-Spirit via the way of essences and were the true masters of their generations.

There are four essences in the universe upon which Agrippa and all the learned through the centuries have agreed. These are Fire, Water, Earth and Air. However, there is a fifth essence, or quintessence, which permeates everything above in the stars and below upon earth. It is the world Soul-Spirit which animates all bodies. It is heavy earth and never free or visible. Yet it is omnipresent, and he who can free this fifth element from the matter it inhabits shall hold in his hand the creative power with which God has endowed the world of matter.

The ancient goddesses of growth and vegetation, like Isis, were nothing more to the alchemist than the emblems of the quintessence, the generative power that resides in the philosophers' stone.

The hermetic world plan depicts a dualism. Above is the Heavenly Trinity, the Lamb, the Dove, and the Hebrew Jehovah. Surrounded by angels, they send forth rays of divine light. Below is the world of matter. The starry heaven encircles the hermetic work, which is "half above and half below." Its center is the philosophic stone, a triangle inscribed by the double sign of mercury and gold.

The symbol is flanked by the three signs of the alchemist procedure: a triangle, air (signifying the volatile mercury), a reversed triangle, water (the fixed mercury). In the third sign, the two qualities of mercury are superimposed, forming a six-branched star which symbolizes the "fixed volatile." Seven concentric circles surround the sign.

The innermost contains the recommendation to use four degrees of fire for the work. Then follow the trinities of mercury, sulphur, and salt. The philosophers' mercury is not corporeal, but Spiritual; the corporeal mercury meaning the sublimated metal; and the vulgur, mercury.

One circle signifies time, which divides into the solar year, the year of the stars, and that of the winds. They refer to the influences of sun, stars, and atmosphere upon the hermetic work. The outmost circle, finally, shows these influences must be directed.

Favorable constellations have to be awaited: here are the twelve signs of the Zodiac, and the five signs of the planets (sun and moon having special places). The sphere of the fixed stars encircles five hermetic emblems: the raven, the swan, the hermetic dragon, the pelican which feeds it children with its own blood, and the phoenix which resuscitates in the flame.

The world below is dualistic, divided into light and darkness, day and night. Man and woman are chained to the world above. They are the two principles of procreation, with which God has endowed the world of matter. Here below, everything is divided into two, male and female. In God alone both principles are united, as He is the cause of everything.

Various meanings are superimposed on these two figures. The male is the Sun, gold, the fiery dry essence. He is the Soul or the generative principle. With him is the lion of the zodiac, presiding over the month when the heat is strongest. He is Jupiter and Apollo, and fire and air are his elements, because they are dry and warm. The fiery phoenix is his emblem, and the lion is the symbol of gold. Lion and man hold the sun, which is the philosophers' gold as well as the heavenly star, and the emblem of generation.

Woman is the moon, silver, the moist and cool essence; she is the spirit, bearing fruit, conceiving, giving birth and nourishing. In her hand she holds the grape whose many fruits are her true symbol. She is connected with evaporation, rain, and earthly moist exhalation, for her elements are earth and water. From her breast flows the Milky Way, the seed which penetrates everything in this world of bodies, and which the wise men also called the world spirit or world soul. In her left hand she holds the moon in its two extreme phases. Her fugitiveness is symbolized by the eagle.

Other alchemical allegories of the sixth stage represent the Holy Virgin, immaculate, like Diana, standing upon the half-moon.

Not all of these rare men of the royal line may attain to adeptship, since they often exhaust their forces in other directions for the good of humanity. But such Souls alone possess the possibilities or the primary conditions.

When, therefore, these primary conditions exist, the first course to be pursued is to devote as much time as possible to the study of Spiritual subjects and to master each and every branch of Occultism. Simultaneously with this study the body must be trained in regard to matters of diet, and sexual relations. In other words, the human Soul must be wholly evolved up out of the animal Soul. The sphere of undeveloped good in man's constitution must be developed.

The animal forces and appetites, instead of being conquered and chained like a wild beast as taught by Oriental mystics, must be gradually developed and transformed or evolved into the human.

The problem of good and evil must be solved in each individual case. And right here consists the vital point of failure or success, defeat or triumph. As we have labored over and over again to impress upon the reader, man is a composite being and perfection consists in harmonious evolution. It ought by this time to be self-evident to any candid mind that those fearful practices in the East of asceticism, celibacy, and self-mutilations, simply starve and chain the animal into subjection. They do not develop it into a useful obedient and most highly important factor of the perfect man's seven fold nature.

Did the alchemist have valid knowledge about the process? That is not difficult to believe, for alchemy's principles were not scientific. The principles of alchemy were correct and did not belong to science, but to a philosophic wisdom which directed it from its inception toward Mysticism. Alchemy's chief values were of a psychic nature; the Hermetic was the brother of the mystic and Master.

The experiments of the adepts resulted in an impressive series of chemical discoveries. If alchemy failed to discover what it had been seeking, it certainly stumbled upon things it had not anticipated.

It may be worthwhile to mention some of these true alchemic adepts:

1. Albertus Magnus (1193-1280) is credited with the preparation of caustic potash. He was the first to describe the chemical composition of cinnabar, ceruse, and minium.
2. Raymond Lully (1235-1315) prepared bicarbonate of potassium.
3. Basil Valentine (fifteenth century) discovered sulphuric ether and hydrochloric acid.
4. Theophrastus Paracelsus (1493-1541) was the first to describe zinc. He also introduced the use of chemical compounds.
5. Jean Baptiste Van Helmont (1577-1644) recognized the existence of gas.

6. Johann Rudolf Glauber (1604-1668) discovered sodium sulphate (Glauber salt) which he believed to be the philosophers' stone.
7. Brandt (1692) of Hamburg, discovered phosphorus.
8. Giambattista della Porta (1541-1615) prepared tin oxide.
9. Johann Friedrich Boetticher (1682-1719) was the first European who made porcelain.
10. Blaise Vigenere (1523-1596) discovered benzoid acid.

These few examples suffice to illustrate that the alchemists' researches, though lacking scientific direction, produced a benefit to humanity at large, not merely for the chosen.

The ascetic, whether ignorant or selfish, who starts out to attain magical powers for himself, and who enters upon a cold, rigid use of the will to crush and annihilate his animal passions, may succeed. But he will find out too late that his powers over the elements and forces of Nature have been purchased at the awful expense of the destruction of the feminine portion of his own Soul by gradual absorption into himself of the being upon whose development in harmony with his own depends his immortality.

Did this happen to some of the alchemists? I think not, for they realized the essences of the universe. They understood how souls must unite. One must realize that union with the twin Soul constitutes the Divine Self. One cannot deny there is aught in the universe beyond his state except false Nirvana to which he is drifting. This is practically a condition of annihilation. But often one fondly pictures Nirvana in as vague and pleasing terms as possible, as "absorption into the Infinite." Then he denies point blank (since they no longer exist for him) the angelic and celestial states, and devotes himself to a systematic dissemination of the dogmas of Karma and reincarnation. These in their essence are the most subtle and enervating forms of fatality conceivable by the human mind, since they sap the Soul of all true inspiration toward the higher self and perfect life.

As there may be many roads which will ultimately lead

us to the same mountain top, so there are many systems of Occult training. The end in view of every system is the same. It is to first evolve conscious lucidity, the rest will then follow.

When once the aspirant becomes an accepted neophyte, whether he personally sees Him or internally realizes the Master makes no difference. Future progress depends upon his strict obedience to the commands received, unselfish motives, and a pure life. The alchemists were able to do this and so may you.

6

Mortality and Immortality

In attempting to elucidate the problems of "Mortality and Immortality" (life and death), it must be understood we are dealing with questions which depend upon the construction which is placed in the terms used. It is not our province to enter into the scientific minutia of these problems, nor to present an abstract of learned nonsense concerning the various derivations from which the words reached us. Equally unimportant to our purpose is the sense in which our hoary ancestors may have used them, seeing such questions must ever remain matters of speculation and opinion. "When doctors disagree, who shall decide?"

At present we are concerned with the Occult side of the problems, and with the laws which are far removed from the realms of mere opinion and constitute eternal realities. The manifestations of these laws can be realized and verified by each individual Soul for itself.

Simply and briefly stated, immortality means life or continued life. Mortality means death or the extinction of life, and therefore is the antithesis of life and immortality. These are the generally accepted sense in which the words are now used. Mortality and immortality in their external relation towards each other stand as the polar opposites, and as such they are the alpha and omega of cyclic existence. They represent "the evening and the morning" of every phase of infinite creation, upon the outer planes of manifested being. Life and death form the grand spiral axis of time, and the resultants to the human mind are seen in the world of phenomena.

For the sake of convenience we will consider each problem by itself. Then, as a stimulant towards mental reflection, we will leave their relationship to each other to be thought out by the reader.

Mortality, as stated, means death and extinction upon the material plane. But when viewed from the higher and more interior standpoint, death simply means a change of form and function. There can be no absolute extinction in the strict sense of the term. Atoms are immortal, eternal, and indestructible. But a universe or an organism which is composed of an infinite number of atoms may be dissolved, destroyed and forever lost. It is lost as an organic whole, but not lost as regards its separate atomic parts.

The mental being which bound these atoms together loses its force during the process of change or death, thus death is simply change of polarity. In order to see this, it must be understood the Moons, Planets, Suns, and systems have their own special individuality exactly like men. On the contrary, an atom has no individuality, so far as its external form is concerned, but it possesses a cosmic individuality. This is an attraction and repulsion of its own, by virtue of its differentiation from the universal atom. It is the complex expression of the myriad atoms which compose the organism or the universe which produce individuality. This individuality gives expression to a form suitable to Nature, and constitutes the personal or external appearance of a material object. These facts must be borne in mind, or the real meaning of this material will be misunderstood.

As a general principle of phenomenal expression, Nature embodies, within some external form, every idea, thought, and motive which mankind evolves. The only limit to her possibilities in this direction is the mental and magnetic condition of the race. In fact, every organic form which we see around us is Nature's expression of various thoughts and ideas. These thoughts and ideas are representative of Spiritual qualities which react upon the Astral light. These Spiritual qualities emanate from the Mind or mental being, either human or divine.

As illustrations of the process of death and change, let us select two cases, one from the vegetable world, and one from the animal kingdom — a tree and a tigress. The tree dies, decay sets in, and soon it appears to be gone forever. But this disappearance is only an illusion, for the tree not only exists but exerts a very powerful influence upon the material plane.

The tree, so far as its phenomenal outcome is concerned, has only been a means by which the progressive cycle of evolution works upward from the mineral state. It is composed of millions of atoms of life undergoing their various cyclic rounds within the vegetable circuit, and as a natural consequence of this internal spiritual activity the tree possesses a Karmic sphere within the Astral spaces of its life wave. The Astral tree, if we may so call this Karmic counterpart, is far more beautiful in its wonderful details, and more perfect in its symmetry and geometrical proportions than the material physical organism of earth.

When the material tree no longer exists as a living earthly organism, the arboreal image within Nature's wonderful laboratory becomes the means of reflecting the outlines of a still more perfect vegetable organism upon the outward planes of matter. These outlines of Astral skeletons of future trees possess the attractive force which draws within them the living germs of the young seedlings growing upon the earth.

The greatest perfection of one tree becomes impressed within the astral light and also the means of developing a more perfect organism of its kind in the next generation. The ideal of the tree becomes externalized in its offspring.

The trained psychic, and those also who naturally possess some spiritual lucidity, can see this ethereal vegetation within the Astral world. Therefore, proofs may be

quickly obtained of the two planes of existence should they
ever be required. The internal plane is more alive than the
external. The physical tree disappears, but it does not die as
we suppose. When physical death transpires it undergoes an
evolutionary change; the sphere of its activities becomes
translated, removed from the external to the internal. This is
in strict obedience to the higher laws of its internal nature.
Thus we see the tree, having served its purpose on earth,
vanishes from external sight, while its ethereal counterpart
performs another cycle upon a higher plane of being.

When each has fulfilled its great purpose, the various
evolving atoms which constituted its life form, obeying the
interior laws of their cyclic round, seek their reincarnation.
They separate and the cycle is complete. The individual tree
no longer exists as a tree. But there has been no death; only a
change of form. The atomic forces of the tree reappear upon
a higher plane in a million other varying forms throughout
every department of nature.

Since ancient times philosophy has striven to separate
the good from the evil, and the pure from the impure. This is
the same as saying all things die and that only the Soul lives
eternal. The Soul endures while the body decays, and you
may recall that correspondingly a seed must rot away if it is
to bear fruit. But what does it mean to rot? It means only
this — that the body decays while its essence, the good, the
Soul, subsists. Once we have understood this, we possess the
knowledge which contains all virtues.

Decay is the beginning of all birth! It transforms shape
and essence which are the forces and virtues of nature. Just as
the transformation of all foods in the stomach prepares them
and makes them into a digested pulp, so it happens outside
the stomach. Decay is the midwife of very great natural
things! It causes many things to change so that a noble fruit
may be born. It is the reversal, the death and destruction of
the original essence of all natural things. It brings about the
birth and rebirth of forms a thousand times improved. And
this is the highest and greatest mysterium of the Spirit, the

deepest mystery and miracle that has been revealed to mortal man.

Having considered death and decay in regard to the tree, let us now examine the animal kingdom or the case of a tigress. We have already stated Nature ever strives to externalize ideas and thoughts in some form or other. This statement must always be borne in mind. The tigress presents us with a fine illustration of this law of transformation upon the outward planes of existence.

What the tigress is when endowed with physical life we all should know. Her chief qualities are selfishness and destructiveness! She is, in fact, a complete expression of cruelty. When death transpires, the astral tigress like the astral tree, becomes indrawn within the karmic sphere of its astral world. There it is to perform the higher evolutions of its special round until the life atoms, which constitute it, become "rounded out." Then it is ready to externalize in some higher form.

Thus the tigress, like the tree, is one of nature's countless mediums for the expression of mental force. By the interior laws of its constitution, it forms a central vortex or focus for the materialization of the purely selfish and destructive elements of humanity. When death removes the physical tigress, the ethereal tigress becomes the sphere of action until the tigerish qualities have run their full cycle.

But we cannot say there has been any real extinction, or death hath come upon the tigress, anymore than we can say the heat of the sunbeam is destroyed because the solar ray is no longer brought to a focus. The eye of the newest psychic initiate can distinctly see the ferocity of the animal in the inhumanity of the man.

Mortality or death, then, can only exist and be a truth in reference to the individual material forms. It has no existence when brought face-to-face with the spiritual qualities and mental force, which actually created these forms. Changes of sphere and changes of action are the only realities of death.

Ever onward, ever upward, forever and ever more! Eternal progression is the anthem of evolution and the cycles of action are but intervals of time as measured out to the life forces by the pendulum of creation.

The second portion of our subject — "Immortality" — is the polar opposite of death and mortality. Individual forms and characteristics are the only things which change and die. This death as we have shown, is not an extinction of the life atoms in the literal sense of the term, but simply a change of sphere and function.

Death is the grand terminus of one cycle of existence, and the commencement of another. Mortality is the harbinger of a still higher state of life. Consequently it is the forerunner of immortality. There are exceptions to the general rule, though they are very few.

There are two distinct phases of immortal life: conscious immortality, and unconscious immortality. One relates to mind, the other to matter; one to intelligence, the other to substance.

There is only one grade of external life which can be said to inherit immortality in the occult sense of the term. This is the eternal conscious life or immortal individuality. Not as we know and recognize individuals, but, rather an individuality consisting of Soul qualities. This is a purely Spiritual state which can only be partially expressed by the word Identity.

All the states below the human plane are only so many radiating lines which converge to a point, and are brought to a focus within the human organism. Therefore, every quality and force upon the planet or within the system of which the organism forms a part must find expression within this womb of Nature. If this were not so, man would not constitute a microcosm or universe in miniature.

In the grades below the human state, we do not find complete organisms. They are mere temporary shapes of matter continually dying out of existence to give place to something more nearly perfect. The forces they were evolved to express are exhausted, they evolve to a higher cycle. They are not souls in the true sense, but refracted attributes of

Souls. They are qualities and functions in the process of evolution. They are isolated parts and characteristics of a whole; organs, but not organisms.

Commencing at the very lowest point of animated existence we discover only the most rudimentary expression of the simplest function of organic life or a desire to live. As we ascend higher, the organs become multiplied, and the desire to live is increased. This gradual scale expands right up to man, where we find a miniature universe, absolute and complete within itself.

The central deific atom, controlling this universe, has traveled all the way up from the crude fire rocks of cosmic evolution. It has conquered every state through which it ascended upon its progressive toilsome journey. At each state, it evolved from within itself a complete attribute corresponding to that state. It polarized and bound the atoms of life and annexed them as a portion of its spiritual empire, thereby forming the means for their progression. Until, at last, the deific atom sits upon the spiritual throne as kind of the microcosm, capable of thinking, creating, and evolving from within itself.

It is therefore an occult truth to declare: All things below man are mortal, and all above immortal! Man, alone, contains within himself the forces of life and death, of mortality and immortality. Man, then, contains "the promise and potency of life" and constitutes, upon the spiritual plane, what protoplasm does upon the physical. It has the possibilities of infinite progression.

To attain unto immortality it is necessary, as we have shown, for the central life atom to conquer every state below the human; to become externalized upon earth as an individual human being; and to undergo the trials and become subjected to the responsibilities of a conscious, reasoning, individual human being in the struggle for life. The nature and quality of the soul, combined with the polarity of the organism, will launch the individual into the exact conditions and circumstances which are best adapted to arouse all the latent qualities.

It is not a previous karma which determines an

individual's condition in life, but the nature and quality of the Soul conflicting or harmonizing with the external conditions. This turmoil of life, this ceaseless human warfare, is just as necessary for the Soul's final development as are the earlier struggles through the lower states of the Great Chain of Being. Man possesses the possibilities of such immortal life in such a potent degree as to nearly always succeed. There are, however, a few solitary exceptions.

When man has passed through the travail of human life, he then meets the struggle of his karma in the realm of Spirit. Here he may even sink forever, because he does not actually possess immortality; but only the promise of possibility of it. Not until the four realms of the astral world are passed and man enters the sixth state of the Soul world, where he becomes reunited with his Soul mate, his missing half, can he attain the exalted state. Until this union is complete there is, and can be, no actual Immortality! Previous to this he is but a part of himself, and has control only of half of his spiritual nature.

It is the union of the two which forms the absolute One. "And they twain shall be one flesh," saith the old Jewish Scripture.

"As it is above, so it is below."

It is seen that it is the reunion of the twin Souls in the realm of Spirit which confers upon man the state of angelhood. He is human no longer and he is then Divine. As a Deific being he possesses the attributes of eternal progression and immortal life.

Virgil, richest of the ancients in Philosophy, says thusly:

> "And first the Heaven, Earth, and liquid plain,
> The Moon's bright globe and stars Titanian
> A spirit fed within, spread through the whole
> And with the huge heap mix'd infused a soul:
> Hence man and beasts, and birds derive their strain
> And monsters floating in the marbled main;
> These seeds have fiery vigor, and a birth
> of Heavenly race, but clog'd with heavy earth."

What do these verses mean other than the world should have not only a Spirit-Soul but also should partake of the Divine Mind. The original virtue and vigor of all inferior things depends upon the Soul of the world! Plato, the Pythagoreans, Orpheus, Trismegistus, Aristotle, Theophrastus, Avicenna, Algazel, Plotinus, and all the Peripatetics confess and confirm this truth.

There are four essences in the universe on which all the learned through the centuries have agreed. These are Fire, Water, Earth, and Air! There is, however, a fifth essence, or quintessence, which permeates everything above in the stars and below upon earth. It is the world Soul-Spirit which animates all bodies. It is "clog'd with heavy earth" and never free or visible. Yet it is omnipresent, and he who can free this fifth element from the matter it inhabits shall hold in his hand the creative power with which God has been endowed upon the world of matter. The ancient goddesses of growth and vegetation, like Isis, were nothing more to the Alchemist than the emblems of the quintessence, the generative power which resides in the Philosophers' Stone.

Thus we have a transcendental field as the only real from which the material universe emerges in a series. The properties of this material world reveal the Supreme Chain of Being. The basic polarities of consciousness or Spirit and matter or Soul energy make up life, as it appears as a material form or species.

In a sense, life is the direct reflection of the transcendent Supreme; hence, biological thinking is privileged. The cycles of life are perceived in body (material), psyche (Self), Soul, and Spirit. The lesser of these is the reincarnation of the impersonal Soul in many men. But in others, a larger epoch evolves over the vast periods of astral time as the "cycle of necessity," and Spirit pervades all of their being.

When this has occurred, the Soul is no longer conscious of the body, and cannot tell whether it is man or a living being or anything real at all; for then the contemplation of such things would seem unworthy. It has no leisure for them;

but when, after having sought the Astral Spirit, it finds itself in its presence, it goes to meet It and contemplates It instead of itself. What itself is when It gazes, it has no leisure to see.

When in this state, the Soul would not exchange its present condition for anything, not for the very heaven of heavens. There is nothing better, nothing more blessed than this! For it can mount no higher; all other things are below it, however exalted they be!

It is then it judges rightly and knows it has what it truly desired, and there is nothing higher. It is now the Macrocosm! There is no deception; where could one find anything truer than Truth? What it says, that it is, and it speaks afterwards, and speaks in silence, and is happy, and is not deceived in its happiness.

Its happiness is no titillation of the bodily senses; it is the Soul which has become again what it was formerly, when it was thrice blessed.

All the things which once pleased it — power, wealth, beauty, science — it declares it despises. It could not say this if it had not met with something better than these. It fears no evil while it is with the Astral Spirit, or even while it sees Him; though all else perish around it, it is content, if it can only be with Him, so happy is it.

The Soul is so exalted that it thinks lightly even of that spiritual intuition which it formerly treasured. For spiritual perception involves movement, and the Soul now does not wish to move. It does not call the object of its vision Spirit, although it has itself been transformed into Spirit before the vision and lifted up into the abode of Spirits.

When the Soul arrives at the intuition of the Astral One, it leaves the mode of spiritual perception. Even so, as a recent traveler and entering into the palace, it admires at first the various beauties which adorn it. But when the Astral Master appears, he alone is the object of attention. By continually contemplating the object before him, the evolved Soul sees It no more. The vision is confounded with the object seen, and that which was Him becomes to the state of seeing.

The Astral Spirit has two powers. By one of them it has

a spiritual perception of what is within Itself, the other is the receptive intuition by which It perceives what is above. The former is the vision of the thinking Spirit, the latter is the Spirit in Love. For when the Spirit is inebriated with the nectar, it falls in Love, in simple contentment and satisfaction. It is better for the evolved Soul to be so intoxicated than to be too proud for such Spiritual intoxication of Love.

As it is above, so it is below!

7

The Dark Satellite

When we look about us with the physical senses, Nature seems to be in continual warfare with Herself. In fact, it seems utterly impossible to find anything not in deadly conflict with something else. Observing this, mankind has unconsciously, from time immemorial formulated the idea of two great powers — the "good" and the "evil." From this idea the grand dogma of all theology — "God" and the "Devil" — sprang into existence. It soon became the chief cornerstone of every sacerdotalism which the world has witnessed.

While there is some basic truth in this idea, as in every popular conception, it has its false premises as well. Mankind as a whole cannot formulate any idea which is wholly and absolutely false in every detail. Yet owing to the fact that man, while existing upon the material plane, cannot grasp the Divine idea of absolute Truth, nor realize the logical absurdity of more than one Absolute.

He, therefore, utterly fails to comprehend how that which is relative evil can be harmonized into an Absolute Good.

To the majority of mankind this mighty problem of good and evil is still unsolved. But a few, a very few indeed, of the profoundly learned students of Occult lore have arrived at a true conception of the subject.

Countless legends and allegories have evolved, during the lapse of the ages. These embody the facts and the processes connected with this great arcane mystery, but the metaphysics of these legends has never been revealed to the uninitiated. Especially this is the case in regard to the Dark Satellite. However, the time has now come when certain facts in regard to this orb of evil may be given to the world for the first time.

In the first place, certain misconceptions in regard to the dark orb need to be corrected. Many earnest students have thought it to be "The Lost Orb" of the Grecian mysteries. This would make it similar to the Egyptian conception of the spiritual "fall." But there is, in fact, no connection between the two at all.

Another misconception has regarded the Moon as identical with the dark orb. Many assert, in a very mysterious manner, the Moon is not only the eighth sphere, or the orb of death and dissolution, but it is "the dust bin of the universe." This conception is radically false as regards the Moon. It approaches the realm of truth in some respects regarding the nature of the mysterious Dark Satellite itself.

With these brief remarks it now is possible to point out a perfectly correct conception of what this Dark Satellite is, and also to understand its fearful importance at the present crisis in the world's history.

During the Golden and Silver Ages of our Earth's evolution, this Dark Satellite was in the aphelion of its orbit and then its influence was scarcely felt. Its influence then was seen and recognized in its true relation of animal force and undeveloped good. As a factor of evil it was still imperceptible. But during the Copper and Iron Ages the orb gradually approached the Earth, and its dark shadows became more and more bewildering and more potent until the year

1881. Then it passed its grand perihelion point. It is now slowly but surely receding, and although the clouds are not completely lifted from the mental horizon, the fact is the fearful conflict which occurred at the perihelion is over. Yet, the confusion and chaos of today seem more widespread and more rampant than ever before in the world's history. Still it is past its darkest portion of the orb and its culminating point.

As it is often darkest just before break of day, so even now the dawn of a brighter morn is at hand. Then the faithful, resolute truth-seeker shall be able to solve for himself this awful problem of good and evil. Therefore, we must be sustained by the knowledge of the ultimate victory of order and equilibrium over chaos and opposing forces. Even though enveloped in the darkness of battle and involved in the vortices of the defeated legions of error, let us turn our attention more closely to the satellite itself. It has been such a disturbing factor to our planet's mental equilibrium we must consider it with special reverence. The implications and responsibility forced upon every Soul seeking light and Immortality are very great at present.

In the first place, this orb possesses a complete organization of its own, and is governed by well defined laws. The nature of these laws may be known only too well by patiently observing the merciless instincts of the lower animal nature manifested in man. There the moral consciousness is absolutely wanting. Throughout this whole sphere are numerous races of Spiritual beings, many of them possessing the highest forms of cunning and intelligence possible on the animal plane. It is these beings who are neither elementals nor elementaries, but who are the producers of the greatest portion of the suffering and misery which afflicts all humanity.

From within the dark center of the Astral realms of these beings, the Spirit of lies, murder, fraud, and religious imposture are first formulated. It is then projected to the human fraternity as the means of its continued existence.

From these human centers it is reformulated to suit the spirit and temper of the times. Then its psychological influence is projected into the mental whirl of the human race. Its silent, subtle influx poisons the dimensional spaces which constitute the magnetic planes of all human life.

The unseen Occult current penetrates the innermost recesses of the human mind and possesses the Soul to such an extent that deep down in the heart of man there is an evil. No matter how pure and disinterested one may appear, there lurks the slimy reptile of selfishness inside the Soul. It is there even when he least suspects it. It is this grim monster which each aspirant to Occult truth seeks to conquer. When this Goliath of the Soul is struck dead by the smooth white pebble of the Spirit, the ordeal is over. It is slung with the neophyte's full will and the crown of Immortality won. "To the victor belong the spoils."

It is the dark satellite which formulates the Spirit of lies, murder, and frauds and this was well known to the initiates of the greater Hermetic mysteries. We find the idea very clearly defined in the mystical language of the ancients. The following extract from one of the supposed lost magical works of Hermes Trismegistus shows this clearly. He was speaking of the magical rulers of the Dark Satellite as they sit in council, creating all delusion, when he wrote:

> *"So they called forth a form*
> *From the Deep dark abyss*
> *To embody their evil desires.*
> *Obedient it came*
> *From the realms of the dead,*
> *Arrayed in its magic attire.*
> *As it passed o'er the earth*
> *The fair flowers fell dead,*
> *From its breath of poisonous fire."*

Indeed, so thoroughly has this poisonous fire of self-interest permeated the world, the fair flowers of disinterestedness are an almost entirely extinct species.

Should the real state of unselfish unworldliness of the true Mystic become known, he would be either regarded with pity as "non compos mentis," or else looked upon with suspicion as acting from motives much more subtle than those which govern the ordinary mortal.

The manner in which this dark magnetic energy is projected from the satellite to the earth is inversive. The rulers and magical hierophants make use of this inversive force to distort and corrupt truth in every form as it struggles to become manifest upon the Earth. The powers and influences attributed to certain races of the Astrals, belong in reality to the rulers and principalities of the Dark Satellite. They mercilessly distort every arcane truth into theological dogma of partial error, thus causing it to assume to the human mind the delusive form of the externals of truth and logic.

But the delusive form is, after all, only a very flimsy sophistry when subjected to the keen searching eye of the Soul. Consequently, it is always those who are half informed of nature's mysteries who fall into the snare. Herein is seen the Occult truth in the old proverb, "A little learning is a dangerous thing."

Just as the Dark Satellite was at its perihelion, these inversive brethren achieved the greatest theological and metaphysical success by the relaunching forth throughout the world of the doctrines of "Reincarnation," "Karma," and "Disembodied Shells." These were formulated and taught by the decaying priesthoods of the dreamy Orient. Viewed in its true light this gigantic movement of the inversive brethren was aimed as a death blow to the rapidly spreading Spiritualism of the Occident.

Such a movement, however, was doomed to ultimate failure as there were certain absolute Truths connected with this Spiritualism. This Truth was there notwithstanding the ignorance of its expounders and the many errors and gross impostures. These truths were neither to be suppressed by inversive magic, nor smothered by any oriental theory.

These truths were well expressed in the Book *Yetzirah*, which stated:

God is the matter and form of the universe. Everything exists in Him; He is at the bottom of all things and beings, which carry the symbols of His intelligence. The Whole, God and the universe, is a perfect unity. The uniting bond in creation are the twenty-two letters of the Hebrew alphabet and the first ten numbers (expressed by the first ten letters). These two types of signs are called the thirty-two marvelous ways of wisdom, upon which God has founded His name. They are identified with thought rendered visible, and they are superior to bodies and substances. God's breath is in the Hebrew letters. They are equally of man and of God.

The ten numbers are the essential form of all that is; the number ten is the basis of the world plan. Through them intelligence perceives the world's existence and the divine action. These numbers are called the *Sefirot.*

Their names are: *Kether,* Crown, the ideal principle of all entities, and which in itself embraces all other beings; *Chochma,* Wisdom, the principle of all life; *Binah,* Intelligence, the principle of everything that has understanding; *Chesed,* Goodness, the model of all grace; *Geburah,* Power, the principle of the distribution of reward or punishment; *Tiferet,* Glory, the principle toward which converges all that is beautiful and perfect; *Nisah,* Victory, to which conforms the permanent and the lasting; *Hod,* Honor, the principle of all that flows down to inferior beings; *Malchut,* Kingdom, the link which transmits all things from the superior to the inferior, and which helps the inferior to assimilate itself to the superior.

At this point the question naturally arises: "Of what personal or selfish benefit is the propagation of error to the inhabitants of the Dark Satellite?" The answer is simply this, it furnishes them with the means of prolonging their external existence while on Earth. It also supplies them with an additional lease of life in the world to come, as will be made manifest from the Hermetic laws of death as given below.

According to these laws, death is now what is known as physical dissolution, but is a failure on the part of the human being to polarize the atoms which constitute the Soul and thus realize Immortality. It is a falling from the human to the animal plane, where conscious existence may be prolonged indefinitely.

The Laws of Death (Hermes Trismegistus):

1. As it is below, so it is above; as on the earth, so in the sky.
2. There are two states of being: one is mortal; the other Immortal.
3. That which is mortal is dissolvable, and dissolvable bodies pass away like a mist in the morning.
4. An Immortal body is an essence which is eternal and incorruptible.
5. But the twain, the mortal and the Immortal, cannot exist together forever, but each returneth to the place from whence it came.
6. The mortal body is sensible, but the Immortal is reasonable.
7. The former contains nothing that is perfect, the latter nothing that is imperfect; for the one is the essence of the Spirit, the other the essence of matter, and man, the microcosm, holds the balance of the twain.
8. And there is a fierce warfare for the Victory, between the upper and lower, as they both desire to obtain the body as their prize; for the state of man is envied by the lower and glorified as a noble state by the higher.
9. Now as the man inclines toward the lower Nature which is mortal, he thereby aids the lower imperfect powers to oppose the higher which is Immortal, and must suffer the pains of slavery for his disobedience to the workman his maker. But if he inclines to the higher, then he is truly wise and blest.
10. Should man, after being attracted by the vanities of the world and then after obtaining a knowledge of the things that really are, return to the vanities of the world, he will be punished with torments and fire in the darkest states of disembodied Souls.
11. Should a man, after knowing the things that are, become rebellious of restraint to that part which is Immortal, and return to the vanities of the world, the higher essence will straightway depart from him, and he will become the slave of the lower essence which will seize upon him and drive him to all sorts of wicked arts and evil ways.

12. When man has thus impiously disobeyed nature and turned his face away from that which is Immortal, behold he is then disinherited from his birthright, and is no longer counted among the children of Nature because he has become an evil, perverse thing, possessing only those things which are mortal, and he is punished with death.

13. And so death is meted out to all those who rebel against Nature impiously, because they know the things that are. But to those foolish souls who are ignorant, and who have not knowingly rejected Nature, behold, they are purified after much suffering and are sent to the world again.

The teachings in the above laws are so clear, so simple, and so divinely just, that to attempt in any way to explain or annotate them would only sow the first seeds of error and misunderstanding. We will, therefore, leave them with the reader as they are, pure and free from the mental bias of any mortal being.

Man alone, possesses the elements of both life and death. The laws of life have been fully elucidated, and the Soul which imperfectly obeys them will, "After it has been purified by much suffering," ultimately reap the reward of eternal conscious existence. Consequently, the great majority of those Souls who are really human beings, will inherit Immortality as the natural consequence of their humanity.

But there are exceptions, which though few in number, require special notice. These exceptions may, for the sake of convenience, be divided into three distinct classes. The first and most numerous consists of imperfectly organized, sensitive, weak-natured individuals, with little or no mental bias, but who possess strong mediumistic magnetisms. Individuals of this class, though perfectly human to begin with, soon lose the actual control of the external organism, and in consequence the body becomes the obedient instrument for any and every class of disembodied earth bound spirits. But what is still worse, it may become the slave of some vicious elementary.

In this case, there was no real or true individuality, therefore, no one can assert truthfully he was actually acquainted with the true personage. The real Soul had departed in the very early infancy of the organism's physical existence. Just how, or when, or where, none but the trained seer can tell. In every individual case the Astral causes which produced the Soul's abortion widely differ.

The second class are those who fall victims to premeditated obsession, and are by no means so numerous as the first class. In this case the organism is generally very fine, insofar as the magnetic temperament is concerned, but the Soul is utterly wanting in Spiritual volition or will. The magnetic polarity of their Soul is of such a nature the Spiritual will of the Soul is almost powerless to act. The absence of this essential element of human life may be the result of the mental condition of the mother during her pregnancy, or of a mental coma of both parents at the moment of conception.

This mental coma externalizes itself in the offspring as a lack of vim, verve, and fire. Hence we often see this condition manifested in the children of kings, noblemen, and those from parents of great wealth. These people have the means to pander to and gratify a fashionable sentimental lassitude. In addition to this lack of Spiritual volition, the magnetic constitution is always strongly mediumistic. Such an individual, if left quite free from the control of others, would be naturally good, highly sensitive, and in the true sense of Spiritual parlance, "A spirit medium." Such a person would be inspirational, physical, or clairvoyant, according to the peculiar magnetic grade. This is why they often fall victim of premeditated obsession.

When such an obsession transpires, it is generally found some potent external mind, that of an evil sorceress, or black magician, requires the organism for the purpose of prolonging their own personal world existence. When a suitable mediumistic body is found, they bring the whole of their powerful magnetic will to bear upon the almost will-less brain of their victim. Slowly but surely they eject the rightful occupant, and then by virtue of their Occult powers and magic arts, inhabit the organism themselves.

The near friends and relatives of the victim are often surprised at the remarkable change which they notice has taken place in the temperament and the disposition of their friend. They seldom if ever suspect the terrible truth which such a change implies. They can never be brought to fully understand the individual moving among them as usual has nothing whatever in common with their silently departed recent friend.

The third, and the least in number, of these classes includes those who are born into the world under strangely conflicting conditions. Possessing all the essential elements of manhood, they also possess a powerful current of the most potent and concentrated form of selfishness and pride. In addition to this undesirable acquisition, they express the highest form of intellect combined with a powerful will and mediumistic temperament. These dominating conditions predispose them to the study of psychology and Occultism, hence they fall an easy prey to the members of the Black magic and their inversive Astral Brethren.

Their selfishness, combined with their unbounded ambition and desire for power, precipitate them headlong into the most frightful practices, where, surrounded by the infernal rites of their diabolical seducers, they become helpless to the very powers they sought to control. Henceforward they are lost!

As the Hermetic law states: "They are punishd with death." They know it and consequently are compelled, for their own safety, to remain faithful to the order which entrapped them. Their only motto is Self, their only desire is to live, and this they will do at any cost. For their own lives they would sacrifice the entire balance of creation, if such a thing were possible. Death to them is death in reality.

In the first and second classes of so-called lost Souls, the true individual does not become lost; he is the foolish, ignorant Soul. He simply loses his physical organism! This personality, along with the animal and Astral portion of it, becomes a lifeless shadow at death, and slowly disintegrates within the magnetic spaces of the Astral light. It is a misty form, incapable of personating its original owner, or of being "galvanized into temporary life."

While the counterfeiting, obsessing forces, after running the cycle of the magnetic existence within the electrovital spaces of the planet, become attached to the eighth sphere; the Dark Satellite or orb of death. This attraction is brought into force by virtue of their affinity with the realms of elemental being. They have sunk beneath the plane of humanity, and consequently are no longer human. When once they become enclosed within the fatal magnetic whirl of death, they lose the polarity over the feeble atoms which constitute their only being, and gradually dissolve, atom by atom, like poisonous miasmatic mists before the rising sun.

The Deific atoms themselves are imperishable as ever, and enter upon a new cycle of involution and evolution. Thus they are slowly building up new individualities for themselves. Not on this planet, the scene of their failure and suffering; but on a higher plane, in worlds more ethereal than ours.

The higher they are placed, the closer they are to the divine. Kether, the first emanation, is the Spirit. The elements issued from each other, and the more remote they were from the Highest, the more gross they became. Air is the highest and the most subtle element; earth (condensed water) is the least noble among them. With such a conception, substance is resolved into one principle and brought under one law.

The letters partaking of the intelligible and physical world leave their imprint upon all things; they are signs by which we recognize the supreme intelligence in the universe. And through their mediation, the holy spirit reveals itself in nature. With letters, God has created the Soul of every form, in mingling them and combining them in infinite ways. Upon letters, He has established His ineffable and sublime Name. Through word and writ, man can penetrate the most hidden divine secrets, and with words and signs work wonders.

The Hebrew letters are grouped into three types: the mother letters, which are Aleph — A, Mem — M, Shin — Sh;

the seven double letters, which have two sounds; and the twelve single letters. Aleph is air, because the letter is pronounced with a slight aspiration. Mem is water, being "mute." Shin is fire, because of its hissing sound. Three, seven, and twelve are the numbers with which the world is built. They recur in the three realms of Nature:

> In the general composition of the world,
> In the division of time,
> In man.

Fire is the substance of heaven, water the substance of earth; air is the mediator between the two, the dominator and also reconciler. God's breath or word. Fire is summer; water, winter; and air, spring and fall. For either time or season contains the same number arrangement as Man and World. In man, the number three is head, heart and stomach. The seven double letters are twofold in their essence, their effect being ambivalent, either good or bad. The seven planets influence changes according to their position. In the realm of time, seven are the days and nights of the week, in man they are the openings of his head: the eyes, the nostrils, the ears, and the mouth.

In the universe there are twelve signs of the zodiac; in time, twelve months of the year; in man, twelve capacities: sight, smell, speech, hearing, nutrition, generation, touch, locomotion, wrath, laughter, thought, and sleep. Summing up: the material form of intelligence, represented by the twenty-two letters of the alphabet, is also the form of all that exists; for, outside man, time and the universe, only the infinite is conceivable. Therefore, the three realms are called the faithful witnesses of Truth.

The world of letters and words is built in steps. One dominates three, three governs seven, and seven is superior to twelve, yet each part of the system is inseparable from the others. They are one, although many of their elements are in opposition, arrayed against one another. Finally, above man, above the universe, beyond time, above the letters and numbers is the Spirit, Who tolerates no duality or any definition, as He is the Infinite, yet partaking of everything.

But He does not submit to the law, which He embodies: He is the law. The closer things and beings are to Him, the more they are bathed in His light. Evil is not a separate force, but rather the scarcity or absence of true light.

The significance of numbers was developed in a somewhat curious manner, which it may be worth while to summarize:

1. In the moral order, a Word incarnate in the bosom of a virgin. In the physical order, a Spirit embodied in the virgin earth, or Nature. It is the generative number in the order, because the monad supposes the duad, and thence, through the triad, all numbers are evolved.

2. In the moral order, man and woman. In the physical, active and passive. It is the generative number in created things.

3. In the moral order, the three theological virtues. In the physical, the three principles of bodies. The reference here is to Salt, Sulphur and Mercury, thus indicating the Hermetic connections. Three also denotes the triple Divine Essence.

4. The four cardinal virtues, the four elementary qualities and it is, moreover, the most mysterious of numbers, because it contains all the Mysteries of Nature.

5. The quintessence of religion, and the quintessence of matter — which again is alchemical. It is also the most Occult number, because it is enclosed in the center of the series.

6. The theological cube and the physical cube. It is the most salutary number, because it contains the source of our spiritual and corporeal happiness.

7. The seven sacraments and the seven Planets. It is the most fortunate number, because it leads us to the decade, the perfect number.

8. The small number of the elect, or the wise. It is the most desirable number, because he who possesses it is the cohort of the Sages.

9. The exaltation of matter. It is the most sublime number because Nature is exalted.

10. The ten commandments and the ten precepts of Nature. It
     is the most perfect number, because it includes unity and
     zero, the symbols of matter and chaos, whence everything
     emerged. In its figures it comprehends the created and
     uncreated, the beginning and end, power and force, life and
     annihilation.
11. The multiplication of Religion and the multiplication of
     Nature. It is the most multiplying number, "Because with
     the possession of two units, we arrive at the multiplication
     of things."
12. The twelve articles of faith. The twelve apostles and the
     foundation of the Holy City. The twelve operations of
     Nature. The twelve signs of the Zodiac, and the foundation
     of the *Primum Mobile*. It is the most solid number, being
     the basis of our Spiritual and corporeal happiness.

Hermetic and Kabbalistic Philosophies are ascribed to a
common source, and this has been the case with sympathetic
as well as hostile critics. I am sure that as regards the branch
of Hermetic Philosophy which is known under the
name of Alchemy, we should accept this statement. The
earlier books ascribed to Hermes Trismegistus, and not
concerned with the transmutation of metals, make use of
many of the doctrines of the Kabbalah, more or less veiled.

The symbol of chemistry is drawn from creation (in the
eyes of its adepts) who save and purify the divine Soul
enchained in the elements, and above all, who separate the
divine Spirit confounded with the flesh. As there is a Sun, the
flower of fire, a celestial Sun, the right eye of the world, so
copper, if it become flower by purification, becomes then a
terrestrial Sun, which is king on earth, as the Sun is king in
the sky. There is no doubt that this is a very important
citation. It shows why early Hermetic books came to be
regarded as Alchemical in later times, and it institutes a
striking parallel between Egyptian and Jewish science. But
the latter is the science of the Kabbalah.

But we shall do well to remember that the doctrine of
the Macrocosm and the Microcosm, the analogy between
Spiritual and material, the Zoharistic symbolism of the

balance, have all been traced to the oldest sacred books of the world.

The great Hermes Trismegistus used these sacred Occult books in his studies of magic and the forces of Good and Evil. He was one of the few profoundly learned students of Occult lore among the ancients. To him we owe much of our knowledge of the dark satellite and its fearful importance.

8

The Astral World

The oldest Occult teachings, as well as the latest, inform us that there are Seven Planes of Being. The lowest of these planes is known as the Material Plane. Second in order is known as the Plane of Forces. The third is known as the Astral Plane. The fourth is known as the Mental Plane.

Above these four planes are three higher planes which have no modern names which can be understood by those dwelling only on the lower planes. These higher planes are incapable of explanation to those on the lower planes; yet I shall refer briefly to some of these higher planes, as we proceed with our study.

It should be mentioned that each of the Seven Planes has seven sub-planes; and each of these sub-planes has its own seven subdivisions; and so on to the seventh degree of subdivision. So, you see, there is a minute classification in these Occult teachings about the Planes of Being.

According to Occultists, these seven are as follows (the older Sanskrit names, which are now superseded, are only being given for reference): Divine or *Adi,* Monadic or *Anutadaka,* Spiritual or *Nirvana,* Intuitional or *Buddhi,* Mental or *Manas,* Astral or *Kama,* and Physical or *Sthula.* These worlds are not physically separate in the manner which planets appear to be, but interpenetrate each other. They depend for their differences on the relative density of the matter which composes them, and the consequent difference in the rates at which the matter vibrates.

Except for the physical world (densest) our knowledge of them, so far as it extends, is dependent on Occultism, and the more exalted the vision of the Occultist the higher the world to which Astral Vision can perceive. Each world has its appropriate inhabitants, clothed in appropriate bodies, and possessing the appropriate states of consciousness. The two highest worlds, the Divine and the Monadic, are at present incapable of attainment by human powers, the remaining five are attainable to a greater or lesser degree. The Monad for the purpose of gathering experience and for development, often finds it necessary to pass downwards into the material sphere. When it has taken possession of the Spiritual, intuitional, and higher Mental worlds, it may be looked on as a Self or Soul embodying the will, intuition, and intellect. It continues eternally as the same entity, never altering itself except by reason of increasing development, and hence is Immortal.

These higher Worlds, however, do not afford sufficient scope to the absolute Monad and it presses still farther down into matter, through the lower Mental, into the Astral and Physical Worlds. The bodies with which it is there clothed form its personality and this personality suffers and is renewed. At the death of the physical body, the Self has merely cast aside a garment and thereafter continues to live in the next higher world, the Astral Plane or Astral World.

At the death of the Astral body, another garment is cast aside and the Self is clear of all appendages. It is as it was before its descent into the denser matter, having now returned to the Mental World. The Self finds itself somewhat strange to this world or plane owing to insufficient development, and it again descends into matter. The round is completed again and again, and each time the Self returns with a fresh store of experience and knowledge, which strengthens and perfects the mental body. When at last this process is complete, this body is cast aside and the Self is clothed with its casual body.

Again it finds itself strange to this plane and the round of descents into matter again begins and continues till the casual body is fully developed. The two remaining worlds are but imperfectly known, but the Intuitional, as its name indicates, is that plane where the Self's vision is quickened to see things as they really are. In the Spiritual world the Divine and the human become unified and the Divine Purpose is fulfilled and the Great Chain of Being is completed.

To those who may find it difficult to form the idea of a number of manifestations with each having its own rate of vibration, and occupying the same point of space at the same time, a consideration of the phenomena of the physical world will serve as an aid in understanding. For instance, every student of physics knows a single point of space may contain vibrations of heat, light, magnetism, electricity, X-rays, and other various electromagnetic forces each manifesting its own rate of vibration, and yet not interfering with each other.

Every beam of sunlight contains many different colors, each with its own rate of vibration, and yet none crowd out the others. By the proper laboratory apparatus each color of light may be separated from the others, and the ray is thus split. The difference in the colors is simply from the different rate of etheric vibrations of the light.

Again, it is possible to send many telegrams along the same wire and at the same time, by using senders and receivers of different vibratory frequencies. The same thing has its corresponding analogy in the case of radio and T.V. So, you see, even on the physical plane we find many forms of vibratory manifestation occupying the same point in space at the same time.

The Material Plane, with which we are all familiar, has its seven sub-planes, and likewise its seven-times-seven series of subdivisions. At first we are apt to think we are perfectly familiar with every form of matter, but this is far from being the case. We are familiar with only a few common forms. The Occult teachings show us that on certain of the fixed Stars, and on some of the Planets of our own system, there are forms and kinds of matter lower in vibration than the densest form of matter known to us. There are in existence in other worlds, and even in our own, forms and kinds of matter as much higher than the highest forms of ultra-gaseous matter known to us. This may be a startling statement, but every advanced Occultist knows it to be true.

Physical science formerly classified matter as follows: (1) solids; (2) liquids; and (3) gaseous. But modern science has found many forms of matter more tenuous and rarer than even the finest gas. It now calls this fourth class the "ultra-gaseous matter." But Occultists know beyond this fourth sub-plane of matter, which science is just now discovering, there lie three other planes, and still finer sub-planes.

Next higher in the scale of manifested Being, we find what is known as the Plane of Forces, of which very little is known outside of Occult Science. Although physical science has been breaking into this field, it will take the next century for physical science to proceed further in this direction. The research into radio activity is leading toward such further knowledge regarding this plane of manifestation.

On the Plane of Forces we find the seven sub-planes, and likewise, the seven-times-seven subdivisions. These are forces far below the scale of the ordinary forces of Nature known to man. And, likewise, there is a great series of Nature's Finer Forces at the other end of the scale, of which the ordinary man knows nothing. It is these finer forces which account for many of the wonders of Occult Science. In particular, the fine force called "prana" or "vital force" plays a most important part in all Occult phenomena.

Next above the scale of the Plane of Forces, we find the great Astral Plane. The term "Astral" is derived from the Greek word meaning "related to a star", and was originally used in describing the heavens of the Greeks and the abodes of their gods. From this sense and usage the term has widened in its application. It was employed to indicate what might be called the "ghostland" of the Ancient peoples. This ghostland was believed to be inhabited by beings of an ethereal nature; not only disembodied Spirits, but also angelic beings of a very high order.

The Ancient Occultists of Greece, and other Western lands, thus naturally fell into the custom of using the familiar term, "Astral", to indicate what we now know as the Astral Plane. Of course, the Oriental Occultists had their own terms for this plane of manifestation, and these terms were derived from old Sanscrit roots. But, as the use of Sanscrit terms has a tendency to confuse most western students, the best Oriental teachers of today almost always use the old Greek Occult words.

Each of the physical senses of man has its Astral counterpart which functions on the Astral Plane, just as the physical senses do upon the material plane. Thus every man has in latency, the power of seeing, hearing, feeling, smelling, and tasting on the Astral Plane by means of his five Astral Senses. All advanced Occultists know man really has seven physical senses instead of five, though these two additional two senses are poorly developed in the average person. Even these two extra physical senses have their Astral counterparts.

In the cases of persons who, accidentally or through careful training, have developed the power of Astral Vision or perception through Astral Sight, the scenes of the Astral Plane are perceived just as clearly as are those of the material plane. The ordinary Clairvoyant has flashes of this Astral Vision, as a rule, but is not able to sense Astrally by an act of will. The well trained Occultists, on the other hand, are able to shift from one set of senses to another by the act of will. In fact, such an Occultist may function and perceive on both planes at the same time.

In cases of Clairvoyance, or Astral visioning, the Occultist remains in his physical body and senses the phenomena of the Astral Plane quite naturally. It is not necessary for him to enter into a trance or any other abnormal mental state. It is not necessary for him to leave his physical body in such cases. In the higher form of

Clairvoyance, he may even sense distant events both on the physical plane, as well as on the Astral Plane. Strictly speaking this power belongs to a somewhat different order of Occult phenomena.

To vision Astrally, the Occultist has merely to shift his sensory mechanism, just as the operator on the typewriter shifts from the small letter type to the capitals. This, then, is the simplest and most common way of Occult sensing on the Astral Plane, and it is possible for many persons.

The second avenue of approach to the Astral Plane is that in which the individual leaves his physical body, and actually travels on the Astral Plane in his Astral Body. The Astral Body is composed of an ethereal substance of a very, very high degree of vibration. It is not mere matter, and yet is not pure force. It is composed of Astral substance which resembles very fine matter, but which is more tenuous than anything known as matter. Ordinarily the Astral Body can be sensed only by means of the Astral Vision, but under certain other conditions it takes on the semblance of a vapory form or matter and is perceptible to the ordinary physical senses as a "ghost" or "apparition."

The Astral Body is an exact counterpart of the physical body, but survives the latter by a number of years. It is not Immortal, however, and finally it disintegrates and is resolved into its original elements just as does the physical body. The advanced Occultist, in his Astral Body, is able to leave his physical body (which remains in a state of sleep or trance) and may visit at will on the Astral Plane, even to points in space far removed from his physical body.

One of the hardest things to realize is the Astral is just as real, abiding, and fixed as is the material world. Just as steam is actually as real as water or ice, so is the Astral just as real as the world of matter. It is not a great body of solid fixed matter, but rather is an aggregation of an infinite number of the tiniest particles built into atoms which then are built into molecules and solid masses of matter.

The space between the electrons of the material atom is

as comparatively great as the space between the Planets of our Solar System. And every electron, atom, and molecule is in constant and intense vibratory motion. There is nothing solid in the material world. If a magnifying glass were built to an infinite power, even the electrons would melt into seething, nothingness. There would be nothing left but the ether which has no weight and which is imperceptible to the senses. So you see, the solidity of things is merely relative and comparative. The vibration of substances on the Astral Plane is higher than those on the material plane. But even the Astral vibrations are far slower than those of the next higher plane.

To the traveler on the Astral Plane, the scenery and everything connected therewith seems as solid as the most solid material does to the physical eye. It really is just as solid as is the Astral Body in which you visit it. As for reality, the Astral is just as real as is the material.

The Forces of Nature are not perceptible to the physical eye, except as they are manifested through matter. But they are very real as all of us know by experience. You cannot see electricity, but you may receive a shock and realize its reality. You cannot see the force of gravity, but you become painfully aware of its reality when you fall. It is realized by all advanced Occultists, that if there really are any degrees in reality, the balance is in favor of the finer forms of substance and force.

The Astral has its scenery, geography, and things just as the material world. These things are just as real as the Great Redwood Trees of California or the Grand Canyon. Its inhabitants are just as real as any of the great men of our country.

The law of constant change operates on the Astral just as on the material plane. There, things come and go just as they do here on the material plane. Concentrate on the matter, and you will see the difference between the things of the two planes is simply a difference in the rate of the vibration of the substance.

Moreover, and this is quite important to the student, the Astral has its laws just as has the material world. These laws must be learned and observed, otherwise the inhabitants of the Astral, as well as the visitor, will reap the painful result which always comes from a broken Natural law.

Again, there exists the "geography" of the Astral. There are regions, points of space, places, kingdoms, and countries on the Astral, just as on the material plane. Sometimes these Astral regions have no connection with any on the material plane. In other cases they have a very direct connection with material places and the material plane inhabitants.

One may travel from one region of the Astral to another, by simply an act of will. This raises the vibrations of the Astral Body without it moving in space. Again, one may travel in space from one point to another on the Astral plane. This is possible in cases where these points have some relation to certain points on the material plane.

As an example of this form of travel, I would say one may travel in the Astral from Berlin to Bombay by merely wishing or willing to do so. Time and space have their manifestation on the Astral Plane. But certain Astral manifestations, on its seven-times-seven sub-planes, may be and likely are, present therein, at, and on, the exact point of material space which you are occupying at this very moment on the material plane.

If you have the knowledge and power, you may traverse all of these sub-planes, one after the other, witness their scenery and inhabitants, their phenomena and activity, and then return to the material plane. This may be done in a moment of time and without changing a single point in space.

Or, if you prefer, you may travel to any of these sub-planes of the Astral and then travel in space on the Astral Plane to some other place. Then you have the choice of returning either the same way, or else descending to the material plane, and traveling on it, in your Astral Body, back to where your physical body is resting.

In traveling on the Astral Plane, one meets with many strange inhabitants of the wonderful realm of Nature. Some are pleasant and others are unpleasant. Some of these inhabitants have passed on from the material plane, while others have never dwelt on it. These forms are natives of the Astral Plane and peculiar to it.

When you find yourself outside of your physical form or body, and clad in your Astral form, you glance at your body and you find it appears no different from your ordinary body. Even your clothing is the same and this phenomena occurs through perfectly Natural laws on the Astral Plane.

You realize you are indeed out of the physical body when you turn your head and perceive your own physical form, sunk in apparent sleep in the chair in which you were seated just a few moments ago.

Looking a little closer you will see that your Astral form is connected with its physical counterpart by a tiny, thin, tenuous filament of ethereal substance, resembling a strand of shiny spiderweb. This filament is capable of expansion and contraction, which enables you to move about freely.

Now concentrate your will so that your vibrations increase in rate. You will find yourself in a strange atmosphere, although you have not moved an inch. Behind you, you perceive dimly the room in which you were just living. Ahead of you, you perceive strange flashes and streaks of phosphorescent light of many different hues and tints. These are vibrations and waves of force, for you are now passing through the Plane of Force.

You will notice a peculiar faint vibratory glow around every physical object. This is the force of atomic and molecular attraction. Still fainter, you will find a peculiar radiance permeating the entire atmosphere. This is the outward sign of the force of gravitation.

Now, you feel your life force vibrating at a higher rate, and realize the sense of weight seems to be dropping away from you. You feel as though you could move without any effort.

You may walk through the wall of the room, and out into the street. Now walk down the street. Step out just as if you were in the flesh. Stop a moment! There you let a man walk right through you! Do you realize you are a ghost? Just as much a ghost as was Hamlet's father, except his physical body was mouldering in the ground. A dog will see you or a cat feels your presence! Animals possess very keen psychic senses!

But cease thinking of yourself, and look closely at the person passing by. You notice each one is surrounded by an egg-shaped aura extending on all sides to the distance of about two or three feet. Do you notice the kaleidoscopic play of blending colors in the aura? Notice the difference in the shades and tints of these colors, and also observe the predominance of certain colors.

Notice the beautiful Spiritual blue around that woman's head, and see the ugly muddy red around the man passing. An intellectual giant with a beautiful golden yellow around his head, like a nimbus, comes into view.

Notice those great clouds of semiluminous substance, which are slowly floating along and notice how the colors vary. Those are clouds of thought vibrations, representing the composite thought of a multitude. Notice how each body of thought is drawing to itself little fragments of similar thought forms and energy. Here is the tendency of thought forces to attract others of their kind. Thoughts come home!

Speaking of atmospheres, notice each shop has its own peculiar thought atmosphere. The houses and the street itself have their own atmospheres, created by the composite thought of those inhabiting and frequenting them.

From above the level of the housetops, look down and see a great multitude of tiny lights, each of them represents a human soul. A few brighter lights and some which shine like a brilliant electric spark are the Auric symbols of advanced Souls.

Enter the vibrations of the lower sub-planes of the Astral, but nerve yourself to witness some unpleasant sights. The first impression is that the material world is still around, with all its scenes visible. As one looks one will find there seems to be a peculiar veil between those scenes and the Plane upon which you are temporarily dwelling. This veil, while semitransparent, nevertheless seems to have a peculiar appearance of resistant solidity, and one instinctively realizes it would be a barrier to the passage of the Astral entities back to the material plane.

Gazing around on all sides, one sees what appears to be the disintegrating forms of human beings. These forms seem to be floating in space. They seem real, and yet, in some ways, not real. They are not physical bodies, but still they bear too close a resemblance to physical corpses to be pleasant.

These disintegrating Astral forms are what Occultists know as the "Astral shells." The Astral shell is really an Astral corpse, just as the physical body in the grave is the material corpse. The disembodied Soul eventually leaves the Astral and moves on to what the Occultists know as the mental or Spiritual planes of being. These are symbolized by the conception of "the heavens." When the Soul passes on, it leaves behind it the Astral body it has inhabited while on the Astral Plane. This Astral body, or form, then begins to disintegrate, and in time disappears altogether and is resolved to its original elements. During this resolution process, it dwells on this particular division which has no other purpose and is separate and apart from the other subdivisions of the Astral Plane.

There is a great difference between the Astral shells of different individuals, so far the duration of the shells in this place of disintegration. For instance, the Astral shell of a person of high Spirituality and Ideals will disintegrate very rapidly, as its atoms have little or no cohesive attraction when once it is discarded. But, on the other hand, the Astral shell of a person of Earthly ideals and material tendencies will hold together for a long time. The attractive force generated while the shell is occupied by its owner is very strong.

Those Astral bodies are "dead" and have no consciousness or intelligence, and as a rule cannot even be galvanized into life as can the class of Astral forms known as the "spectres," or "shades."

A momentary glimpse of the subdivision of the Astral

Plane upon which the spectral forms abide is never a pleasant one, but it is interesting since it explains some peculiar features of Psychic or Occult phenomena which are often misinterpreted. Instead of floating about in Astral space, as did the shells, these spectres act like shadowy human beings in a dazed or dreamlike condition. They walk dreamily about without set object or purpose and are a weird, unpleasant sight.

These spectres are really Astral shells from which the Souls have departed, but which have left in them sufficient power from the thought and will vibrations of their former owners, to give them a temporary semblance of life and action.

In the case of the Soul with high ideals and Spiritual aspirations there are practically no material thought vibrations remaining to "galvanize" the Astral Body after the Soul has withdrawn. But in the case of the Soul retaining strong material thoughts and desires, the power is stronger. In these, even after the higher Nature of the Soul has drawn it upward and above the Astral, these lower mental vibrations may persist in the deserted Astral form. Thus they give a semblance of life and activity which, though a counterfeit, may manifest considerable power for a time.

The counterfeit power of these spectral forms steadily decreases, but in certain cases it is used up, as a spark is rendered bright by blowing upon it. This is by means of a Psychic stimulus from persons living on the material plane. This is the power generated in "circles," and mediumistic persons, on the material plane of Earth life. The Psychic power so generated, coupled with the strong mental attractions set up between certain persons in earth life and the spectral form, may cause the form to manifest itself, either by more or less complete materialization, or partially through the physical organism of the medium or mediums present in the circle.

In such a case, the spectre, reanimated and galvanized into life by means of the Psychic power of the medium, or the psychic circle, will strive to manifest itself by speech, automatic writing, raps, or in various other ways. But at the best, its effort will be feeble and faulty, and the persons witnessing the phenomena will always remember the event with the dim idea that "there was something wrong about it." In some cases, the vibration of old memories will survive in the spectral form and will enable it to answer questions fairly well. But even then, there will be a shadow of unreality which will impress the careful observer.

There are many other forms of "Spirit return," partial or complete, but much which passes for the real phenomena is really but a manifestation of the presence of spectral forms. Moreover, these entities borrow ideas and impressions from the minds of the mediums or persons in the circle, which in addition to their own shadowy memories, doubly become reflections or counterfeits of Spirit.

These spectres have really no Soul. The Soul which formerly occupied the form has departed to a higher plane. It is in ignorance of the performance of its discarded shell. It is pathetic to witness cases where these counterfeit spectral forms are accepted as the departed Soul of the loved individual. A lack of knowledge of true Occultism often permits of deplorable mistakes of this kind. The true Occultist is never deceived in this manner since these spectres are no more "departed Souls" or "Spirits" than a physical corpse is the individual which once inhabited it. It remains a corpse and discarded shell, and that is just what the spectral form is.

Where are the disembodied Souls themselves? Most persons expected to see them as soon as they crossed the border of the Astral. This is the general expectation of the neophyte in Occultism, as he gets his first glimpse into the Astral Plane. But, unless he happens to stumble by accident upon certain sub-planes, he is apt to be disappointed. The better way is to learn by viewing the various sub-planes.

You notice the vibrations are changing, and growing more intense. You are now entering upon a very wonderful sub-plane, or rather, upon one of the subdivisions of such a sub-plane. This region, is one which is strictly guarded by the

law of the Astral, and watched over by certain very high
Spiritual influences. It is a sacred place! No one is admitted
here just as a visitor, unless he be of high Spirituality and
pure heart. Even a trained Occultist, unless he possesses these
qualifications, finds it impossible to enter.

This region is the resting place of the disembodied Souls
for a time after they have left the physical body. In it they
dwell in peaceful slumber, unfil Nature performs certain
work in preparing them for their new plane of life. This state
has been compared to the cocoon stage of the caterpillar, a
stage where complete transformation is effected. Here the
new life form is developed to take the place of the old form.

You must enter upon a contemplation of its wonders,
with all reverence and Love of all mankind. On all sides,
stretching away as far as the eye can see, one perceives the
slumbering forms of the disembodied Souls, each Astral form
resting in dreamless sleep. Yet even if you were not so
informed, you would recognize these forms are not dead, but
are merely sleeping. There is none of the atmosphere of death
about this region. Nothing depressing, but there is a sense of
infinite calm and peace. Being Spiritually developed yourself,
you feel the presence of certain great Spiritual entities. Their
vibrations are too high for you to see them even by Astral
Vision. These are the great Spiritual guardians of this realm,
who protect the slumber of the Souls at rest; the "Great
Watchers of the Sleeping Souls."

If you watch carefully, you will notice here and there a
movement indicating the awakening of some of these resting
forms. A moment later the form disappears, it seemingly
melts into nothingness. But it is still existent for its vibrations
simply have changed, and it has moved on to another
sub-plane. It has begun its real life after death.

It is a common teaching of many religions that the
disembodied Soul enters at once upon its Heaven or Hell. The
Roman Catholic Church and some branches of Buddhism,
however, teach of an intermediate state called Purgatory.
Some denominations of the Church hold all Souls slumber in
unconsciousness until the call of the great trumpet of

Judgment Day. Then all awaken from their long sleep, are judged and sent to the place of reward or punishment as their cases deserve. On the Astral Plane, you see some things which show you all of these views have a basis in fact, and yet are imperfect conceptions.

All Occultists know, however, that nearly all of the original religious teachers had a complete knowledge of the real facts of the Astral, and higher planes. They merely handed down to their followers such fragments of the Truth as they thought could be assimilated. All of the theological teachings regarding Life After Death and Heavens or Hells contain some truth, but none contain all the Truth.

In the majority of cases, the mind of the dying person sinks into the slumber of so-called death and awakens only after a period of restful, transforming slumber upon the Astral Plane. In some cases, however, there is a brief waking, shortly after the departure from the physical body. Then the Astral Body may appear visibly to some friend, associate, or loved one. This accounts for the occasional instances of the disembodied person appearing. But even in such event, the disembodied Soul soon becomes drowsy, and sinks into the preliminary sleep of the Astral Plane.

There is a great difference in the length of time during which the disembodied Soul slumbers in this state. Strange and paradoxical as it may appear, the highest and lowest Souls in the scale of development awaken first. The average Soul slumbers longer than either.

The highly Spiritual person, needing but comparatively little transformation to fit him for higher planes, may slumber here only a short time. In cases of very high development, they may omit these Astral planes, and pass on at once to the plane or planes above the Astral and directly into what Occultists know as the "Heavens." Technically, these are regions of the Mental Plane, and the ones even higher. The average Soul, however, slumbers many years perhaps, and then awakens upon the Astral Plane.

The low, material Soul, as a rule, awakens very speedily, and passes at once to the low plane for which it has an affinity. The highly developed Soul awakens speedily, for it has less to slough off and be transformed into higher attributes. The average Soul, on the other hand, requires a much greater transformation for its higher activities, and so remains much longer in the transforming sleep. The low material Soul awakens speedily, not because it has been transformed easily for the higher scenes, but because it is not destined for these higher planes. It never reaches them, but descends to a lower plane of the Astral, where it lives out its low inclinations and ideals.

On the Heaven Planes, the Spiritual Souls spend great periods of time enjoying the well-earned bliss. Souls lower in development spend less time there. The low, material Souls, scarcely taste the experience of those high regions. Let us change the vibrations, and visit some of the scenes of Astral life, in which the awakened Souls are living, moving, and having their Being. Let us begin at some of the lowest sub-planes, and their divisions.

You are vibrating on a very low subdivision of the lowest sub-plane of the Astral. You are conscious of a very unpleasant feeling, and an almost physical repulsion to the atmosphere around you. Some very sensitive Natures experience a feeling of being surrounded by a dense, sticky, foul, foggy atmosphere, through which they must almost force their way. It is akin to the feelings experienced by a highminded Spiritual person on the Earth plane, if he happens to enter a place inhabited by persons of a lewd, vulgar, depraved nature.

It is no wonder one of the old Egyptian writers, whose work survives graven on stone said: "What manner of foul region is this into which I have foolishly come? It is without water; without air; it is unfathomably deep; it has darkness of the blackest night, when the sky is overcast with dense clouds, and no ray of light penetrates their curtain. Souls wander hopelessly and helplessly about herein; in it there is no peace, no calm, no rest, no quiet of the heart or mind. It is an abomination and desolation. Woe is the soul that abideth herein!"

Looking around you, in the dim, ghastly light of this

region, you perceive countless human forms, of the most repulsive appearance. Some of them are so low in the scale as to seem almost beastlike rather than human. These creatures are disembodied Souls, in the Astral Body, living on the low plane to which they descended when awakening from their very brief Astral sleep.

If you will peer through the fog, you become conscious of the presence of the material world as a sort of background. To you it appears detached and removed in space, but to these creatures, the two planes seem to be blended. To them, they appear actually to be abiding in the scenes and among the persons of the lowest phases of Earth life. Even you find you can see only the very low Earth scenes in the background. To these poor Souls there is no Earth world except these scenes which are in accord with their old vile desires.

But while apparently living amid these old familiar and congenial low earth scenes, these Souls are really suffering the fate of Tantalus. For while they plainly see these scenes and all that is going on, they cannot participate in the revels and debaucheries which they perceive. They can see only! This renders the place a veritable Hell for them, for they are constantly tantalized and tormented by revels in which they cannot participate.

They can exercise simply "the lust of the eye," which is but as a thorn in the flesh. On all sides, on Earth, they see their kind eating, drinking, gambling, engaging in all forms of debauchery and brutality, while they eagerly cluster around and cannot make their presence felt. The lack of the physical body is indeed a very hell to them.

The Astral atmosphere of low dramshops, pool rooms, gambling halls, race tracks, "free-and-easies," brothels, "redlight" districts, and their more fashionable counterparts, are filled with these low Astral forms of Souls just across the Astral border. Occasionally, they are able to influence some earth companion, who is saturated with liquor, or overcome by drugs. When they do, they strive to lead him into further degradation and debauchery.

In some instances the sojourn on this low Astral

sub-plane sets up such a strong desire for rebirth in the flesh, the poor Soul eagerly presses forward toward reincarnation on a similar low plane. In other cases, the experience so sickens and disgusts the poor Soul it experiences a revulsion and disgust for such things. Then the current of its desires naturally carries it in the opposite direction, and it is given the opportunity to rise on the scale of the Astral.

At the end, however, in nearly all cases "living-out" results in "out-living," and even the lowest rises in time. Some few Souls, however, sink so low as to be incapable of rising and they meet the final fate of annihilation. In these Hells of the Astral, however, the degraded Souls are "punished not for their sins, but by them."

But this scene is not the only one on this sub-plane of the Astral. There the punishment, by the sin rather than for it, is similar. They are tormented by the sight, but are tantalized by not being able to participate. The result is similar, and some find desire increased and others find disgust and nausea and thus seek the way to higher things.

There are hundreds of similar regions on the lower Astral Plane, which are higher than those we have just considered. All of them serve as a Purgatory, or place of the burning-out of desires of a low kind. This idea of burning away or purging of the low desires is found to permeate nearly all religions, and has its basis in the facts of the Astral Plane.

What I have just said regarding the nature of the Astral scenery must not be taken as indicating the Astral, itself, is merely imaginary or unreal. Nor is the substance of which the scenery is composed any less real than the substance of which the material world is composed. On the material plane, substance manifests in a finer form of "stuff" or material. Again, on the material plane, the material, or matter, is shaped by the physical forces of Nature, or, perhaps, by the mind of man to build "artificial" structures.

On the Astral, on the other hand, the Astral material is not thrown into shape by physical forces, but is shaped and formed only by thought and imaginative power of the minds of those inhabiting the plane. But these shapes, forms, and structures of the Astral material are not to be thought of as existing merely in the mind of the Astral dwellers. They have an independent existence of their own, being composed of Astral material.

The Astral scenery survives the passing away of the mind which built it and disintegrates only after the passage of considerable time. As for the power of the imagination of man, do not be deceived for a moment, for this is one of the most efficient powers in Nature. It operates strongly even on the material plane, though on the Astral its power is easily recognized by the senses. To the dwellers on the Astral Plane their scenery, buildings, and objects are as solid as are those of the material plane.

Passing through the various sub-planes and their divisions, on the Astral you notice a great variety, and a great difference in the character and occupations of the inhabitants. But, you notice one general characteristic underlying all of the differences, namely the fact that all of these Astral dwellers seem to be filled with an intense earnestness, and manifest a degree of concentration which gives to them the appearance of being preoccupied. Everyone seems to be busy, even when their tasks are those of sport or play.

The key to the occupation and pursuits of these dwellers is found in the principle that the life of the Soul on the higher divisions of the Astral consists in a working out of the intellectual desires, tendencies, tastes, likes, and aspirations which they were unable to manifest fully on Earth. I do not mean the low sensual desires, or purely animal tastes, but rather ambitions and similar forms of higher desire. Many of these inclinations may be very creditable and praiseworthy, but they are all concerned with the physical manifestations, rather than with Spiritual unfoldment and evolution. The higher planes are those in which the Spritual forces bud, flower, and bear fruit. The Astral Plane is the scene of the living-out and working-out of earthly intellectual ambitions and aspirations.

Raising our vibrations, we find ourselves on a higher plane. Here we see men engaged in what would be called "useful work" on Earth. But they are performing it not as labor, but rather as a joyous recreation. You will see the work is all of an inventive and constructive nature. The men and women are improving on their work, and are filled with the joy of creation. On some of these divisions we see the artist busily at work, turning out wonderful masterpieces, and musicians are creating great compositions. The architect builds great structures and the inventor discovers great things. All are filled with the joy of work and the ecstasy of creative imagination.

But, do not regard this as merely play, or as possibly a form of reward. The main thing to remember is that in this work on the Astral Plane, there is an actual mental advance and progress.

In many cases, here on these very planes of the Astral there is being built the mould for inventive and creative achievements on the material plane. The Astral is the great pattern shop. Its patterns are reproduced in matter when the Soul revisits the Earth. Many a work of art, musical composition, great piece of literature, or great invention, is but a reproduction of an Astral pattern.

The soul is always at work using up old ideas, aspirations, and discarding them. In this way, real progress is made, for after all, even earth-life is largely a matter of "living-out and out-living." In the work of the Astral many old ideas are worked out and discarded; many old ambitions manifested and then left behind. There is a certain "burning up, and burning out" of old mental material, and a place made for new and better material on the Earth. Often there is accomplished as much in the direction of improvement and progress, as would be possible only in quite a number of earth lives. Life on the Astral is very earnest and intense and the vibrations are much higher than those of the material plane.

Bearing this in mind, these Astral scenes which you are now witnessing take on a great and new meaning. You recognize them as very important schoolrooms in the great school of life. Everything has its meaning! There is no waste effort! The Astral is no joke of the universe! It is one of the great workshops and laboratories of the Soul.

Raising vibrations a little, you now enter upon the great second sub-plane of the Astral, with its seven subdivisions. Almost before I tell you, you feel the religious atmosphere pervading this plane. This is the plane upon which the religious aspirations and emotions find full power of expression. On this sub-plane are many Souls who have spent some time on the other sub-planes of the Astral, doing their work there and then passing on in order to manifest this part of their Natures.

But, I wish to call your attention to the Occult distinction between "Spirituality" and "religion." Spirituality is the recognition of the divine spark within the Soul, and the unfoldment of the same into consciousness. Religion, in the Occult sense, consists of observance of certain forms of worship, rites, ceremonies, the holding to certain forms of theology, and the manifestation of what may be called religious emotions. The religious instinct is deeply implanted in the hearts of men, and may be called the stepping stone toward true Spirituality. It is a beautiful thing! But in its lower forms, it leads to narrowness and bigotry!

This sub-plane of the Astral is filled with a multitude of Souls each of whom is endeavoring to manifest and express his own particular shade of religious conception. It may be said to contain all the heavens that have ever been dreamed of. Each of the great religions has its own particular region in which its disciples gather, worship and rejoice. In each region the religious Soul finds "just what he had expected" and hoped to find on "the other shore."

All forms of religion, high and low, Oriental and Occidental, ancient and modern, are represented on this plane. Each has its own particular abode. There are some beautiful and inspiring scenes and regions on this plane, filled with advanced Souls and beautiful characters. But, alas! there are some repulsive ones. It is marvelous to realize how many forms religion and theology have taken in their evolution. Every form of deity has its region, with its worshippers. It is interesting to visit the scenes once filled with the worshippers of the most ancient religions. Many have only a handful remaining, while in some cases, the worshipers have entirely disappeared, and the temples and shrines are crumbling away and disappearing.

On the highest of the sub-planes of the Astral, we find the regions inhabited by the philosophers, scientists, and metaphysicians, of man; those who used their intellectual powers in striving to solve the Riddle of the Universe, and to peer Behind the Veil. There are as many schools of philosophy and metaphysics here, as there were religious sects on the plane below. Some are pitifully weak, crude and childish in their conceptions while others have advanced so far that they seem like demi-gods. But even this is not true "Spiritually" any more than are the religious formalism and dogmas.

It is interesting to note that on this plane, and the one below are found groups of disembodied Souls who persist in declaring "there is no hereafter for the Soul." These deluded Souls believe they are still on the material plane and they have built up quite a good counterfeit Earth to sustain them. They sneer and sniff at all talk of life outside of the physical body and bang their Astral tables with their Astral fists. This, indeed is the very irony of Astral life.

You noticed certain glorious forms on these regions. These were those highly evolved beings, once men like ourselves, who have voluntarily returned from the higher spheres to teach and instruct religion and philosophy, combining the best of both, and leading upward toward the Truth. It is true, on the Astral as well as on the Earth, that "when the pupil is ready, the Master appears." The Astral has many of the Elder Brothers of the Race, working diligently and earnestly for the uplift of those struggling on the Path.

I may say here, that an understanding of the Nature of the various regions of the Astral, and the scenes thereof, will throw light upon the varying reports of "the other side" given by disembodied Souls at Spiritualistic seances. The secret is each is telling the truth as he sees it in the Astral, without realizing the Nature of what they have seen. Contrast the varying "heavens," and see how different the reports would be coming from some of their inhabitants. When the nature of Astral phenomena is once understood, the difficulty vanishes and each report is recognized as being an attempt to describe the Astral as seen by the disembodied entity.

The planes higher than the Astral transcend adequate description. Enough to say, here, that each Soul on the Astral, even the very lowest, finally sinks into an Astral slumber when it has completed its work on that plane. Before passing on to rebirth, however, it awakens for a time upon one of the subdivisions of the next highest plane. It may remain awake on this plane, in its appropriate subdivision, for merely a moment of time, or for many centuries. It depends upon its state of Spiritual unfoldment. During this stay on these higher planes, the Soul communes with the higher phase of itself — the divine fragment of Spirit — and is strengthened and invigorated. In this period of communion, much of the dross of Nature is burnt out and dissolved into nothingness, and the higher part of the Nature is nourished and encouraged.

These higher planes of being constitute the real "Heaven world" of the Soul. The more highly advanced the Soul, the longer does it abide between incarnations on these planes. Just as the mind is developed and enabled to express its longings and ambitions, on the Astral, so are the higher portions of the Soul strengthened and developed on these higher planes. The joy, happiness, and Spiritual blessedness of these higher planes are beyond ordinary words. So wonderful are they, that even long after the Soul has been born again on Earth, there will arise within it memories of its experiences.

These, then, are the real "Heaven worlds" of the Occult teachings, something far different from even the highest Astral planes. The reports of the mystics are based on experiences on these planes, not upon those of the Astral. Your Soul has truly informed you regarding the reality of the existence of these wonderful regions. Therefore, hold fast to the ideal and the vision!

The Astral is not simply a plane of Nature created for a place of temporary abode and development for Souls which have passed out of the physical body. Important as are the planes of the Astral in the progress of the disembodied Souls, they form but one phase of the activities of Nature. There are strange and wonderful phenomena on the Astral plane, as well as enough wonderful inhabitants and dwellers on some of its sub-planes, to still render it the place and region of interest that it always has been to Occultists. Let us take a glance at these wonderful phases of Astral phenomena and Life:

THE ASTRAL LIGHT

Changing vibrations, we find ourselves entering a strange region, the nature of which at first one fails to discern. After the Astral Vision becomes attuned to the peculiar vibrations of this region, you find you are becoming aware of what may be called an immense picture gallery, spreading out in all directions.

At first it is difficult to decipher the meaning of this great array of pictures. They are arranged not one after the other in sequence on a flat plane, but rather in sequence, one after another in a peculiar order which may be called the order of "Oneness in space." It is neither one of length, breadth, or depth. It is practically the order of the fourth dimension, which cannot be described in terms of ordinary spatial dimensions.

Upon closely examining the pictures one sees they are very minute (practically microscopic in size) and require the use of the peculiar magnifying power of Astral Vision to bring them to a size capable of being recognized.

The Astral Vision, when developed, is capable of magnifying any object, material or Astral, to an enormous degree. The trained Occultist is able to perceive the whirling atoms and corpuscles of physical matter, by means of this peculiarity of the Astral Vision. Likewise one is able to plainly perceive many vibrations of light. The Astral Light which pervades this region is due to the power of the Astral Vision to receive and register these vibrations of light.

By bringing this power of magnification into operation, you will see each of the little points and details of the great world pictures is really a complete scene of a certain place on Earth, and at a definite period in the history of the Earth. It is fixed and not in motion and yet we can move forward along the fourth dimension, and thus obtain a moving picture of the history of any point on the surface of the earth. One can even combine the various points into a larger moving picture.

For a moment we will travel back in time along the series of these Astral records, for they travel back to the beginning of the history of the Earth. Looking around, you perceive the pictured representation of strange scenes filled with persons wearing peculiar garbs. But all is still, no life, no motion!

Let us move forward in time, at a much higher rate than that in which these Astral views were registered. You see before you the great movement of Life on a point of space in a far distant past. From birth to death you see the life of these people, all in the space of a few moments. Great battles are fought, and cities rise before your eyes. All in a great moving picture flying by at a tremendous speed.

Now let us move backward in time, still gazing at the picture. You see everything moving backward. Cities are crumbling into nothingness, men are rising from their graves, and growing younger each second, everything is moving backward in time.

You can witness any great historical event, or follow the career of any great personage from birth to death. You will notice everything is semitransparent, and you can see the picture of what is going on inside of the buildings as well. Nothing escapes the Astral Light Records. Nothing can be concealed from it.

You gazed at the great World Picture in the Records of Astral Light (the great Akashic Records). In these records are found pictures of every single event, without exception, that has ever happened in the history of the Earth.

By traveling to a point in time, on the fourth dimension, you may begin at that point, and see a moving picture of the history of any part of the Earth from that time on to the present. You may even reverse the sequence by traveling backward. You may also travel on the Astral Plane, on ordinary space dimensions, and see what happened simultaneously all over the Earth, at any moment of time.

As a matter of Truth, however, I must inform you the real records of the past, the great Akashic Records, really exist on a much higher plane than the Astral Plane. What you have witnessed is but a reflection of the original records.

It requires a high degree of Occult development in order to perceive even this reflection in the Astral Light. An ordinary Clairvoyant is often able to catch occasional glimpses of these Astral pictures. He may thus describe fairly accurately the happenings of the past. In the same way, the Psychometrist, given any object, may be able to give the past history of the object, including a description of the persons associated with it.

On certain planes of the Astral, there exist certain entities or living beings, which never were human, and never will be. They belong to an entirely different order of Nature.

These strange entities are ordinarily invisible to human beings, but under certain conditions they may be sensed by Astral Vision. Strictly speaking, these strange beings do not dwell upon the Astral Plane at all. We call them Astral entities simply because they become visible for the first time to man, when he is able to see on the Astral.

So far as place, or space, is concerned these entities or beings dwell upon the Earth just as do the human beings. They vibrate differently from us and they are usually of a microscopic size. The Astral Vision not only senses their vibrations, but also it magnifies their forms into a perceptible size.

Some of these Astral entities are known as Nature

Spirits, and inhabit the streams, rocks, mountains, and forests. Their occasional appearance to persons of Psychic temperament, or ones with a degree of Astral Vision, has given rise to the numerous tales and legends in folklore regarding strange beings. Various names have been given them, for instance: fairies, pixies, elves, brownies, peris, djinns, trolls, satyrs, fauns, kobolds, imps, goblins, little folk, and tiny people. The old Occultists called the Earth entities of this class by the name of "gnomes"; the air entities as "sylphs"; the water being as "undines"; and the fire beings as "salamanders."

This class of Astral entities, as a rule, avoid the presence of man, and fly from the places in which man dwells. They avoid large cities for they prefer the solitudes of Nature. They do not object to the physical presence of man, so much as they do his mental vibrations which are very distasteful to them.

A certain class may be called "good fellows," and these, once in awhile, seem to find pleasure in helping and aiding human beings. Many such cases are told in the old folklore, but modern life has driven these friendly helpers from the scene.

Another class, now very uncommon, finds delight in playing elfish and childish pranks, particularly practical jokes on peasants. At Spiritualistic seances these elfish pranks are often in evidence.

The Ancient magicians and wonder workers were often assisted by creatures of this class. And, today in India, Persia, China, and the other Oriental lands, such assistance is known. Many of the wonderful feats of these magicians are attributable to such aid.

These creatures are not unfriendly to man, though they may play a prank with him occasionally. They seem particularly apt to play tricks upon neophytes in Psychic research, who seek to penetrate the Astral without the proper instruction. To neophytes they may appear as hideous forms or monsters, and drive them away from the plane where their presence is apparent.

However, they usually pay no attention to the advanced

Occultist, and either severely let him alone, or else flee his presence. Some of these little folk seem anxious and willing to be of aid to the earnest, conscientious inquirer, who recognizes them as a part of Nature's great manifestations, and not as unnatural creatures, or vile monstrosities.

ARTIFICIAL ENTITIES

In addition to the nonhuman entities which are perceived by Astral Vision, or on the Astral Plane, there are found on the Astral or on the Earth plane, a great class of entities, or semi-entities, which Occultists know as "artificial entities."

These artificial entities were not born in the Natural manner, nor created by the ordinary creative forces of Nature. They are the creations of the minds of men, and are really a highly concentrated class of thought forms. They are not entities, in the strict sense of the term, having no life or vitality except that which they borrow, or have been given by their creators. The student of Occultism who has grasped the principle of the creation of thought-forms, will readily grasp the Nature, power, and limitations of this class of dwellers.

The majority of these artificial entities, or thought-forms, are created unconsciously by persons who manifest a strong desire-force, which is accompanied by definite mental pictures of that which they desire. But many magicians have learned the art of creating them consciously, in an elementary form of magic, white or black. Much of the effect of thought force, or mind-power, is due to the creation of these thought-forms. Strong wishes for good, as well as strong curses for evil, tend to manifest form and a semblance of vitality in these artificial entities. These entities, however, are under the law of thought-attraction and go only where they are attracted. Moreover, they may be neutralized and even destroyed by a positive thought properly directed.

Another and quite a large class of these artificial Astral entities, consists of thought-forms of supernatural beings, sent out by the strong mental pictures of the persons creating them, the creator usually being unconscious of his results.

For instance, a strongly religious mother, who prays for the protective influence of the Angels around and about her children, frequently actually creates thought-forms of such Angel guardians around her children. These are given a degree of Life and mind vibrations from the Soul of the mother. In this way, such guardian Angels, so created, serve to protect the children and warn them from evil and against temptation.

Many a pious mother has accomplished more than she realized by her prayers and earnest good desires. The early fathers of the churches, Occidental or Oriental, were aware of this, and consequently bade their followers to use this form of prayer and thought. They did not explain the true unyielding reason behind such actions. Even after the mother has passed to the higher planes, her loving memory may serve to keep alive these thought-form entities, and thus serve to guard her loved ones.

In a similar way, many "family ghosts" were created and kept in the same way. All by the constantly repeated tale and belief in their reality, on the part of generation after generation. In this class are the celebrated historical ghosts who warn royal or noble families of approaching death or sorrow. The familiar family ghost, walking the walls of old castles on certain anniversaries, is usually found to belong to this class of thought-form entities.

Many haunted houses are explained in this manner. The ghost may be "laid" by anyone familiar with the laws of thought-forms. These artificial entities are of purely human creation, and obtain all their form and mind from the action of the thought-force of their creators. Repeated thought, and repeated belief, will serve to keep them alive and to strengthen these entities.

Many supernatural visitors, saints, and semi-divine beings, of all the religions have been formed in this way. In many cases, they are kept in being by the faith of the devotees of the church. In many temples in the Oriental countries, there have been created and kept alive for many centuries the thought-form entities of the minor gods and saints. These are endowed by thought with great powers of response to prayer. Those accepting the belief in these powers are brought into harmony with the vibrations and are affected by them for good or evil.

The power of the devils of savage races (devil-worshipers) arise in the same way. Even in the early history of the Western religions, we find many references to the appearances of the Devil, and of his evil work. Witchcraft, and diabolical presences, are all created thought-form entities. Many of the effects of sorcery and black-magic are produced in this way. It is the element of belief, of course, which adds to the effect. The Voodoo practices of Africa, and later of Martinique, and the Kahuna practices of Hawaii, are based on these same principles. The effect of "charms" depends on these same laws.

Even certain forms of the "Spirits" in certain forms of Spiritualistic seances arise from this principle. An understanding of this principle will aid in the interpretation of many phases of Psychic phenomena.

SPIRIT RETURN

Nothing I have said must be taken as denying the reality and validity of what the Western world knows as "Spirit return." On the other hand, I am fully familiar with very many instances of the real return to earth-life of disembodied Souls. But at the same time, advanced Occultists are equally aware of the many chances of mistake in this class of Psychic phenomena. Shades, and even Astral shells, too often are mistaken for departed loved ones. Again, many apparently real "Spirit forms" are nothing more or less than semivitalized thought-form entities.

Again, many mediums are really Clairvoyant, and are able to unconsciously draw to some extent upon the Astral Records for their information regarding the past. They do this instead of receiving the communications from the disembodied Soul. This is in all honesty and in good faith. Occultism does not deny the phenomena of modern Western spiritualism; it merely seeks to explain its true Nature. Above all it desires to verify, while pointing out the real Nature of other phenomena. It should be welcomed as an ally, by all true Spiritualists.

ASTRAL VISION

The Astral Vision is a matter of slow, gradual development in most cases. Many persons possess it to a faint degree, and fail to develop it, for want of proper instruction. Many persons have occasional flashes of it, and are entirely without it at other times. Many "feel" the Astral vibrations rather than seeing with the Astral Vision. Others gain a degree of Astral Vision by means of crystal gazing. The Psychic power which is frequently referred to as "Psychic sight," or "Psychic sensing," is a form of Astral Visioning or sensing. Psychism is bound up with Astral phenomena, in all cases.

I have sought to give you the great underlying facts of the Astral Plane. I have crowded very much into a very small space. You will have to read and study carefully in order to get the full meaning. In fact, this is not to be read and then laid aside. It should be reread and restudied, until all the essence is extracted.

9

Mind Power

We see in this world a constant change, and it is these changes we call birth and death. The body and our mind, being a compound, are subject to change. Is there anything that does not change? No, all things change from one condition, state, or appearance to another. Why is this true? Because things "as such" being in time, exist in time, and end in time.

But is Man a "Thing?" I do not think so, but we will have to go further than the mere assertion to establish this in consciousness. If this is true, we must have a foundation based on Knowledge rather than belief, as our "belief" is apt to change our search for Truth.

We must study and have experience in order to gain Knowledge. What is the value of such Knowledge? For one thing, it is the principle remedy for ignorance. Who can deny this? Knowledge then, will be the power to destroy the cause of misery. Will the study of what we are, the nature of our mind and "Thought Power," have any effect? If so, in what way? Have we any way of learning how to control our thoughts? Assuredly: The power to make and change the Mind dwells within, for this Mind is only an instrument in the hands of the "Self" (the intelligence in the body), but we must realize this and not just believe it. Therefore, the reading of this chapter, showing how the Mind is created (and the difference between your "Real Self" and the Mind) will be the beginning of a Knowledge that will give you a foundation for a Practical Psychology.

These subjects are logically formulated, thus, the student is not given just a mere theory or the opinion of the writer. The subject is reasoned out under the law of cause and effect.

Has the Mind any sense? No! Has it any light of its own? No! Of course, many of you will perhaps doubt me when I say "No," but analysis of how the mind is created will show you I am right in making this assertion.

Can we truthfully say a phonograph record has any sense or light of its own? We must realize the distinction between Intelligence and our Mind, and I will show that this difference is established. Those whom the reading of Psychology has left a "Jumble of Thoughts" will perhaps appreciate my teachings.

Have we a Mind? I assume all of us will answer "yes," but when questioned as to where or what it is, nearly everyone will commence by telling about the Brain and mixing the idea of "God," "Soul," "Spirit," and "Intelligence" as being the Mind. I shall attempt to make tangible what is really an abstraction: *The Mind.*

When we speak of our Mind, what do we mean by the word "Mind?" In order that we may understand what we talk about, a clear definition of the meaning of the terms used is necessary. Unless we know what the words mean, how can we understand the discussion?

When referring to our Mind, will the using of terms such as "God," "Soul," "Spirit" or "Intelligence" give one the definition of "Mind?" No! Why? Because we have not defined the terms. Is it possible to attain Knowledge of the nature of our Mind without making use of the terms? Let us see. But before doing so, I must establish a basis, the nature of which is the creative power. Therefore, Intelligence must be our basis. This Intelligence is distinct from Mind, however, and we shall see that this is True.

This Mind of ours is a compound and created in the following manner: when we have any kind of an experience an impression is made upon the brain and these impressions contain the "Nature of that which is experienced." Who or what has the experience? The Intelligence of "Self" of Man. This aggregation of impressions constitute our Mind.

How is that? All our Knowledge comes from experience, does it not? What I believe is not what I know! So when we say "I know it in my mind," we certainly are not referring to those impressions recorded upon the brain which contain that particular experience. This experience may have been study, observation, or some other sensory impression. Our Mind, then, as such, is but a group of these impressions.

We often hear the remark, a "bright Mind." How can the Mind be bright if it is only a group of impressions? It seems to us as "bright," but this is because of Intelligence shining through these layers of impressions. Thus, it is only the reflection of Intelligence which makes the Mind appear to be bright.

In dealing with the subject of Mind, many psychologists convey the idea of "conscious" and "subconscious." I do not accept this statement because I have shown our Mind to be a product of experience, and the total of these impressions make only one Mind. Thus, the terms conscious or subconscious are only states of the one Mind. But the activity of the Mind, or past impressions, must work on two planes: One is called "conscious" and the other "subconscious," for the intelligence in man reacts, and Mind (the instrument) functions, and appears to think (consciously) and control (subconsciously). Our Mind is subject to change, and these changes I call modifications through which are experienced painful or pleasurable "states of mind."

When our experience with anything demonstrates the true Nature of that particular thing, we then have the modification existing known as correct cognition. But if we accept the statement of someone and blindly believe, we will then not have conscious knowledge, and, therefore, not "correct cognition." Lacking this, we will not see or know the real facts. The other modifications of our Mind are: Sleep, Memory, Fancy or Imagination, and Misconceived Ideas. We also have degrees of the modifications and one is a Weakened State in which we cry and blame others for our own foolishness. Scattering occurs when the thoughts are not controlled and we are not able to concentrate. Gathering Inwardly, Indifference, and Illuminating, are the other states of Mind.

BREATHING AND MEDITATION

While sitting for these breathing exercises, it is necessary to have the head, neck, and chest straight so as to avoid having pressure on the nerves of the spinal column. Have your posture as natural and as easy as possible, since new sorts of vibrations will occur in the body as a result of the exercises.

The first type of breathing to do is to breathe in an easy, natural manner. One should count ten during the intake of breath and ten during exhalation. This form of breathing is to establish a rhythm, that is, so the molecules of the body will have a tendency to go in one direction. This, in turn, generates "Nerve Energy" which flows over our nerves and feeds the nervous system.

Count slowly up to ten — same number while breath is being exhaled. After you have practiced this exercise for five minutes, rest two minutes, then try this exercise: close the right nostril by pressing forefinger against it, fill the lungs with air through left nostril to your capacity, immediately close left nostril with finger, remove pressure from nostril and exhale through it. Keep the left nostril closed, inhale through right nostril to full capacity, remove finger from left nostril and exhale through it.

Repeat the alternate nostril breathing three times at each setting and practice the exercise three times a day. Have the periods about eight hours apart. It is a good plan to use a time when you feel free from other things, so you must use your best judgment about the time for practice.

These exercises are to be practiced every day for thirty days. Consistent practice is absolutely necessary! How can we expect good results if we do not practice?

The purpose of the nostril breathing is to bring about an internal purification, especially to the nerves. After finishing the required (daily) thirty days, practice another form of breathing. First, get the body in a harmonious condition by regular breathing (counting ten as before) and practice the following: Inhale in four seconds, retain air for sixteen seconds, exhale in eight seconds. Practice only twice a day, morning and evening, for a period of twenty days to establish a good condition for concentration. The power to concentrate is the central "secret" for getting results.

I shall quote from an authority on breathing, Paul Tyner: "The proportions of oxygen, nitrogen, and hydrogen in the body of an individual at any time are not only an indication of his bodily condition, but will also indicate his spiritual condition. That is to say, the character and development of the Self itself determines the composition of the body and the proportions of oxygen and nitrogen will be blended in exact relative proportions with the good and evil in the man's Nature."

Every good thought increases the proportions of oxygen, as a deep breath does, and lessens that of nitrogen, thus making the body more refined. Every evil thought or impulse increases the nitrogen, thus having a reverse effect on body and Soul.

The flywheel of an engine, when set in motion, conveys motion to the finer parts, and the breath acts in a similar manner in regard to the body and Mind. This action establishes rhythm or harmony in the body. The breath must contain in a very subtle form the Life principle we call "Vital Energy," and we certainly know we can live longer without food or drink than we can without air. There is another thing we must remember. The breath is the highest and most subtle manifestation of the Physical Man. And "thought," is the greatest manifestation of the Intelligence in Man.

We will deal with the philosophy and value of certain kinds of Thought for our Meditations. The kind of thoughts we project or "think within" will determine our action under a certain environment. What we call the "impulse to do" this or that thing, must be caused from the "seed" of past thoughts. How do we know this? Because there is not anything that will come out of us unless it is within. One cannot get something out of nothing! Experience which is the real Teacher, proves this. So we see it will make a difference "what we think." I put before you a few wonderful meditations.

We meditate upon the Nature of that Being who produced the Universe, may he enlighten my Mind. What is the philosophy of this form of meditation? We will take the word "Being" — what does it signify here? I interpret "Being" as a verb; therefore, it denotes action, and action in this case means the creative principle, or Power. Now, the Power that created the Universe must also be the light that shines through its own creations. This "Being" must exist! If so, "It" cannot exist without Knowledge because there cannot be existence without Knowledge and no Knowledge without existence. If there is any light or Knowledge anywhere, it must be contained in that "Being" which is the cause of creation.

The concept, then, is to get a Reaction from the thought or meditation upon "That Being."

I AM THE BIRTHLESS AND THE DEATHLESS, THE OMNIPOTENT, OMNISCIENT EVER GLORIOUS ONE. I AM HE! I AM HE!

I have stated that our thoughts first become involved when we use auto-suggestion (tell ourselves something). The suggestion acts upon the "Intelligence within", and this reacts in the form of vibration. That vibration, which is a thought wave, becomes involved in the brain substance, and from the brain it comes out in the form of an action, impulse, or belief.

If you recall that Man is not the body nor the Mind, you

will understand the above meditation as a means to strengthen the Mind and free it from the fear of death.

MAY ALL THAT LIVES BE JOYFUL, LET ALL BEINGS BE BLISSFUL.

Send this thought to the east, west, north, and south, above and below. Is this not a much greater thought than the narrow one of "God bless me and my wife, my son John and his wife, us four and no more?"

Try sending out thoughts which are liberal and you will feel much better for it. Practice one of these meditations each day.

Thought is a great power to create not only "Things" but a happy or unhappy state of mind. The evil or good we do is caused mostly from our thinking, for all thoughts act upon the "Self" and the reaction from within will be in accordance with the nature of the active thought. Thought also manifests itself as a "force."

Are there any signs which would indicate we have attained concentration? Yes! And the best sign is when we have no consciousness of "Time." Where is Time? Time is in our thought, for it is only when we think that "time" begins. Suppose one is very much interested in his or her work or perhaps reading a book. Several hours elapse and we are not conscious of the "time", and we say; "I did not know it was so late." What does this show? It is proof that we were concentrating so hard on what we were doing that nothing else was present in consciousness during this period.

Concentration proper is when the thought is only upon one subject or object, whether the thought is held inside or outside. The main object is to make the Mind pointed. I will now tell how to do this: Sit with the eyes closed, let the Mind run along for a few minutes, do not try to stop any kind of a thought. After the waves of these various thoughts have run down and subsided, as they will if you let them alone, they will become finer and less disturbing. Now, bring up in your Mind the thing you want to think about. If any thought other than that particular one enters the Mind, knock it down with an opposite thought. Do not mentally accept any thought other than what you have first selected. You may find this a little hard to do at the beginning because the "Seeds" of old thoughts and their associations are there ready to oppose your "New Idea." If you do not believe this, try to break away from some of your old habits and superstitions.

We are to control the outgoing tendency of our Minds by the practice of "non-attachment." When we are greatly attached, whether to the home, business, clothes, or when we are afraid to let go of superstitions, all this clinging to things prevents the free action of thought. How, then, can you hope to concentrate on other things when all this "stuff" holds you down?

The acquiring of knowledge and the Truth about things (not beliefs) gives one a great help in gaining concentration. When we have knowledge, our mental state is better organized because it is more one-pointed. Without knowing the Truth about things, our thoughts are diverse or scattered. That which is good is to be thought upon. One Truth held will have a tendency to steady the Mind. Ignorance and Knowledge are widely separated and lead to opposite points. If we persist in being heedless and ignorant, our thoughts become more branched, causing us to "go round and round" and have no poise. Without poise, how can we succeed in attaining the power of concentration?

One must practice restraint of the "outgoing" energy, or the thought force. Our thought should be upon what is essential only, for if we choose the nonessential, we do not act directly upon the thing we are dealing with. If you have not the discriminating faculty, you can develop it by not jumping to conclusions about things you have no knowledge of. Stop saying you know a thing when the best you have is a belief about it. Check up, reason things out; thus, you will have more control of the Mind. The better the control, the easier it is to concentrate!

Think of a space in your heart and that this space is filled with light. Think of the ocean as calm, or think of the stability of the earth and its immovability. The constant practice of Nonattachment and drawing the thought within when it seems to want to "go out" will enable one to gain control of the Mind; therefore, concentrations results in a powerful force.

As pointed out, all thoughts act and react upon the intelligence, and the effect of the reaction is according to the nature of the active thought. How are these fine impressions to be controlled? As stated, by raising an opposing thought wave. Suppose you have a big wave of anger! How are you to control or prevent it from affecting you? Think of *Love*. This thought is the opposite of hate, and by raising opposite waves of thought, we can conquer those which we want to reject from the Mind.

By meditation, you can make the Mind subdue the waves which hinder concentration. The unbroken practice of discrimination is a means for the destruction of ignorance. All modifying factors are fine. What are these fine factors? Thought is "fine" or invisible. What is a greater factor than "thought," either to intensify or modify an existing condition?

How do we know thought is a force? Is it not true that the thought of a thing will make you angry or glad? Also, the feeling of fear is caused by the thought of danger. What does this show? Simply this, if we control those thought waves and prevent them arising in the brain, we will then master our emotions. The power to create the wave of anger, love, hate, or fear lies in a particular thought wave pattern.

SUGGESTION

In order to secure the best results, we must first gain control of our Minds, and the exercises given in the lessons will enable you to do this. It is not so much that you have a stronger will than the other person, but it is the cooperation, or mental willingness of the one you are working with, which makes the magnetic connection. You can now understand why it is necessary to establish confidence within yourself and the other party. That is, he must have confidence in you. A very good way to gain the confidence of another is to be sincere in your attitude. The manner in which we go about doing a thing is noted by those around us. If they detect any weakness or hesitation on our part that will be a psychological factor against our success with them.

In using suggestion, the voice must be under control so as to be distinct and sound to the listener as calm and pleasant. But be sure you have their attention before giving any suggestions. One should use constructive suggestion by telling them that they are being restored to a healthy condition mentally and physically and the organs of the body are being strengthened and are performing their function.

Having established the conditions necessary, or the willingness and attention of the person, give the kind of suggestion which will cause that person's intelligence to react in accordance with the desired results. If you are attempting to cure him of a bad habit, tell the patient that he no longer has the desire. The cause for that action is destroyed, and you, the operator, are doing this while you are using suggestion. But under no circumstances ever tell anyone what you are doing or what you think about any form of psychological treatment, that is, if you care to keep your psychic powers.

You must remember this "Intelligence" is not only the Real Man, but it is both conscious and subconscious. It is the conscious actor and the subconscious receiver; therefore, because the operator is positive and the patient negative, we can see it is quite "natural" that this Intelligence, although in separate bodies, would influence itself.

"Auto-suggestions" are the inverse of oral suggestions and are practiced by the person himself. While it is true many of us unconsciously practice auto-suggestion, it is better to do so consciously and be more scientific about it. Those who understand anatomy and the effect of thought will get better results because of intelligent direction to the proper centers of the brain.

There are contained in the cosmos the Three Principles: *Substance, Motion* and *Consciousness.* From these three Principles, we have manifestations of *mind, energy and matter.*

THE COSMIC LAWS

1. ORDERLY TREND: Under this law, we have order in the cosmos, from the Sun to the atoms, and the law of cause and effect. Thus, there is no "chance" or "accident" in the Nature of things.

2. The Law of ANALOGY: Under this law, we have correspondence and agreement regarding the various forms of manifestations and when we know one, we know "as above, so below."

3. Under the Law of OPPOSITES: A thing is and is not. A thing is subject to change; therefore, it is and it is not at the same time. Also, if we carry opposite things to the extremes, they are alike, as in extreme light, we cannot see, or in the darkness we do not see.

4. The Law of SEQUENCE: Under this law, we learn that everything proceeds from something and it is succeeded by something.

5. The Law of BALANCE: We find that everything has its opposites: Love, Hate, Pleasure, Pain. As we can see, it requires the opposite to give us balance.

6. The Law of CYCLICITY: Everything seems to move in circles, but by wisdom and strength of Mind we are able to work the circles into spirals for the purpose of progress and attainment.

When we speak of the law, we regard it as an abstract principle of Power. "That" we can neither represent with words nor by symbols. It is an Absolute principle or the cause of Being, yet it transcends all of this or that which the finite Mind conceives.

In the external existence of "That" which is the omnipresent reality, the following five forms are contained: *Omnipresence, Potential Power, Illusion in the Potential Power, Knowledge,* and *Bliss.* When the Mind retains consciousness of the first three forms mentioned, realization is the Reality. But if we become separately conscious of the ideal of Bliss, then the Mind separates its identity with reality and the following five forms emerge. Salvation and Freedom are for those who perceive beyond the form in which we dwell.

What is meant by the external existence of "That"? By

"That" is meant the intelligence which we observe is everywhere. By Potential Power we mean that we have within us the Power to Create. What is Illusion in Potential Power? To say in the separated sense of the sort, I do this or that entirely independent of something else, or as a man might say, "I am a self-made man." We are self-made plus the assistance of something or someone else.

As to Knowledge and Bliss: If this experience causes us to forget the first three forms (consciousness of "That", which is the real "I Am") then illusion is added to illusion and we lose consciousness of our Real Nature.

SUMMARY

It was shown that the Real Man is not the body nor the Mind but something back of both, and he is using the Mind and Body as an instrument to manifest in the physical world.

I do not think it necessary to comment on "Thought," as no doubt we are aware that thought is the Power which creates states of mind and "Things."

The different practices have, as their object, to quiet the body and Mind for the purpose of having the power to concentrate. This seems to be the Key or Power to unlock or strike the necessary blow, to get results from that on which we concentrate.

When anyone tells you they "will think it over" or, "I haven't time," you know they are using an alibi. If you have clearly stated your proposition, and those to whom you are talking are sane, they have already decided. Therefore, all else they say is so much evasion or "bunk." I base this upon over twenty years of experience with the public, and I have found but rare exceptions.

This is only one of the reasons why we must develop and use "Discrimination." The practice of Psychology simply means to use our knowledge of the more "subtle law" and govern ourselves accordingly. The "Finer" is the cause and the "Grosser" is the effect. This applies both to conduct and creation.

By controlling our thoughts, speech is more discriminating. Speech is "Thought" in "Manifestation."

Those who control the "Finer," control also the "Grosser."

Our "invisible" powers are Thought, Intelligence, and the breath.

You will recall about the breath and the value of relaxation from a Psychological standpoint. Slow and regulated breathing must be used in connection with the thought which must be concentrated upon. We know the body does not rest when it is tense in either the waking or sleeping state.

When the body and Mind are under control and we are calm, the better and more work we can do. We lose a great amount of energy through emotion or attachment or clinging to things. This energy should be directed to constructive work.

If you are practicing in the Psychic Arts, you will find you will get better results when you have your patient relaxed and you yourself are calm.

The student should know about "how to eat." There are several good books on the market and also charts which show food values. Be informed. The cost is small; why remain ignorant of one of our most important subjects or "Discrimination in eating?"

Perhaps you will remember about the five faculties of the Mind, of which the Intellect, Reason, Perception, Discrimination, and the Will form the principal ones. I think that contained in those five faculties are all other attributes or phases of "Mind in Action." The Mind cannot function without faculties any more than the body can function without "organs." The degree to which we have those faculties developed, determines the manifestations of the mind as rational or irrational.

Remember the "Illusion of Time" which is in me and not "I in Time." Of that from whence the thought returns, unable to reach with speech, that is the greatest of the Great. Realize the "I Am" as "That."

Life, we sometimes say, is what we make it. This is an incorrect statement. We do not make "Life" but express it in various forms. What we do make or create is the state of consciousness we experienced in "Life."

Perhaps I should repeat that results come from work! This means we must practice! All of the external powers of man are developed by practice upon the "Potential Energy" within our own body, which is the only other real power outside of Intelligence.

When you practice the exercises you should always be alone, and do not practice in a dirty place.

Cheerfulness, poise, and desire to eat are the best conditions for one to have at meal time. Discuss no disagreeable topics at the meal. It is much better to talk of things elevating and healthful. As a comparison between persons who practice and those who do not, temperament and characteristics are in favor of those who practice. The chemical action of food is much better in its effect upon a person of a calm, cheerful state of Mind than upon those whose emotions are of an angry, envious, and dissatisfied nature.

10

Mediumship-Its
Nature and Mysteries

"What is mediumship and who are the Mediums?" is the question often asked of the initiated Masters of Occult Science. The answer is as broad in its application as the universe itself. "Everything is Mediumistic, and every atom is a medium for the expression of Spiritual force." We find throughout the vast infinitude of our universe that the Spiritual and the material are so intimate that to classify and separate them, or to account for phenomena on the basis of either alone, would be like erecting an edifice without a foundation.

Modern science commences with matter and confines its research strictly to the domain of material forms and forces. It terminates at the very moment when its path impinges on the border of the imponderable or the unknowable. The real starting point of all true science is within the Spiritual spaces. Its vast orbit sweeps downward throughout the whole universe of matter, recognizing the different attributes and manifestations of the Divine Force in every form of creation. Its decisions culminate in the realm of Spirit. Divinity is unity! The two great attributes of the Divine Soul coalesce as matter and Spirit in the great universe of manifested being. Matter is visible and solidified Spirit or the passive or negative principle in a concrete, condensed, or material form. Spirit is the movable, ever active, positive principle in motion.

Matter ranges and transforms itself from the lower and denser state of the mineral upward to the aerial and invisible gases, terminating in the "universal ether" of Science. In this refined condition, the active and positive principles of Divinity become united and are transformed into creative Force. Hence, the universal ether contains within itself all that is, that was, or that ever will be. Such are the actual facts of the case. What, then, are the logical conclusions Spiritual philosophy may draw therefrom?

That the universe is one mighty, inconceivable medium, and Deity the controlling, the omnipotent Spirit.

That Deity becomes the medium of Wisdom, the passive becomes the medium of the active state. Matter is and must be the absolute medium of Mind.

The passive Nature of the Divine Soul is the only means whereby the active Spirit can manifest itself, and upon this rests all the mysteries of the cosmos.

In view of these facts, we find the universal will, utilized by the imperial Soul of man, is alone the true center of all magical and Spiritual power manifested upon Earth. Man is the great pivot around which revolves every phase of magical, magnetic, and mental phenomena embraced within mundane psychology.

Mediumship is a well-known term and is applied to that state of sensibility which, though found pure and natural in some individuals, has been developed in others. They then are able to come in rapport with invisible intelligences and other powers. Their magnetic aura has received a degree of sensitiveness compatible with their becoming mediums of communication for these forces. A medium, therefore, is, properly speaking, a person or object in whom the capacity of reception and transmission is fully evolved and of practical value. All human beings in their natural state are forces.

A medium is not necessarily Clairvoyant and usually is not. A person in whose body the etheric matter easily separates from the denser matter is a medium and can readily be utilized as a sort of telephone between the visible and the invisible planes. A medium is an abnormal person and is a good medium in proportion to the degree of abnormality. If the etheric matter of the body is easily extruded, the physical body readily falls into the trance condition, and the mechanism of conversation can be operated by the so-called "dead" person who has temporarily taken possession of it.

In such cases it is not the medium who speaks for the "dead" communicator. He is speaking directly himself, but he may often do it with great difficulty and not always succeed in accurately expressing the thought in mind. He may have to contend with other thoughts, moods, and emotions than his own, and to those who understand something of his difficulties, it is not strange that such communications are frequently unsatisfactory.

It is not often that an analogy can be found which will give a physical plane comprehension of a super-physical condition, but perhaps a slight understanding may be had by thinking of a "party line" telephone which any one of several people may use at any moment. A listener attempting to communicate with one of them may find that others are constantly "switching in." If distinction of voices were eliminated and then a stenographic record were made of all words reaching the listener, he would find it would often be fragmentary and trivial.

It seems to be a common opinion that the evidential value of such Psychic communications, even under the direction of a skillful scientist, cannot be very great. But it is not at all difficult for the investigator to direct his work not only to incidents unknown to the medium, but to scientific facts which the medium cannot possibly comprehend. It is a matter of common knowledge that mediums are usually people without technical, scientific knowledge. A few of them have a fair degree of education, but many of them are illiterate. Some of the most celebrated belong to the peasant class of Europe.

Therefore, when considering the various forms and phases of mediumship, instead of viewing them in the light of "Spiritual gifts," they must be viewed as the natural attributes of internal Nature or as the positive potentialities of the human Soul. The various forms and degrees of mediumship are not Spiritual gifts. They are the senses of the Soul and hold the same relation to the Spirit as our five external senses do to the physical body. Just as our objective organism is governed and controlled by absolute and eternal laws, the internal, imponderable constitution is under the government of transcendental laws in harmony with its purely subjective Nature. These laws constitute the "Science of the Soul," and it is only by a thorough knowledge of this science that we can see the true realities of mediumship. By understanding it we guard ourselves from its terrible dangers and enjoy without fear its countless and unlimited blessings. By the aid of this glorious knowledge, we are able to perceive the action and interaction of the great planes of existence.

The flower which blooms in beauty, breathing forth to the air its fragrance, is pleasant to the senses and stimulating to the nerves. It is a perfect emblem of Nature's faultless mediumship. Herein may be seen some of the mysteries of incense and the great value of its use, especially in various ceremonies.

The Spirit inheres in every grade of matter as the instigator of life, force, and motion, being attendant upon the ethereal currents which permeate all worlds and bind the universe together. In exact proportion to the refinement of substance is the sphere vitalized by Spirit. The brain and nervous system of the human represents the climax of material vitalization. Here Spirit blends with matter with such force and grade sufficient to form the astro-magnetic link of connection between the two worlds of cause and effect. The mental powers are vitalized from the great Deific fountain of Wisdom; Sympathy and affection are derived from the same divine Soul as Love.

It is the grand prerogative of each grade of Being, differing in degree of evolution, to transmit that which it receives from the realms above to the planes immediately below. From the glorious, pulsating Soul of the central Spiritual sun, descending through every sphere of creation, deep down into the very bowels of matter, one eternal and harmonious chain of Spirit mediumship prevails. Each plane depends upon the next ascending one.

When the whole of this mighty scheme is taken into consideration, we see how necessary it is for those who wish to develop their Spiritual possibilities to live upon a pure diet. At the same time, it demonstrates the fact that a life spent amid the flowery fields and pine-clad mountains is the only existence which can fit the Mind and educate the Soul to the highest point. The thinking Mind will not fail to see that those who live in close, unhealthy, and densely populated towns become subject to the very lowest planes of Spiritual activity. Under such antagonistic conditions, progress is absolutely impossible, and those laboring under such adverse circumstances should avoid practical interference with magic, Spiritual phenomena, and mediumship.

Mediums — unless of very pure and noble character — are special objects of attack, and too often the weaker ones, weakened still further by the passive yielding of their bodies for the temporary habitation of other excarnate Souls, are obsessed by these creatures and are driven into intemperance or madness.

It now becomes our duty to elucidate the laws and mysteries of mediumship, and here we are met with the mightiest subject within the whole of Occultism. No branch is of greater importance in the study of Truth, nor more completely unknown and misunderstood.

Mediumship is governed by well-defined laws, insofar as its general principles are concerned. Yet, it is so subtle and intricate in its different degrees, forms, and phases as to be absolutely beyond the grasp of the ordinary Mind. Its ramifications and the results of its actions are as unlimited as the Infinite. Only the more prominent and apparent forms will be outlined in the present chapter. As a matter of convenience, we shall divide the general laws of mediumship into two general classes: (1) that of the controlling force, and (2) that of the mediumistic instrument. These are known to initiates as the laws of *Reception* and *Transmission*.

In order to grasp the significance of the laws and their interrelationship, it must be borne in mind that the lower states of life are always the mediums of, and consequently subject to, the higher. Therefore, every realm must not only possess the quality of mediumship, but also exercise the power of Spirit control.

Many Souls unnecessarily lengthen their stay by seeking to communicate with the Earth, in whose interests they are entangled by means of mediums who allow them to use their physical bodies for this purpose. From them comes most of the mere twaddle with which everyone is familiar who has had experience of public Spiritualistic seances, the gossip and trite morality of the petty. As these Earthbound Souls are generally of small intelligence, their communications are of no more interest (to those already convinced of the existence of the Soul after death) than was their conversation when they were in the body. Just as on earth, they are positive in proportion to their ignorance, representing the whole Astral world as identical with their own very limited area.

> They think the rustic cackle of their burgh
> The murmur of the world.

It is from this region that people who have died with some anxiety on their minds will sometimes seek to communicate with their friends in order to arrange the Earthly matter that troubles them. If they cannot succeed in showing themselves or in impressing their wishes by a dream on some friend, they will often cause much annoyance by knocking and making other noises directly intended to draw attention. These noise are sometimes caused unconsciously by their restless efforts.

To illustrate this idea, let us take the organism of man. Man, as we know him, is the mediumistic instrument through which higher states manifest their wisdom and power. This mediumship, on general lines, extends from the lowest specimen in the scale of humanity upwards to the highest initiated adept; the only difference between the two is that of development.

Man, according to his state, assimilates the specific grade of life essence from the Universal Force which corresponds exactly to the quality and development of his Soul. As man ascends higher in the scale of Spiritual development, he becomes the recipient of finer essence; the coarser atoms are repelled and transmitted to less perfect organisms. The primal Life Force, in its original purity, contains all the requisite grades of Spiritual nutriment for every form of existence in the universe.

Within each realm the same laws are in force. Those forms of Life which, by comparison, are passive, become the mediums for those which are active. Ascending to the Mental plane, we find it precisely the same with knowledge. The active research of powerful, penetrating Minds accumulates this knowledge and then formulates the same into systems composed of more or less Truth and error. This combination of wisdom and ignorance constitutes a religious sect or school of philosophy.

The ignorant become the mediums of the wise. This wisdom may only merit such a name, however, by comparing it with the ignorance by which it is surrounded. The sum total of any nation's wisdom or ignorance may always be found by examining its laws, politics, constitution, and religion. A great political leader, a giant Mind, impresses his force upon a circle of kindred but less positive Minds. The millions are simply the mediums for the expression of Mental Force. Again, the visible head or center of this force may, in his turn, be the medium of some other but invisible head. Such invisible power may be mortal or Spiritual, embodied or disembodied.

All of these forms and phases, however, are to be classed as unconscious mediumship because the operator is seldom conscious of the magical powers he is using.

The prominent form of mediumship recognized as having a direct connection with practical Occultism is the mediumship of Spiritualism and some of its more recondite phases.

The basis of all trance, or physical mediumship, is embraced in the term passivity. The degree of passivity attained is in proportion to the power or strength of a person's mediumship. The question as to whether a given person will develop into a trance speaker or into a physical medium depends upon the brain conformation and upon the magnetic temperament of the body. Some individuals are so complex that they may become either the one or the other, according to the will of the circle. The chief point in these forms of mediumship is that they tend toward the destruction of individuality. They can only be attained in the totally passive state. The developing process is a means of destroying whatever amount of will the medium may have originally possessed.

This destruction of the human will is the greatest curse of mediumship. The controlling forces of such will-less creatures may be anything and everything, according to "conditions" and circumstances. A medium said to be "developed" stands upon the public platform and is controlled by some disembodied Intelligence.

But in nine cases out of every ten, it is the psychological influx of the audience centering upon the sensitive medium which produces the peculiar semi-mesmeric state known as a trance. Under such conditions, the inspired oration will harmonize with the majority of the Minds present, and, in numberless cases, the exact thoughts of individuals in the audience are reproduced.

Spiritualists should learn that mediums can be controlled by a Spirit and can be equally controlled by a living person. Of all places, the public platform is the least likely spot to be the center of Spiritual inspiration which emanates from ascended human Souls.

Those forms of mediumship known as Psychometry and Clairvoyance depend upon the degree of sensitiveness. Brain formation and magnetic temperament are only secondary in their evolution. Consequently, animals as well as humans may possess these phases.

Two of the most subtle, and so far almost entirely unsuspected, forms of this Spirit mediumship are "semi-transfer of identity" and "thought diffusion."

In a previous chapter we showed how a person who during Life possessed an active Mind will leave within the spaces of the Astral light thought forms or Psychic thought embryos. These thought forms are the Earth karma of the human Soul. Now, under certain conditions, this karma of disembodied Souls can be, and is, contacted by those still in the flesh. Thus, a person of strong, positive Mind, having rendered his Soul sphere contactable by partial development while his brain still remains positive, becomes a true medium. Being self-conscious, as far as the Mind and brain are concerned, he scorns the idea of mediumship, but in real truth he is as much a medium as a trance speaker. In this state he comes into magnetic rapport with certain thought forms within the Astral karmas of the disembodied.

In this condition a semi-transfer of identity takes place, and he seems to exist in some previous age. He becomes identified with the karmic form controlling his sensitive sphere. Under these circumstances, he becomes deceived by his ignorance and imagines he is recalling some incarnation of the past or simply puts the whole matter down as a sort of daydreaming. Esoteric Buddhists, unable to account for such phenomena, have in their benighted ignorance invented their "reawakened memory" theories. They consider these phenomena as veritable recollections of their past experiences. Yet, they are nothing of the kind. They are, indeed, past experiences, but not theirs!

The forms they contact are those of individuals who belong to the same Spiritual state of life, and who possessed, when upon the Earth, a similar mental and magnetic temperament. All such evidences of reincarnation are due to the simple action of mediumship.

When the Soul receives its true spiritual initiation, all these Earthly errors vanish, and the fleeting phantoms of the Astral world appear in their true light. There is no evidence obtained in the support of that which is fundamentally false, neither is there any experience which appears to favor or sustain a reincarnation theory that cannot be explained by the laws of mediumship.

Another form of the recondite phase of mediumship is that of thought diffusion. It is by this means that the potent, self-willed Minds behind outward Buddhism are silently subjecting certain sensitive Minds. This is in order to regain their lost sacerdotal power upon humanity. Thought diffusion is the power of diffusing to others certain thought forms and certain positive ideas. These currents of thought circulate around the various mental chambers of the human Mind. Wherever they contact a sensitive sphere possessing magnetic affinity, they gradually impress their force and ultimately subject the Soul to those ideas. In this way, by the subtle mental magic of its devotees, religious theology obtained its first foothold within the human Mind.

This diffusion of ideas is in active operation upon every mental plane; thus, one potent Mind evolving thought forms in this country may suddenly set in vibration hundreds of sympathetic Minds upon the other side of the Atlantic. They begin to think similar ideas and to form similar conclusions. These ideas may then become universal and constitute public opinion. Only a few are conscious of these ramifications of mental magic.

Esoteric Buddhism owes its origin to such magic and depends absolutely and entirely upon such Occult processes for its existence. Its followers never dream that instead of being independent, self-conscious Minds, they are the mediumistic sensitives of Oriental control. One must never forget that upon the external plane there is nothing so potent as the magic of the human Mind.

Many mediums believe all the various forms and phases of Spiritualistic phenomena are produced by one or more of the following agencies, either singly or in combination.

1. Elemental Spirits.
2. Human elementaries (i.e., the lost souls of depraved mortals).
3. Disembodied shells (the lifeless forms of disembodied mortals).
4. The mesmeric influence of living individuals.

The actual truth is midway between these extremes. It is a most glorious fact that disembodied human Souls can and do return and commune through various mediumistic Natures with embodied humanity. Still, the action of these Souls is chiefly confined to and manifested upon the impressional and inspirational planes of mediumship. The Spiritualist is correct, and there is much truth, together with much that is false, in this theory.

The "memory of nature" is not merely a poetic name. It is a phrase that designates a part of the marvelously complex mechanism by which human evolution is accomplished. In the earlier history of physical science, such a term would have been meaningless, but in the light of more recent discoveries, there is nothing startling in the idea.

Our conceptions of matter have been revolutionized in recent years. We have learned that even in its grosser grades it is enormously more impressionable than had been supposed. The sensitiveness of the ether which permits wireless communications gives some suggestion of the degree of responsiveness. If, in addition, we take into account the work of the superintending intelligences, we have, in toto, a plan of human evolution in which each of us is his own recorder of thought, emotion, motive, and act.

Those who study the Occult laws which shape human destiny may learn to use them for their rapid progress and for insuring a comfortable, as well as a Spiritually profitable, life journey.

Most people seem to believe that there is no law which will certainly bring them the results of their evil thoughts and acts. Others believe that, if there is such a law, they can in some way elude it and escape the consequences of its violation. We see them pass through life always doing the selfish thing or the thoughtless thing. They falsify facts. They harbor evil thoughts. They engage in gossip. They have their enemies and hate them. They scheme to bring discomfort and humiliation upon those whom they dislike.

And then, when the harvest from this misdirected energy is ripe, they are misled by the falsehoods of others to their loss and injury. They merely call it so much bad luck and go blindly on with their generation of wrong forces that will, in due time, bring them another enforced reaping of pain.

Let us, therefore, consider the agencies mentioned:

Elemental Spirits, often termed spooks, are the innumerable classes and species of impersonal elementals in the various rounds and spaces. But only three classes of them have any influence upon mediums and Spiritualistic phenomena. The first and lowest on the scale of intelligence is the class of cosmic elementals, generated in the four realms of Occultism (Fire, Earth, Air, and Water). These creatures cannot deceive the medium. They are incapable of impersonating or imitating anything beyond themselves unless they are impelled by the medium's internal desire for such deception. In such cases they may obey the impulse of the medium's Mind.

They are completely subjective to the human will, when psychically directed, and they possess no real individuality of their own. They are simply the blind forces of Nature, either active or latent according to the magnetic conditions. Therefore, they would be more correctly designated as the undeveloped Mind of matter.

The second class of Spirits on the scale of intelligence is the *Animal Elementals.* These beings are the Souls of animal forms of life undergoing the magnetic cycle of their impersonal existence within the Astral spaces. When any animal dies upon the Earth, it undergoes another cycle of life within the karmic spaces of its kind in the Astral World. There it evolves the forces and conditions to be utilized for its next incarnation. These Souls, if we may call them such, especially those of the domesticated animals, frequently become attached to various human beings on Earth. These are people with whom they have some peculiar magnetic affinity or to whom they were attached during their external Earth-life. It is these beings who become the innocent instruments of fraud.

They respond to the desires of the medium or to the

secret wish of the circle or to those who may consult the medium. Under these circumstances, it will always transpire that when a person consults a medium upon any subject about which he possesses a positive opinion, the answer he receives will correspond to this opinion. It makes no difference whether it be correct or incorrect.

The same thing happens when the client asks the advice or the opinion of a medium upon a worldly matter. The answer will always respond to the secret desire which the animal elemental perceives in the Mental sphere of the client. This type of "control" cannot be called fraud any more than a pet dog can be so charged when it fulfills his master's desire. The benighted ignorance of both medium and client is the only cause for such an apparent fraud.

Mediums who become the instruments of this class of intelligence are generally those of unbounded personal egotism. They formulate the idea that their Spirit guides cannot be any other than the most exalted of personages and Souls. The obliging, imitative Soul of the animal elemental feels the full force of the medium's egotistical thought desire, immediately responds and fulfills this mental idea. But no matter who they claim to be, they will always correspond to the ideal image of that personage existing in the medium's Mind. Should the medium be ignorant of the lives, times, and circumstantial surroundings of their idealized guide when on Earth, then their ideal guide will be equally ignorant of self.

The third class in the scale of intelligence is the *Magnetic Elementals* of the seven planetary divisions of Nature. These intelligent creatures are much too bright and ethereal ever to be guilty of fraud. They are generated by the Life forces of the planetary chain existing within each orb. They are the intermediate agents of the physical results of the planetary influences manifested on the Earth. They are the attendant familiars of certain classes of mystical students, especially those devoted to Alchemy and Astrology. It is these beings who usually produce the visions in crystals and magic mirros or vases of water. In consequence of this, they have often been wrongly termed planetary angels by certain schools of magical research.

They are planetary in Nature, but they do not belong to the physical planet to whose Nature they correspond. They pertain to our own orb equally as much as man himself and can give much information regarding the orb under whose dominion they act. If any deception transpires, it is but the reflection of the deception existing in the Minds of those who use them. They do not and cannot control mediums by mesmerism or by trance. Their sole influence is manifested in the impressional and Clairvoyant phases of mediumship.

Disembodied Human Elementaries are a class of agents made up of the animal Souls of depraved, wicked mortals who have sunk beneath the human plane. Thus, they caused a separation of their Divine Soul from their conscious individuality. Those who fall as low as this are generally evil magicians and sorceresses. These mortals are far more numerous than civilized society realizes. This class is made up of magnetic vampires who prolong their vicious existence by sapping the life blood of their mediumistic victims. They will impersonate anything and everything!

They are almost irresistibly impelled by longings to try and influence the affairs to which their passions and feelings still cling. They are bound to the earth even though they have lost all accustomed organs of activity. Their only hope of peace lies in resolutely turning away from Earth and fixing their minds on higher things. But comparatively few are strong enough to make this effort, even with the help always offered to them by workers on the Astral Plane.

Too often, such sufferers, impatient of their helpless inactivity, seek the assistance of sensitives with whom they can communicate and so mix themselves up once more in terrestrial affairs. They sometimes seek even to obsess convenient mediums and thus to utilize the bodies of others for their own purposes. Their only aim is to completely demoralize the mediums and plunge them into all kinds of depravity. The chief characteristic of the Human Elementary is obsession.

Nearly all those mortals who go insane through their religious excitement are the victims of elementary obsession. It is needless to add that these vampires are lost to all that is redemptive and good. They have gravitated to the lowest realms of brute animality in Nature, and ultimately they become indrawn within the death whirl of the magnetic orb known as the Dark Satellite. There they are swept to their final doom and extinction.

Disembodied Shells are the magnetic forms of those who have lived, died, and been buried upon the Earth. They are perfectly lifeless; they hover around the grave which conceals the lifeless corpse to which they are bound. As this slowly decomposes, the magnetic shell of phantom also slowly dissolves. They cannot be drawn away from the grave. They cannot be made to answer any mediumistic purpose whatsoever. Those who assert, as some do, that they can be regalvanized into a temporary life and made to simulate the deceased individual are sadly in error. These mediums know not whereof they speak.

The *Mesmeric influence* of living individuals is a potent factor. It is evident that any Spirit medium will feel, and to some extent respond to, the mesmeric will of a potent, positive, and magnetic Mind.

Under conditions of weak health or nervous excitement, the medium then becomes very dully conscious, or entranced, according to the lesser or greater amount of the etheric matter extruded. Mesmeric will may drive out the greater part of the etheric double, so that consciousness cannot affect or be affected; its bridge of communication with the other planes is broken.

In the abnormally organized persons called mediums, dislocation of the etheric and dense bodies easily occurs.

In sleep, when the consciousness leaves the physical vehicle which it uses during waking life, the dense and etheric bodies remain together, but in the physical dream-life they function to some extent independently. Impressions experienced during waking life are reproduced by the automatic action of the body, and both the physical and etheric brains are filled with disjointed, fragmentary pictures, the vibrations jostling each other.

Vibrations from the outside also affect both, and combinations often set up during waking life are easily called into activity by currents from the Astral World of Nature. The purity or impurity of waking thoughts will largely govern the pictures arising in dreams, whether spontaneously set up or induced from without by mesmeric influences.

By the tremendous pressure of Nature's disregarded laws, we are learning of the existence of those laws and the misery that accrues from ignoring them in Life and conduct. The lesson they would not learn during Earth-life is whirled away on the torrent of lusts and desires. It is pressed on them and will be pressed on them in their succeeding lives, until the evils are eradicated and Man has risen into a better Life.

Nature's lessons are sharp, but in the long run they are merciful. They lead to the evolution of the Soul and guide it to the winning of its Immortality.

BOOK II

All Western peoples have a double line of ancestors, their own forefathers and the Eastern civilizations. Both sets of ancestors have contributed much to modern methods of prophecy. Thus, only very few prophetic beliefs are original to a given people since most are mankind's common cultural heritage. They have been transmitted to us along the paths of civilization from the ancient East via Greece and Rome. This is particularly true of the most scientific and most common branch of prophecy, Astrology.

Prophecy originated in Mesopatamia, the country between the rivers Euphrates and Tigris, much more than 5000 years ago. It was in Babylon and in the other cultural centers of Mesopotamia the brilliant men first systematized these occult arts and raised them to the status of a pure science. Astrology in particular!

All of us are prophets, not so much from choice as from sheer necessity. Whenever we cross a road and fail to take into account traffic conditions or misjudge distances and speeds, we may have to pay dearly for our lack of prophecy or foresight. The foresight needed in this case is not on a very high level since it resembles the instinctive reaction of animals sensing danger.

However, man is born with it! Very small children are capable of dealing with such simple situations, and can do much more than scream at approaching danger. Many adults fare worse, for their inability to estimate the immediate future is borne out by the mounting toll which auto traffic accidents take of drivers and pedestrians.

The type of foresight we are discussing consists of immediate responses to external signals. The responses of fear, thought, and escape are the most primitive and also the most persistent of human reactions. Civilization has not reduced our general anxieties, but instead has merely shifted their causes. The builders of the Pyramids had a different set of anxieties from those of the modern motorist and took many different precautions. No doubt they took too few! Man has become more prophetic, or more civilized.

The foresight needed to avoid accidents is occasionally called "presence of mind," though "mind" plays only a little part in it. In essence, it involves making good use of the intuition and the fraction of time between the discovery of the source of danger and evasive action, then acting appropriately within very circumscribed conditions.

Everyday prophecies are by no means restricted to the kind of short range predictions we have been discussing. Most people can predict where they and other people will be at a given future date, and for what purpose. The fact that they can organize does not mean they know nothing about the rest of their time. Quite the contrary is the case!

The uncertainty factors involved in everyday living are considered so negligible that people who tell you they will be in Madeira, in Iceland, or in Hawaii in six months' time are not credited with possessing any special prophetic gifts. Not so long ago anyone claiming he would reach some distant place on a given day would have been taken for a ridiculous braggart, or if successful, for a divine Seer.

From this alone it must be obvious that the art of predicting the future has made tremendous advances. What was previously a matter for prophets has become a commonplace activity. Our certainty has become much greater!

Man lives in a world of predictions and the question whether human beings are capable of foretelling the future is purely rhetorical. All we can ask is what events human beings cannot predict at all or only with a small degree of probability and what are the limits of man's true foresight. This leads to a question: Is there any means of extending these limits?

What we are really concerned with is simply the wealth and complexity of the methods with which mankind attempts to form a picture of the future, for only in this way can we overcome the prejudice that true prediction and prophetic speculation are not identical, but are charlatanism and black magic.

Human beings have always wanted to look ahead, and to a large extent they are capable of doing so. Methods of prediction have changed over the ages. Some have been discarded, others, no less confused, have been retained, but many new and valuable occult facts have come to be appreciated.

Only by taking complete stock of the available material can we hope to choose correctly.

1

The Great Prophets

In the primitive dualistic world, the powers of light and darkness were worshipped alike. The equal strength of both good and evil had arisen in the mind of man when he observed nature and meditated upon his own life. Man is inhabited by contradictory forces; in his thought and action, good and evil are intimately mingled, and he cannot always distinguish between them. Moreover, good intentions sometimes generate evil, or criminal desires even become the servant of good. Both principles seemingly are everlasting, and in nature all things carry out the idea that light should overcome darkness.

With civilization, man became increasingly aware of his capacities and his responsibility. The Chaldean star taught that luck and disaster were not haphazard events dependent upon the caprices of spirits, but rather that they derive from the heavenly bodies, which send good and bad according to mathematical laws. Man, it seemed, was incapable of fighting the will of the planet divinities. Yet, the more this system evolved, the more did the wise men read ethical values in man's fate. The will of the stars was not completely independent from man's will.

ZOROASTER

It was probably in the Seventh century B.C. that Zoroaster, the Median prophet, preached the doctrine that evil, powerful and everpresent, can be avoided and defeated. Zoroaster purified the ancient belief in the hosts of good and evil spirits; the rulers of a split universe. He traced these legions back to their principles: Ormazd (Ahura-Mazda), King of Light; and Ahriman (Anra-Mainyu), Prince of Darkness. The good demons of older traditions were dethroned by Zoroaster; however, they were granted a place in the hierarchy of evil spirits.

Led by Ahriman, these spirits no longer opposed Good in unruly swarms. The Kingdom of Evil had become organized like that of Good. The two armies were marshaled in warlike array. Figures oppose each other in equal strength; the armies of light and darkness face one another. Victory is not followed by peace because the struggle continues to the end of time. In heaven, as on earth, resounds the battlecry.

Six archdemons were Ahriman's principal underlings, corresponding to the six archangels which surrounded the King of Light. These archangels were Divine Wisdom, Righteousness, Dominion, Devotion, Totality, and Salvation. The archdemons were the spirits of Anarchy, Apostasy, Presumption, Destruction, Decay, and Fury.

Many other demons in the Zoroastrian religion, daevas of lower rank, tempted one away from the true worship: Paromaiti, Arrogance; Mitox, the Falsely Spoken Word; Zaurvan, Decrepitude; Akatasa, Meddlesomeness; Vereno, Lust.

Still lower in fiendish hierarchy ranked the Drujs, the Yatus, the Nasus, enchantresses, malevolent beings, deceivers, and monsters. Just as great was the circle of heavenly legions, the good Yazatas.

The originality of Zoroaster resides in something beyond his elaborate angelology and demonology. He conceived periods of time in which the fate of the material world and of the good and bad principle would be decided.

The outcome was good; defeat awaited Ahriman. Zoroaster distinguished between two types of time — boundless time or eternity and sovereign time, a long period which Ormazd "carved out" from the bulk of eternity.

Sovereign time will last twelve thousand years; it was divided into four cycles of three thousand. Each millennium was presided over by a sign of the Zodiac, an indication that sovereign time is an enormous celestial year whose smallest fraction is the circle of the twelve daily and nightly hours. Three, four, and twelve are the mystical numbers. They are the base from which evolves the number seven, the six archdemons together with Ahriman their ruler, and the six archangels and Ormazd.

The first three thousand years were those of spiritual creation during which all creatures remained in their transcendental form. The second triad was that of material creation, of celestial beings, of spirits, sky, water, earth, plants, animals, and mankind. The third period was that of the irruption of the Evil One, which dominated man's history before the coming of revelation. The last period started with the advent of Zoroaster and will end with the Day of Judgment.

Zoroaster stated that creation began in this manner: Akaron produced light by emanation; from light sprang Ormazd, the first-born, who created the pure world. He ordered the hierarchy of angels and the myriad concepts of things he intended to bring into being. Another emanation of Boundless Time was Ahriman, second-born of the Eternal, who was jealous and hungry for power.

He envied Ormazd and was banished to the realm of darkness, where he reigned in night while the struggle between good and evil was being fought.

The war began when after a thousand years Ormazd created light patterned after the supermundane, the celestial light. He fashioned the source of life, a power he called Bull, and Ahriman destroyed the bull-being.

From its scattered seed, Ormazd then fashioned the first man and the first woman. With milk and fruit Ahriman seduced the woman, and man fell into sin. And as evil counterparts of the good animals, Ahriman created harmful beasts, reptiles and snakes, the Khraftstras. And the war goes on; the strength of evil grows. Yet, at the moment when Ahriman seems to triumph, redemption was at hand.

Redemption awaits the Day of Judgment, the advent of the Saviour, when a flood of molten metal shall sear the wicked while the righteous shall pass unharmed.

As good and evil are parted finally from one another, Ormazd will establish his Good Kingdom. The dead shall rise and hell shall be purified for the enlargement of the regenerated world, deathless and everlasting.

HERMES TRISMEGISTUS

Hermes Trismegistus was the master of alchemical philosophy. Hermes was the Greek god who conducted the souls to the dark kingdom of Hades, the underworld. He opened the doors of birth and of death. He controlled exchange, commerce, and learning; he was the gods' messenger, the mediator, the reconciler.

Trismegistus meant "three times the greatest," an epithet which reveals his high status. He was not a Greek god, but a divinity of the Greek colonists in Egypt. These Greco-Egyptians admired the ancient religious doctrines of the Nile.

From the colossal amount of writing ascribed to Hermes Trismegistus not much has survived except fourteen short texts written in Greek and a series of fragments preserved by Christian authors. These express mystical and philosophical ideas, which, viewed as a whole, recall Gnosticism. The best known among them is *Poimandres, the Good Shepherd.* Some of its passages bear a striking resemblance to the *Gospel of St. John,* while others are reminiscent of Plato's *Timaeus.* Jewish thought, as is expressed by Philo, can be discerned in them.

In addition to these writings, a few magical treatises were ascribed to Trismegistus. Their main theme was astrology; alchemy was treated somewhat vaguely.

His hermetic books were considered by the alchemists as Hermes' bequest to them of the secrets which were veiled in allegories to prevent the precious wisdom from falling into the hands of the profane. Only the wise were able to find their way in this mystical labyrinth.

Hermes' passage, cited frequently, the Credo of the adepts, was the inscription found on an emerald tablet "in the hands of Hermes' mummy, in an obscure pit where his interred body lay," situated, according to tradition, in the great pyramid of Gizeh.

> Tis true, without falsehood, and most real: that which is above is like that which is below, to perpetrate the miracles of One thing. And as all things have been derived from one, by the thought of one, so all things are born from this thing, by adoption. The Sun is its Father, the Moon is its Mother. Wind has carried it in its belly, the Earth is its nurse. Here is the father of every perfection in the world. His strength and power are absolute when changed into earth; thou wilt separate the earth from fire, the subtle from the gross, gently and with care. It ascends from earth to heaven, and descends again to earth to receive the power of the superior and the inferior things. By this means, thou wilt have the glory of the world. And because of this, all obscurity will flee from thee. Within this is the power, most powerful of all powers. For it will overcome all subtle things, and penetrate every solid thing. Thus the world was created. From this will be, and will emerge, admirable adaptations of which the means are here. And for this reason, I am called Hermes Trismegistus, having the three parts of the philosophy of the world. What I have said of the Sun's operations is accomplished.

ALBERTUS MAGNUS

In the thirteenth century, the men of the faith dwelt peaceably together with the wise men of antiquity, admitting the presumable inventor of all magic, Zoroaster. A more profound understanding of the past, a wider conception of wisdom produced this world, which although not universal, was well-ordered with all its elements fully understood.

Albertus' importance in scientific matters lies more in his attitude than his achievements. His description of the marvelous virtues which dwell in crystals may serve as an example: If you hold a crystal toward the sun, you can light a fire.

Albertus had within himself a curiosity which was laudable, together with the disciplined methods of a scholar. These methods test particular statements by the general law concerning living beings as it was established by Aristotle.

He never doubted that magical wonders were effected. True, there existed jugglery and illusion; people believed they were seeing things which did not exist. True, evil demons led men astray with magic, which was considerably worse than the deception of the eyes. Yet, there also existed in Albertus' opinion *natural magic,* which was of the good, and a great deal of good was found in the writings of the Arabs as well as hermetic literature. There were wonderful virtues in herbs and stones of which the patristic writings did not speak. Betony conferred the power of divination; verbena was used as a love charm; the herb meropis opened the seas.

Many other marvels were induced with plants, as was written in Costa ben Luca and Hermes. There were also magical stones which cured diseases. In his work on minerals, Albertus spoke extensively of the hidden virtues of stones.

Some of these marvels he had experienced himself. *"Lapides preciosi praeter alliis habent mariabiles virtutes."* *(Precious stones have more miraculous virtues than others.)*

Albertus was an alchemist; like his pupil, St. Thomas Aquinas, he believed that alchemy was a difficult but true art. In his chemical experiments, he was less hampered by philosophy, perhaps because the early Greeks were not acquainted with alchemy. He describes his operations with accuracy and expresses original ideas.

Among the numerous volumes he bequeathed to posterity, his alchemical treatise is perhaps the best. In the book on minerals, he finds much to criticize in alchemical theories, and sometimes he seems opposed to the art of

Hermes, but in his treatise *On Alchemy,* which is authentic, he champions alchemical operations.

This is what he recommends in his book to his fellow alchemists:

"The alchemist must be silent and discreet. To no one should he reveal the results of his operations . . . He shall live in loneliness, remote from men. His house should have two or three rooms consecrated entirely to the work."

Contemporaries of Albertus affirm that he built an automaton, the android. Shaped like a man, with each part of its body welded under the influence of a particular star, the android was Albertus' servant. He was endowed with the gift of speech so much so that his gibberish disturbed the studious Aquinas who destroyed the machine. Did such an automaton really exist? Eliphas Levi, the nineteenth-century occultist, remarked subtly that it was only a symbol of Albertus' scholasticism, human in form, but an artificial being controlled by a mechanism and not by life.

ROGER BACON

Like Albertus, Roger Bacon, the Franciscan Friar, based his knowledge upon Aristotelian philosophy. Not only did he gather wisdom by philosophical methods or through observation and reasoning, but also, like Albertus, he emphasized the importance of experimentation.

Bacon's writings have a vivacity which we do not often find in scholasticism, and his impatience, mingled with clairvoyance, compelled him at times to make truly astounding predictions:

"First, I will tell you about the admirable works of art and nature. Afterwards, I shall describe their causes and their form. There is no magic connected with this, for magic is inferior to such things and unworthy of them. Namely: Machines of navigation can be made, huge ships for rivers and the seas. They move without oars; a single man can maneuver them better than if they were manned fully.

"Then there are also cars, moving along without horses

and at a colossal speed, and we believe that such were the battle wagons of old furnished with sickles.

"Flying machines can be made also. A man sitting in the center controls something which makes the machine's artificial wings flap like those of birds.

"A device, small in size, for lowering heavy weights can be made, most useful in emergencies. For by a machine, three fingers high and wide, and less in bulk, a man could free himself and his friends from all dangers of prison, and could rise and descend.

"A machine can be constructed for submarine journeys, for seas and rivers. It dives to the bottom without danger to man. Alexander the Great has made use of such a device, as we know from Ethicus the Astronomer. Such things have been made long ago and they are still made in our days, except perhaps the flying machine."

Magic existed for Roger Bacon as it did with his contemporaries. He admitted there were difficulties in discerning between science and the black arts. He accepted natural magic, which is not evil. We find the scholar's conceptions were not unlike those of the philosophers. Magic aiming at the good was permissible and was called natural magic; the black arts promoting what was evil were to be rejected.

Alchemy is related to physics, said Bacon. It treats of colors and other substances, of burning bitumen, of salt and sulphur, of gold and other metals, and though nothing concerning the alchemical art was written by Aristotle, he was necessary for the study of natural philosophy and speculative medicine.

Through alchemy, gold can be made, and thus the hermetic art can provide for the expenses of the state. It prolongs man's life. But there were few who worked alchemically, and still fewer who could produce works which would prolong life. The art was suited only to the wisest, who knew the meaning of the eagle, the deer, the serpent, the phoenix, creatures who renew their lives through the virtues of herbs and stones.

Like Rabbi Moses Maimonides, Bacon believed that Holy Writ was the basic source of Astrology. This made the study of the stars and their influence a legitimate occupation. Bacon's opinion in this matter was not shared by all, for in spite of the growing influence of Astrology on medieval learning, the official attitude of the Church was rather adverse.

Bacon implied a belief that philosophy, which he identified with astrology and mathematics, should lead to and confirm theology. He went even further, asserting that without Astrology or philosophy, Church doctrine was not complete.

In his *Opus Majus,* he said: "If the truth of philosophy is impaired, damage is inflicted upon theology whose function it is to use the power of philosophy, not absolutely but in controlling the Church, directing the commonwealth of believers, and aiding the conversion of predestined unbelievers."

And of the theologians who opposed such ideas, he said, "But they err not only in this, that they ignorantly condemn knowledge of the future secured through mathematics."

Bacon's teachings were not of the Faustian character which enthusiastic investigators claimed. He was the enlightened forerunner of a scientific time, whose voice was unheard in the scholastic desert. In his determination to unify all learning, wisdom, and faith, he produced a unique work, the *Opus Majus,* which he arranged and coordinated according to his own original views.

PICO, COUNT OF MIRANDOLA

Pico, Count of Mirandola, was born in 1463 near Modena. His precocity was considered comparable to that of the painter Masaccio who died at twenty-seven after having given a decisive impetus to the plastic arts. At twenty-four Pico went to Rome, where he posted his nine hundred theses for public debate.

Among these, many were concerned with magic and the Kabbalah, a secret doctrine which was discussed in earlier chapters. These occult systems were to prove the divinity of Christ. Pico's plan did not win the approval of the Church. Pope Innocent VIII, who had a rigorous attitude toward matters of witchcraft, appointed a commission to examine the whole of Pico's theories. The verdict was unfavorable: Four were judged to be rash and heretical; six others were condemned; three were called false, heretical, and erroneous.

In his work, Pico favored the prediction of the future by dreams, sibyls, spirits, portents, and also by birds and the intestines. The two latter methods, being undoubtedly pagan, certainly were not tolerated by the Roman theologians. His leanings toward Chaldean oracles, Orphic hymns, and the like were not acceptable to them. Some of his propositions have a Neo-Platonic and Gnostic flavor.

But Pico's ultimate goal went beyond that of reviving old, more or less known magical ideas and of introducing new ones. His ambition was to reconcile the officially sanctioned Aristotelianism and Platonism which the scholars were studying again. He strove to accomplish this with the help of the Kabbalah.

TRITHEMIUS

During the time Trithemius was a student in Heidelberg, he met a mysterious teacher who instructed him in the secret sciences. When in 1482 Trithemius decided to return to his native town, the teacher informed him that on his journey he would find the key to his life. As Trithemius reached Sponheim, snow was falling heavily and he sheltered in the Benedictine monastery. There, life appeared so attractive that he decided to become a monk. This was the famous key of which the secret master had spoken.

Though most of his works were ecclesiastical treatises, Trithemius wrote on magic. Alchemy attracted him greatly, and he declared in his books that transmutations can be made and the philosophers' stone can be attained. This stone, he said, was the soul of the world, or *spiritus mundi*, rendered visible. One might call it the petrification of God's breath, as the abbot affirms the world soul was the breath emanating from its divine source. In this sense, we understand his saying God permeates everything.

In the midst of the sixteenth century, Copernicus discovered a new world, that of the planets circulating together with the earth around their central star, the sun. This discovery demolished the old Christian dogmatic hierarchy. God could not be above, as there was no above and no below, and there was nothing outside the world. Therefore, a new dwelling had to be found for Him.

Trithemius was very modest and timid, and he did not wish to do anything which was contrary to the established tradition. So he invented all sorts of secret methods of writing by which profound thoughts could be disguised in apparently harmless texts.

The fact that he influenced Paracelsus and Agrippa shows he was sympathetic to magic learning. He speaks often in dissembling terms; for instance, the Golden Age would arrive when the lion and the lamb would dwell together. In this Biblical symbol he clothed the thought that the philosophers' stone was attained when the Fire of God, the lion, and the Divine Light are joined mystically.

According to modern Occultists, these contain an enormous amount of magic wisdom. It is expressed in a code, each word having a double meaning, but the key to this mystical work Trithemius carried to his grave. The words should be read according to certain combinations, and the book loses sense completely when translated from its original Latin.

AGRIPPA

In the whirlpool of the Renaissance, Henry Cornelius Agrippa von Nettesheim, the most important figure among the Occultists of that age, was driven from country to country, from high favor to prison, from silent study to the battlefield, and from wealth to poverty.

Agrippa was encouraged by Trithemius to commit to writing his knowledge of the Occult. His acceptance of Neo-Platonism was championed by the Humanists as opposed to the Aristotelianism of the Middle Ages. In his study of the Neo-Platonists, such as Plotinus, Iamblichus and Prophyry, Agrippa became immersed in the supernatural and the occult. His enthusiasm for these philosophers overwhelmed his sense of criticism.

With a mind open to every current of occult thought, he strove to reconcile various magical doctrines. In his later years, Agrippa recanted his magical writings. Now, as incredulous as he had been credulous before, he professed nothing was certain either in the arts or in the sciences. The only reliable thing in the world was religious faith.

He was imprisoned at Brussels and released after one year. Now his *Occult Philosophy*, which he had written in his early days, was published. The belated publication created incredible confusion because its contents had already been recanted by his work *On The Vanity of Arts and Sciences*. The *Occult Philosophy*, on the contrary, indulged in the belief that men were able to work miracles by the power of their wisdom.

The *Occult Philosophy* greatly influenced Western occultism and deserves a brief resume: Magic is a powerful faculty, full of mystery and comprising a profound knowledge of the most secret things, their nature, power, quality, substance, and effects, as well as their relationships and antagonisms. It is a philosophical science; it is physics, mathematics, and theology. Through physics we learn the nature of things; through mathematics we comprehend their dimensions and extent, and the movement of heavenly bodies can be calculated; through theology we come to know God, angels, demons, intelligence, soul, and thought. Physcis is terrestrial; mathematics, celestial; theology is concerned with the archetype world.

PARACELSUS

There is no one comparable to Paracelsus, physician, astrologer, anthroposophist, theologian, mystic, and Magus. At a time when knowledge was assuming many ramifications, when faith was divided into dogmas, and when the old unified world structure collapsed, Paracelsus achieved the impossible. He wove his knowledge, practice, and faith into one.

Pursuing this magic ideal, he betrayed himself as being solidly tied to bygone Middle Ages, an epoch in which unification of every branch of thought was still possible.

But contrary to his fondness for the past, he publicly burned the works of Galen, denouncing the sterility of his fellow physicians, and he made it clear that his own world was to be welded into one by other means than those offered by conventions. He wanted to know the true nature of things through investigation and not through the study of dusty volumes.

These bold views guided his critical attitude toward classical authorities. Paracelsus believed nature was the highest authority because nature, unlike man, does not commit errors.

Everything in nature partook of the world machine, built according to a divine plan. The various forms and events of the corporeal world had their profound meaning and were just so many manifestations of the divine.

Man's first doctor was God, the maker of health, for the body was not a thing apart, but a house for the soul. The physician, therefore, must treat the two simultaneously and strive at bringing them into harmony, which was the only true health. Such inner accord harmoniously united in man the things of the world with the divine.

Religion was derived from the Latin *re-liqare* (to unite again). The curative process shared this characteristic. Religion was the basis of medicine. In his prophecies, Paracelsus predicted an evil end for people who fail to achieve self-recognition. They did not know the true nature with which they were endowed. Living rightly and healthily was the attainment of harmony with one's true self.

Therefore, the physician must be an astrologer as well; he should know about the harmony of the spheres and their influence. Moreover, he must be a theologian to comprehend the needs of the soul. He must be an anthropologist in order to understand the needs of the body. He must be an alchemist to perceive the universal substances which are found in harmonious mixtures everywhere in the material world.

He should be conscious of the primary creative cosmic forces because they are universal and are in man himself. And he must be a mystic in order to recognize that there exists something beyond logic, as the ancients have demonstrated.

Paracelsus affirms that God had given various qualities to things at their creation, forces which enabled them to exist independently. The divine intervention was, therefore, not constantly to be sought after, for man has the capacity to help himself, like the stars which move by their own initiative.

The heavenly bodies influenced man. They were inhabited by the Greco-Roman divinities who emit a mortal light, for everything in creation was mortal.

God alone sends forth a divine light which is immortal and which is received by that which is immortal in man. These two kinds of light are the essence of all.

The astrologer inquires into the mortal light of the stars, by whose contemplation he gains knowledge. Man was molded from the dust of the stars, his older brothers.

Man was receptive to the radiance of the stars, and to be attracted to their light was godly, but mortal at the same time. It existed before the coming of Christ; it still exists and grows even stronger.

NOSTRADAMUS

Nostradamus (Michel de Nostre-Dame), the greatest of all seers and astrologers, was born in St. Remy, France in 1503. Though his prophecies are styled in scurrilous language, many lent themselves to striking interpretations of happenings which have occurred centuries after the stargazer's death. Even names mentioned by the seer coincide with those connected with the predicted events.

The great seer had written an often-reprinted work on cosmetics, on perfumes, and on the art of making jam with sugar, honey, and cooked wine. This indicated that Doctor Nostradamus was also well-versed in the science of herbs and minerals, like his grandfather, Jacques de Nostre-Dame.

Michel was one of the greatest physicians of his epoch. When studying medicine at Montpellier University, he interrupted his studies and helped to stamp out an epidemic of the Black Death. Nostradamus, apparently immune to the pestilence, traveled from city to city to perform miraculous cures.

His prophecies, which he called *Centuries,* were published in 1555, long after his book on cosmetics. These predictions made an enormous impression, and people from all classes traveled to Salon seeking the seer's prophecy and advice.

PORTA

When practicing medicine in the late 1500's, Porta had many occasions to observe his patients and to study their character and complexion. The results of this studious inquiry were laid down in his book *Physiognomy,* a striking and convincing system not to be dismissed.

Porta's early experiments in physiognomy influenced the eighteenth century philosopher, Johann Kaspar Lavater, who wrote many volumes on the art of judging men by their features. The elaborate system includes morphological, anthropological, anatomical, histrionical, and graphical studies. Lavater quoted long excerpts from Porta's books and inserted illustrations from the works.

Many other wonderful things were described in Porta's book on magic. He vouched for the frequently described marvel of animals being produced spontaneously from putrefaction. He described the dangerous art of making bread heavier by increasing the weight of wheat. He gave instruction for the counterfeiting of precious stones and for similar arts which his readers were most eager to learn.

The chapter on physics contains items such as how to make a man mad for a day, or how to cause sleep with a mandrake. This chapter deals with the art of causing pleasant and troublesome dreams. Special parts of Porta's work were devoted to distillation, fireworks, cookery, hunting and fishing, and other activities which rendered life agreeable.

CAGLIOSTRO

Among the Magi, the Zurich pastor Johann Kaspar Lavater was foremost as a promoter of tolerance. This modest author of a famous work on physiognomy had his own views on religion. He observed his fellow men with deep insight, for the physiognomic art was the study of man's features as the signs and characters formed by nature to reveal the inner man. His urbanity often proved more effective than the tempestuousness of his fellow magicians.

One would think such a learned and influential man would not need advice from a fellow Magus. Yet, in 1780, Lavater traveled to Strassburg where he hoped to gather more wisdom from the Count Cagliostro. The Count, however, refused to see him. They exchanged letters. To Lavater's question, "In what precisely does your knowledge reside," Cagliostro answered laconically: *"In verbis, herbis et lapidibus,"* (In words, herbs, and stones.) thus alluding to his marvelous cures.

He performed these cures with simples concocted from minerals and vegetables and with the suggestive power of his word. Such an answer was unusually modest, as the "count" made little secret of his knowledge. Cagliostro was less talkative in referring to his stay in London where he had committed several frauds.

In spite of Cagliostro's shady past, even his enemies could not deny the magician's astounding intelligence. And many friends and followers acknowledged their master's scandals and lies as extravagances to be weighed against his wisdom, his charity, and truly superhuman talents of a seer, healer, and Hermetic.

Cagliostro was the founder of the Egyptian Lodge. The power of his word attracted numerous adherents and whole groups of Freemasons abandoned their rites to follow those invented by the Grand Kophta, as Cagliostro called himself.

Brothers of every creed were accepted. The only postulate was to believe in the immortality of the soul.

During the seances, magical ceremonies were performed with the intention of communicating with the seven "pure spirits." An innocent girl, the "Dove," was led to a table where a glass bottle was flanked by two torches. The girl would stare into the bottle in which absent persons, future happenings, or angels would appear. She was often led behind a screen where she would experience a mystical union with an angel.

SAINT-GERMAIN

The riddle of Saint-Germain has never been solved. The dates of his birth and death are unknown. Incredible things are claimed of him. Frederick the Great called him the man who could not die. The count himself asserted he had lived 2000 years based on the professed discovery of the liquid which could prolong human life.

He would speak familiarly of a chat with the Queen of Sheba and of wonderful happenings at the marriage of Cana. He knew the gossip of the court of Babylon, tales a thousand years old.

His knowledge of European history was uncanny. He would mention various happenings in the reigns of Henry IV and Francis I. To an astounded lady, he would whisper family secrets. True things, the lady said, which he heard from her ancestor on the battlefield of Marignano.

The count was neither tall nor very handsome; he always appeared about forty and dressed exquisitely. He was dark-haired, lively, and smiling. His clothes were covered with precious jewels. He spoke and wrote Greek, Latin, Sanskrit, Arabic, Chinese, French, German, English, Italian, Portuguese, and Spanish.

He verged on the supernatural. He was a talented painter, a virtuoso on the harpsichord and violin, and his alchemical knowledge far surpassed any of his contemporaries.

From the lives of these men, we may learn many lessons applicable to our studies: The Magi in their study of nature will increase their wisdom by degrees: Through the study of stones they will learn the essence of the stars; from the Planets their knowledge will be led to the sublime.

Agrippa started with the four elements, Fire, Water, Earth, and Air. These elements occur in three types: Here on earth they are mixed, impure. In the Stars, they are pure. Thirdly, there are composite elements which can change and which are the vehicle of all transformations. The elements are found here below, in the whole universe, in spirits and angels, and even in God.

From the elements were born the natural virtues of things, but not occult virtues. The latter were infused into things through ideas by means of the world-Soul.

In order to ascertain occult virtues, we should explore the world by means of resemblances. For instance, fire here on earth excites celestial fire, the eye cures the eye, sterility produces sterility.

As there is accord between things akin, there is discord between things hostile. Experience has shown, for instance, between the sunflower and the sun there is accord, whereas between the lion and the cock there is hostility. It is the task of the Magi to recognize these sympathies and antipathies in order to operate magically through nature.

Similar dispositions are found in the planets, whether friendly or hostile to one another. Such relations, when made use of, yield magical results, for all things inferior submit to those above.

Not only single objects depend upon the Stars, but whole provinces, countries, and kingdoms, to which planetary and zodiacal signs are allotted. In tracing such celestial signs, the Magi propitiates virtues from above. The sign of Sagittarius brings down the virtues of that constellation.

Thus, through various contrivances well-prepared and coordinated, favorable influences are attracted, not only from the Stars, but also from good Spirits and from God.

2

Psychic Power

Development

There have been attempted explanations of and theories regarding the phenomena of Psychic powers, some of which are more or less plausible while others are quite visionary, "wild," and fantastic. I shall give you plainly, clearly, and simply the time-honored teachings of the advanced Occultists, those which have been tested and tried by centuries of investigation and experiment.

The Occult Teachings inform us in addition to the five physical senses possessed by man (Seeing, Feeling, Hearing, Tasting, and Smelling) which have their appropriate sense organ, every individual is also possessed of Five Astral Senses. These form a part of what is know to Occultists as the Astral Body. These Astral Senses, which are the astral counterparts of the five physical senses, operate upon the Astral Plane. This is next above the Physical Plane.

By means of these Astral Senses, one may sense outside objects without the use of the physical senses. It is through such sensing by the Astral Senses that the phenomena of Psychic power occurs. Just as the Physical Senses operate upon the Physical Plane, so do the Astral Senses operate upon the Astral Plane.

The Occultist believes that by using the Astral Sense of Seeing, a person is able to perceive occurrences and scenes at a distance almost incredibly far. One may see through solid objects, see records of past occurrences in the Astral Ether, and see the future as it is thrown ahead of Time. Like the shadows cast by material objects, "coming events cast their shadows before." Such events may travel immense distances and often after great periods of time because the Astral Vibrations continue.

The Astral Senses of Taste and Smell are seldom used although there are abundant proofs of their existence. The Astral Sense of Feeling allows one to become aware of certain occurrences on the Astral Plane and to perceive mental impressions which are manifested at a distance. The Astral Sense of Feeling may be explained as a sense of "Awareness" not just a mere "Feeling." It may well be called "Sensing" for want of a better name. But still we must not overlook the fact there are many instances of true "feeling" on the Astral Plane. An example would be when one actually "feels" the pain of another, commonly known as "sympathetic pains."

To understand the Astral Senses, one must be acquainted with the existence of "The Astral Body." There is no point in Occult teachings better established, longer held, or more thoroughly proven than the existence of this Astral Body.

The Astral Body is an exact counterpart of the physical body of the person. It is composed of a fine ethereal matter and is usually encased in the physical body. In ordinary cases, detaching of the Astral Body from its physical counterpart is accomplished only with great difficulty. But in dreams, when under great mental stress, and under conditions of occult development, the Astral Body may become detached and sent on long journeys. It may travel at a rate of speed even greater than that of light. The Astral Body exists after the death of the physical body, but it disintegrates in time.

The Astral Body of a dying person is often projected to the presence of friends and loved ones a few moments before

the actual physical death. Such a phenomenon arises from
the strong desire of the dying person to see and be seen. The
Astral Body frequently travels in psychic phenomena and
visits far distant places, there sensing what is occurring. The
jumbled and distorted recollections of these places are due to
the brain not having received perfect impressions. The result
is like a blurred or distorted photographic plate.

In order to grasp the underlying principles of this
phenomena and its allied subjects, you must familiarize
yourself with the Astral Senses. Unless you understand and
accept these truths and facts, you will not be able to grasp
the principles underlying psychic phenomena, but will be lost
in the quagmire of idle theories and fantastic explanations.
Investigators of Psychic phenomena who have not made
themselves acquainted with the Occult Teachings are always
lost in such realms of fantasy.

The phenomena of the Psychic powers may be grouped
into three classes, each being produced by its own special
cause. In either or all cases, the impressions are received by
and through the Astral Senses. But there are three distinct
ways in which these impressions are received. They may be
classified under the following terms: (1) "Clairaudience" is a
term sometimes used to indicate Astral Hearing. Astral
Hearing functions on the Astral Plane, just as the physical
sense of Hearing functions on the Physical Plane. In many
cases of Psychomantic Vision there is Clairaudience while in
other cases it might not occur. Likewise, Psychomantic
Vision is usually accompanied by Clairaudience although one
may be able to hear Astrally, and see nothing. An example of
this is the story of Saint Joan. She told of hearing a message
while praying before a shrine.

Psychic Powers lie dormant in every person since the
Astral Senses are present in everyone. The possibility of their
being awakened into activity is always present. The different
degrees of Psychic Power seen in different persons depends
chiefly upon the degree of their development, or unfoldment,
and not upon the comparative strength of the faculties. In
some persons, of certain temperaments, the Astral Senses are

very near to the manifesting point at all times. Flashes of intuition and premonitions are really manifestations of the psychic mind.

In other persons the Astral Senses are almost atrophied, for they are merged in materialistic thought and physical life. The element of Faith plays an important point in this phenomena as it does in all Occult phenomena. One's belief tends to open up the latent Psychic Powers and faculty in man, while disbelief tends to prevent their unfoldment. There is a very good psychological reason for this; belief and disbelief are two potent factors on all planes of action.

Occultists know, and teach, that the Astral Senses and faculties of the human race will unfold as the race progresses. Then Psychic power will be a common possession of all persons, just as is the use of the physical senses at the present time. In the meantime, there are persons who are beginning to manifest this power in a greater or lesser degree. There are many more persons in this stage of development than is generally realized. In fact, many persons manifesting Psychic Power are apt to pass by the phenomena as imagination and foolishness. Then many persons manifest the power during sleeping hours and dismiss the matter as merely a dream, etc.

Students often ask how this Psychic faculty will first be manifested in themselves or how they may know when they have reached the stage at which its first faint foreshadowings are beginning to be felt. Cases differ so widely it is impossible to give to this question an answer which will be universally applicable. Some people begin under some unusual stimulus and become able just for one time to see some striking vision. Very often in such a case, because the experience does not repeat itself, the newest seer comes to believe that he was the victim of a hallucination. Others begin by becoming intermittently conscious of the brilliant colors and vibrations of the human aura, while still others find themselves seeing and hearing something to which those around them are blind and deaf. Others see faces, landscapes, or colored clouds floating before their eyes in the dark just before they fall asleep. The commonest experience of all is in those who begin to recollect with greater and greater clarity what they have seen and heard on other planes during their sleep.

Very many persons possess respectable degrees of the full manifestation of Psychic Power. Such persons have intuitions, notions, presentiments, and the faculty of getting ideas other than by the usual physical mental processes. Others manifest certain special degrees of Psychic Powers, which develop rapidly by practice. The phases of Time Psychomancy (Past and Future) and of space Psychomancy, in its higher degrees, are rare; few persons possess them. Still fewer persist in the practice until they develop it since they are lacking the patience, persistence, and application necessary.

While it is difficult to lay down a method of instruction in the Development of Psychic Power, there is a plan of giving general information which, if followed, will put the student upon the right path.

DEVELOPMENT METHODS

1. Concentration: In the first place, the student should cultivate the basic faculty of Concentration. This is the power to hold one's attention upon an object for some length of time. Very few possess this power, although many think they do. The best way to develop Concentration is to practice on some familiar and common object – a pencil, a book, or an ornament. Take up the object and study it in great detail. Force the mind to examine and consider it in every part until every small detail has been observed. Then lay the object aside. A few hours later pick it up again and repeat the study; you will be surprised to see how many points you missed on the first trial. Repeat this again and again until you feel you have exhausted your object. The next day take up another object and repeat the study.

2. Visualizing: The second point of development is the faculty of Visualization. In order to Visualize you must cultivate the faculty of forming Mental Pictures of distant scenes, places, and people. Do this until you can summon them before you at will whenever you place yourself in the proper mental condition. Another plan is to place yourself in the proper mental position, then make a mental journey

to some place you have visited. Mentally, see yourself starting on your trip, see all the intermediate places and points, arrive at your destination and visit the points of interest, and return home. Later, try to visit places you have never seen, in the same way. This is not clairvoyance, but is training of the mental faculties for Concentration and Visualization.

After you have developed along the lines of Concentration and Visualization, you may begin to practice your psychic powers. Take a lock of hair, a handkerchief, a ribbon, or a ring belonging to someone else. Press it against your forehead lightly, closing your eyes, and assume a receptive and passive mental state. Desire calmly that you will visualize the past history of the object. Do not be in too much of a hurry; await calmly the impressions.

You will begin to receive impressions concerning the person owning the object and will form a mental picture of the person. Soon you will begin to receive impressions about him. You should practice with a number of objects, at different times, and gradually you will develop your Psychic Powers. Remember, you are developing what is practically a new sense, and you must have perseverance and patience in unfolding it.

3. Another form of Psychic development is of tracing the past history and surroundings of metals and minerals. The process is identical to that just described. The mineral is pressed against the forehead, and with closed eyes the person awaits the impressions. Some who have highly developed faculties were able to describe the veins of mineral ore and give much valuable information regarding them. There are other cases on record in which underground streams of water were discovered by the clue given by a bit of earth or stone from the surface.

In this, as mentioned, practice, practice, practice is the general instruction regarding psychic development.

4. Crystal Gazing: We consider the use of the Crystal Ball or other forms of the ancient "Magic Mirror" to be the best plan of developing Psychic Powers. This method serves to focus the concentrated desire, will, and thought of the person. Thereby it becomes the starting point for the Astral Tube. The student passes by easy, gradual, and natural

stages to the higher and more complex phases. The "Magic Mirror" was used by the ancient Occultist in developing the powers of their students.

In all countries and in all ages, it has played a great part in the process of developing Psychic Powers by serving as a focal point for the erection and operation of the Astral Tube.

There is no special virtue or magical properties or qualities in the Crystal itself. It is merely an instrument for Astral Vision, just as the telescope, microscope, and other optical instruments are instruments employed in physical vision. It is the materialistic atomic and molecular characteristics of glass or crystal which allow its use. But there is no special "Magic" in the crystal itself, so do not fall into any of the superstitions regarding its use.

All the old talk about magic ceremonies and incantations necessary in manufacturing the "Magic Mirror" is pure nonsense. The simple direction is for the gazer to practice by himself. At first, practice in a quiet room sitting with the back toward the light. The Crystal is placed on a piece of black cloth, and then you calmly gaze at the Crystal. Do not be afraid of winking, and do not strain or tire the eyes. If you fail to see anything at first, do not be discouraged. Persevere. A number of trials are necessary at first.

The first signs of the actual "seeing" come in the form of a cloudiness, or milky-mist in the Crystal. This slowly resolves itself into a form or scene. It appears gradually like a photograph upon a sensitive plate in the developing room. In some cases, the misty cloud deepens into a black one before the picture appears.

There is no royal road or magic word which once pronounced will prove an "open sesame" to the Doors of Psychomancy. There is no "Secret" to be imparted. It is a matter of general understanding, practice, and work. To some it comes easier than to others, but the higher degrees mean work and practice.

The simple use of the Psychic Powers is much more common than is generally supposed. Many people are quite sensitive to "impressions" coming to them, which, while akin to the impressions of Telepathy, nevertheless belong to the higher degree of Psychic Phenomena known as Psychomancy. The differences between ordinary telepathic impressions and those of Simple Psychomancy perplexes many students. The similarity between the two phenomena causes this confusion.

Telepathy is the passage of Thought waves or Currents from one brain to another, just as the waves of heat, light, and electricity pass through the ether. In telepathy, the brain of the Transmitter sends out the vibrations, waves, or currents, and the brain of the Receiver registers these, receiving them by means of the Pineal Gland. It acts in a manner similar to a TV set. Telepathy is merely the sending and receiving of thought vibrations via the physical organs inside the brain.

By the use of true Psychic Powers, the person may, and does, receive the thought vibrations emanating from the mind of another. But not via physical channels, as in Telepathy, but by means of the Astral Senses. This is the difference! Now, it follows since the Astral Senses are far more keen and acute than the Physical senses that they will register vibrations and impressions more readily and will often register impressions the Physical Senses (even the Pineal Gland) overlook. The person in whom the Astral Senses are even partially developed will receive impressions of thoughts of others that even the most acute Mind Reader will fail to notice. Words actually spoken by the other person and ideas forming in the mind of the other person not yet expressed in active thought-waves are all received equally well.

But the development of one's telepathic powers frequently grows into a development of their Psychic Powers. So telepathy is one of the easiest paths to Psychic Power and may be used in developing true clairvoyant power, along with unfolding the Astral Senses. The person possessing even a moderate degree of Psychic Power often "feels" the thoughts, ideas, emotions, and other mental states of the people around him and knows without words being used just what the others are thinking and feeling. This is perceived by

the increased power to receive and register Thought
Vibrations. In some cases the ability to sense the "Aura" of
the other person heightens the impressions.

All persons and objects are surrounded by an emanation
called an "Aura" or the egg-shaped psychic emanation which
extends several feet around them. This Aura is charged with
the Thought Vibrations of the person, and it is really the
"atmosphere" we feel surrounding people. We feel attracted
or repelled as the case may be by this Aura. The trained and
developed Psychic is able to see the colors of the various
emotions and thoughts. But even when that degree of power
is lacking, one may feel the general character of the various
component parts of a person's Aura.

When you have developed your Psychic Powers, you will
be able to look at a person and will see him surrounded by
the luminous mist of the Astral Aura which is flashing with
all sorts of brilliant colors. These are constantly changing in
hue and brilliancy with every variation of that person's
thoughts and feelings. You will see this Aura flooded with
the beautiful rose color of pure affection, the rich blue of
devotion, the hard dull brown of selfishness, the deep scarlet
of anger, the lurid red of sensuality, the livid grey of fear, the
black clouds of hatred and malice, or any of the other
indications so easily read by a practiced eye. Thus, it will be
impossible for any person to conceal from you the real state
of their feelings on any subject.

Only a comparatively few students ever develop to the
degree where they are able to distinctly see these Auric
colors. But a great number of people are able to feel the
subtle vibrations which give rise to these Auric colors. Just as
there are authenticated cases of blind men and women being
able to distinguish by the sense of touch the various colors,
so are thousands of people able to feel the Auric shades,
which their partially developed clairvoyant vision fails to
perceive clearly.

It is interesting that science informs us that the sense of
feeling was the first developed of the physical senses; in fact,

all the other senses are extensions of this original sense of feeling. There is a close correspondence between this phenomena of the Physical Senses, and those of the Astral Senses.

But there are other, and perhaps more wonderful, features of Simple Psychomancy. It is a well-established scientific fact that nearly all objects are constantly emanating streams of electrons. The delicate instruments of physical science are able to detect and register some of the coarser vibrations of this pure energy. Yet the most delicate instruments have yet to register the finer vibrations. The Astral Senses of the developed Psychic register and record these finer vibrations, and in this way many so-called "miracles" of Occultism are explained.

It becomes clearly apparent to any student of the subject, early in one's investigations, that the Psychic is able to "see" things hidden by other objects or surrounded by the densest of matter. In other words, one is able to see through solid objects — to see through a brick wall, to use a familiar phrase. This may seem incredible to one on the first mention of the subject. But the skeptic's attention is directed to X-rays and similar energy forms of modern science. These crude waves readily pierce through solid objects and may be actually "seen" by the eye on a fluoroscope or recorded on a photographic plate. Now the impossible feat of seeing through a brick wall becomes a very simple, understandable matter. In an almost identical manner, the Psychic sees through any solid object since the most solid, dense material becomes transparent to Astral Sight.

The fine streams or waves of energy invisible to the naked eye, which are constantly being emanated by all objects, are registered and recorded by the Astral Sense of Sight. The Psychic, by means of the elementary power of Simple Psychomancy, is able to see what is going on in an adjoining room, to read the contents of a sealed letter, to describe the contents of a locked steel safe, or to read a chosen passage in a closed book.

The Astral Plane is composed of an ethereal form of matter very much rarer and finer than the matter of the Physical Plane. But it is matter, nevertheless, and is subject to fixed laws and conditions. Just as it is possible to establish "lines of force" in the physical ether, so corresponding lines of force may be established in Astral Matter. And the Astral Tube is really such a LINE OF FORCE. It is possible to set up and establish a line of force on the Astral Plane which will serve as a conductor of Astral vibrations. This affords a highly efficient channel of communication between objects far removed from each other in material space. This channel is actually created and used in a variety of Occult phenomena.

When the human Will is directed toward a distant person or object, under psychic conditions, it tends to "polarize" a path, or channel through the Astral atmosphere (Astral Tube). This channel becomes at once an easy path of Psychic communication for the transmission or receiving of Psychic impressions or expressions. In the case of Psychomancy and kindred phenomena, the Astral Senses of the person are able to readily "sense" the impressions being manifested at a distant point in material space.

Through this polarized Astral Tube, the Astral Senses actually sense objects. The sights and sounds being manifested at a distance are sensed, just as one may see distant sights through a telescope or hear distant sounds through a telephone. The Astral Tube may also be used as a microscope. Attention is directed toward the fact that in this form of phenomena the Psychic remains within the physical body. One does not travel in the Astral Plane at all. Consciousness remains within the physical body.

The Astral Tube unconsciously springs into existence spontaneously under the power of some strong emotion, desire, or will. It is also present in some cases of hypnotic phenomena when the hypnotist uses his will to cause the subject to form an Astral Tube and report the impressions. It is used by the trained Psychic, without any starting point, or "focal center," by the exercise of well-trained, developed, and concentrated willpower. The "starting point" is generally either what is known as the Associated object or else a glass or Crystal Ball, or a similar polished reflecting surface.

The phenomena commonly known as Psychometry is only one phase of Psychomancy. It may be said to be only a method employed to bring into action the Astral Senses. The Psychic gets the rapport with the distant scene, period of time, person, or object by using some bit of physical material associated with them. This is in order to "open up communications" along the lines of Psychomancy. This is compared to the use of associated objects in the case of memory. We all know how the sight of some object will recall at once memories of things long since forgotten. These are readily recalled when the association is furnished. What association is in the case of memory, so is the material object presented as the "Associated Object" in Psychometry.

The Occult teachings inform us there is a Psychic connection existing between all things once associated. When we throw ourselves into the Psychic current surrounding an object we may follow the current back until we reach the associated object which we are seeking on the Astral Plane. All memories are registered and permanently recorded, and if we have a good starting point we may travel back until we find that which we desire. In the same way, the associated object furnishes us with a means of starting our Astral Tube. This is the secret of the use of the lock of hair, the bit of clothing, the piece of metal, or mineral.

It may be asked how it is possible, amid the bewildering confusion of the records of the past, to find any particular picture when it is wanted. As a matter of fact, the untrained Psychic usually cannot do so without some special link to put one in rapport. It seems as though there is a sort of magnetic attachment or affinity between any particle of matter and the Astral record which contains its history. This enables it to act as a kind of conductor between the record and the faculties of the Psychic.

In many respects, the Crystal acts in a manner akin to the associated object, but there is one point which should not be overlooked. The associated object gives to the Psychometrist a starting point for the Astral Tube and serves to point the Astral Telescope in the right direction. But the Crystal does not, for it is not closely allied to or in sympathy with any other things when used in the usual manner. Instead of being the eyepiece of the Astral Telescope, it is really a Magic Mirror which is turned first this way and then that. It reflects whatever comes within its field just as does any other mirror. The trained and developed Crystal Gazer, however, may direct his Mirror to any desired point and may hold it there by means of a concentrated Psychic Will.

The favor which Crystal Gazing meets with at the hands of beginners is due to the fact it is the easiest method known by which the Astral Vision may be trained. With the majority of people, the power may be awakened and trained only by the aid of some physical object which acts as a starting-point for the Astral Tube. Any number of objects may be so used, but the Crystal is the best because of certain atomic and molecular arrangements which tend to promote the Psychic Powers and faculties.

Crystal Gazing, as a method for inducing Psychic vision, is quite common among all peoples and in all times. There are some people who cannot look into an ordinary bottle without seeing pictures form and this without any effort or will on their part. Crystal Gazing seems to be the least dangerous and most simple of all forms of experimenting. You simply look into the Crystal and look at it. You make no incantations and engage in no mumbo jumbo. You simply look at it for two or three minutes, taking care not to tire yourself, winking as much as you please, but fixing your thoughts upon whatever you wish to see. THEN IF YOU HAVE THE FACULTY, the glass will cloud over with a milky mist, and in the center the image is gradually precipitated in the same way as a photograph forms on the sensitive silver plate.

There is another phase of Psychic phenomena where the consciousness of the person does not remain within the physical organism but is actually projected along with the Astral Body to the point being examined. Here physical consciousness is temporarily suspended, and the Astral Body is projected to some far distant point with the rapidity of thought. There it examines objects and receives their sensations through the Astral Senses. This phenomena may occur while the person is in a trance, asleep, in a moment of concentrated abstraction, or when one is daydreaming. When one returns to the physical body, he "comes to himself," and what was seen or heard seems to be a daydream or fantasy. If one is a trained Seer, the two planes of consciousness will be closely related and almost continuous.

The trained Psychic has the advantage of being able to search about on the Astral Plane for what is desired. One is able to direct his Astral Body to definite places by means similar to finding one's way on the material physical plane or by following up the Psychic clue afforded by an associated object. Of course, the person whose powers are not highly developed is not able to have true control over his Astral Body. He is like a child learning to walk; he is awkward and must learn to direct his movements. There are many degrees of power, from the occasional, spontaneous travel on the Astral Plane to travel even more easy than that on the physical plane, and with the same degree of control.

LOOKING INTO THE PAST

The questions which naturally arise in one's mind in connection with this phase of the Psychic phenomena are: "How is the person able to sense past events and objects of the past? There are no vibrations emanating from past scenes, and as they no longer exist, how can anyone see them by Astral Vision or by any other means?" The Secret of Past Time Psychomancy is found in the Occult Teachings of the "Akashic Records." On the higher planes of Universal

Substance, there are found records of all that has happened and occurred during the entire World Cycle of which the present time forms only a part. These records are preserved until the termination of the World Cycle, then they pass away with the world of which they are a record.

This does not mean there is a Great Book in which the doings, good and bad, of people are written down by the Recording Angel. But it does mean there is a scientific, Occult basis for such popular legend. We may turn to modern science for the proof. It is taught by scientists that there is no such thing as destruction of energy, because energy always exists in some form. The Occult teachings verify this and go even further. They state every action, thought, happening, event, and occurrence, no matter how small or insignificant, leaves an indelible record on the Universal Ether. In other words, every action or scene which has ever occurred or existed in the past left an impression on the Universal Ether. There it may be read by one's developed Psychic Powers.

There is nothing especially wonderful about this when you compare it with the other facts of nature. Astronomy teaches us that light travels at the rate of 186,000 miles a second and that there are fixed stars in space so far removed from the Earth that the light leaving them hundreds, yes thousands, of years ago is only now visible. When we look at some of the fixed stars, we do not see them as they now are, or where they now are, but rather as they were and where they were hundreds of years ago. Astronomers tell us that if one of these stars happened to be destroyed hundreds of years ago, we would still be seeing the light which left them before the event occurred. We would be seeing these stars hundreds of years after they had ceased to exist.

The vibrations of light they set into motion would persist for centuries, even after their source disappeared. This is not Occult knowledge but a well-proven and thoroughly established materialistic scientific fact, as anyone may see by reference to a work on astronomy. The same is true of waves of electricity, electronic emanations, or waves of any kind of energy. Even in the physical view of things, nothing can exist without leaving a record on the Universal Ether. So the Occult teachings find their corroboration in modern science.

Another illustration is found in the phenomena of the Memory of Man. Stored away in our brain cells are the records of all past things, events, scenes, occurrences, people, and objects. You often find yourself thinking about people, things, and events of years long since passed. By a mere effort of the will you may bring the records of these people, things, or events before your mental vision and see them reproduced in detail. Dissect a brain cell and you will find no trace of memory. Nevertheless, every exercise of memory proves the record is there.

There is nothing wonderful or miraculous in the Psychic record of past events. The Universal Ether has within itself a true and full record of anything and everything which has ever existed within its space. If one develops the power to read these records, one can have a full and complete key to all of the past.

In order to avoid a misapprehension, it must be emphasized that none but the most advanced and highly developed Occultists and Masters have clear access to the planes upon which these records are found. The majority of Psychics merely see the Lower Astral Plane. This vision can be compared to the reflections of trees and landscapes in a pond of still water — reflections which are often distorted and disturbed by the ripples and waves created by a passing breeze. The records of the past open to the average Psychic are merely reflections of records and are apt to be distorted or cloudy. This is a brief and simple statement of an important Occult scientific truth, which would require many pages to explain technically. In actual practice we find the phenomena of Past Time Psychomancy manifested principally in crystal gazing. There are also many instances of a partial manifestation of this power among individuals in everyday life. Such individuals, when meeting a person, frequently get some impressions of his or her past life.

LOOKING INTO THE FUTURE

It will be sufficient to understand that in the Astral as well as on the physical plane, "Coming Events cast their shadows Before." Without entering into a metaphysical discussion of Destiny or Fate, it may be stated: "When Causes are set into motion, the Effects follow unless other Causes intervene." In some cases effects have been averted by reason of a previous Vision, then another cause intervened. This shows that the event was not wholly cut-and-dried. It is like a man walking toward a precipice which he will walk off unless warned in some way.

The phenomena of Premonitions, Previsions, and Second Sight are all forms or phases of Future Time Psychomancy. In these various forms, the phenomenon is quite common. Many times Psychic visions manifest themselves during sleep. The reason for this is that in the majority of people the physical holds the attention of the individual and prevents him from manifesting the Psychic faculties. When the physical body sinks into sleep, however, the field is clear for the exercise of the Astral Senses. In fact, a majority of persons do manifest Psychomancy during sleep, but have little or no recollection of it when awake. Only indistinct recollections of dreams may persist. Still, many of you who read these lines will have a memory of certain dreams in which you seemed to visit other places, scenes, lands, or countries. Upon awakening, you were somewhat annoyed at having been brought back from your pleasant travels to other lands.

Psychomancy frequently manifests itself in your dreams; yet precisely the same principle is at work in both waking and dream Psychic phenomena. The apparent difference is that the dreamer seldom carries back with him a clear and connected memory of the visions. The awake Psychic person is able to impress his Astral Vision upon a wide-awake physcial brain, and there it is remembered and recorded.

3

The Stars and Science

To understand the wonderful order which rules the world and the ever-changing position of man in relation to it, we have to discover the means by which the heavenly influences may be measured. We must examine the world clock to find the laws which govern its wheels. From the dial plate, we must be able to know when the clock is going to strike and what it means.

Mathematical knowledge of heavenly movement is as old as civilization. The Chaldeans, Egyptians, Assyrians, Greeks, and Persians were masters of Astrology — cunning mathematicians who without telescopes or delicate instruments discovered important astronomical facts. Remember, spyglasses were first made at the beginning of the seventeenth century and the first telescope was not in use until 1663. Throughout the Renaissance the stargazers used in their observations a stick or ruler whose function it was to guide the eye. Copernicus and Tycho Brahe worked with such simple aids.

Astrologers are scholars, not charlatans, and Astrological wisdom requires a knowledge of languages for the study of original texts, as well as considerable mathematical skill.

The stars either are favorable or unfavorable to man's health and activities and to those of the state. Nothing depends upon chance; everything is regulated and guided in a world built on order. When a man is born, the aspect of the heavens impresses its seal upon his future. This is not its only influence; after this original impetus, the stars continue to exert power. Rulers once retained astrologers at court for their own benefit, as well as for that of the state. No war was declared, no building begun, no financial transaction made until the stars were consulted. The Astrologer made a horoscope, a scheme which showed the stars exerting their influence at the hour for which the action was planned. Such horoscopes were elaborated according to basic principles and methods.

The planets and the signs of the Zodiac are always present in the heavens, but not all are visible. It is necessary for Astrologers to establish rules by which the quality of the visible heavenly bodies may be judged in order to know their influence, their strength, and weakness — their exaltation and rejection. Certain planets or stars are powerful; the influence of others is negligible. The basis of the method is, therefore, to define these areas and thus establish a system for the starry globe.

The planets are considered the most important of heavenly bodies, since they exhibit power by their individual course, according to their own laws, and move in a direction contrary to the fixed stars. The circuits of the Planets cover varying spans. The orb described by the Moon is smaller in diameter than that of Saturn. In one month, the Moon achieves its journey around the Earth, whereas Saturn requires thirty years.

In starting this elucidation of the heavenly bodies, it is necessary to inform the reader that the system to be elaborated is purely empirical and constitutes a special branch of the primeval "wisdom religion" which made the ancient Occult schools of Egypt and Chaldea so justly famous.

It is necessary to explain several matters of great importance in forming a true conception of Astral Law. The reader must not suppose the Planets are the primary cause of all fortunes and misfortunes which fall to the lot of mankind. This is by no means the case, for the primary cause has its origin within the Soul. The sexual relationship between man and woman has its laws, its harmonies, and discords. It is man's duty to investigate and know these laws. When we bear in mind that there is neither morality nor sentiment in the cold inflexible justice of nature, we learn that "Unto every violation of the law there is meted out a penalty."

If the attributes of a thief are conceived, a thief will be born into the world. It matters not what his circumstances or position in life may be; the individual so conceived will be a thief in his heart. There is no real difference, except in magnitude, between the man who legally by some commercial sharp practice steals a railroad and the one who lives above his income to the detriment of his creditors. Even the poor devil who, under the influence of criminal temptations, robs a bank or steals your watch is just a thief. All three, when viewed in their true light, are natural-born thieves, and each is equally deserving of the same term of penance.

The false glamour and artificial conventionalities of modern society, however, praise and bow down in adoration to the gifted thief of a railroad. They pity and condone as unfortunate the man who terminates his career in bankruptcy. But they, with neither pity nor mercy, hurry off to jail the poor wretch who steals a watch or robs a bank of a few paltry dollars. As a rule, it is this poor devil who is most deserving of our sympathy.

Ignorance and a neglected childhood have often intensified the evil influences of such a man's conception and birth to an inconceivable extent. If the world would only let him, he might become a better and wiser man. It is equally in accordance with the same immutable laws that every species of crime is born into the world. When inflamed passions and cruel thoughts are latent within us and remain uncontrolled by the higher Self during the conjugal union, a child with a similar nature is always conceived. There is no benevolent God to graciously interfere and prevent a criminal from being launched upon society.

Man has the privilege and possesses the possibilities of choosing the good and preventing the conception of evil. Therefore, if either by choice or ignorance man risks all the natural consequences, Mother Nature will write *murderer* across the brow of the unborn infant.

When the embryonic potentialities of a human Soul are launched forth into the matrix, they remain there. Slowly they evolve their organic powers and are imprisoned within the womb until their magnetic period of gestation is complete. It is not possible for a child to be born and live until the Astral influx corresponds exactly to the external polarity of its Soul. Only when the heavens are harmonious can that which we term good become manifest upon the Earth. If the heavens are evil, the opposite becomes eternalized.

We are, to a very great extent, what the ignorance or wisdom of our ancestors have made us. As the world progresses, mankind obtains more knowledge. The rising generations become wiser than their parents. This mental evolution moves forward until the intellectuality of the race becomes exhausted. After a rest, mankind declines from the summit of its genius to relapse into ignorant barbarism; after having regained a supply of latent mental force, the race once more advances.

Intellectual forces correspond in their apparent motion, to the motions of the planets, becoming alternately direct, swift, stationary, or retrograde. Men, like plants, have their times of germination, growth, maturity, and decay. The races of man are no exception to this universal law of change. They move in greater cycles and their climax of civilization corresponds to the flowering season of the vegetable kingdom, then they run to seed and decay. But the racial

Soul is treasured like the precious seeds from the flowers, which while lying dormant, await the necessary magnetic and spiritual conditions for its next glorious unfoldment.

Such are the sublime facts of nature's immutable laws which have made the science of the Stars true for all time and in all ages. When Uranus and Neptune were shining in their distant heavens undiscovered, mankind was, as a body, impervious to their action. Their organism did not vibrate with a higher state of action. Thus, we see that as man evolves his higher powers, more ethereal orbs appear in the celestial hierarchies of the heavens for the purpose of controlling and directing him.

The old and now much abused Chaldean sages were thoroughly acquainted with the facts. In order to teach these principles to their youth, they elaborated beautiful imagery in the form of fables and allegories. They gave the nature and power of each group of organs to the character of that planet which they knew controlled its activities. Then they worked out the facts into a series of mythical histories of gods and divine personages, who incarnated themselves for the benefit of man.

Thus, Mars took the character of Vulcan, the God of War; Venus and her innocent companion, Cupid, were assigned the character of Love and the sympathetic tendencies of the human heart; while the benevolent Jupiter assumed the position of Father, the kindly, generous parent, good to all his offspring; and so on.

From this you will perceive that when they taught their children that their gods had existed in human bodies, they did not mean to convey the idea of Divine incarnation, but that a portion of the divinity had centered in man and expressed itself in a special form. Thus, a great warrior who brought honor and riches to his tribe or country through his brilliant military victories was properly considered a son of Mars. His nature expressed the Martial Spirit in what was considered its highest and most potent form. If the planet is dignified and aspected by benefic rays, then all that is noble, honorable, and manly will be the result.

You should perceive that sympathy and antipathy are the two great laws by which the Planets affect the human organism. These two forces, or rather let us say the dual action of this one force, constitute the two modes of motion by which every cosmic principle expresses itself. The two actions, the action and the reaction, are true polar opposites. Upon the physical plane their effects are correlated as harmony and discord.

The powers of harmony and discord possess forms which are peculiar to themselves. These forms in Astrological science are angular and are denominated aspects. The more perfect or complete the angle is, the greater the power its influence exerts upon matter. The symbol of discord is called a square, and every inharmonious, angular ray constitutes a portion of the square or the angle of 90 degrees. The symbol of harmony is a triangle and every benefic angular ray constitutes a portion of the trine or an angle of 120 degrees. Thus, we have the geometric expression of good and evil.

The discordant rays of magnetic force strike each other crossways from opposing angles. This conflict produces a violent commotion. There is a fight, as it were, in the current between two powers, while the contrary result is produced in the action of the benefic rays of magnetic force. They impinge upon each other like the two forks of a river, and then with their united forces flow onward in harmony.

We see that when the combinations of stellar force flow in straight lines and cut through each other from cross angles, the result upon the physical plane is discord and evil. But when the rays of force flow in straight but convergent angles from or towards each other, then harmony, love, and prosperity reign.

The next subject which requires our thoughtful attention is the four Triplicities. These trigons correspond to the four ancient elements, Fire (Fiery), Earth (Earthy), Air (Airy), and Water (Watery). Each triplicity of "Trigon" contains three Zodiacal signs. The Fiery trigon embraces the signs of Aries, Leo, and Saggitarius. The Earthy trigon embraces the signs of Taurus, Virgo, and Capricorn. The Airy trigon embraces the signs Gemini, Libra, and Aquarius. The Watery trigon embraces the signs of Cancer, Scorpio, and Pisces.

In practical Astrology, these triplicities are of great importance. They shed their potent influence upon the sign at the birth of every living thing and impress their particular nature upon the temperament of the native.

Magnetic and electric forces vary in their spirituality like everything else in the universe. That which is superior, by virtue of its higher or more interior emanation, will demonstrate its superiority upon every plane. For example, Aries is the first and highest representative of the fiery trigon, and those born with this sign rising upon the ascendant of their horoscope will always move higher, mentally and spiritually, than those born under Leo or Sagittarius. But externally, people born under Aries will show their superiority from a purely intellectual point of view. Their nature will be chiefly fiery and mental, consequently, they are quick in action and prompt in decision.

Leo is the second representative of the Fiery trigon, and persons born in this sign will always move upon the sensitive and emotional planes. Their nature will be chiefly fiery and sensitive, consequently, they are hasty and impulsive. They will act without thinking, upon the spur of the moment, under the dominating influence of their susceptible emotional natures. In this we see the difference between Aries, which rules the head, and Leo, which represents the heart. Leo persons, when aroused to a pitch of passional fury, are violent in their wild and erratic actions. An Aries person, though susceptible to an equal degree of furious temper, never becomes blind with emotion. Even in their most outrageous conduct an impartial observer will see that "there is method in Aries madness."

Sagittarius is the third of the Fiery trigon, or the most external emanation of the fiery triplicity. It illustrates the law of contradiction to perfection. Those born under this sign actually live and move, when mentally and spiritually considered, upon the third plane of the fiery emanation. Externally and in the eyes of the world they seem to move in the very highest plane. Their natures are warm, sympathetic, and active; consequently, they are generous and benevolent, ambitious and truly jovial. They do as the world does, for they progress not of their own internal volition, but by the gentle attraction of the social tide of their surroundings.

In everything they are external. They are great admirers of all outdoor sports, recreations, and pastimes, and as such they are totally incapable of grasping any form of the higher mental and metaphysical studies. They are considered by the masses and the world as sound logical reasoners and possessed of good common sense. Externally they do possess all these desirable qualities.

In Aries we have the Fiery imperial brain, which molds, guides, and acts for itself, independent of the opinions of others. Such persons, when unmodified by other influences, are either despots, cranks, or fanatics, according to their peculiar bent and station in life. In Leo we see the emotions and sensitive feelings of the heart. These souls follow impulsively the lead of some mental genius and form the enthusiastic followers and admirers of those who depart from the beaten path of custom. But they require the thinking brain to direct them. They cannot strike out upon a new path for themselves.

In Sagittarius we see the genial, sympathetic, courteous neutrality which represents the external true gentleman. They are simply waiting to be led in any direction that the strongest mental force desires to carry them. They love the world and its varied delights and are consequently contented and willing to let others do all the thinking for them.

These remarks are to be considered in a general sense only, and in speaking of any given sign it is, of course, presupposed that the position and aspect of the Sun, Moon, and planets do not contradict the general tendencies of the sign upon the ascendant. What we have thus far stated in reference to the Fiery trigon will also apply to the other triplicities. It is unnecessary to go over the same ground with each trigon, as the above will suffice to explain the varying powers of each Sign.

We have only to bear in mind when forming our opinion that our premises and our conclusion must occupy the same plane. Thus, the Fiery trigon manifests itself in the combative, aggressive, imperious, commanding, and courageous planes of action. The Earthy trigon manifests itself in the patient, laborious, plodding, obedient, and inert planes of action. The Airy trigon manifests itself in the aspiring, philosophical, musical, artistical, and volatile planes of action. The Watery trigon manifests itself in the dreamy, romantic, changeable, timid, and submissive planes of action.

The person born will possess deep down and latent the qualities of the specific trigon and under proper conditions and circumstances it will rise dominantly to the surface and manifest the true internal characteristics of the person's nature. The purely esoteric aspect of the four triplicities have their Hermetic and Occult meanings. The four ancient elements have been symbolized from time immemorial as the Man, the Bull, the Eagle, and the Lion. Astrologically these are *Aquarius,* "the water bearer," symbolical of the Man; *Taurus,* the sign of the Bull; *Leo,* represented by the Lion; and lastly, *Scorpio,* ancient symbol of the Eagle.

In this change of symbols "hereby hangs a tale." In the esoteric planisphere of the twelve signs, Adam Kadmon, the primordial man, pure and in perfect accord with the Father, occupied a point of the planisphere now designated by the sign Libra. This signifies the point of equilibrium in the Zodiac. This esoteric point is where day and night, winter and summer, light and darkness, good and evil, are all one. Adam Kadmon represents the ideal Man, and the very fact that we can form an ideal conception is the absolute proof we possess the possibilities of attaining unto the ideas and realizing our conception.

The modern English name for this point of the Zodiac, "The Balance," which means Justice, is a fitting one. Justice discriminates upon the external plane between good and evil and metes out rewards and punishments. Life, Light, and Truth are the same and consist of spiritual reflection. They are Spiritual rays, and when these rays become refracted by passing through the prism of matter, Truth becomes illusion, Life becomes limited by assuming the appearance of death. The Spiritually beautiful and eternally True have no existence in the world where all is change, strife, discord, and death. Therefore, the divine Spiritual ray of Good, when it becomes refracted, presents all the forms and colors of evil.

This celestial point in Libra is represented by Enoch in the mysteries of the Jewish Temple, the Man who walked with God "and was not." This theological idea was plagiarized by the early fathers of the Christian Church when they elaborated their Christian mysteries. They make Libra symbolic of their Day of Judgment, when celestial "Justice" will be meted out to all. This is the point of the planisphere occupied by their divine Man. The Kabbalistical Adam Kadmon, the Enoch of Judaism, becomes the Emmanuel of the new. Jesus is the sacrifice required by the Divine Justice of God's anger for the awful errors of a sinful world. Judas, who as a disciple of the Son of God was able to' soar heavenward upon the wings of an Eagle (the inward inspirations), falls into temptation and betrays his Master into the hands of his murderers. Thence comes the fall, the Divine Eagle of the Celestial Heavens becomes the lowly reptile, the Scorpion whose sting is concealed in the tail.

By Nature the Zodiac is divided into equal arcs of Light and Darkness, Winter and Summer, which in the technical terms of the science are termed the northern and the southern Signs. When the Earth in her annual orbit round the Sun enters the sign of Libra, the Sun appears to enter the first degree of Aries. This occurs about the 21st of March and is called the Vernal Equinox. Our Sun apparently moves forward through the signs until about the 21st of June when the first point of the tropical sign Cancer is reached and the greatest noonday altitude is attained in the northern hemisphere. On or about the 21st of September, the Sun appears to enter the first degree of Libra, which completes the Solar passage through the six northern signs, and the arc of light is over. Libra, Scorpio, Sagittarius, Capricorn, Aquarius, and Pisces constitute the southern arc and are termed the arc of darkness.

From the time of the Winter Solstice (about the 21st of December) the sluggish life forces of matter begin to expand. All things increase in vitality until the Sun enters the sign of Cancer. This is the highest point of intensity in the northern hemispheres of the Cosmic Life Forces. For a time these forces remain stationary, then reaction slowly sets in; the trees begin to change their tints, fruits begin to ripen, and the days grow shorter as the Life wave recedes.

The actual duration of life of people shows a startling contrast between those born from December to June, and those born between July and the end of November. The longest livers were born in March, April, and May, and a majority of the short-lived population would be found to be born during the months of August, September, and October. This is true on general principles and does not apply to any one individual horoscope. The increase of the Solar light simply governs the vitalizing capacity of the race, and not the individual.

Everything in Nature, though constituting a trinity in itself, possesses a fourfold application when viewed from the external plane. At least we find this fourfoldness a truth so far as "the things of Earth" are concerned. Therefore, by laws of correspondences, the same application must hold good in regard to the Celestial objects in the Heavens. The Hermetic rule is very precise upon this: "As on the earth, so in the sky."

Therefore, we will describe the fourfold aspect of the Stars. It is well known to people of Occult literature that behind the external personalities of the twelve sons of Jacob were concealed the various powers of the twelve constellations of the Zodiac. Until quite recently, their correct tabulation has been carefully concealed. In fact, the Kabbalistical and esoteric aspect of this science was never committed to writing, except under the dense veil of extremely vague allegorical symbols. This knowledge formed a portion of "the greater Ancient Mysteries," and as such was necessarily confined to the favored few.

Time, however, which regulates all things harmoniously, arranges the supply of Spiritual truth in exact proportion to the real demand. Since a real, earnest demand has arisen for light upon the Spiritual side of Nature, we begin to see the bright rays of Truth. The recipients of Occult knowledge are now distributing their hoarded treasures, with delighted hands, to the daily increasing number of seekers after Occult truth.

ARIES: THE RAM

The Sign of Aries, in its symbolical aspect, represents the sacrifice. The flocks and herds bring forth their young during the portion of the year the Sun occupies this sign. In addition to the sacrifice, the Ram also symbolizes the Spring and the commencement of a New Year when life, light, and love are to be bestowed upon the sons of the Earth. The Sun has once more gained victory over the realms of winter and death.

Aries represents the head and brains of the Grand Man of the Cosmos. It is the acting, thinking principle in Nature called instinct and intelligence. Upon the esoteric planisphere, this Sign is occupied by Benjamin, of whom Jacob, in his blessing to the twelve sons said, "Benjamin shall rave as a wolf, in the morning he shall devour the prey, and at night divide the spoils."

Above all other animals the wolf is sacred to the planet Mars, and the sign Aries is under the special and peculiar control of this Fiery planet. Mars is the most Fiery of all the planets, and Aries is the first constellation of the Fiery triplicity. The gem of this sign is the Diamond, and those born with Aries rising upon the ascendant of their Horoscope possess in this stone a powerful magnetic talisman.

TAURUS: THE BULL

The Sign of Taurus, in its symbolical aspect, represents the powers of fecundity and the procreative forces in Nature. Its genius was symbolized as Aphrodite, who was represented as wearing the two horns upon her head in imitation of a Bull. Many mythologists were deceived by this symbol and took it to represent a figure of the crescent Moon upon the head of Isis. It was the planet Venus which the Ancients intended to so symbolize because she rules the constellation of the Bull by her sympathetic forces. Apis, the sacred Bull of the Egyptians, is another conception of Taurus, since as the Sun passed through this sign during their plowing month, we also find this sign used as the symbol of Egyptian husbandry.

The Sign of Taurus represents the ears, neck, and throat of the Grand Man, hence this Sign is the silent, patient, attentive principle of humanity. The gem of this Sign is the Sapphire and this gem constitutes their natural talisman. Taurus is the highest emanation of the Earthy Trigon and is the constellation of the planet Venus.

GEMINI: THE TWINS

The Sign of Gemini, in its symbolical aspect, represents unity and the strength of united action. The two bright stars, Castor and Pollux, represent the twin Souls. The Greek myth of Castor and Pollux avenging the rape of Helen is only a repetition of the biblical story of Simeon and Levi slaughtering the men of Schechem for the rape of their sister Dinah.

The Sign Gemini represents the hands and arms of the Grand Man and expresses the projecting and executive forces of humanity in all mechanical departments. Upon the esoteric planisphere, the sign is occupied by Simeon and Levi. "They are brethren and instruments of cruelty are in their habitation."

Fearfully potent powers of production lie concealed

within the magnetic constitution of all those who are dominated by this Sign. The mystical symbol of the Twins conceals the doctrine of Soul-Mates and other important Truths. The mystical gem is the Emerald and, consequently, forms the talisman stone. Gemini is the first and highest emanation of the Airy Trigon and is the constellation of the planet Mercury.

CANCER: THE CRAB

The Sign of Cancer symbolizes tenacity for Life. The crab, in order to move forward, is compelled to walk backwards, which illustrates the Sun's apparent motion when in this Sign. It also represents the fruitful, sustaining essence of the life forces. We see the symbol of the Crab occupying a prominent position upon the breast of the statue of Isis, the Universal Mother and sustainer of all.

The Sign of Cancer signifies the vital organs of the Grand Man and represents the breathing and digestive functions of the human family. It also indicates the magnetic control of this constellation over the Spiritual, ethereal, and vital essences. Cancer governs the powers of Inspiration and Respiration. The Sign of Cancer upon the esoteric planisphere is occupied by Zebulon, of whom his patriarchal father declares, "Zebulon shall dwell at the haven of the sea, and he shall be haven for ships."

Astrologically it intimates the home of the crab, which is upon the seashore. It also expresses the varied powers of cohesion and the paradoxical truths found in all contradictories. The mystical gem of the sign is the Agate. The stone constitutes a powerful talisman for all natives of Cancer, which is the highest emanation of the Watery Trigon and is the constellation of the Moon.

LEO: THE LION

The Sign Leo symbolizes strength, courage, and Fire. The hottest portion of the year, in the northern hemisphere, is when the Sun is passing through this Sign. It is the solar

Lion of the mysteries which ripen with their own internal heat, the fruits brought forth from the Earth by the moisture of Isis.

The Sign Leo signifies the heart of the Grand Man and represents the life center of the fluidic circulatory system of humanity. It is also the Fire vortex of physical life. Those born under this influx are noted for the superior strength of their physical constitution and for their wonderful recuperative powers after being exhausted by sickness. The Sign of Leo upon the esoteric planisphere is occupied by Judah, of whom his dying parent says, "Judah is a lion's whelp. He stooped down, he crouched as a lion."

This Sign reveals to us the mysteries of the ancient sacrifice and the laws of compensation. The mystical gem of Leo is the Ruby, and it forms the talisman for all governed by the Leonine influx. Leo is the second emanation of the Fiery triplicity and is the constellation of the Sun.

VIRGO: THE VIRGIN

The Sign Virgo symbolizes chastity and forms the central idea of a great number of myths. When the Sun passes through this Sign the harvest is ready for the reaper, so Virgo is symbolized as the gleaning maid with two ears of wheat in her hand.

The Sign Virgo signifies the solar plexus of the Grand Man and represents the assimilating and distributing functions of the human organism. Consequently, we find those born under this influence possess fine discriminating powers. This constellation, governing the bowels of humanity, is highly important since the intestines comprise a vital section of the digestive organism and vital fluids.

Upon the esoteric planisphere, Virgo is occupied by Asher. "Out of Asher his bread shall be fat," says Jacob, "and he shall yield royal dainties."

This Sign expresses the fulfillment of the creative design and the mysteries of maternity are concealed under this symbol. The mystical gem of Virgo is the Sardonyx, a stone possessing great virtues. Virgo is the second emanation of the Earthy Trigon and is the constellation of Mercury.

LIBRA: THE BALANCE

This constellation in its symbolical aspect typifies Justice. Most of our readers have seen the goddess of Justice represented as a female, blindfolded, holding in her hand a pair of scales. This is a purely Astrological concept and dates back to Ancient times.

The Sign Libra signifies the reins and loins of the Grand Man and represents the central conservatory or storehouse of the reproductive fluids. It is the magnetic vortex of procreative strength. This constellation also represents, in its most interior aspect, the equinoctial point of the arc in the ascending and descending cycle of the Life atom. This Sign contains the unification of the Cosmic forces as the grand central point of equilibrium of the Sphere. Libra upon the esoteric planisphere is occupied by Dan, the patriarch. In his blessing he refers to his celestial Nature: "Dan shall judge his people as one of the tribes of Israel."

Libra represents the interior equilibrium of Nature's forces and contains the mystery of the Divine Equality of the Ancient initiations. Upon the universal chart, this sign becomes Enoch, the perfect Man. Its mystical gem is the wonderful Chrysolite. Libra is the second emanation of the Airy triplicity and is the constellation of Venus.

SCORPIO: THE SCORPION

The Sign of Scorpio symbolizes death and deceit. It is the allegorical serpent mentioned in Genesis as tempting Eve. Hence the so-called fall of man from Libra, the point of equilibrium, to degradation and death by the deceit of Scorpio. No wonder the primitive Mind, when elaborating this symbol, tried to express a spirit of retalation.

The Sign Scorpio typifies the generative organs of the Grand Man and, consequently, represents the sexual and procreative system of all humanity. It is the emblem of generation and Life, and the natives of Scorpio excell in fruitfulness of the seminal fluids which creates a corresponding increase in sexual desire. A reference to the fruitfulness of this Sign will be found in Genesis, Chap. XXX: 10-12, where Leah, when she beheld the birth of Zilpah's son, exclaimed, "A troop cometh."

Scorpio, upon the esoteric planisphere, is occupied by Gad, of whom the dying Jacob says, "Gad, a troop shall overcome him, but he shall overcome at the last."

It is symbolic of the fall of man from a state of innocence and purity through the multitude of sensual delights and his final victory over the realms of matter as a Spiritual entity. This sign represents the physical plane of the attributes of procreation. It contains the Mystery of Sex and the secrets of the Ancient phallic rites. The mystical gem of Scorpio is the Topaz, the talisman of those born under its influence. Scorpio is the second emanation of the Water Trigon and is the constellation of Mars.

SAGITTARIUS: THE ARCHER

This constellation, in its symbolical aspect, represents a dual nature, as it symbolizes retribution and all outdoor sports. We find it depicted as a Centaur with the bow and arrow drawn ready for shooting. Hence it was frequently used to designate the autumnal chase. The Centaur is a symbol of authority and worldly wisdom.

The Sign Sagittarius signifies the thighs of the Grand Man. It represents the muscular foundation of the seat of locomotion in humanity. It is the emblem of stability, foundation, and physical power. This Sign also represents the centers of physical, external, authority and command.

Sagittarius, upon the esoteric planisphere, is occupied by Joseph. "His bow abode in strength," says the patriarch, "and the arms of his hands were made strong."

It represents the powers of "Church and State" and the necessity of legalized codes. It indicates to us the organizing powers of humanity and the absolute necessity of "the powers that be." We see in Joseph, the Egyptian ruler and law-giver, a true type of authority. The mystical gem of this influx is the Turquoise, and Sagittarius is the third emanation of the Fiery Trigon and is the constellation of Jove or the planet Jupiter.

CAPRICORN: THE GOAT

This Sign, in its symbolical aspect, typifies sin. It is the scapegoat of the Israelites and the universal offering of a young goat as an atoning sacrifice for man's sin. The different qualities of the sheep and the goat, from a symbolical standpoint, are used by St. John in his mystical Apocalypse. The Redeemer of Mankind, or Sun God, is always born at midnight as soon as Sol enters this Sign, or the Winter Solstice. "The young child is born in the stable and laid in the manger of the goat, in order that he may conquer the remaining signs of winter or death, and thus save mankind from destruction."

The Sign Capricorn signifies the knees of the Grand Man and represents the first principle in the trinity of locomotion, or the joints. It is the emblem of material servitude and as such is worthy of notice. Capricorn, upon the esoteric planisphere, is occupied by Naphtali, of whom Jacob says, "If a hind let loose, he giveth goodly words."

Here we have two distinct references. The first is to the symbol of a hind or young deer or a goat with horns, the second, to the Christmas proclamation, he giveth goodly words, "Peace on earth, good will toward men."

This sign represents regeneration or rebirth and reveals the necessity of new dispensations. The mystical gem of this constellation is the Onyx. Capricorn is the third emanation of the Earthy Trigon and is the constellation of the planet Saturn.

AQUARIUS: THE WATER BEARER

This Sign symbolizes Judgment and forms the starry original of the Urn of Minos from which flow wrath and condemnation or blessings and reward. The earlier baptismal urns of the primitive Christians and the elaborate stone fonts of the modern churches are relics of this great Astral religion.

The Sign Aquarius signifies the legs of the Grand Man and represents the locomotive functions of the human organism. It is the natural emblem of the changeable, movable, and migratory forces of the body. The Water-Bearer, upon the esoteric planisphere, is occupied by Reuben, "The excellency of dignity and the excellency of power. Unstable as water thou shalt not excel."

A simple but magnificent Astrological description of this Sign, symbolized by two wavy lines, are the ripples of running water. This Sign signifies consecration, and not only contains the rites and mysteries of consecration, but reveals the potency of all sacred and dedicated works. The mystical gem is the Amethyst. Aquarius is the third emanation of the Airy Trigon and the constellation of Uranus.

PISCES: THE FISHES

This Sign symbolizes the flood, chiefly because when Sol passes through this Sign the rainy season commences, clearing away the snow of Winter. This Sign is also the terminus of Apollo's journey through the twelve Signs of the Zodiac.

Pisces signifies the feet of the Grand Man and represents the basis or foundation of all external things, as well as the mechanical forces of humanity. It is the natural emblem of patient servitude and obedience. This Sign, upon the esoteric planisphere, is occupied by Ephraim and Manasseh, the two sons of Joseph who received their portion in Israel as the two feet of the Grand Archetypal Man.

It signifies confirmation and indicates to us the Divine purpose of the great cycle of necessity. This cycle commences with the disruptive, flashing, dominating fire of Aries and terminates with its polar opposite, Water, the symbol of universal equilibrium. The mystical gem of Pisces is the Bloodstone. Pisces is the third emanation of the Watery Trigon and is the constellation of Neptune.

The four triplicites symbolize the four cardinal points of the universe. To us on our present external and physical plane, they signify the four opposite points of space as represented in the compass and cross and the four Occult elements (Fire, Earth, Air, and Water). They each correspond to a particular quarter of the heavens, as the Fiery trigon corresponds to the positive azoth. It is expressed in the glowing, flaming, eastern horizon at sunrise. It is the beginning of the present order of things and stands for the principle of heat termed caloric.

Upon the intellectual plane, Fire represents Zeal, animal courage, daring, and all that pertains to action and activity. While on the higher plane, the esoteric Fire implies the interior apprehension of the meaning and significance of action as displayed in the Trinity and expressed by the Fire of Aries, Leo, and Sagittarius.

The Earthy triplicity stands for the frozen, inert North as a symbol of frigidness and death. It is concerned with all phenomena which are most external and palpable to the senses. Upon the Intellectual Plane, it is concerned with the relations of solids to each other, from which is evolved form, proportion, and sound. Esoterically, the Earthy Trigon denotes the comprehension of the Spiritual qualities evolved from the earthy activities or the one Spiritual quality of the threefold formation or Taurus, Virgo, and Capricorn. Capricorn is the result of the union of Taurus and Virgo, and it leads either to the higher plane in the spiral of existence or to the lower plane of the downward course.

The Airy Triplicity represents the West, the scene of the setting Sun which signifies the dying of the day. Yet it is only the promise of another day or an advance to a higher plane of Being. This brighter day is denoted by the Airy trigon and is concerned with the priestly, political, and social relations of human life. It represents the higher qualities of these relations. It is symbolized by the invisible element, Air, or the great medium of motion. Its esoteric significance is comprised in the arcana of the one True Science.

The Watery Triplicity, symbolic of the South, is the exact opposite of the earthy North. It is the frozen melted, the hardened liquified, the renewal of the crystal into other forms, and the resurrection of death to Life. The Water Trigon signifies the constant effort in Nature to adjust opposites and contradictions and to bring about chemical change and affinities. On the external planes of human life, the Watery Trigon denotes Love and offspring, the external results of the union of love and sex. On the more esoteric planes, Cancer symbolizes tenacity for life, hence the desire for immortality which leads the Immortal Soul to the termination of its earthy pilgrimage and material incarnations. Having passed from the lower arc of matter, the Soul enters once more upon the Spiritual path of eternal conscious life.

The four great Trigons are but the different attributes within the human Soul (microcosm), and the twelve constellations of the Zodiac reveal the mystical signification of Adam Kadmon. Thus, we begin with Fire and terminate with Water. These constitute the two poles of the human magnet.

PLANETARY INFLUENCES

Before describing the nature and influence of the Planets, it is necessary to explain the difference between the Nature of a planet and the Nature of a constellation. The twelve Signs constitute the innate, latent possibilities of the organism, and as such represent the constitution as a whole. While on the other hand, the Planets constitute the active forces which arouse these latent possibilities. In this duplex action of Sign and Planet, both Natures come into play and produce the results of external life. Man, the microcosm, is merely the sounding board or the reacting point for their ethereal and magnetic vibrations.

While the twelve Signs represent the human organism as a form containing possibilities, the Sun, Moon and Planets represent the Spirit, Soul, and Senses of the organism. Man consists of Body and Soul and Spirit. The constellations are the Body; the Moon is the Soul; the Sun, the Spirit; and the five Planets Saturn, Jupiter, Mars, Venus, and Mercury, represent and express the five physical senses. It is in this light that we must consider the various Natures of the planetary influx.

THE SUN

The symbolical aspect of the glorious orb of day undoubtedly first occupied the attention, veneration, and worship of the primitive races of mankind. Everything in Nature depends absolutely upon the presence and kindly support of the shining Sun. The literal interpretation of the Hebrew name for the Sun, Ashahed, is "The all bountiful fire."

The Sun represents the central Spiritual source of All. It is the divine Self of the Grand Man and thus signifies the Spiritual potentialities of creative power. It is the great *I AM* of all things, both Spiritual and temporal. It is the grand conservatory of Life, Light, and Love. Upon the esoteric planisphere, the Sun becomes the great archangel Michael who defeats Satan and tramples upon the head of the serpent of matter and thence guards the way of Life and Immortality with its flaming swords of solar power. In this sense, the Sun represents the positive aggressive, controlling forces of the Cosmos.

Astrologically considered, the Sun constitutes the central Life Principle of all physical things. His influx determines the absolute measure of physical vitality within each human organism. When the Solar Ray is not vitiated by the discordant configurations of malefic stars, the individual born then will enjoy a sound constitution.

Upon the Intellectual Plane, the Sun governs the higher group of the selfish sentiments and lower group of the Moral qualities. These are firmness and self-esteem and hope and conscientiousness. Those dominated by this influx are the natural born leaders of mankind. By their high-minded presence, they proclaim their "right divine to govern." They are proud and ambitious yet magnanimous and noble. Hating all mean, petty, and sordid action, they express the very highest form of true dignified manhood.

Upon the Physical Plane, the position of the Sun in the Horoscope is one of vital importance. On this hangs the vital thread of Life, and if evil rays are concentrated, the life will be of short duration.

When the Sun is afflicted at birth, His influence upon the native through life will be malefic. When this is so, even minor evil directions to the Sun and Moon combined will bring about the destruction of Life. For prosperity and success in life, it is essential that the luminaries be well aspected and favorably situated in the celestial figure. When the Sun and Moon are afflicted at birth, that person will have a very hard struggle against an adverse fate all the days of his life. It will not require the powers of an inspired prophet to foretell his general destiny: "From evil, discord and suffering are born."

THE MOON

The symbolical aspect of Luna, like the Sun, has been known from time immemorial. The fair goddess of night has always been venerated and worshipped as the universal mother, the feminine fructifying principle of all things. In the poetical conception of the Hebrews, the Moon was called Ash-nem or Shenim, the state of slumber and change. Without a complete knowledge of Astrological science, the weird truths concealed beneath the veil of Isis can never be properly understood. The secret of the tides, the mysteries of gestation, and the alternate periods of sterility and fruitfulness are caused by the ebb and flow of the magnetic life currents throughout every department of Nature. This knowledge was the sublime attainment of the sages who, "first discovered the starry truths that shone upon the great Shemaia of the Chaldean lore."

The Moon represents the Soul of the Grand Man. It is the celestial virgin of the world. Upon the esoteric planisphere, Luna becomes transformed into the Angel Gabriel. Upon the universal chart, we see Her expressed as the divine Isis, the woman clothed with the Sun. As Isis, She represents the grand initiatrix of the Soul into the sublime mysteries of the Spirit. The Moon represents the molding, formative attributes of the Astral Light. She stands as the representative of matter. Hence, in her dual character, She reveals to us Her forces which are purely magnetic, and as such, they stand as the polar opposite of the Sun, which are electric. In their relation to each other, they are male and female.

Astrologically considered, volumes were written regarding this orb. When we consider Her proximity to our Earth and Her affinity with it, as well as the rapidity of Her motions, we cannot help granting to her the highest position as an active agent in every branch of judicial Astrology. Her influence is purely negative, and when void of the configurations of the Sun and planets, She is neither fortunate nor unfortunate. But when configurated with other orbs, Her influx becomes exceedingly potent, as she receives and transmits to us the intensified influence of those stars aspecting Her. The Moon, therefore, may be called the great Astrological Medium of the Skies.

Upon the Intellectual Plane, Luna governs the physical senses and the animal passions. She controls the lower forms of the domestic qualities and lower group of intellectual faculties. Those dominated by Her influx are changeable in their Nature, submissive, and very inoffensive. Magnetically their odylic sphere is pure mediumistic or inactive and dreamy. Generally, Luna natives are rather indifferent characters, lacking anything and everything which may be called strong and decisive. They are given to roaming about or constantly moving their residences from one place to another.

Upon the Physical Plane, the influence of the Moon is convertible in its Nature, being harmonious or discordant according to Her relative position to the Sun and the major planets. If the Moon be dignified at birth, She renders the native more refined, engaging, and courteous. Should She be well-aspected, such a position will confer refined, artistic tastes, easy disposition, and good abilities on the native. Should the Moon be evilly aspected, however, the native born then will be a shallow-minded, evil character, prone to dissipation, slothful and void of proper business foresight, consequently, improvident.

MERCURY

In its symbolical aspect, the planet Mercury was prominent as "the messenger of the gods." A thousand myths were elaborated regarding "the fleet-footed Mercury." In the fertile imaginations of the early Greeks, the spirit of Mercury was ever on the alert to manifest its powers. His actions, though sometimes mischievous, were most often beneficial. It seems the central idea of the Ancients was to typify or express in external form the restless activities of the mercurial Mind; hence wings were placed upon his head and feet.

The planet Mercury signifies perception and represents the power of sight within the Grand Body of the Celestial Man. It is the active power of Self and consciousness within humanity. It is the ability to see, perceive, and reason. Upon the esoteric planisphere, Mercury becomes transformed into the angelic Raphael, the genius of wisdom and art. We, therefore, see the esoteric forces of this orb are those which tend to elevate mankind from the animal planes.

Astrologically, the influx of Mercury is mental and restless. No system of mere human invention would have dedicated to an almost invisible star the government of man's intellectual Nature. Any fanciful system would have attributed such an important group of mental qualities to the Sun or to the lordly Jupiter. The experience of the Ancients, however, showed them that neither the Sun nor Jupiter possess such influence. It is upon the experience of the ages that the truths of Astrology are founded.

The qualities of Mercury may be expressed by energy, intellect, and imprudence. There is nothing too hot or too heavy for His ingenuity, nor is there anything too great for His fertile brain.

Upon the Intellectual Plane, the planet Mercury is truly the genius of wisdom and governs those mental qualities called perceptive. The oratorical powers are ruled by this planet. Those dominated by its influx are ingenious, inventive, witty, sarcastic, scientific, and possess a remarkable penetrative power. They are profound investigators of all those sciences which aid in the promotion of commerce and the investigation of space.

Upon the Physical Plane, Mercury rules the brain and tongue. When strongly placed at birth, the person will possess a vivid imagination and retentive memory. One will be noted for mental capacity and the power of persuasion. Such a position, if configured with the moon, will give an unwearying fancy and strongly incline the mind towards the curious and inventive.

VENUS

In Her mythological and symbolical aspect, the planet Venus has been venerated the wide world over in Her dual character of Love and Wisdom. The bright star of the morning is the harbinger and genius of wisdom. None of the stars of the Heavens can compare with the brilliance and glory of Venus when She shines as the herald of the new day. As the goddess of Love, She is equally prominent. The ancient Greeks also represented her as Aphrodite, wearing the horns of her most sacred bull, Taurus.

The planet Venus signifies Love within the Soul of the Grand Archetypal Man, and thus represents the sense of true feeling embodied in humanity. It expresses the clinging, yielding feminine portion of the human constitution. Upon the esoteric planisphere, Venus becomes the celestial Angel, princess of the Astral Light. In this character we behold Her powers of transformation and the "conservation of forces." As Isis (Moon) represents the Astral Fluids in a state of rest, Venus represents the same fluid in action. Therefore, the Moon and Venus form the symbols for the two modes of motion within the Soul of the Universe.

Astrologically, the planet Venus represents mirth, joy and conviviality as the influx inclines those under Her rule to pleasureseeking and grand display. The pleasures of society are especially governed by Venus. Balls, parties, concerts, and receptions possess almost irresistible attractions to those born under Her influence. If afflicted in a feminine Horoscope without strong counteracting rays, the native becomes "unfortunate" and suffers from the loss of virtue.

Upon the Intellectual Plane, Venus controls the higher group of the domestic qualities and also the ideal, artistic, and musical sentiments. Those dominated by her influx excel in music, art, and poetry and become noted for their refined accomplishments. But they may lack true moral power. They are impulsively guided by their sentiments, passions, and desires.

Upon the Physical Plane, Venus has chief dominion over the Mind of the native. She induces a strong predilection for society and confers a good humored, witty, kind, and charitable disposition. Men dominated by Venus are always great favorites with the fair sex, but they are thoroughly deficient in firmness and self-control. It has been truly said, "The general disposition derived from Venus is that of mildness and genuine good nature, and whatever defects may fall to the lot of the native, they are seldom great ones and are more the result of weakness and a strong animal Nature than constitutional wickedness and/or a great desire to do wrong."

MARS

This Planet, in its symbolical aspect, was the object of Divine honors more than all others in the eyes of the Ancient world. Mars was the most sincerely worshipped of all the gods by our northern Ancestors. The greatest glory, in their rude times, was enjoyed by the greatest warrior. Hence Mars, in His universal character, represents the God of War. He was also symbolized as Vulcan, the celestial blacksmith, who forged the thunderbolts of Jove. This indicates the rule of Mars over Iron, Steel, Fire, and edged tools.

The Planet Mars signifies alimentiveness within the Grand Man and represents the sense of taste. We have a direct reference to the expression of these martial forces in reference to the physical sensations in the New Testament, "Eat, drink and be merry for tomorrow we die."

Upon the esoteric planisphere, Mars becomes transformed into the angel Samael (Zamael), wherein are shown the highest attributes of this Spirit. Mars represents the power and ability to appreciate the higher, finer, and more ethereal essences of the Life wave and to have dominion over the powers of absorption and assimilation.

Astrologically considered, Mars typifies and embodies in his Astral expression the spirit of cruelty, bloodshed, and of indiscriminate destruction. The true son of Mars is a genuine pugilist and is never so happy as when thoroughly engaged in vanquishing his opponent.

Upon the Intellectual Plane, Mars represents the Spirit of enterprise, energy, and courage. Without a spice of this planet, all men would be shiftless, effeminate cowards. Those dominated by the Martial influx are mechanical in the highest degree and possess an unconquerable, untiring energy and potent will.

Upon the Physical Plane, Mars signifies all those who are engaged in the production of Iron and Steel. All martial men prefer some business where sharp instruments are used. When the planet is rising at birth, it imparts a kind of ruddiness either upon the face or hair, a Fiery look, or gives to the native a dauntless, manly appearance. If located in the negative angle, it causes the native to become improvident and to spend money thoughtlessly. Located in the mid-heaven, Mars never fails to cause the native much suffering from slander and consequent detriment of character. When we compare the native of Mars with that of Saturn, we find them as the polar opposites.

JUPITER

Under its symbolical aspect, we find Jupiter universally recognized among the Ancient Greeks as Jove. Under the remoter Aryan symbolism, it is represented as the "all Father of Heaven." Both conceptions, Greek and Aryan, are identical. The rude conceptions of the hardy sons of the North see the planet Jupiter depicted as Thor, from which comes the Saxon Thors-day or the modern English Thursday.

The planet Jupiter signifies ethereal absorption within the Grand Man. It, therefore, represents the power of scent or smell within the body of humanity. It is the sense which the developed Soul perceives and partakes of the finer aromatic essences of Nature. Upon the esoteric planisphere, Jupiter becomes transformed into the celestial Zachariel of Zadkiel, and thus represents the impartial Spirit of disinterestedness. In this capacity, it signifies the principles and philosophy of arbitration, the perfect adjustment of equilibrium by the withdrawal of any disturbing forces.

Astrologically, the planet Jupiter is the largest, and next to Saturn, the most potent planet in our Solar system. He signifies all that is truly good and charitable in human life. His action is truly noble, far removed from the sheepish timidity of Saturn or the impudent forwardness of Mars. The genuine son of Jupiter fills the atmosphere around him with genial warmth. His Soul is brimming full of honest good Nature. Utterly incapable of practicing fraud, He never suspects it in others, and often becomes the victim of others. This planet's Nature suggests that the native takes every man to be honest until he is proven to be a rogue.

Upon the Intellectual Plane, Jupiter signifies the higher Moral Nature, the humanitarian qualities, and is the author of all noble and charitable institutions and enterprises. Those dominated by His influx express the highest form of human nature. There is something truly royal in this planet's influence, a mixture of the father, patriarch, and king. Such natives do much to redeem mankind from their general depravity. There is always a fine sense of discrimination, and they possess rare qualities of Justice which entitle them to be the judges of the people.

Upon the Physical Plane, Jupiter may be called the Greater Fortune when he rules over a nativity. He gives a sober, manly, commanding presence. The native is sober and grave, but at the same time kind and sympathetic. If well dignified, He makes the native sincere, honest and faithful, generous, liberal, prudent, and aspiring, strongly given to religious and moral sentiments.

SATURN

Old Father Time with his skeleton-like form and deathly scythe is well known. This is one of the many forms assumed by Saturn in his symbolical aspect. With the Ancient Greeks he was known as Kronos, holding the cycle of necessity and eternity in one hand and the symbol of death in the other. Saturn then was typifying eternal change of form, sphere, and function. Among the ancient Hebrews, Saturn was called Shebo, a name which literally means seven. It is composed of Ashehed, which means the star of old age and expressed the symbol of the planet.

The planet Saturn signifies silent meditation and corresponds to the auricular attributes of the Grand Man. It represents the sense and powers of hearing and listening. We see the mystical significance of the conception of this orb as silent meditation. In order to meditate, there must be silence. Meditation is but the listening of the Mind to the inspirations of the Soul. Upon the esoteric planisphere, Saturn becomes the angel Cassiel or the genius of reflection in the Astral Light. It also presents to us the Occult side of all theological mysteries; hence the medieval conception of this planet as the isolated hermit of the sky.

Astrologically, the planet Saturn is the most potent and malignant of all the planets. This is not because of the marked character of his influence, rather it is the imperceptible, subtle manner in which His influx undermines the vitality of the physical organism. Mars comes like a thunderclap and gives every one to understand there is something decidedly wrong. But Saturn is exactly the reverse. His Nature is slow and patient, cunning and stealthy. At least a good half of our world's suffering is due to the action of this malignant planet. In fact, nine-tenths of the ills of human life are due to the malignant rays of Mars and Saturn when combined. Mars commits crimes in a passionate and unthinking manner and is seldom guilty of premeditated wrong. Saturn is the reverse! He thinks over all His plans very carefully before He attempts to put them into execution and seldom makes a mistake.

Upon the Intellectual Plane, Saturn governs the higher group of the selfish sentiments and the whole of the reflective qualities. Those dominated by His influx are retired, reserved, slow in speech and action. They express the highest form of reflection; consequently, they are studious, scientific, and close reasoners. They generally tend to exclusiveness, and the hermit is a true type of this planet's action.

Upon the Physical Plane, the only good Saturn can do is to strengthen the mentality, cool the passions, and make the native selfish and careful of his own interests. When a person can claim these favors, he is exceedingly fortunate because almost every aspect and position of this planet is more of a misfortune than a blessing. In Nature it is cold and selfish and is very apt to create a miserly disposition.

We have now completed our description of the Ancient seven planetary principles of Occult philosophy, but we will add an outline of the remaining orbs (Uranus, Neptune, and Pluto). They belong to another octave and were not known to the wise Ancients.

URANUS

Uranus, the mythological parent of Saturn, commences the first series of a higher round or cycle of celestial influence. His nature is that of Mercury upon a more interior plane and that of Mars and Saturn combined upon the lower or physical plane.

Astrologically considered, the planet Uranus has not exerted His full power upon the Earth. The age is not yet ripe for His total influence.

Upon the Intellectual Plane, Uranus rules the ideal sentiments and the imagination. Those dominated by His influx possess the most extraordinary abilities in various special directions. They are real geniuses whose talents are so strange and erratic that they seldom become appreciated.

Upon the Physical Plane, Uranus tends to make the native an object of comment. Those under His influence are odd in their many ways. They are strongly argumentative and opinionated. What they say is to the point and asserted with a startling amount of confidence. This planet is the great significator of the Occult, and His influence never fails to produce true Mystics.

NEPTUNE

At present the influence of Neptune is small, except upon certain organisms. We are not prepared for the revolutions of still more ethereal forces. As the race evolves higher susceptibilities, the influence of Uranus and Neptune will increase and that of Mercury and Venus will wane. Neptune expresses all higher qualities at present known to us.

Astrologically considered, Neptune is the octave expression of the planet Venus. Its influx relates to the affectional and emotional qualities. This love is purely platonic and idealistic.

Upon the Physical Plane, His aspects (when powerful) with the Sun and Moon tend towards the production of Clairvoyance.

PLUTO

Strange as it may seem, it is, nevertheless, a fact that Pluto was the long missing planet. It has been allegorically expressed as the Prodigal Son. In our esoteric system there are ten celestial bodies — the Sun and the nine planets. Until 1933 we had only nine in all. Where was the lost one? Now we know! Pluto symbolizes the missing Soul within the human constitution. Pushed out of the line of march by disturbing forces, Pluto became the prey of disruptive actions. The ring of planetoids between the orbits of Mars and Jupiter indicated to us the empty throne of Abel, whom Cain (Mars) slew in his anger. The time ultimately came when this orb was reconstituted, and until that time the missing

Soul sought its physical mate in vain. The affect of Pluto
upon our modern lives is still poorly understood.

The wise men of Chaldea inspected the beautiful
constellations of heaven and learned therefrom the mighty
secrets of the Soul's origin and destiny as well as the material
details of their physical lives. The same book of Nature is
open now as then, but only the pure in heart can read its
pages and trace the Great Chain of Being and Life from
Nature through the Stars.

THE SOUL AND THE STARS

The beautiful, twinkling, glittering stars,
The rivals in splendor of Venus and Mars,
They come and they go,
Molding the powers of our weal or our woe.

Shining serene in the heavens above,
Nightly teaching us lessons of love,
No discords nor jars
Appear to disturb these beautiful stars.

The soul seems to claim these jewels on high,
And struggles to soar to its source in the sky,
But sorrow and pain,
Are the pathways that carry it homeward again.

How oft have we dreamed, when gazing above,
That the purified soul — the offspring of love,
When freed from earth's load,
Would find in the stars its peaceful abode.

So fondly we think of our homes in the sky,
Joined with the soul for whose presence we sigh;
Where Saturn nor Mars
Can embitter our joys mid the beautiful stars.

4

Astrology Lessons For Beginners

What is Astrology? It seems best to answer this question at the beginning. Astrology is the science of the Stars. It teaches that each of the nine planets in the sky which are within our Universe has a special or individual influence upon the earth and all things on the earth. There are thousands of stars in the sky which can be seen on a clear night. Only nine of them are within our Solar system. The others are beyond and too far away to have any great influence upon us. In Astrology, we are mainly concerned with the Sun, Moon, Mercury, Venus, Mars, Saturn, Uranus, Jupiter, and Neptune.

These orbs appear to revolve constantly around the earth at different rates of speed. The path they apparently take in traveling through space is called the Zodiac. The Zodiac has been divided into twelve sections from time immemorial by ancient and modern Astrologers and named Signs. We can trace or follow the motion of these planets (the Sun and Moon are called planets in Astrology) through the Zodiac or Signs. These are called Aries, Taurus, Gemini, Cancer, Leo, Virgo, Libra, Scorpio, Sagittarius, Capricorn, Aquarius, and Pisces, in the order named.

Since there are 360 degrees in a circle and there are twelve signs, each sign is 30 degrees in length. Each degree is

divided into minutes (60) and seconds (60). Thus one may, if
he knows how, find the exact position of each planet at any
time in degrees, minutes, and seconds at any time of the day
or night or at any day of any year. An Ephemeris is a book of
tables for any year, giving the exact positions of each planet
in degrees, minutes, and seconds for any day and month.
These tables are prepared in advance by the U.S. Naval
Observatory at Washington, D.C. and by other countries, and
Astrologers adapt these tables to their own use and purpose.

Each of the twelve Zodiacal Signs is said to have a
Ruling Planet. Since there are only nine "planets," some of
them rule more than one sign. After years of observation,
Astrologers have determined that the influence of some
planets in some signs is stronger than when they are in other
signs. Therefore, each sign was given a ruling planet on the
theory that the influence of the planet is peculiar to that
sign.

The next thing is that each sign corresponds to certain
dates of the calendar. Thousands of years ago it was
discovered how at certain times of the year the Sun was in
the same sign of the Zodiac. It was found that the Sun was
always in Aries when the Spring began, that it had just
entered Cancer when the Summer begins. Therefore, each
sign was given the corresponding dates for the sign.

Formerly, the first of the year began on the 21st of
March, for this is really the beginning of a new year when
Spring revives all Nature from its long, wintery slumber. That
is why Aries, which rules from March 21st to April 20th, is
called the first sign of the Zodiac. But while the calendar has
been changed several times, the planets and signs rule the
same time of the year, regardless of how many times the
names of the months are changed.

The planets move at different speeds through the sky.
Thus, the faster moving planets will pass those which do not
move so fast. Therefore, they form certain ASPECTS with
each other as they move across the sky. When two planets are
120 degrees apart, they are Trine or good aspects to each

other and their influence upon the earth is favorable. When two planets are 90 degrees apart, they are in adverse aspect to each other and their combined influence upon the earth is unfavorable. As these nine celestial bodies move majestically around the Zodiac, you can see why it is unlikely that in one generation they will ever entirely repeat themselves, and their Aspects will constantly change. No two people are exactly alike in every way, and this is why it is necessary to construct a chart of the positions of the planets at the time of the birth of the individual in each case in order to get details of the influences.

The speed of the planets is as follows:

The MOON passes entirely around the Zodiac through all of the twelve signs every 28 days.

MERCURY passes through the entire Zodiac every 88 days.

VENUS takes 32 weeks to go through the entire Zodiac.

The Sun goes through the entire Zodiac once in each year, remaining in each sign about a month. The Sun is considered the Giver of Life, and so whatever sign the Sun is in at your birthday is your birth sign.

MARS takes about two years to go through the Zodiac.

JUPITER takes about twelve years to pass through the entire Zodiac and may be said to remain in each sign about a year.

SATURN takes about 29 years to pass through the entire Zodiac, and so remains in each sign approximately two and one half years.

URANUS takes 84 years to go around the entire Zodiac, and so remains in each sign roughly seven years.

NEPTUNE moves through the entire Zodiac in about 164 years, and so remains in each sign about 14 years.

It should be plain why no two people are alike, for these different transits and aspects of the Sun, Moon, and Planets can hardly be repeated exactly within one lifetime, especially as it takes some planets more than one lifetime to transit the complete Zodiac.

Astrology should not be classed with fortune telling. One does not need any "supernatural gifts" to learn and practice Astrology. It is an art and science which anyone with an ordinary school education and a fairly good memory should be able to learn and practice. Astrology is a science in the sense it predicts the positions of the Sun, Moon, and Planets in advance or bases its analysis of the character and future of a subject on such positions at the time of birth. It is an art in the sense that certain conclusions are drawn from the relative positions of these orbs at any time in the past or the future. The positions of the planets are obtained from Ephermerides based upon astronomical observations and calculations by competent astronomers.

This chapter teaches the Nativity Horoscope, based upon the date and hour of birth. Later, you may wish to study the Radical and Progressed Horoscope. These are more advanced and more complicated studies necessary to become a professional Astrologer. An Ephemeris of any given year may be purchased from large dealers in Astrological literature. Consult any magazine on Astrology, found on most large bookstands or in large book stores, for such information.

Astrology is returning to public favor rapidly of late years. It is the oldest science in the world, and evidently has its beginnings in very early civilizations. The ancient Egyptians and the ancient Hebrews were familiar with it. In fact, it has been said that the twelve tribes of the Hebrews were named after the twelve signs of the Zodiac. However, this art and science could only be practiced and understood by the learned and more intelligent, while the mass of people were relatively ignorant. And so, as the age of darkness of learning and intellect deepened and was encouraged by selfish and tyrranical rulers, this art and science of Astrology fell largely into disuse.

As intelligence and education increased in more modern times, these studies were again revived. The modern art of Astronomy which consists merely of the study of the celestial orbs of the skies, their positions, distances, sizes, and many other kinds of information useful to modern physical science, is the result of the studies of such men as Copernicus, Keplar, and others who lived hundreds of years ago and who were really Astrologers in origin.

As a matter of fact, the name Astronomy was originally Astrology (Astro, meaning stars, and ology meaning study or science of) but to distinguish physical Astronomy from Astrology, its name was changed in recent years.

Newspaper reports of more or less recent investigations of Sun spots and their causes seem to indicate, statistically at least, that they have an apparent effect on the affairs of men aş well as on the periodic growth of vegetation. There have been indications that the periodic appearance of Sun spots might be coordinated with the periodic outbreak of dormant volcanos. However, a study by some astronomers would seem to coordinate the periodic outbreak of Sun spots (roughly every twelve years) with the position of the planet Jupiter at perihelion (nearest position to the Sun) which also occurs every twelve years.

Astrologers, of course, have long considered the influence of the Sun, Moon, and Planets on the Earth and its people to be a reality. The influence of the Sun and Moon is, of course, stronger since these bodies are nearer the earth and such influences as they have on tides are the most easily noted.

Incidentally, the ancient Roman name of our Moon was Luna, and the word "lunatic" for an insane person evidently was derived from the Roman name for the Moon. This would indicate that there was a popular idea or superstition that the Moon's light made some people crazy. Of course, scientists laugh at this notion and perhaps rightly. Yet, the fact in itself would argue that the Ancients, at least, found some sort of baleful influence of the Moon on certain persons at certain times.

While a true Horoscope should rightly be based on the hour, date, and place of birth, many persons do not know the exact hour of their birth. Modern Astrologers have compromised by the use of the date of birth only for such cases. They are not so accurate a source of a Horoscope, but by making the Sign which is based on the birth date the rising sign, or first sign, they have been able to furnish what they call a Nativity as distinguished from a true Horoscope. The true horoscopes of young children can often be made because the parents will be able to recall the actual or approximate hour of birth of the child.

THE SIGNS AND SYMBOLS USED IN ASTROLOGY

To enable you to study Astrology, it is necessary that you first become familiar with the symbols used by Astrologers.

The Planets in the sky are constantly moving through space. These movements and positions are listed in a book called an Ephemeris. An Ephemeris is a table or list of the Planets and the signs they occupy from day to day. The astronomers, scientists, and mathematicians who determine these day-to-day positions have adopted a universal system of symbols so that a person who speaks any language may read the English Ephemeris. The same thing applies to other languages. Once you have learned the symbols for each Planet and each sign, you will be able to read the positions from any Ephemeris. The names of the planets and signs are not spelled out in the Ephemeris. Therefore, it is necessary that you thoroughly fix those symbols in your mind and learn to make or draw them yourself.

The Symbols of the Signs of the Zodiac are as follows:

ARIES	♈	LIBRA	♎
TAURUS	♉	SCORPIO	♏
GEMINI	♊	SAGITTARIUS	♐
CANCER	♋	CAPRICORN	♑
LEO	♌	AQUARIUS	♒
VIRGO	♍	PISCES	♓

The Symbols of the Planets are as follows:

MOON	☽	SUN	☉
MERCURY	☿	VENUS	♀
MARS	♂	JUPITER	♃
SATURN	♄	URANUS	♂
	NEPTUNE	♆	

When writing down the Planets and Signs, get into the habit of using the symbols instead of spelling out the words. If you will examine the symbols closely, you will find that each one of them is very easy to draw.

DATES AND QUALITIES OF THE ZODIAC SIGNS

Everyone is born in one of the twelve signs of the Zodiac. These Signs also have the qualities called Fire, Earth, Air, and Water named after the ancient, supposed, four elements in Nature. Fire and Water signs do not harmonize readily, nor do Earth and Air signs.

The following are the dates and qualities of the twelve signs:

NAME OF THE SIGN	BIRTH DATES	GENDER	ELEMENT
ARIES	March 21 to Arpil 20	Masculine	Fire
TAURUS	April 21 to May 20	Feminime	Earth
GEMINI	May 21 to June 21	Masculine	Air
CANCER	June 22 to July 22	Feminine	Water
LEO	July 23 to August 22	Masculine	Fire
VIRGO	Aug. 23 to Sept. 22	Feminine	Earth
LIBRA	Sept. 23 to Oct. 22	Masculine	Air
SCORPIO	Oct. 23 to Nov. 21	Feminine	Water
SAGITTARIUS	Nov. 22 to Dec. 21	Masculine	Fire
CAPRICORN	Dec. 22 to Jan. 19	Feminine	Earth
AQUARIUS	Jan. 20 to Feb. 18	Masculine	Air
PISCES	Feb. 19 to March 20	Feminine	Water

It is interesting to note that physiologists and embryologists recognize the fact that all individuals have, basically, qualities of both sexes, but which will predominate in the final sex of the individual depends on certain interesting genetic qualities.

If you will now refer to the sample chart, you will notice the Zodiac signs or their symbols are on the outside. Each sign has 30 degrees. Every 10th and 20th degree is indicated with a longer line. The 5th, 15th, and 25th degrees are indicated by shorter lines or dots between the numbers. Each sign is separated from the next with a dividing line which goes through the second and third circles of the chart. The first degree of Aries is exactly on that long line at the left edge of the chart. If the planet is in the eighth degree of the sign, it would be entered halfway between the 10 and the dot which indicates 5 degrees. You may draw a little line from the symbol of the planet on the outer circle to the exact degree on the inner circle if you wish. This may make it easier to judge the aspects which will be described later.

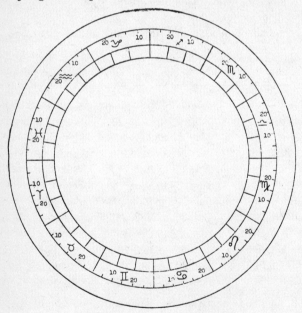

ASTROLOGICAL CHART

To construct a chart for one born October 2nd, 1924, we find in a purchased Emphemeris on October 2nd, the Sun was 9 degrees in the sign Libra. Find the sign Libra on the chart and place the symbol of the Sun (a circle with a dot in the center) near the 9th degree of Libra. We note the Moon, whose symbol is a crescent, is 27 degrees in Scorpio. Place the symbol for the Moon near the 27th degree of the chart. Also, place the symbols of the planets on the proper places, thus: Neptune 21 degrees in Leo, Uranus 18 degrees in Pisces, Saturn 2 degrees in Scorpio, Jupiter 14 degrees in Sagittarius, Mars 26 degrees in Aquarius, Venus 24 degrees in Leo, and Mercury 22 degrees in Virgo.

ASPECTS: An aspect is the number of degrees on the chart between two planets. If they are 90 degrees apart, this is an adverse aspect. If they are 120 degrees apart, this is a favorable or good aspect. Because of the different rates of speed through the Zodiac, the Planets form different aspects or angles at different times.

It was, originally, necessary to find the aspects by making tedious calculations to find the angles between the transiting Planets. This is not now necessary, for there is a mechanical process for doing this. An aspect finder is sold by Astrological supply firms. On a diagram of the Zodiac, the disc is placed over it at the center and a thumb tack put at the exact center around which the disc will turn. Turn the disc until the initial arrow points to the degree or near it at which the Moon is placed. Look at the place where the nearest Planet is touching. We enter on the recording chart the adverse or favorable aspects of the Planets. When taking the Moon's aspects, ignore any aspect which is more than 10 degrees from the line.

All the Planets will not have aspects to each other. When recording aspects for Planets, ignore those more than 5 degrees from any of the lines. The adverse aspects are 180 degrees, 150 degrees, and 90 degrees. The good or favorable aspects are 60 degrees and 120 degrees. When two Planets are within 5 degrees of each other, they are said to be in conjunction.

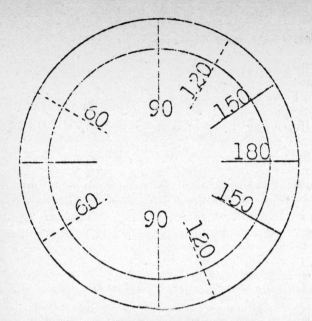

ASPECT FINDER
Numbers refer to degrees of space. Solid lines Bad. Dotted lines Good. Refer to these degrees on the Aspectarian so as to tell which are good and which are bad aspects.

When finding aspects, you eliminate one each time you go from one Planet to the other. To make this clear, you indicate the aspects of the Sun and Moon when you take the aspect of the Moon. Thus, taking the aspect of the Sun again would only repeat the same thing.

THE ORDER IN WHICH TO RECORD ASPECTS

Moon to Mercury, Venus, Sun, Mars, Jupiter, Saturn, Uranus, Neptune.
Mercury to Venus, Sun, Mars, Jupiter, Saturn, Uranus, Neptune.
Venus to Sun, Mars, Jupiter, Saturn, Uranus, Neptune.
Sun to Mars, Jupiter, Saturn, Uranus, Neptune.
Mars to Jupiter, Uranus, Neptune.
Jupiter to Uranus, Neptune.
Uranus to Neptune.

By looking them up and recording in this manner, you will avoid repeating any aspects. When recording aspects it would be well to draw a line after the Planets with no aspects to avoid confusion.

If you have a recording sheet properly filled out, you are ready to begin reading the Horoscope.

Start at the top of the page and then look up the indications of the Sign under which you were born, or the sign written on top. Then, one by one, look up the meaning of the Planets in the Signs you have recorded. You will find them in the chart reader. Make a note of all that you discover in the indications. Next, look up in the chart reader the good and adverse or bad indications, also making note of them. After that, look up the meanings of the conjunctions, if any. Incidentally, the word "bad" or adverse does not really mean as unfortunate as it sounds. It has a limited meaning, since the Stars incline but do not impel.

Where indications of different aspects seem to conflict, this kills or neutralizes one another. Thus, if an indication says a happy marriage and another aspect means an unhappy marriage, these just mean the unhappy one has been neutralized by the happy one. You thus have to balance once aspect with another in this way when they relate to the same thing.

As an Astrologer, it is your job to adjust these aspects, always remembering that this is not fortunetelling, and the stars incline but do not impel.

If you read more advanced books on Astrology, you may note that a Table of Houses of the Horoscope is needed. After you have mastered this course and become thoroughly familiar with it, you may be interested in the more advanced courses. There are numerous good handbooks on the market.

But for some time all you will need is an Ephemeris of each year because a different horoscope requires a different Ephemeris if the year of birth is different.

ASTROLOGICAL WORDS

AIRY SIGNS: Gemini, Libra, Aquarius.
ASPECT: The number of degrees between two Planets on the Aspect Chart.

ASPECT FINDER: A mechanical disc placed over the Aspect Chart, etc.

CONJUNCTION: When two Planets are within 5 degrees of each other.

CHART: A graphic map of the heavens showing Signs and Planets at the time of birth.

DIRECT MOTION: When a Planet is apparently moving steadily ahead.

DEGREE: The 30th part of a Sign. Each Sign is divided into 30 degrees, 60 minutes, and 60 seconds. You may disregard the minutes and seconds except when the total is almost a degree.

EARTHY SIGNS: Taurus, Virgo, Capricorn.

EPHEMERIS: A table of the positions of Planets, Sun, and Moon for each year.

FIXED SIGNS: Taurus, Leo, Scorpio, Aquarius.

FIERY SIGNS: Aries, Leo, Saggitarius.

HOROSCOPE: A series of interpretations and forecasts regarding life of an individual. Information derived from individual Star Map at the time of birth.

PARALLEL: When two Planets are at equal distance from the Equator. Same value as a conjunction.

RETROGRADE: When a Planet appears to be moving backward, or opposite to direct. This is only an apparent motion because of the motion of the earth and its relation to the motion of the Planet, etc.

SIGN: An arbitrary section of the Zodiac of 30 degrees angular length. It may be said to be the path of the earth, or a twelfth section.

WATERY SIGNS: Cancer, Scorpio, Pisces.

ZODIAC: A representation in the heavens of the angular path of the Earth around the Sun. The ancients believed the Earth went around the Sun, whereas the Zodiac is its apparent path as seen from the Earth.

FORECAST DAILY OR MONTHLY CONDITIONS

After you have become familiar with the general procedure and secure an Ephemeris for the current year, find the date for any month and day you wish to look up and note the location of the Moon. Turn the aspect finder until the pointer or arrow is at the degree and sign of the Moon for the month and day. Now, see if it makes any aspects with the Sun and any of the Planets. If the aspects are all favorable for the day, then the day is favorable. If the majority of the aspects are adverse, then caution is needed for that day.

If you will go through the same procedure for the Sun for any month, you can find out the favorable or unfavorable conditions for that month. Watch the aspects of the Sun for a fortunate month in advance. As the Sun changes its position a degree a day, there will be some variations, but the balance or majority of aspects, good or bad, will govern events.

The illustration is a device which is called a Mechanical Aspectarian. These devices are constructed of good quality cardboard so that they will last a lifetime and may be procured for a reasonable sum from the concerns that sell Ephemerides. This chapter has been prepared to incorporate the use of an Aspectarian, since it is then very easy for the student to find his own aspects and read his Horoscope.

The illustration is for the purpose of acquainting you with the appearance of an Aspectarian so you will know what you are buying when you purchase one. Various manufacturers of these Aspectarians have differently decorated disks, yet they all serve the same purpose.

The use of an Aspectarian saves the student many hours of hard work and mathematical calculation since it is automatic in its showing of the planetary aspects and absolutely accurate as to the relative distance of the Planets from each other in the Horoscope chart.

The Chart Reader gives the inclinations or influences and the probable results unless something is done to change them. The principle of Astrology, as distinguished from fortunetelling, is that forewarned is forearmed against adversities or adverse characteristics.

When people drift through life without an attempt to correct adverse inclinations, the latter will largely prevail, modified by the environment. Because your chart may show some adversities is no reason for your experience to be like them. Man is not a creature without will. He can control his destiny if he is strong enough to do it. In other words, fatality and Astrology are not the same thing. Emerson once said, "Astrology is astronomy brought to earth and applied to the affairs of men." As Shakespeare once said in his play *Julius Caesar:* "The fault ... is not in our stars but in ourselves ...." Take counsel from the stars but reserve judgment and action for yourself.

Incidentally, the names of the signs of the Zodiac are actually the names of stellar constellations enormously more distant than the Planets in our solar system. Many thousands of years ago these constellations could be seen at the parts of the heavens corresponding to the signs. But during this great period of time there has been a shift, so that Pisces now appears where Aries should be. This is an interesting point which you might look up later when you have learned more about Astrology.

CHART READER

The following pages are devoted to a reading of the supposed influence of the Planets in all the signs and the aspects they make with each other at different times. No one person, of course, will have all the indications for each case, but it is necessary to give all indications for all cases or nativities as they occur. This section is called the "Chart Reader" because it is to be distinguished from the making of the chart and the tabulation of the Planets for each nativity.

There is no hard and fast rule as to the influences given. As you eliminate conflicting influences and outline those which agree, you will find that no two horoscopes are exactly alike because you will have to change the given indications somewhat and put them into your own words to fit every individual. Experience and practice in constructing charts and reading them will enable you to give better interpretations.

CHARACTERISTICS OF THE ZODIACAL SIGNS

ARIES: (March 21st to April 20th inclusive, any year) A masculine sign. Ruling planet Mars. Denotes much mental energy. A natural leader. Very ambitious. Dislikes a master and limitations. Quick temper and quick witted. Love of justice but apt to go to extremes if indignant. Philosophically minded. Will go to extremes if ambitious. Can do best work when at the head of things. Usually kind, considerate, and thoughtful. Thinks no one can do better than himself when well educated or trained. Hard worker, honest, and sincere in friendships. Desires home comforts. High ambitions, but may lack patience in attaining them. May be destined to rise high in life, perhaps.

TAURUS: (April 21st to May 21st) A feminine, earth sign. Ruling planet Venus. Self reliant and firm in convictions. Careful or cautious. Usually patient and will wait a long time for hopes to mature. Kind and gentle unless provoked unduly, furious and headstrong when fully aroused. Energetic and talented. Retiring and somewhat shy, often. Keen appreciation of art, music, nature, literature, and scientific things, especially if educated along these lines. Inclined to romance, love of travel, and dealing with public. Eager for education. Humanitarian. Kind to animals. Usually a loving, trusting disposition.

GEMINI: (May 22nd to June 21st) A masculine, airy sign. Ruling planet Mercury. Changeable in opinions. Great love of home and family. Too easily influenced by kindness and apt to place confidence in the wrong kind of persons. Vivid imagination and quite studious. Always striving for self-improvement. Quick in decision or judgment. Keen observer. Dislikes idleness and must be busy at something. Ambitious but sometimes visionary. Confiding, honest, sincere. Quite skillful with hands. May be clever and witty and a good sense of humor. Fond of travel and change as well as intellectual pursuits. Forgives easily. A magnetic personality. Inclined to go to extremes in jealousy, sympathy and other emotions.

CANCER: (June 22nd to July 22nd) A feminine, watery sign with ruling planet the Moon. Sensitive disposition. Versatile but retiring and timid at first acquaintance. A fertile imagination with many worthwhile talents capable of development. Fond of adventure, travel, music, books, drama, romance, and the arts. Too easily influenced by environment. Often inclined to self-pity. Also often too generous for own good. Greatly attached to home and family. May have many talents and fail to concentrate on one, to his detriment. Inclined to worry about many things. Inventive and dramatic talents, perhaps. Often too easily influenced by others.

LEO: (July 23rd to August 22nd) A masculine, fiery sign. Ruling planet the Sun. A natural leader. Full of energy but sometimes somewhat nervous and restless. Philosophical, determined, high tempered, with a sunny disposition. Dislikes a master and not to be forced to do anything against his will. Not satisfied in subordinate positions, perhaps. Ardent, sincere, and affectionate. Love of praise but honorable in dealings. Some have inventive minds. Others love music, the arts, natural beauties, and intellectual pursuits. Some have clairvoyant ability. Hard to convince and must have their own way, quite often. Will not be driven but can be persuaded. Fond of travel, sports, exercise, mechanics and often have a number of interesting hobbies. A magnetic personality.

VIRGO: (August 23rd to September 22nd) A feminine, earthy sign. Ruling planet Mercury. Very critical at times. Easily offended but modest and generous, thoughtful, artistic, talented, and romantic. Great respect for wealth. Quick, perceptive mind. Good memory. Very active but seldom contented for long. Philosophically inclined with good reasoning powers. Idealistic in many ways but yet rather practical. Fond of reading and other intellectual activities. Sometimes given to worry without important cause. May then be irritable and unhappy. Quick to learn and worth educating or training. Somewhat quick-tempered but seldom get into serious quarrels. Love of reasonable argument. Adults often have a good command of the language after proper education and much reading. Have the patience to rise high in life.

LIBRA: (September 23rd to October 22nd) A masculine, airy sign. Ruling planet Venus. Quite romantic. Often in love with someone or their work. Peace-loving. Just, sincere, and sympathetic. Love of friendships. Sensitive and sometimes secretive. Are said to be great idealists. Love of poetry, music, art, literature, beautiful scenes, singing, dancing, drama, traveling, and many refined amusements or occupations. Tends to refinement and dislikes coarseness in work or pleasures. May have many love affairs, especially when young. May make the warmest friends and greatest lovers. Love of justice and fair play.

SCORPIO: (October 23rd to November 22nd) A feminine, watery sign with Mars the ruling planet. Keen judgment, shrewd, critical, and often rather skeptical. May be inclined to be suspicious with little cause. Fond of beauty and luxury. Love travel, beautiful natural scenery, harmony, but unintentionally could stir up trouble for others at times. Can be quite sarcastic if angered. Daring, brave, capable, strong-minded, and determined. Unyielding if they think they are right. Forceful character. Strong likes and dislikes. More practical than romantic. Aggressive, progressive, and precise. Quick-tempered and may be inclined to nagging. Sometimes rather unfeeling but just, honest, and honorable. Trustworthy and dependable in business dealings and agreements. Inclined to go to extremes at times.

SAGITTARIUS: (November 23rd to December 22nd) A masculine, fiery sign. The ruling planet is Jupiter. Most people born under this sign have a generous and charitable nature, perhaps too generous for their own good. They are frank and plain spoken, honest, ambitious, persevering, and not easily discouraged. They love harmony and freedom and cannot stand oppression or restrictions. They possess intuition and good judgment, and are sometimes mediumistic or psychic. They usually aim high and generally hit the mark. They are often misunderstood and may be wrongly accused of things they did not say. They dislike idleness and must be doing something all the time. They do best in occupations where they are self-employed, professional, or otherwise. They have strong tempers but generally hold no grudge. Inclined to be romantic, affectionate, cheerful, and sometimes rather jealous.

CAPRICORN: (December 23rd to January 20th) A feminine, earthy sign with ruling planet Saturn. They are usually practical minded, are often disappointed but never discouraged. They can also be headstrong and unyielding, are hard workers and persistent. Have good reasoning powers and can figure things out according to past experience. They meet many obstacles but soon figure out a way to overcome them. They are natural fighters, long-suffering and have strong will power. They also have strong likes and dislikes and are not easily swerved from their course. Will go to extremes to carry out their plans.

AQUARIUS: (January 21st to February 18th) A masculine, airy sign. The ruling planet is Uranus. They have a quiet, patient, faithful, and persevering nature. Usually philosophical, refined, and ambitious. They can discriminate and concentrate and are both theoretical and practical. They sometimes have quite advanced ideas, have a strong temper, but it is easily controlled. They love liberty and freedom and will not be driven. They may be interested in occult or psychic matters and in the mystical things of life. Are literal success-finders and often too generous for their own good. Therefore, they may be imposed upon. They can bear responsibilities and have high ideals. They tend to be straightforward, artistic, retiring, sincere, ambitious, and magnetic.

PISCES: (February 19th to March 20th) A feminine, watery sign. The ruling planet is Neptune. They are industrious, ambitious, amiable, and have a kind, loving nature. Are imaginative, creative, sympathetic, and tend to be neat and well dressed. Very fond of natural or scenic beauty. They also love music, art, romance, and quite often interested in occult matters. They may also have powers of magnetic healing and be somewhat mediumistic. May also be somewhat timid with strangers but usually are good talkers when they are in familiar surroundings. It may be difficult to get the best of them in an argument. Usually have a deep love for their families and are also often trying to help others. They have strong humanitarian principles.

INFLUENCE OF THE SUN

SUN IN ARIES: Gives health, strength, willingness, energy, independence of thought, and capacity for public work. Musically and intellectually inclined. Fond of travel, exploring, and scientific work. A good leader.

SUN IN TAURUS: Gives warm-heartedness, determination, and firmness. Ambitious to rise above the common levels. Will have more than one occupation. Gain in money or property through parents or relatives.

SUN IN GEMINI: Gives strong versatile mind. Can adapt talents to any line. Female horoscope shows two marriages, birth of twins. Man's horoscope shows he will be in before the public, many journeys.

SUN IN CANCER: Love for home, long life, desire for pleasures, good lawyer, doctor, nurse, political leader. Obstacles or disappointments may be overcome with patience, etc.

SUN IN LEO: Loves authority, ambitious, generous, sympathetic. Somewhat irritable, nervous, and restless sometimes. Good actors, teachers, or instructors. Often have psychic tendencies. Many capabilities.

SUN IN VIRGO: Many talents, analytical, love of details, musical or artistic inclinations. Fond of material gain. May have an unfortunate marriage unless discriminating. Must have a mate to encourage him or her. Feels cramped in subordinate positions.

SUN IN LIBRA: Sociable, romantic, affectionate nature. Love of beauty and the arts, music, etc. Possibility of disappointment in marriage or trouble in courtship. Short journeys. Imaginative. Attachment for parents, relatives.

SUN IN SCORPIO: Prideful, firm, strong character. May be jealous or sarcastic at the wrong time. Will assume many obligations. Gain of money by marriage late in life. Love of occult investigations.

SUN IN SAGITTARIUS: Generous, alert mind, jovial disposition. Will travel land and sea. Honest, cannot tolerate secretiveness. More than one occupation. Rather impatient. Many problems to solve.

SUN IN CAPRICORN: Serious and determined nature. Practical and qualified to direct others. Love of material gains. Inclined to fault-finding and pessimism. Few intimate friends. May become prominent during life.

SUN IN AQUARIUS: Broad-minded. Deep sympathies, prudence, liberal, and generous. Always helping relatives or friends. May travel much. Occult or mediumistic tendencies.

SUN IN PISCES: Restless, changeable disposition. May go to extremes in feelings and actions. Many successes but also some opposition. May have periods of depression and anxiety. May lack perseverance. Responsibilities. May have latent psychic ability.

The influence of the Sun in the twelve signs can be very important and deserves careful study. Sun is the Giver of Life and by general study you should be better able to divide people by characteristics according to the signs under which they are born.

INFLUENCE OF THE MOON

MOON IN ARIES: An enthusiast but apt to go to extremes. Impulsive and dislikes a master. Not too conventional. May be susceptible to head complaints. Early estrangement from parents possible. Secret love affairs. Occult.

MOON IN TAURUS: A quiet person, persistent, determined, ambitious to get ahead. Interested in music and painting (art). Occupations on water or residence near water. Good disposition. Somewhat sensuous. Romantic. Mysterious experience.

MOON IN GEMINI: A lover of intellectual subjects. An active mind and skillful with hands. Writer, journalist, designer, sculptor, engraver, salesman, or traveler. Money from mother's side. May resemble mother in mind or body. May make many trips away from home.

MOON IN CANCER: Fond of home. Imaginative, emotional, sympathetic, proud, determined. Some acting ability. Also may be interested in mediumistic and intellectual studies. Success on or near water. Parent of many children.

MOON IN LEO: A good manager. High-minded, candid, and honest. Sincere lover, favorite with opposite sex. Love of luxury, perfumes, and fine clothes. Capable of assuming authority and responsibility. Possible inheritance.

MOON IN VIRGO: Has good memory, also good and true friends. Many journeys probable. May be good druggist, doctor, or herbalist. Quiet and persevering. Also witty. Some ill-health possible but nothing serious.

MOON IN LIBRA: Popular, affectionate, ability in music and other arts. Has a companion in undertakings; seldom works alone. Great difference in age between marriage and business partner. Strange friendship experience.

MOON IN SCORPIO: Self-reliant, abrupt, plain-spoken, fond of natural phenomena. Hard to influence. Can fight own battles. May be extravagant. Incompatibility in marriage sometimes, also trouble over legacy.

MOON IN SAGITTARIUS: Quick to action and decision, restless, unsettled, kind-hearted, good-humored, lover of the great outdoors. Fond of travel; inclined to mysticism and the occult. Faithful worker. May have two jobs or change often. A step-parent possible or may be adopted.

MOON IN CAPRICORN: A public personage; administrative ability, good reasoning powers. Idealistic. Fond of show, sometimes selfish in money matters. May have trouble with parents. Some drawbacks to a marriage.

MOON IN AQUARIUS: Broad minded, thorough, keen imagination, intuitive, lover of luxury, fond of travel, interested in national affairs, good company. Inclined to day-dreaming; may have healing or mystical powers. Slight tendency to nervous ailments.

MOON IN PISCES: A retiring but pleasant personality. Easily discouraged, impatient, and restless. Love of study and romance. Secret enemies but harmless. Other people may try to interfere or rule.

THE OTHER PLANETS

To every Planet, the Astrologers attribute two houses, or headquarters — one of the night, the other of the day. Sun and Moon, being the heavenly bodies of day and night par excellence, have only one house each. The Sun resides in Leo, the Moon in Cancer. The Zodiac was partitioned into the halves of Sun and Moon. Each half contains six signs. Those of the Moon, or night, are Aquarius, Pisces, Aries, Taurus, Gemini, Cancer; those of the Sun, or day, are Leo, Virgo, Libra, Scorpio, Sagittarius, Capricorn.

This is the primary partition made by Astrology. The important thing now is that each Planet gains power or influence when entering his house. At night, he is most powerful in his night House; by day, in his day House (see Chapter 3).

Things are more complicated, for the greatest power of each Planet is not in his headquarters, but upon another degree. The Sun, for instance, has, according to tradition, His greatest influence upon the nineteenth degree of Aries, and his weakest spot is exactly opposite to his *exaltation,* upon the nineteenth degree of Libra. This position of extreme weakness is called *dejection* or fall.

A third demarcation of the power of the planets is one which played an important role in Ancient Astrology. The whole heavenly globe being marked by 360 degrees, each sign of the Zodiac is 30 degrees. Ten degrees of each sign are consecrated to a Planet which becomes influential when passing through this *decan,* so-called. There are thirty-six such decans at 10 degrees, in which the Planets alternate, the Sun and Moon being excluded.

With the day and night Houses, exaltation and dejection, and the decans, the Astrologers established a system of correspondence between the Zodiacal signs and the Planets. By these means, they will be able to judge various good or bad influences according to the favorable or unfavorable position of the Planets. Their individual qualities are little changed since the time of Chaldea.

Here in capsule form are the Planets and Signs with their interrelationships in the Horoscope.

SUN: The masculine principle; spirit, mind, the living being, the will to live, vitality, willpower, determination, health and the heart, the man, the father, authority. Sign: LEO

MOON: The feminine principle; the soul, the psyche, the mother, fecundity, adaptation, the wife, the family, the nation, hereditary qualities. Sign: CANCER

MERCURY: Intellect, mediation, transmission of knowledge, judgment, critical ability, analysis. Sign: GEMINI AND VIRGO

VENUS: Love and art, physical attraction, feeling, sense of harmony and beauty, girl or maiden, sweetheart or mistress. Sign: TAURUS AND LIBRA

MARS: Energy and action, courage and determination, impulsiveness, ruthlessness, brutality, soldiers, sportsmen, technicians, craftsmen, surgeons. Sign: ARIES AND SCORPIO

JUPITER: Harmony, law, and religion, expansion and enlargement, ownership, moral and religious aspirations, judges, high ecclesiastics, bankers, wealthy people, fortune hunters. Sign: SAGITTARIUS AND PISCES

SATURN: Inhibition and concentration, consolidation, perseverance, seriousness, caution and economy, melancholy, reserve and taciturnity, segregation and seclusion, calcification, old age, agriculture, mining, and real estate. Sign: CAPRICORN AND AQUARIUS

URANUS: Suddenness, revolution, transmutation, independence, excitability, and impulsiveness, innovators, reformers, inventors, and technicians; magicians, occultists, and astrologers (the "paranormal"). Sign: AQUARIUS

NEPTUNE: Impressionability, fantasy and imagination, inclination to mysticism, vagueness, confusion, deception, people of doubtful character, confidence man. Sign: PISCES

PLUTO: Higher power or providence, invisible forces or

powers, the will to exercise power, to influence the masses, propagandists and politicians, actors and orators.

CONJUNCTIONS

A conjunction of planets occurs when they are within 5 degrees of each other.

PLANETS	TABLE OF CONJUNCTIONS AND MEANINGS
Moon & Mercury	Sudden opportunities but not very fortunate. Intelligent.
Moon & Venus	General good fortune. Social prominence. Loving nature.
Moon & Sun	Gain from superiors. An energetic, cheerful nature.
Moon & Mars	Loss through haste. Lack of caution and judgment.
Moon & Jupiter	Fortunate. Prosperity and wealth(?) Kind and generous.
Moon & Saturn	Unfortunate. Disappointments. Apt to be moody.
Moon & Uranus	Alternate gains and losses. Adventures. Impulsiveness.
Moon & Neptune	Peculiar dreams. Psychic experiences (?) Intellectual.
Mercury & Venus	Musical, cheerful nature. Successful enterprises.
Mercury & Sun	Big achievements. High minded. Full of energy.
Mercury & Mars	Loss through fraud, bad temper. Too restless.
Mercury & Jupiter ...	Gain through travel, law, adventures, very cheerful.
Merucry & Saturn ...	Loss through deceit or treachery. Pessimistic.
Mercury & Uranus ...	A remarkable career. Original talent. Unusual mind.
Mercury & Neptune ..	Changeable conditions. Ups and downs. Possible sorrows.
Venus & Sun	Fortunate. Gain in the arts. Successful love affair.

Venus & Mars	Dangers from opposite sex. Deceitful friends.
Venus & Jupiter	Fortunate. Gains by marriage. Peaceful, successful life.
Venus & Saturn	Possible scandal. Jealous partner. Many delays.
Venus & Uranus	Strange experiences. Strange successes. Loving nature.
Venus & Neptune ...	Love entanglements. Dual attachments. Many delays.

Sun & Mars	Inflammatory complaints. Loss through haste. Restless.
Sun & Jupiter	Good health, success, sudden improvement. Good judgment.
Sun & Saturn	Possible accidents, sudden reverses. Easily confused.
Sun & Uranus	Trouble through recklessness. Sudden turn of events.
Sun & Neptune	Strange succession of events. Odd attachments. Psychic.

Mars & Jupiter	Gain through friends or relatives. Many powerful friends.
Mars & Saturn	Accidents, minor sicknesses, danger of loss of business.
Mars & Uranus	Lack of caution. Possible losses. Danger from trickery.
Mars & Neptune	Strange experiences. Ups and downs. Must fight alone.

Jupiter & Saturn	Rather successful. Many impositions. Sudden changes.
Jupiter & Uranus	Sudden good luck. Travel abroad. Pleasant experiences.
Jupiter & Neptune ...	Engage in financial schemes. Strong psychic nature.

| Saturn & Uranus .... | Sudden reversals. Losses. Possible loss of liberty. |
| Saturn & Neptune ... | Serious obstacles. Danger of imprisonment. Too careless. |

| Uranus & Neptune ... | Enemies. Delays. Unexpected turns of events. |

It is necessary to know from which point in the heavens the Astrologer will receive the answers to his questions. The most important spot is the degree of the ecliptic or Sun trajectory, which rises on the eastern horizon at the very moment of the birth or enterprise, of which a Horoscope shall be drawn. Originally, it was not the mathematical point but some important star rising in the east which was considered.

The rising degree of the ecliptic was called *ascendant*. The rising sign of the Zodiac in which this degree lay was called Horoscope. The name was given later to the entire constellation, the theme which was to be examined. Two other points were of importance: the degree in the west (that is, the disappearing point of the ecliptic), and the center between these extremes in the middle of the way of the Sun. Starting from the rising degree in the east, twelve partitions of loci were made, which contained the answers to the twelve questions.

They were: 1. life, 2. wealth, 3. inheritance, 4. land and ancestral tombs, 5. wife or city, children, brothers and parents, 6. health and disease, 7. marriage, 8. death, 9. gods, religion, travels, 10. habitation, state, honors, art, character, etc., 11. friends, charity, and 12. enemies and captivity.

The twelve loci are divisions which contain the questions and correspond to twelve strips in the visible heaven and are inscribed in a scheme which is commonly quadrangular.

From the above it should be plain why no two people are ever exactly alike. Astrology is based on the wonderful order which rules the world in an ever-changing evolution of new and different aspects and the position of man in relation to these heavenly influences. It is thus a science and not some mystical quackery.

5

Your Stars and Their Influences

Astrology, the Science of the Stars, teaches that the Earth, Sun, Moon, and all the other Planets play their part in the universal system or scheme of things and that they have a definite influence upon the destinies of man.

From the beginning of history humanity has observed and recorded the positions of the planetary bodies and has noted the effect on earthly conditions caused by these various combinations of planetary forces. Since it was discovered that the destinies of individuals, nations, and humanity in general is written in the Stars, these forces have been studied and analyzed more and more thoroughly.

Why or how these Planets influence each other is too lengthy an explanation to give here. Suffice it to know that certain combinations of Planets foretell certain accurate results. Astronomy teaches that the universe is governed by a perfect system, accurately timed with marvelous precision and accomplished with unerring exactness. Always the Sun rises and sets; the tides come and go, and the seasons follow each other around the calendar, but these are merely visible manifestations of nature's laws. The planetary forces are flowing around us at all times in invisible channels, directing our lives toward certain conditions and experiences which can be avoided or improved by knowing in advance what to expect.

Astrology does not conflict with the Bible. As a matter of fact, there are numerous passages that refer to the influence of the stars. It dates back to the time of Adam. "For then it was that Adam obtained wisdom, even from the stars in the heavens." In Isaiah, Chapter XLVII:13, we read: "Thou art wearied in the multitude of thy counsels; let now the Astrologers, the star-gazers, the monthly forecasters stand up and save thee from these things that shall come upon thee."

The names of the twelve Tribes of Israel translated from the Hebrew are the names of the twelve Zodiacal Signs. The Bible was written in Hebrew, and the letters of that alphabet are the names of the Signs, Planets, and Constellations. Therefore, the very foundation of the Bible is Astrological.

The following work is the cream of Astrological observation, culled from the author's many years of successful practice of the Science of Astrology and condensed to convenient, practical proportions.

The varying conditions of the Astral and magnetic forces are caused by the various angles at which, in their apparent motions or in the stellar influx, they are reflected to any given point of the Earth. The cardinal points of the day (Sunrise, Noon, Sunset, and Midnight) indicate the greatest changes. But these changes from one to the other are gradual. To measure this gradual angular change, the Ancient Astrologers divided the space of the Heavens visible at any moment into six Houses, and the opposite or invisible arc also into six. These twelve were designated as the diurnal (day) and nocturnal (night) Houses of the Heaven. Modern Astrologers follow the same principles because they are founded upon the rock of Absolute Truth. Their influences can be verified in every correctly calculated Horoscope.

These twelve houses (or divisions) contain, like the signs of the Zodiac, 30 degrees of space each, but unlike them, their distance is measured by degrees of right ascension (or time) instead of celestial longitude. This is the only relation existing between the twelve Houses and the twelve Signs.

If we divide a circle into quadrants, we see the angles which represent the four cardinal points of the day, and upon a more extensive scale, the four seasons of the year. These are no mere fanciful ideas, but are external symbols of living realities upon the external plane of phenomena. If the reader will now divide the circle into twelve equal parts, he will possess an outline representing the twelve Houses of the Heavens with the Earth in the center. The horizontal line upon the left represents the Eastern horizon or the point which is occupied by the Sun at sunrise. The perpendicular line above the horizon, marking off one quadrant of the circle, represents the zenith or meridian occupied by the Sun at noon.

Now, between these two points, the horizon and the meridian, we have two angular lines which divide the quadrant of 90 degrees into three parts containing 30 degrees each. These are the three southeastern Houses which mark off the angular changes of Solar and Astral influx between sunrise and noon. The horizontal line opposite to and parallel with the line of the horizon shows the point of the Heavens which is occupied by the Sun at sunset. The two angular lines between it and the meridian indicate the changes of terrestrial and celestial conditions between noon and sunset. Thus, the Sun, Stars, and Planets which make the transit of the diurnal are of six Houses. During this time every conceivable change of polarity is possible under the Solar influx and may be manifested upon the Earth. The same holds true for the six nocturnal Houses.

The earth is divided into positive and negative halves which are continually changing from one to the other; the half under the Sun's rays is always positive; that portion under the shades of dark is negative. Day and night then, like the Sun and Moon, are the polar opposites of each other, and so are the individuals born under the two conditions.

From the foregoing it will be seen that any individuals born during the course of a single day and at different times will differ widely in their physical temperament and mental bias. Also, they will differ widely in their fortunes and destiny. Herein we see the grand basic principles of this Science which accounts, in a most philosophical manner, for the wonderful diversity of all human beings. Scarcely any two are alike either in Mind, form, or feature, because no two are born at exactly the same moment of time under exactly the same position of the Heavens. Suppose one hundred children in different parts of the world were born at the same precise moment in time; the difference in latitude and longitude of their respective birthplaces would render no two alike. The reader has only to bear in mind that it is sunrise, noon, sunset, and midnight every moment at some point on the Earth.

The secondary causes which regulate and modify the Astral and planetary influx are the apparent motions of the Sun, Moon, and Planets in their orbits. It is the real motion of a Planet which affects our inhabitants. When our Earth is situated so as to appear to an observer, were he on the Sun, to be moving through Cancer, the Sun appears, to the inhabitants on Earth, to be passing through the opposite sign, Capricorn. So far as the Earth is concerned, it really is, because the Solar center stands between the Earth and the Sign. The Solar influx is impregnated with the magnetic qualities of Capricorn with which it permeates the Earth. When we speak of the influence of the Sun in Capricorn or any other Sign, though only an Astronomical appearance, we mean exactly what we say.

Further, when the Earth by its progressive motion moves faster or slower in a different direction from the other Planets, it causes them to become alternately stationary, direct in motion, or retrograde. We know these are purely appearances, so far as the Planets themselves are concerned, but their influx is just the same on Earth as if it were a reality. The real movements of our Earth place them in those positions in reference to the apparent position of the Sun. The various angular distances so formed, termed aspects, are so potent in their magnetic effects that sometimes the whole good or evil influx of a given Planet is completely polarized. Always these aspects are found to constitute some very important factors in the native's Horoscope.

From the foregoing statement of Astral principles and in order to properly gauge and apply the actual influences in operation at a person's nativity, two primary considerations are necessary: the time and place of a person's physical birth. Without these nothing reliable can be scientifically determined. And any system of Astral, planetary, or Solar influences which pretends to determine the celestial influences upon man and ignores these essential elements is naturally only partially correct.

Ancient astrology is not, as so many seem to think, "an exploded science," and, further, we wish to point out that many superficially learned individuals think the old geocentric system of Claudius Ptolemy was the only foundation upon which the Ancient Astrology rested. When the present Copernican system overturned the Ptolemaic theory of a "primum mobile," the Astrology of the ancients was not buried amid the ruins. Such superficial minds are in sad need of a little True Light! The observed effects of certain positions of the heavens, be they apparent or real, is the only foundation of judicial Astrology.

It was upon the continuous observation of ages that the old Chaldean sages formulated their wonderful Science of the Stars. The eclipses of the Sun and Moon, conjunctions of the Planets, and the exact length of the Solar year were all correctly computed ages before the days of Abraham. In reality, it makes little difference to Astrology whether the earth moves about the Sun or the Sun about the Earth. Astrology rests upon the absolute fact that one of them does indeed move.

So far as the physical organism of man is concerned, the Planet of birth is its center and the focus of all the celestial influences; hence, the Earth and its motions are the only ones of vital importance upon the material plane of man.

THE HOUSES

The significance of the Houses on you, the native, born under a particular Sign is as follows:

ARIES

The first HOUSE shows your personality. You are determined, practical, industrious, usually quite frank and plain-spoken, eloquent, progressive, energetic and a natural trail-blazer. You are inclinced to be irritable and impatient. You regard your opinions and judgment to be as good as others.

The second HOUSE deals with your financial affairs. It is controlled by Taurus and ruled by Venus. You are inclined to be impulsive. This must be overcome if you would succeed in life. You are capable of attaining financial independence through your own activities if you do not scatter your efforts over too many lines of endeavor. Learn to coordinate your Mind and body; do your best, and success will be assured.

The third HOUSE deals with travel and the Mind. It is controlled by Gemini and ruled by Mercury. This shows some stubbornness, keen perception, originality of thought, inventive ideas, a fertile imagination, and good judgment. Sudden journeys will be taken, some leading to drastic changes in your life's routine.

The fourth HOUSE deals with your home affairs. It is controlled by Cancer and ruled by the Moon. Some difficulties in home life will develop at an early stage. After maturity most Aries people roam a great deal and are only occasionally concerned with home ties. You are extremely interested in your home and will spare no effort to achieve an artistic; homelike atmosphere.

The fifth HOUSE deals with your affections and romantic experiences. It is controlled by Leo and ruled by the Sun. Some sad experiences attend your affections through life. You will often be taken advantage of and imposed upon because of your sentimental qualities. You are not necessarily demonstrative, but usually show your devotion to others by service and loyalty.

The sixth HOUSE deals with your health and work. It is controlled by Virgo and ruled by Mercury. Headaches, colds, catarrh of the head, and bowel complaints will be likely ailments unless you guard your health at all times. More than the average person, you require plenty of outdoor exercise, sleep, and rest. In your work you are very practical, painstaking with details, and always trying to improve your methods of doing things.

The seventh HOUSE deals with marriage. It is controlled by Libra and ruled by Venus. This is where you will have to be careful, as you are apt to be hurried into an emotional marriage that will not last. For complete harmony, your marriage must be to someone who is intellectual and philosophical and who respects your ideas. Marriage to someone in Leo is best if your individual Horoscopes blend.

The eighth HOUSE deals with length of life and Spiritual gifts. It is controlled by Scorpio and ruled by Mars. You have great recuperative powers and with ordinary care will live a long and useful life. You possess an uncanny intuitive faculty, and your ability to read people's minds should be developed and used in your social and business activities. You have your own philosophy of life and usually live up to it.

The ninth HOUSE deals with journeys and religion. It is controlled by Sagittarius and ruled by Jupiter. This shows you will travel extensively and your journeys generally will prove profitable and exciting. Nothing thrills you more than preparations for a trip. You follow scientific trends of thought and are philosophical. You have great respect for piety, though not deeply religious.

The tenth HOUSE deals with professions and ambitions. It is controlled by Capricorn and ruled by Saturn. There is no reason why you should not be successful if you make the most of your opportunities. Your most fortunate lines of business or occupations are music, literature, art, journalism, banking, medicine, nursing, decorating, designing, contracting, managing large enterprises, and handling real estate.

The eleventh HOUSE deals with friends and companions. It is controlled by Aquarius and ruled by Uranus. You will have hosts of friends and admirers. Favors and promotions will come frequently from companions. You will go to extremes to defend a friend or anyone you feel is unjustly wronged. You need never be lonely since you are a good mixer socially and a clever entertainer.

The twelfth HOUSE deals with your limitations. It is controlled by Pisces and ruled by Neptune. You are likely to engage in too many lines of endeavor and will go out of your way to help others, even at a sacrifice to your own interests. You resent opposition to your plans and will profit from experience in early life, so in later years you will settle down to a prosperous and useful life career.

TAURUS

The first HOUSE shows your personality. You are ambitious, determined, cautious, perservering, firm, magnetic, patient, brave, affectionate, courteous, and honest. At times you are inclined to be peculiar, stubborn, stolid, and emotional. Once your Mind is made up you are hard to win over to some other idea. You are cheerful and optimistic and do not become discouraged if your hopes and plans fail to develop as rapidly as desired.

The second HOUSE deals with your financial affairs. It is controlled by Gemini and ruled by Mercury. You have a good earning capacity, but your tendency to spend money too freely will handicap you. You can become financially independent if you learn to save money early in life, invest in land, buildings, successful business enterprises, or corporations. Not much gain is shown through speculation.

The third HOUSE deals with travel and the Mind. It is controlled by Cancer and ruled by Moon. You are very set in your ways and capable of being extremely agreeable or extremely stubborn. You have a constructive Mind and great power of concentration. You are very fond of travel and this pleasure will be gratified many times in life.

The fourth HOUSE deals with your home and home affairs. It is controlled by Leo and ruled by the Sun. A happy home life is necessary to your success, for home means much to you. There is nothing you appreciate more than the comforts of a cozy home. You are devoted to your parents and make a charming host or hostess.

The fifth HOUSE deals with your affections and romantic experiences. It is controlled by Virgo and ruled by Mercury. You probably will have several love affairs which will bring some disappointments. You are highly emotional and are a strong admirer of people of culture, refinement, and social standing. You are rather demonstrative in the bestowal of your affections and get much pleasure in bringing gifts to those you love.

The sixth HOUSE deals with your health and work. It is controlled by Libra and ruled by Venus. You are likely to suffer from throat trouble, pneumonia, stomach disorders, rheumatism, and slight liver, kidney, and bladder troubles. By strict daily caution these may be prevented. You usually apply yourself to any work you undertake conscientiously and with great interest. You are a valuable employee.

The seventh HOUSE deals with marriage. It is controlled by Scorpio and ruled by Mars. Because of your emotional Nature, you should select your mate with great care. With the proper life partner, no one will be happier than you in marriage; an unfortunate marriage will make you irritable and disagreeable. You should marry someone born in Scorpio, provided individual Horoscopes blend.

The eighth HOUSE deals with length of life and Spiritual gifts. It is controlled by Sagittarius and ruled by Jupiter. This gives promise of a long life if you take reasonable care of yourself. You are more or less interested in the mysteries of Nature and possess a great deal of natural intuition and foresight.

The ninth HOUSE deals with journeys and religion. It is controlled by Capricorn and ruled by Saturn. In religious views you are very sensitive, but broadminded. Before you condemn any other creed, you will study it carefully. If dissatisfied after investigation, you will no longer be concerned with that particular creed or cult. You have a longing for travel either for pleasure or educational purposes, and you will usually find some way to satisfy this desire.

The tenth HOUSE deals with professions and ambitions.

It is controlled by Aquarius and ruled by Uranus. Some of the following lines are best for you: teaching, music, art, mediumship, acting either on the stage or screen, writing, law, medicine, work along mechanical lines, and governmental work. You are versatile enough to prepare yourself for almost any profession and succeed in it. You are ambitious to excel in some unusual, uncrowded line of endeavor, and if at all possible, you will not be contented until you have achieved in some such activity.

The eleventh HOUSE deals with friends and companions. It is controlled by Pisces and ruled by Neptune. Your dynamic, magnetic personality attracts many people to you, and you are likely to have the admiration and respect of many who are more prominent than you. You stick to your friends through thick and thin. You will find your most harmonious association among those who were born in Cancer, Virgo, Scorpio, Capricorn, and Pisces.

The twelfth HOUSE deals with your limitations and debts to destiny. It is controlled by Aries and ruled by Mars. Beauty, harmony, and change are essential to you for a happy life, and you do not seem to realize them in your daily routine. When you overcome your impatience in striving to attain them, you will live the kind of life for which you yearn and will be happy, successful, and secure.

GEMINI

The first HOUSE shows your personality. You are changeable in opinion, alert, careful, intuitive, talented, magnetic, sensitive, active, restless, and of a nervous temperament. You have a constructive mind capable of entertaining big ideas. You are too readily influenced through your sympathies and have a roving nature. You are quick-tempered but easily pacified. You have a deep understanding, keen judgment, and foresight.

The second HOUSE deals with your financial affairs. It is controlled by Cancer and ruled by the Moon. This shows that your finances will fluctuate very much through life. At times you will have a great deal of money and at other times your financial status will be very unsettled. You seem particular about investments and should not tamper with stocks, bonds, or government papers. It is best for you to invest in lands, buildings, mines, aviation, or radio enterprises.

The third HOUSE deals with travel and the Mind. It is controlled by Leo and ruled by the Sun. You have keen intuition, but liable to change your opinion in the flash of a moment. You have a strong Mind, but are inclined to worry too much over incidentals. You have a vivid imagination likely to run away with you at times. A fondness for travel is shown, and in the course of your life you will take many long journeys.

The fourth HOUSE deals with your home affairs. It is controlled by Virgo and ruled by Mercury. You are very particular about your home life and take special pride in a neat, cozy home. Since childhood you have pictured an elaborate home which you hope to possess. You will always do your part to create a harmonious home.

The fifth HOUSE deals with your affections and romantic experiences. It is controlled by Libra and ruled by Venus. You are extremely fond of unusual amusements, and your affectionate ties are deep rooted. You will go to almost any extreme for anyone you love, but if once deceived you can never care for that person again. Varied and interesting romances are assured.

The sixth HOUSE deals with your health and work. It is controlled by Scorpio and ruled by Mars. You are subject to the following ailments: colds, pneumonia, poor circulation, constipation, and kidney or bladder disorders. By care and caution you may prevent these ailments. In your work you are capable, honest, conscientious, and progressive. You are always ready to adopt newer and better methods and modern improvements.

The seventh HOUSE deals with marriage. It is controlled by Sagittarius and ruled by Jupiter. Many times Gemini people marry someone older than themselves. You should not marry until you overcome your natural roving disposition and are ready to settle down. Marriage to someone in Sagittarius is best, if your individual Horoscopes blend. You will make a success of marriage if your mate will permit you to do so and will cooperate with you.

The eighth HOUSE deals with the length of life and Spiritual gifts. It is controlled by Capricorn and ruled by Saturn. This shows a reasonably long and interesting as well as a variable life. Some gifts through legacies and insurances after middle life. You are highly intuitive and possess mediumistic qualities that should be developed and utilized.

The ninth HOUSE deals with your religion and journeys. It is controlled by Aquarius and ruled by Uranus. It is quite possible throughout your life that frequent opportunities will come to enable you to take long journeys to all parts of the world. Travel appeals to you very much, and you need the change in environment travel will bring to you. In religious views you are tolerant and philosophic. You are inclined to regard religion from a scientific viewpoint and are friendly to almost all creeds.

The tenth HOUSE deals with professions and ambitions. It is controlled by Pisces and ruled by Neptune. You should succeed in any occupation that enables you to develop your brilliant and active imagination, ingenuity, and skill with your hands. The following are some of the best lines for you to concentrate upon: writing, acting, music, secretarial work, expert accounting, editing, lecturing, barbering, or beauty culture. You are untiring in your quest for knowledge and a great reader. You are highly idealistic in your ambitions and usually strive to realize these ideals.

The eleventh HOUSE deals with friends and companions. It is controlled by Aries and ruled by Mars. Your friendships and associations are a very necessary part of your life. You will do everything in your power to help friends in sickness or sorrow. The men of Gemini usually form attachments with people who do not always harmonize with them and should be careful in their choice of friends. The ladies of Gemini, because of their dual personality, will be unable to single out one to regard as their best friend.

Those born in the following signs will be most apt to harmonize with you: Aries, Leo, Libra, Sagittarius and Aquarius.

The twelfth HOUSE deals with your limitations and debts to destiny. It is controlled by Taurus and ruled by Venus. Your greatest handicap will be your tendency to worry and the fear you are not going to be able to accomplish your desires. If you control your oversensitiveness and do not scatter your forces, you will enjoy a long, useful life and will be able to reach the heights you have dreamed about since childhood.

CANCER

The first HOUSE shows your personality. You are extremely sensitive, adventurous, friendly, romantic, secretive, and often irritable. You are a very positive person and usually move in a world of your own. You never like anyone to know your intimate affairs, yet are interested in the welfare of others. You usually attract many friends and are very popular.

The second HOUSE deals with your financial affairs. It is controlled by Leo and ruled by the Sun. This shows an intense desire to accumulate money, which is not easy for you. You like to speculate and, at times are fortunate, but you should always follow your intuition in such ventures. For good financial gain you should invest in government bonds, land, real estate, and mines.

The third HOUSE deals with travel and the Mind. It is controlled by Virgo and ruled by Mercury. You have a constructive, analytical Mind, are very imaginative, and a good judge of human Nature. You are very well balanced and retain your poise in the face of excitement. You will travel extensively and gain much knowledge in contacts and experiences made in your journeying.

The fourth HOUSE deals with your home affairs. It is controlled by Libra and ruled by Venus. Here is where you take the center of attraction, for you are a great home lover and immaculately neat about everything in the home. The ladies of Cancer are fond of display and are witty. The men of Cancer have more self-assurance, are reserved and resourceful. Great love for parents is shown. In Nature and habits you are very domesticated.

The fifth HOUSE deals with your affections and romantic experiences. It is controlled by Scorpio and ruled by Mars. You are refined and tender in your affections, are not often demonstrative, but show your love in service, loyalty, and material gifts. You possess a strong desire for comfort and ease and are fond of luxury. Few people show such refinement as you show in your love affairs.

The sixth HOUSE deals with your health and work. It is controlled by Sagittarius and ruled by Jupiter. Unless you take good care of yourself, your health will usually give you much concern. The ailments you are subject to are blood disorders, inflammatory complaints, appendicitis, indigestion, constipation, and rheumatism. You are very thorough in your work and like to be complimented upon it. Praise spurs you on to bigger and better things.

The seventh HOUSE deals with marriage. It is controlled by Capricorn and ruled by Saturn. Marriage in this sign is inclined to be a matter of chance and should be considered carefully. Being such a home lover, you need to have a very congenial mate. Your most congenial partner will be found in Capricorn if your individual Horoscopes blend. Do not marry in haste because it will make you either very happy or extremely miserable.

The eighth HOUSE deals with length of life and Spiritual gifts. It is controlled by Aquarius and ruled by Uranus. This house shows a very long life and the realization of your ambitions. Financial benefits will come from many sources, so that after middle life you will be very prosperous. You have a keen, intuitive sense and the ability to see through problems with great clarity and calm judgment. You possess much clairvoyant talent.

The ninth HOUSE deals with journeys and religion. It is controlled by Pisces and ruled by Neptune. This denotes many journeys by land and sea which will bring interesting and exciting experiences to you. In your religious convictions you are very determined and loyal to your creed. It is hard for you to understand a different religious viewpoint.

The tenth HOUSE deals with professions and ambitions. It is controlled by Aries and ruled by Mars. You are not likely to have sudden success, but once started you will achieve without much difficulty. Success will come through your own efforts and by diligent attention to your work. The best lines of endeavor for you are nursing, surgery, law, teaching, music, public speaking, or mercantile pursuits. You will often encounter hindrances in the realization of your ambitions, but if you persist you can make them come true. You are shrewd and are capable of assuming responsibility in all business dealings.

The eleventh HOUSE deals with friends and companions. It is controlled by Taurus and ruled by Venus. You have a large circle of acquaintances, but few real friends. Frequently people whom you have regarded as friends for a long time will turn against you for no real reason at all. You will harmonize best with those born in Capricorn, Taurus, Virgo, Scorpio and Pisces.

The twelfth HOUSE deals with your limitations and debts to destiny. It is controlled by Gemini and ruled by Mercury. Your greatest limitation is probably due to the fact that you help others too much without thought of your own future security. You are constantly giving to public charity or to private philanthropic enterprises.

LEO

The first HOUSE shows your personality. You are proud, ambitious, masterful, good natured, enthusiastic generous, fearless, and determined. You have a strong temper, are quick to anger, but get over it quickly, are inclined to go to extremes in emotions and sympathies. You are very impulsive and restless and sometimes like to follow the lines of least resistance. But you have a versatile Nature and will accomplish what you set out to do, whether it is right or wrong.

The second HOUSE deals with your financial affairs. It is controlled by Virgo and ruled by Mercury. It will be necessary for you to learn to save early in life, for your financial affairs will be varied; you will have many ups and downs. At times you will be thrown entirely upon your own resources, but often you will have financial assistance from others. Speculation is not fortunate for you. It will be better for you to invest in lands, real estate, iron and steel industries, and in manufacturing enterprises.

The third HOUSE deals with travel and the Mind. It is controlled by Libra and ruled by Venus. You are very fond of travel and will be given many opportunities to satisfy this desire. You are optimistic about the future and confident it will bring many changes for the better. You have remarkable insight and the courage of your own convictions.

The fourth HOUSE deals with your home affairs. It is controlled by Scorpio and ruled by Mars. The men of Leo love comfort in the home but are not helpful in making this possible. The ladies of Leo love their homes but do not like its drudgery nor are they especially fond of staying at home. Unless you become more tolerant and sympathetic toward other members of the family, you are likely to have an unsettled domestic life.

The fifth HOUSE deals with your affections and romantic experiences. It is controlled by Sagittarius and ruled by Jupiter. You are likely to have sorrow, trouble, and disappointments in your love affairs unless you curb your emotions, for you are very romantically inclined.

The sixth HOUSE deals with your health and work. It is controlled by Capricorn and ruled by Saturn. You are subject to lung, heart, and stomach troubles, blood disorders, constipation, chills, and headaches. These ailments may be cured by taking good care of your health. In your work you are quick, clever, and competent. You like to be complimented for saving time, making short cuts, and introducing economy measures in operation.

The seventh HOUSE deals with marriage. It is controlled by Aquarius and ruled by Uranus. People born in Leo are usually apt to marry early and to follow their emotions against their better judgment. Marriage is an important institution and you should choose your mate carefully. You are very exacting in all you do, and if your mate is not inclined to be so, there will be no end of trouble. Marriage with someone in Aquarius is best if your individual Horoscopes blend.

The eighth HOUSE deals with length of life and Spiritual gifts. It is controlled by Pisces and ruled by Neptune. This gives promise of a fairly long life. You are extremely sensitive, receptive, and mediumistic. You possess great Psychic powers and your healing and magnetic qualities could heal the sick.

The ninth HOUSE deals with journeys and religion. It is controlled by Aries and ruled by Mars. You have a strong Spiritual side but are inclined to be intolerant of the religious beliefs of others. Unless you try to overcome this tendency, it will make you very unpopular. You are fond of traveling. You will take many trips early in life, then will settle down for a while and later have many opportunities to continue your travels.

The tenth HOUSE deals with professions and ambitions. It is controlled by Taurus and ruled by Venus. It seems hard for you to find your real place in the industrial world, for unless you are careful you will become a Jack of all trades, and master of none. You are likely to succeed in any of the following: managing large business enterprises, practicing law, medicine, or surgery, banking, photography, teaching, music, acting, traffic management, and all educational pursuits. You never will be happy or successful in subordinate positions. You should be in business for yourself, or in some profession where you can take the initiative or practically be your own boss.

The eleventh HOUSE deals with friends and associates. It is controlled by Gemini and ruled by Mercury. You will have many good friends, among them some people of prominence. Because of your generosity, you are likely to be imposed upon by others. People will harmonize best with you whose birthdays occur in Aries, Gemini, Libra, Sagittarius, and Aquarius.

The twelfth HOUSE deals with your limitations and debts to destiny. It is controlled by Cancer and ruled by the Moon. You will be hindered because of your nervousness, impatience, and restlessness. While you never hold a grudge against anyone, you do not forget personal injuries or slights. Early in life you will have to learn to be practical in your ideas and ambitions. If you overcome these limitations, you will have a well-rounded life.

VIRGO

The first HOUSE shows your personality. You are very efficient, progressive, shrewd, methodical in habits, energetic, refined, and intellectual. You are a very discriminating Nature, have an analytical mind and possess a nervous, restless temperament. You are endowed with more artistic and constructive ability than the average person. You have a faculty for handling detail. At times you are inclined to be shy and undemonstrative.

The second HOUSE deals with your financial affairs. It is controlled by Libra and ruled by Venus. Your greatest financial success will be attained in the artistic professions and work requiring close attention to detail. You should become identified with large organizations and concerns producing the better and more refined things of life. Speculation is doubtful for you. Preferably you should invest in land, real estate, and well-established corporations.

The third HOUSE deals with travel and the Mind. It is controlled by Scorpio and ruled by Mars. You have a very practical Mind, keen observation, and good judgement. Your intuition and discriminating qualities cause you to be an asset to any business or society. You will travel extensively and gain beneficial changes and the desire for new experiences. Music and art are important factors in your life. You are also greatly interested in literature, research, and work of an investigating, analytical nature.

The fourth HOUSE deals with your home affairs. It is controlled by Sagittarius and ruled by Jupiter. The men of Virgo have rather unsettled domestic affairs until middle life. The ladies of Virgo are ideal homemakers and usually take great pride in everything pertaining to the home. To make life really worthwhile, you must have peace and harmony and will do all you can to create this atmosphere in your home.

The fifth HOUSE deals with your affections and romantic experiences. It is controlled by Capricorn and ruled by Saturn. You seek to associate with people who are intellectual and artistic. You are extremely sensitive and usually put your heart and Soul into your affections. You will have many sincere attachments before you find the one who is really worthy of your love, and not until then will real happiness come to you.

The sixth HOUSE deals with your health and work. It is controlled by Aquarius and ruled by Uranus. You are likely to have ailments of the neck, eyes, and throat, also bowel disorders and irregularities of the digestive system. However, these are not of serious nature if you observe strict daily hygiene. You are an industrious and conscientious worker. Do not follow any occupation that is distasteful to you and avoid worry.

The seventh HOUSE deals with marriage. It is controlled by Pisces and ruled by Neptune. For happiest marriage your mate should be someone born in Pisces if your personal Horoscopes blend. Because of your exactness and capacity for detail, you must not expect too much from your mate. Marriage will prove a success if you do not require too much attention.

The eighth HOUSE deals with length of life and Spiritual gifts. It is controlled by Aries and ruled by Mars. This shows a fairly long and eventful life. You will have many Psychic experiences. You possess much magnetic power and a fertile imagination. The house also denotes some legacies and possible wealth in later life.

The ninth HOUSE deals with journeys and religion. It is controlled by Taurus and ruled by Venus. This shows you to be very idealistic. Success will usually attend your travels, which will be many on land and sea. You will live a religious life and will be tolerant and broadminded when considering the religious viewpoint of others.

The tenth HOUSE deals with professions and ambitions. It is controlled by Gemini and ruled by Mercury. You are not easily defeated nor swerved from any task you set out to accomplish. You are not likely to become discouraged and will exert every effort to succeed in disputes, temporary setbacks, or hardships. The men of Virgo would make successful artists, musicians, architects, doctors, lawyers, or mechanics. The ladies of Virgo are wonderful nurses, writers, teachers, illustrators, journalists, or demonstrators. Any profession or occupation you select should be one which gives you an opportunity to take the initiative and utilize your originality.

The eleventh HOUSE deals with friends and companions. It is controlled by Cancer and ruled by the Moon. You have a great desire for wealth and many of your associates will be well-to-do people. You prefer to be among those from whom you can learn things, people who are doing things along intellectual and artistic lines. You are very discriminating in your choice of friends, and they are usually of the intellectual type.

The twelfth HOUSE deals with your limitations and debts to destiny. It is controlled by Leo and ruled by the Sun. You should try to overcome self-consciousness and avoid worry because you do not have as much money as you feel you should have. You always feel greatly limited if you are obliged to work on a small margin of profit. Not until you control this tendency to worry, self-pity, and self-consciousness will you enjoy a prosperous, happy life.

LIBRA

The first HOUSE shows your personality. You are extremely well-balanced, have keen perceptive and intuitive powers, are timid, loving, self-willed, slightly selfish, honorable, and idealistic. You are sincere and have implicit faith in others until they prove themselves unworthy. You have a kind, forgiving, affectionate, sympathetic Nature and are inclined to be rather hasty of temper and too generous for your own good.

The second HOUSE deals with your financial affairs. It is controlled by Scorpio and ruled by Mars. You do not realize the value of money and usually spend it as fast as you get your hands on it. You have the personality, ability, and good judgment to earn a great deal of money, but unless you learn to save, you will always be in peculiar financial straits. You should invest some of your earnings in long-time investments — mines, aviation, radio or inventions.

The third HOUSE deals with travel and the Mind. It is controlled by Sagittarius and ruled by Jupiter. Because of your restless, nervous, sensitive temperament, you often long to forget everything, to travel to distant places and start all over again. You have a vivid imagination and often build air castles. You are the greatest idealist of any of the twelve Zodiacal Signs. You will travel much and will profit from such changes.

The fourth HOUSE deals with your home affairs. It is controlled by Capricorn and ruled by Saturn. While inclined to be domestic and kind to and interested in the members of your family, your home affairs are not always pleasant. You will often be accused of being haughty or indifferent, so will seek the comforts of home elsewhere. You are likely to leave home and come back to it several times. You become stifled and unhappy without occasional change of environment or scenery. You will probably establish a home of your own after middle life.

The fifth HOUSE deals with your affections and romantic experiences. It is controlled by Aquarius and ruled by Uranus. You are the most romantic of any of the twelve Zodiacal Signs. You are deeply affected by your love of music and art and beautiful scenery. You make one of the most ideal of lovers.

The sixth HOUSE deals with your health and work. It is controlled by Pisces and ruled by Neptune. You are likely to suffer from stomach disorders, sluggish liver, impurity of blood, diabetes, and a general weak constitution. By observing strict daily hygiene, these ailments may be overcome. You are thorough, capable, and neat in your work and often will be commended for your ability.

The seventh HOUSE deals with marriage. It is controlled by Aries and ruled by Mars. For Libra people, marriage must be a continual romance, and so they are often disillusioned and sad because of their inharmonious domestic life. You should use the utmost care in picking your mate, otherwise your life will be ruined. You should marry someone born in Aries, providing your individual Horoscopes blend.

The eighth HOUSE deals with length of life and Spiritual gifts. It is controlled by Taurus and ruled by Venus. This gives promise of a long, eventful life. You possess great magnetic power, therefore, are intuitive, perceptive, and psychically inclined. You should always be guided by your impressions and hunches.

The ninth HOUSE deals with journeys and religion. It is controlled by Gemini and ruled by Mercury. The greatest thrills of your life will come in your extensive travels. In your religious belief you are firm. You believe in the Golden Rule and try to live up to it. You are broadminded and tolerant about the religious viewpoint of others.

The tenth HOUSE deals with professions and ambitions. It is controlled by Cancer and ruled by the Moon. You have so many talents it will be hard for you to choose a profession or business. You are very interested in music, art, languages, mathematics, and the theatre, and dancing. You are likely to succeed in any profession that enables you to travel or contact with many people. Among the lines of endeavor you should choose are teaching, lecturing, library work, writing, decorating, chemistry, aviation, architecture, carpentry, wood turning, and similar mechanical work.

The eleventh HOUSE deals with friends and companions. It is controlled by Leo and ruled by the Sun. You are usually attracted to people who do not appreciate your refined, sensitive Nature. You prefer to be with people of intelligence and personality rather than of means or social standing. Unless you choose your friends with care, you will have some rather peculiar experiences, since you are greatly influenced by them and conditions associated with them. Those born in Aries, Gemini, Leo, Sagittarius, and Aquarius will best harmonize with you.

The twelfth HOUSE deals with your limitations and debts to destiny. It is controlled by Virgo and ruled by Mercury. Your greatest hindrances will come because you are not practical and are prone to too much daydreaming. You are also too impulsive, inclined to jump at conclusions. You are slow to anger, but once aroused are very brusque in your remarks. It is best for you to follow your own judgment rather than the suggestions of others. You will have to learn to spend less money on luxuries and invest some for future protection. If you conquer these tendencies, you should have an eventful, successful life.

SCORPIO

The first HOUSE deals with your personality. You have great executive ability, are generous, sympathetic, determined, magnetic, progressive and commanding. You are loyal to your friends, but at times are somewhat sarcastic, critical, and harbor an imaginary wrong. You are quick-witted, possess great self-control, and are endowed with Clairvoyant and other Occult powers.

The second HOUSE deals with your financial affairs. It is controlled by Sagittarius and ruled by Jupiter. During the first half of your life you will have financial difficulties and the headway you make will be by diligent application and earnest, conscientious effort. The latter half of your life promises better financial conditions. Investment in mines, shipping industries, corporations, and municipalities are best for you.

The third HOUSE deals with travel and the Mind. It is controlled by Capricorn and ruled by Saturn. This shows great love for travel and you will have occasion to take many trips which will be very advantageous and pleasant. You have a very receptive and inventive Mind, are quick of thought and action, but you are somewhat suspicious, exacting, and inclined to nag. If you strive to retain mental poise and even temper, it will bring you greater happiness in life.

The fourth HOUSE deals with your home affairs. It is controlled by Aquarius and ruled by Uranus. You are a real homemaker and will spare no effort to transform any abode into a homelife atmosphere. The men of Scorpio are usually willing to help in every way to make the home more attractive. The ladies of Scorpio are immaculate housekeepers. Your domestic life, however, is likely to be upset frequently because of interferences of relatives and friends.

The fifth HOUSE deals with your affections and romantic experiences. It is controlled by Pisces and ruled by Neptune. You are very emotional, and once you have accepted a person as your friend you will stick to him through thick and thin. While you have great persuasive power, because you are at times sarcastic and harsh, you are misunderstood and so do not always attract people to you. You are romantically inclined but are not destined to find the kind of romance of which you have always dreamed. Many ups and downs mark your experiences in matters of friendship, love, and courtship.

The sixth HOUSE deals with your health and work. It is controlled by Aries and ruled by Mars. You will need to take more than ordinary care of your health to prevent ailments. Guard particularly against headaches, stomach and liver disorders, rheumatism, poor circulation, and inflammatory complaints. In your work, you are capable and very thorough. Nothing is ever too hard for you to attempt.

The seventh HOUSE deals with marriage. It is controlled by Taurus and ruled by Venus. Here is where most Scorpio people make their mistakes. They must choose their mates with utmost care, for they are usually attracted to the type they should not marry. They should be guided by intellect rather than physical appearance. Those born in Taurus will harmonize best with you if your individual Horoscopes blend.

The eighth HOUSE deals with length of life and Spiritual gifts. It is controlled by Gemini and ruled by Mercury. A changeable but long and prosperous life is denoted. You have great Psychic magnetism, are intuitive, and usually have prophetic dreams. You have great persuasive powers and should learn to project your magnetic personality in your social as well as your business activities.

The ninth HOUSE deals with journeys and religion. It is controlled by Cancer and ruled by the Moon. You are fond of change of scenery, but do not have as many opportunities to travel as you wish. In religious beliefs you are somewhat too dogmatic and severe. You are not tactful in your statements to others who believe in creeds other than your own, which is likely to make you unpopular in religious circles.

The tenth HOUSE deals with professions and ambitions. It is controlled by Leo and ruled by the Sun. You have the determination, self-control, and tenacity to succeed in any undertaking. The lines of endeavor for which you are best suited are music, journalism, teaching, surgery, chemistry, dentistry, law, preaching, nursing, Astrology, physics, dietetics, geology, engineering, farming, or construction work. You have lofty ambitions but must work hard to reach your goals.

The eleventh HOUSE deals with friends and companions. It is controlled by Virgo and ruled by Mercury. You have difficulty in meeting people who are congenial. Usually you are respected and admired, but you seldom care for the people who are fond of you. You like those who have a sense of humor and are musically inclined. You will find your best friends among those who were born in Taurus, Cancer, Virgo, Capricorn and Pisces.

The twelfth HOUSE deals with your limitations and debts to destiny. It is controlled by Libra and ruled by Venus. You are your own worst enemy because of your tendency to domineer over others and your habit of postponing things. You do not have the ability to put yourself on a level with others or see their point of view. Unless you correct these faults, you will not enjoy the happiness and prosperity to which you are entitled.

SAGITTARIUS

The first HOUSE shows your personality. You are a very positive nature, frank, plain-spoken, honest, intelligent, progressive, industrious, magnetic, and forceful. You are a lover of freedom, are of a naturally happy disposition, generous almost to a fault, and a person of discernment and good judgment. But you are inclined to be stubborn and argumentative. You are also somewhat impatient of others who are not as active and energetic as you.

The second HOUSE deals with your finances. It is controlled by Capricorn and ruled by Saturn. You are resourceful and have the faculty of knowing how to make money in many ways. You have a strong tendency to speculate and are not always successful in these ventures. For financial gain you should invest in going enterprises, real estate, transportation lines, construction companies, or financial institutions.

The third HOUSE deals with travel and the mind. It is controlled by Aquarius and ruled by Uranus. Because of your restless Nature, you have a longing for the change which comes from travel. You will take many trips from which you will benefit greatly. You are idealistic, romantic, alert, and belong to the realm of Prophecy, as you have a very receptive Mind. You are a go-getter and endowed with forcefulness and originality of thought.

The fourth HOUSE deals with your home affairs and is controlled by Pisces and ruled by Neptune. It is likely you will leave home because you are misunderstood. You get much pleasure and comfort from a congenial home environment. You are a charming host or hostess and delight in entertaining in your home.

The fifth HOUSE deals with your affections and

romantic experiences. It is controlled by Aries and ruled by Mars. You are extremely romantic and affectionate and usually show your affection in many ways. However, your deepest feelings are seldom realized or understood, so you have many heartaches and disappointments. You do not interfere in affairs of others and never betray a confidence.

The sixth HOUSE deals with your health and work. It is controlled by Taurus and ruled by Venus. You are likely to suffer from over-exertion because of your inability to relax in your work, from poor indigestion, liver, kidney, and bowel complaints, and injuries to the limbs. By strict daily care, none of these ailments will prove serious. Because of your honesty, talents, and close application, you will be valuable to any business organization. You are unusually active and take advantage of every opportunity to advance.

The seventh HOUSE deals with marriage. It is controlled by Gemini and ruled by Mercury. Unless careful, you are likely to marry in haste and repent at leisure. You should be careful in choosing your mate, as you require good companionship to make a success of life. Someone born in Gemini will harmonize best with you, provided your individual Horoscopes blend.

The eighth HOUSE deals with length of life and Spiritual gifts. It is controlled by Cancer and ruled by the Moon. You are promised a long, eventful life. You possess unusual psychic gifts and an almost uncanny faculty of foretelling events. You are naturally so highly attuned to the Cosmos that, at times, you actually give expression to the thoughts of your friends.

The ninth HOUSE deals with journeys and religion. It is controlled by Leo and ruled by the Sun. You will have many journeys which usually will be profitable and successful. In religious beliefs you are very sincere and resent any insinuations against your views. The old-fashioned orthodoxy does not especially appeal to you. You are inclined to be philosophic in your convictions.

The tenth HOUSE deals with professions and ambitions. It is controlled by Virgo and ruled by Mercury. You can follow more than one business or occupation successfully. Your best lines of endeavor are journalism, acting, Astrology, mediumship, law, medicine, nursing, lecturing, inventing, the high arts, work along construction and mechanical lines, photography, designing, printing, or commercial traveling. You aim high and usually reach the mark at which you aim.

The eleventh HOUSE deals with friends and companions. It is controlled by Libra and ruled by Venus. You have a very genial disposition but are often misunderstood by your friends because of your impulsiveness and blunt manner of expression. Your friends are inclined to be jealous, and you often choose the wrong types. For your most intimate associates, choose those who were born in Aries, Gemini, Leo, Libra, and Aquarius.

The twelfth HOUSE deals with your limitations and debts to destiny. It is controlled by Scorpio and ruled by Mars. Your greatest hindrances will come because of your quick temper and extremely generous Nature. You are fond of making a good impression through display and finery and sometimes live beyond your means. If you will overcome these tendencies, your life will be successful and prosperous.

CAPRICORN

The first HOUSE shows your personality. This denotes you are very talented, industrious, courageous, deliberate, truthful, and forceful. But you also have a quick temper, not always under control. You are at times painfully frank and given to fault-finding. Often you say things which you later regret.

The second HOUSE deals with your financial affairs. It is controlled by Aquarius and ruled by Usanus. You show good earning power but sometimes are handicapped by lack of opportunity. You will be successful in partnerships, in dealings with large organizations, and investing in well-established concerns. Speculation and quick turn-overs are not fortunate enough for you to depend on. If you will concentrate upon long-time investments in some going establishment, you will not need to worry. Money seems to be a very important part of your life.

The third HOUSE deals with travel and the Mind. It is controlled by Pisces and ruled by Neptune. You have a very receptive Mind, have great power of concentration, are intuitive and original. When things slow up with you, you become very depressed. You are very fond of travel. Although some journeys are denoted, you will not travel as much as you would like.

The fourth HOUSE deals with your home affairs. It is controlled by Aries and ruled by Mars. You seem to be generally misunderstood in your home circle. You are rather exacting about things pertaining to your home. If you are not pleased with conditions there, it is easy for you to change to more agreeable environments. However, you are devoted to your family and will do what you can for them, whether living at home or not.

The fifth HOUSE deals with your affections and romantic experiences. It is controlled by Taurus and ruled by Venus. You will often be accused of being indifferent, haughty, and undemonstrative, while deep in your heart you do not mean to be so. Your deepest feelings and emotions are seldom expressed. One big and important romance surely is indicated in your life.

The sixth HOUSE deals with your health and work. It is controlled by Gemini and ruled by Mercury. You are liable to nervousness, trembling of the knees, poor circulation, liver complaints, eye strain, back and headaches, and indigestion. Most of these ailments are caused by worry and too close concentration upon work. You will succeed best in business with a partner or under efficient managers. You are conscientious in your work and endeavor to overcome obstacles which seem to stand in your way to better conditions.

The seventh HOUSE deals with marriage. It is controlled by Cancer and ruled by the Moon. With the proper mate, yours will be a very happy married life, but with an improper choice, marriage will be a great disappointment, as you are not a person to make allowances for another's shortcomings,

yet you expect others to make the allowances for you. Someone born in the sign of Cancer will best harmonize with you,
provided your Horoscopes blend.

The eighth HOUSE deals with length of life and
Spiritual gifts. It is controlled by Leo and ruled by the Sun.
This shows a reasonably long life with possibilities of
inheritances and gifts which may create some disturbances
for you. You have great intuitive power and often have
hunches and impressions you do not follow, much to your
regret. Learn to be guided by them and you will make fewer
mistakes.

The ninth HOUSE deals with journeys and religion. It is
controlled by Virgo and ruled by Mercury. Some traveling is
denoted, but not as much as you sometimes desire. You are
liable to have a rather odd religious belief to which you
adhere stubbornly.

The tenth HOUSE deals with professions and ambitions.
It is controlled by Libra and ruled by Venus. You are capable
of making a livelihood in many ways. Among the best lines
for you to engage in are clerking, music, the theatre, radio
work, employment in the automotive industry, law,
brokerage or insurance, agriculture, or work along
construction lines. You are shrewd, have a capacity for work
and are not easily discouraged, but you feel at times you have
to strive twice as hard as is necessary to attain your goal.

The eleventh HOUSE deals with friends and
companions. It is controlled by Scorpio and ruled by Mars.
You will have a large circle of friends but very few with
whom you are really intimate. You are loyal to those you
really care for, but are inclined to be imposed upon by many
because of your good Nature. Your most intimate
companions are those who are born in Taurus, Cancer, Virgo,
Scorpio, or Pisces.

The twelfth HOUSE deals with your limitations and
debts to destiny. It is controlled by Sagittarius and ruled by
Jupiter. Your greatest handicaps in life will be your tendency
to worry and melancholy moods. You must try to control
those weaknesses because they will stand in the way of the
success you can otherwise attain.

AQUARIUS

The first HOUSE shows your personality. You are electric, magnetic, inspirational, impressionistic, studious, affectionate, and intuitive. You have strong powers of concentration and usually attract attention in whatever circle of society you choose to move. You have deep feelings, a great love of beauty, art, music, and Nature. You have a keen appreciation of the Mystical or Occult Sciences.

The second HOUSE deals with your financial affairs. It is controlled by Pisces and ruled by Neptune. This shows that you possess great powers of accumulating wealth but are likely to be too generous and sympathetic so that others force themselves upon you and cause you to lose money. All through life you will be assisting someone financially. You are not very fortunate with speculative ventures or get-rich-quick schemes. It is better for you to invest wisely in real estate, land, and large corporations.

The third HOUSE deals with travel and the Mind. It is controlled by Aries and ruled by Mars. This gives you an observing Mind and shows you have great faculties for meditation, investigation, and constructive thought. You are sensitive, alert, ambitious, and aspire to the finer things of life. Love of travel is denoted, and all things point to several important trips.

The fourth HOUSE deals with your home affairs. It is controlled by Taurus and ruled by Venus. The men of Aquarius are great home lovers and usually exert great effort to maintain a happy home. The ladies of Aquarius are wonderful housekeepers and companions. You are always endeavoring to improve your domestic affairs and take pride in keeping your home cozy and comfortable. The background of a happy, peaceful home seems necessary to enable you to do your best in life.

The fifth HOUSE deals with your affections and romantic experiences. It is controlled by Gemini and ruled by Mercury. You appreciate deep affection more than the average person. However, your affections will likely play over a large keyboard before you find someone who will really appreciate your nature. Not until after middle life does the average Aquarian find the ideal romance. Without love, your life does not seem to amount to much; therefore, you will keep on searching until your desires are realized. With loving companionship you will rise to heights of success and prosperity; without it, you have little ambition.

The sixth HOUSE deals with your health and work. It is controlled by Cancer and ruled by the Moon. You are likely to suffer from nervousness, despondency, liver, kidney, or stomach disorders, but with proper care of your health these ailments may be prevented or overcome. Work wherein beauty is expressed is best for you. In anything you do you are very proficient and conscientious.

The seventh HOUSE deals with marriage. It is controlled by Leo and ruled by the Sun. For the happiest marriage your mate should be someone born in Leo. Most Aquarians marry more than once and have very peculiar experiences. There are exceptions, of course. To them marriage is not usually as romantic as they expected. If you do not make too great demands, your marriage will prove successful.

The eighth HOUSE deals with length of life and Spiritual gifts. It is controlled by Virgo and ruled by Mercury. This shows a fairly long and eventually successful life. Your adversities will really be blessings in disguise. You possess mediumistic gifts and could do much with mental telepathy. You will be the recipient of many gifts, and you will enjoy financial independence throughout the latter part of life. Your natural gifts and talents will give you the opportunity to be much before the public.

The ninth HOUSE deals with journeys and religion. It is controlled by Libra and ruled by Venus. This gives a great love for travel and fondness for out-of-the-way places. A considerable amount of travel is promised you, which will bring new opportunities and many benefits. In your religious views you are very sincere and broadminded. You are inclined to be more philosophical than orthodox.

The tenth HOUSE deals with professions and ambitions. It is controlled by Scorpio and ruled by Mars. This gives you great adaptability and high ideals. The following lines of occupation are best suited to you: teaching, journalism, theatre managing, acting, floristry, interior decorating, illustrating, nursing, medicine, work of mechanical nature, Astrology, and all of the Occult sciences. You should engage in work with an intellectual and refined atmosphere.

The eleventh HOUSE deals with friends and companions. It is controlled by Sagittarius and ruled by Jupiter. You are attracted to people of intelligence. While you are admired by many, you become intimate with but a few. You choose your friends carefully, but once you have made your choice, you will fight for them if necessary, whether they be right or wrong. Your best associates will be found in Aries, Gemini, Leo, Libra, and Sagittarius.

The twelfth HOUSE deals with your limitations and debts to destiny and is controlled by Capricorn and ruled by Saturn. Your greatest handicap in early life will be your inability to rise to your idea of success as rapidly as you would like. In later life your greatest concern will be lack of time to develop your Spiritual understanding. The first part of your life will be given over to the gaining of material things, the latter half to acquiring Spiritual perfection. You will have an unusual but a very thrilling life.

PISCES

The first HOUSE shows your personality. This shows that you have a dual personality and, at times, appear to be two different individuals. You usually have to fight against a tendency to become pessimistic. You are a good conversationalist, are sympathetic and original, possess much foresight and keen judgment. You are thoughtful, truthful, kind hearted, and loyal to your friends.

The second HOUSE deals with your financial affairs. It is controlled by Aries and ruled by Mars. You will have many ups and downs in money matters. At times you will earn money easily; at other times it will be difficult. This does not show very favorably for speculation, and it is well for you to engage in more legitimate ventures, such as the mercantile business and real estate. Subordinate positions do not bring you satisfactory returns and you should be in business for yourself, preferably with a harmonious partner born in a favorable Astrological sign.

The third HOUSE deals with travel and the Mind. It is controlled by Taurus and ruled by Venus. This gives you a romantic Nature and a desire for extensive travel. The men of Pisces will make many agreeable associations among the opposite sex in their travels. The ladies of Pisces will have better success traveling with their own sex. This shows that you are idealistic and fond of the beauties of nature.

The fourth HOUSE deals with your home affairs. It is controlled by Gemini and ruled by Mercury. You are a home lover and take great pride in your home although you do not always have the harmony you desire. Not until about middle life will your domestic affairs come up to your expectations. The men of Pisces have great love for their mothers; the ladies of Pisces adore their fathers.

The fifth HOUSE deals with your affections and romantic experiences. It is controlled by Cancer and ruled by the Moon. Your love affairs will be more successful when the Moon is in watery signs, and in the Full, or Last Quarter. At times you become somewhat jealous and suspicious of a loved one. You are affectionate and very demonstrative to anyone who is loyal to you. It is usually the other person who will do the "cheating," if there is any, for you were not born to be a cheater in love. You like to select one person and shower your affections upon that one only.

The sixth HOUSE deals with your health and work. It is controlled by Leo and ruled by the Sun. If you watch out for your health you need not worry about serious illness. Take care particularly of your chest and the lower limbs, especially the feet. In your work you are diligent and thorough, but you should avoid worry. Outdoor work is best for you.

The seventh HOUSE deals with marriage. It is controlled by Virgo and ruled by Mercury. For the happiest marriage your mate should be someone born in Virgo. Without the proper companion, many ups and downs will beset your married life. If you make the proper choice, you will be a great help to your mate and will go out of your way to make marriage a success.

The eighth HOUSE deals with length of life and Spiritual gifts. It is controlled by Libra and ruled by Venus. If you take good care of your health you are promised a long, eventful life. You possess much Psychic ability and often have hunches you should follow. You are inclined to be very philosophic, have remarkable intuitive faculties which give you power of persuasion and gifts of magnetic healing.

The ninth HOUSE deals with journeys and religion. It is controlled by Scorpio and ruled by Mars. This shows a great yearning for travel. You will likely have successful trips by land, sea, and air throughout your lifetime. You are very orthodox in your religious views and should overcome a tendency to criticize creeds other than your own.

The tenth HOUSE deals with professions and ambitions. It is controlled by Sagittarius and ruled by Jupiter. You should be successful in agricultural pursuits, in merchandising, contracting, teaching, managing large enterprises, acting, writing, nursing, floristry, chiropody, photography, the occult sciences, and in governmental work. You should engage in some line of endeavor where your originality may be advantageously used.

The eleventh HOUSE deals with friends and companions. It is controlled by Capricorn and ruled by Saturn. Because of your generosity and friendliness, you will always have a large circle of admirers among both sexes. You are rather hard to understand because of your dual personality; therefore, choose your friends with care. Generally speaking, your most harmonious associates will be found in Taurus, Cancer, Virgo, Scorpio, and Capricorn.

The twelfth HOUSE deals with your limitations and debts to destiny. It is controlled by Aquarius and ruled by Uranus. If you will develop the positive side of your personality you will succeed, for your greatest hindrances come from your lack of aggressiveness, courage and optimism. Be firmly resolved to let nothing stop you; you will reach the heights of your ambition and enjoy happiness and security.

From the dawn of antiquity, Astrology has played its part in the affairs of mankind, and its popularity persists today. The term means "knowledge of the stars" and as such, Astrology not only served in forecasting coming events, it also included as a by-product the subject now called astronomy. Small wonder that people are impelled by the Signs of the Heavens when the courses of the stars and planets may be calculated to exactitude!

New civilizations inherited Astrology from the old and with it, the scope of the Ancient science was extended. Birthstones were associated with the constellations forming the signs of the Zodiac. Metals were identified with planets, gold with the Sun, silver with the Moon, mercury, because of its elusive quality, with its namesake, Mercury. Everything mundane may be interpreted Astrologically.

All sciences owe much to Astrology. When they branched out on their own, Astrology was not discredited; it merely returned to its original purpose, that of determining the shape of things to come. It is a fact that when Tycho Brahe, the great astronomer, sighted the comet of 1577 and classed it for what it was, he did not even guess at the year when it would next appear. Instead, he used the comet as the basis of an Astrological calculation from which he predicted a prince born in Finland would become a great Swedish king and would invade Germany, meeting his death in the year 1632. That Astrological forecast was fulfilled by King Gustavus Adolphus of Sweden. But astronomers haven't yet found out if Tycho's comet will ever come back.

People do want to know what their birth Signs and planetary influences may mean to them. Often, they would like to check those findings for themselves. That can be done through a study of the pages of these three chapters. There the Science of the Stars is carefully explained.

6
The Science
of Numerology

There are many systems of character analyses and methods of making predictions but none, perhaps, as interesting as Numerology since anyone may work it out. No long hours of tedious study are required since there are only a few simple rules to follow.

The Egyptians, the Greeks, the Romans, and the Arabians had systems of arriving at number vibrations, all of which are remarkably accurate. The teachings of the adepts in Numerology have come down to us from the remotest Antiquity.

All letters have numerical equations; therefore, all combinations of letters in names respond to a certain numerical value. When a name is given to a person, city, book, or anything, it immediately lets loose a certain Occult force expressed in its numbers. Nature in its most primitive form responds to numbers. Note the geometric formation of snowflakes, of growing plant cells, the mathematical precision of the sunrise, the movements of the heavenly bodies, and the procession of the seasons. These and other geometric or mathematical formulas respond to various number values. In everyday life we answer to the numbers of our names, our birth, and our locations by our reactions.

Some names appeal to us immediately, others we pass by unnoticed. It is our reaction to the numerical magnetism which causes us either to ignore or notice them. The Universe is operated with exact mathematical precision calculated to an ultimate fraction of a second.

Every expression of rhythm responds to a numerical measure of time. When you listen to music which thrills you, you are unconsciously harmonizing with certain number influences in the notes of the music. When you dislike certain types of music, it is because the numerical value of such music is not in sympathy with your own name or birth number. Every day of life brings some good or adverse reaction to the magnetic influence of the numbers around you. They are in everything you see, hear, or feel. It is impossible to escape them! The sooner you learn the value of these numbers the better you will be able to harmonize with the life and people around you.

On the following pages the author gives a very simple system of number calculations so you may become familiar with the influences in your daily life and get the best out of your newly acquired knowledge. This is the system taught by the Hebraic Kabbala, which is much less complicated than the other systems.

For instance: the angel who revealed to Adam the Mysteries (Hebr.: Raz) is Raziel; the angel of evil (Hebr.: Sam — poison) is Samael, and the angel of the Moon (Hebr.: Yerah) is Yarhiel.

The simple rules, and also more complicated ones, were formulated in the Talmudic period and elaborated during Middle Ages.

The principal methods of the symbolic Kabbalah which discovers hidden meaning in letter and words of the Hebraic Bible by forming new words, anagrams and numbers, for magical use are now revealed.

Gematria was called a process of discovering relations between words through calculation of their numerical values. Words with the same numerical value may replace one another, or they may by their number indicate a new meaning. In the Hebrew language, as in the Greek, numbers are marked with letters. The numerical value of Jehovah (Yehova), is 10, 5, 6, 5, totalling 26. These numbers contained in the name of God were interpreted mystically, and by similar calculations the Kabbalists discovered the most mighty name of God must contain seventy-two letters. The knowledge of this name was the greatest power man could assume.

As an example of Biblical interpretation by Gematria, the passage Genesis 14:14 may be adduced where Abraham rescues the captive Lot with the help of his three hundred and eighteen slaves. Did Abraham really need so many men, inasmuch as God was on his side? To this Gematria answers the sum of the name of Abraham's majordomus, Eliezer, of Damascus is three hundred and eighteen and Abraham defeated the four kings and rescued Lot with the help of one man. Gematria permitted the magician to melt together words of the same numerical value, thus forming new words which were endowed with power.

The *Notarikon's* method was to consider the Hebrew words as consisting of abbreviations, each letter of a word being the initial of another word. The first and the last letters of words were detached and arrayed in new words. Famous talismans and magical words were invented with the help of Notarikon. The word Agla, so often occurring in Magic, is shaped from the first letters of the benediction, Atha Gibor Leolam Adonai (Thou art mighty for ever, O Lord). Genesis starts with the word Bereshit, "at the beginning." According to Notarikon, this word can be decomposed into the initial letters of the sentence: "He created the firmament, the earth, the heavens, the sea and the abyss."

Temurah substitutes, transposes, and permutes letters of words. Any word may yield a hidden meaning by its anagram. In writing the twenty-two letters of the Hebrew alphabet in a special order and in two lines, the letters above and below placed in relationship may substitute for each other. Arranged in two rows of eleven letters, A is related to L, B to T, G to SH, etc. The result is an alphabet which reads AL BT GSH DR HK WTZ ZP CHI TS YN KM. This secret alphabet is called Albath, from the first two combinations.

Based on similar arrangements, there exist numerous different alphabetical combinations which are called Abgath, Agdath, Adbag, and Abbad, according to their first two combinations. Using such alphabets the Kabbalists would discover hidden meanings everywhere in the Holy Kabbalah and the one word would produce another.

By the power of words and numbers, the Kabbalists summoned Spirits, extinguished fires, and banished diseases. But a few Gentiles used their knowledge for another purpose. They sought to convert the Jewish scholars to Christianity. In the *Zohar* we learn the highest manifestation of the Supreme, Adam Kadmon, is shaped like Man, as the form of Man includes all that is in Heaven and on Earth. For this reason, God has chosen Man's form as His own. God assuming the form of Man could be no one else but Christ. Moreover, we read in *Zohar* that, having created this Celestial Man, God used him as a chariot for His descent.

The Kabbala System of Numerology consists of twenty-two major number vibrations, corresponding to the twenty-two letters in the Hebrew alphabet. We have outlined the various meanings of the digit numbers from one to nine in the appendix and elsewhere in Book I.

The following is the numerical vibrations of the double numbers from 10 to 22 according to the Kabbala.

> Number 10: This number denotes a change in conditions. This number rules the Spiritual and scientific aspects of life. Being under the ruler of the planet Uranus, it signifies sudden and unexpected changes for better or worse.
>
> Number 11: This is considered an emotional number which rules the Psychic Mind. The planet Neptune rules this number and gives the subject strong magnetic influences over others.

Number 12: This number has a strong influence on the deeper human emotions. It is the number of Self sacrifice. It is in harmoney with the sign of Pisces and the twelfth House of the Zodiac. It is the number that rules secret matters and hidden enemies. It also rules hospitals, prisons, and large government institutions.

Number 13: This number corresponds to the Sign of Aries. It rules the pioneer, the military, inventors, and persons with a great deal of daring and courage. It also signifies the beginning of a new cycle.

Number 14: This number corresponds to the Sign of Taurus. It is a materialistic number having great powers of determination which sometimes borders on downright stubbornness. It influences beauty, art, and all gemenine luxuries. It is a strong influence where financial matters are concerned.

Number 15: It is a strong factor where Mental activities are concerned. It helps bring matters down to Earth when thoughts and deeds get out of hand. Ruled by the planet Saturn, it is a stern task maker. It giveth and taketh away.

Number 16: This number governs the passions and physical force for better or worse. It can be aggressive and constructive on the one hand and rash and impulsive and brutal on the other. Being ruled by the planet Mars, it has great force and energy. This vibration produces inventors and explorers.

Number 17: This is the number of faith, hope, and charity. It represents the intellectual force and harmonizes with the Sign of Gemini. Intuition and reason are the major factors for success. When consistency of purpose is learned, it can express the principles of illuminated thinking and action.

Number 18: This number is associated with the Sign of Cancer. It is considered to be a difficult, secretive vibration. It signifies danger through Water, Fire, and explosions. It is more materialistic than Spiritual and is filled with intrigue and oft times deception. Quarrels involving the family with the possibility of deception are common.

Number 19: This is considered a fortunate number. It harmonizes with the Sign of Leo and brings forth good humor and a magnanimous attitude toward Life. It promises success, esteem, and recognition. It is very favorable to the interests of children and is a favorable number for speculation and entertainment.

Number 20: This number is ruled by the Moon, which makes it very changeable. It rules Fate and Spiritual effort upon which the native's fortune depends. A great personal effort is necessary at all times in order to attain success. The fortunes are variable, and there are many ups and downs during the course of a lifetime.

Number 21: This is a number of authority and power. It leads to advancement and contentment. Recognition for work well done with financial rewards for serious effort is shown by this number. The Sun rules this number, which usually brings good fortune with numerous opportunities for financial as well as Spiritual success.

Number 22: This is a weak and unfortunate number. It rules the earth and all of its material failures. It can bring about separations from friends and loved ones. Folly is one of the number's attributes. Vanity and conciet overcome all Spiritual values, usually bringing dissolution and disappointment. Failure, folly, or mistakes can only be overcome after the realization of ones shortcomings.

HOW TO FIND FORTUNATE NUMBERS

These methods, based on the Science of NUMEROLOGY, are different for every person. The author has spent many years studying the Occult meaning of numbers and while we do not guarantee results, many people use them with great success.

Rules:

1. Learn how to tell Magic time! Numbers 1-12 represent a.m. just like a watch, but numbers 13-24 represent the time after noon. For example: a.m. — 1 - 2 - 3 - 4 - 5 - 6 - 7 - 8 - 9 - 10 - 11 - 12 — p.m. — 13 - 14 - 15 - 16 - 17 - 18 - 19 - 20 - 21 - 22 - 23 - 24.

2. Note the day of the week! Monday is 1; Tuesday is 2; Wednesday is 3; Thursday is 4; Friday is 5; Saturday is 6; and Sunday is 7.

3. Count the number of letters in your name. Example: Jack Brown has four letters in his first name and five in his second name. 4-plus 5 equals 9. This number 9 is always lucky for Jack Brown.

4. A lucky number is found by combining the values of the day and month in which you were born. For example: If you were born on June 25th (june is the 6th month), combine 6 and 25 — thus 625 or 67. Add these figures: 6 plus 2 plus 5 equals 13. Add again, 1 plus 3 equals 4. This gives four magic numbers, all with the same strength: 625, 67, 13, 4. Use the one which suits you best. Jan. equals 1, Feb. 2, March 3, April 4, May 5, June 6, July 7, Aug. 8, Sept. 9, Oct. 10, Nov. 11 (or 2), Dec. 12 (or 3).

METHODS FOR USING YOUR FORTUNATE NUMBERS

1. THE MAGIC HOUR: Use the number of the day of the week and the number of the hour at which you play or bet. For example: Suppose it is 4 p.m. on Friday. 4 p.m. is 16 o'clock: Friday is 5. Combine these to make 165 or 75. Then add 1 plus 6 plus 5 equals 12. Add again 1 plus 2 equals 3. This gives four magic numbers: 165, 75, 12, 3 with the same strength. Use the one which suits you best.

2. STRIKE THE KEYNOTE: Use the number of letters in your name and the hour of play. Suppose Jack Brown (9) wants a

Lucky Number at 8 p.m. Combine 9 and 20 to make 920. Add these 9 plus 2 plus 0 equals 11. Add again 1 plus 1 equals 2. This gives four magic numbers: 920, 29, 11, 2. Use the one which suits you best.

3.   YOUR PINNACLE OF SUCCESS: Use the number of the day on which you were born and the number of the month. Suppose you were born on Aug. 24th. Combine 24 and 8. This gives 248 or 68. Add 2 plus 4 plus 8 equals 14. Add again 1 plus 4 equals 5. This gives you four Lucky Numbers of the same magic power: 248, 68, 14, 5.

4.   LADY LUCK METHOD: Count the number of letters in your sweetheart's name and combine with the number of letters in your name. For example, Maybelle Jones (13 letters) and Jack Brown (9 letters) makes 139 or 40. Add these: 1 plus 3 plus 9 equals 13. Add again, 1 plus 3 equals 4. This gives you four lady luck numbers; 139, 49, 13, 4. Use the one which suits you best.

If you want more than one Lucky Number in any day, combine your Lady Luck number with the hour. For example: at 20 o'clock (8 P.M.), combine Maybelle Jones (13) with Jack Brown (9): 20, 139. Add these to suit your convenience. Always note the hour of the day. The time figure changes only when the hour changes. Adding, transposing, or combining a magic number may be used or not used as you wish.

THE ALPHABET

In any system of Numerology, the letters of the alphabet respond to the 9 digits or single numbers. Numbers of two figures are not retained except in the cases of 11 and 22, the reason for this which will be explained later. The letters of the alphabet must be reduced to single numbers, so consequently more than one letter responds to the same number as shown below:

1	2	3	4	5	6	7	8	9
A	B	C	D	E	F	G	H	I
J	K	L	M	N	O	P	Q	R
S	T	U	V	W	X	Y	Z	

You will notice the letters A, J, and S have the same numerical value as the number 1, while B, K, and T have the value of 2, and so on. Whatever number a letter is under, this is its numerical power or number vibration on the Astral Plane.

We are now ready to begin transferring names into magic numbers. We will choose a simple name as the first example. Preferably the first name and last name of a person should be written vertically, as it is easier to add than if written horizontally. We choose the name of Mary Smith for our example:

M 4	S 1
A 1	M 4
R 9	I 9
Y 7	T 2
	H 8
_____	_____
21 or 2 + 1 = 3	24 or 2 + 4 = 6

The name Mary responds to 21 and the name Smith responds to 24. To secure the full name vibration, it is necessary to add 21 plus 24, which equals 45. This is a double number, so we must add 4 plus 5 to get 9. This young lady responds to the name number of 9. You may now refer to the indications of the numbers and find out what the number 9 denotes about her.

We will now suppose Mary Smith's birthdate is June 6, 1947. To transfer this into a numerical value, we would write it thus: 6-6-1947, because June is the sixth month. Now add these numbers together: 6 plus 6 plus 1 plus 9 plus 4 plus 7 equals 27. This total is a double number so we add 2 plus 7 which equals 9. We find Mary Smith's birthdate is 9, the same as her name number. Any number derived from the birthdate is called the Birth Path.

Now we wish to find her Destiny Number. We will add the Name number and the Birth number, thus: 9 plus 9 equals 18. This is a double number, so we have to add 1 plus 8, which equals 9. Mary Smith's Destiny Number is also 9. Refer to 9 in the Destiny Column and read her indication.

Certain numbers have an affinity for each other while others clash seriously. Even numbers harmonize with each other; even numbers and odd numbers harmonize with other odd numbers. But even numbers and odd numbers seldom harmonize except in the cases of 11 and 22. These two numbers are the exception and will harmonize with almost any other number. Eleven is a higher octave of 2, because 1 and 1 equals 2, while 22 is a higher octave of 4, as 2 plus 2 equals 4. However, these two numbers are seldom reduced to a digit because of their very strong individual power. Therefore, when you have arrived at an 11 or 22, you need not reduce it further but look for the indications for those two numbers.

We now propose to find out if Mary Smith with a Destiny Number of 9 would be successful as a typist. Secure the number vibration of the word typist. We find it gives us 2 plus 7 plus 7 plus 9 plus 1 plus 2 which equals 28. This is a double number, so it must be added: 2 plus 8 equals 10. This also is a double number; therefore, 1 plus 0 equals 1. Since the word responds to 1, which is an odd number the same as 9, Mary Smith would be a successful typist.

In the same way we can discover if she would be successful in Chicago, New York, Los Angeles, or any other place by working out the numerical values of such places. We can also find out if a certain street and number is favorable or not, if she should marry her love or not, if travel by land, water, or air is best for her, etc. Many other things will suggest themselves to you that you can work out for yourself or for your friends.

In figuring the numerical values of names, use the one by which the person is known. The name James might have been given a boy at birth, but he always has been called Jim, which is a contraction of James. In this case, use the name Jim. But if you find the name James produces better influences, he should immediately change his name to James and sign it that way at all times. He should insist his friends call him James instead of Jim. The name a person has been called all his life is the name vibration one responds to best. Its constant repetition has stamped upon his destiny the influence of that name, even though it be a nickname.

Therefore, when numberizing a name, the one by which the person is known is the one to be selected. By changing it by adding letters of spelling it differently, a new vibration is produced which will bring different results and a different personality if continued for a long enough time. Many famous people change the spelling of their name when they understand Numerology so as to create better number harmony.

It is sometimes best when a woman marries to retain her given name in addition to her new surname. Sometimes it is best to drop the given name and use her husband's full name, placing a Mrs. before it. By working out the different combinations according to Numerology, the best combination may be found quickly and easily. Once a person decides to change his name, the old one must be forgotten entirely and never again used.

VARIOUS OPERATIONS WITH NUMEROLOGY

There are various ways in which Numerology may be employed to amuse or benefit by those who enjoy working out their numbers. The ideas presented here are just a few suggestions; others will come to mind as you work with the Science of Numbers.

Take a deck of ordinary playing cards and remove the 10 spots. Previous to this you will have worked out your Destiny Number as directed. We will take the Destiny Number of Mary Smith, which was 9. After removing the 10 spots and placing them aside, Mary Smith should shuffle the cards, give them one cut, then shuffle and cut them again. She should go through this operation of shuffling and cutting nine times. She should then deal off nine cards from the top of the pack and put them to one side.

The very next card should be turned up and placed face up on the table. If the card should be a 5, her fortunate number would be 5. If she is seeking a number with two figures, she should deal off nine more cards, place them aside and use the very next card, putting it face up alongside the first one.

If she desires a number with three figures, she will deal off nine more cards and place the next one alongside the other two. Now suppose she has laid down the 5 of diamonds, the 2 of clubs, and the 8 of spades. Her fortunate number if 528. Face cards are to be considered Zero or a cipher. Therefore, if the last card had been the King of Spades instead of the 8, the number would have been 520.

Always shuffle and cut the cards as many times as your Destiny Number. If you have a Destiny Number of 4, you should shuffle and cut four times and deal off four cards from the top. Your Destiny Number is the *Index* to use. This process should not be repeated for the same person more than once in twenty-four hours. To repeat it destroys the vibration of the first Fortunate number and weakens the second one found.

Note: The reason the 10 spots were removed is because 10 is a double number, and in Numerology you are concerned with single numbers only.

We wish to know if 1968 is a fortunate year for Mary

Smith. Add 1968 thus: 1 plus 9 plus 6 plus 8 equals 24. Now add 2 and 4 which equals 6. This result is an even number, so it does not harmonize with Mary Smith's Destiny Number of 9; consequently, 1968 is not as fortunate for her as other years. The digit of the year must be the same or must be in harmony with your Destiny Number to be a Fortunate Year for you. There are more specific directions later in this chapter about Fortunate years.

Any day which adds up to your Destiny Number is the best day for you. Mary Smith's lucky days in any month are 9th, 18th, and 27th. Her fairly good days are those which add to other odd numbers. The days which are neutral or slightly adverse are those which add up to even numbers. Work this out with your own Destiny Number and check off your good and adverse days on your calendar to guide you.

To find out your best hours of any day, find the time of Sunrise from your local daily paper. For example, suppose the Sun rises at 6:15 a.m. The first hour after sunrise will be from 6:15 a.m. to 7:15 a.m., Mary Smith's best hours are the 9th hour after Sunrise and any other hour which adds up to 9, which would be the 18th hour after Sunrise. These hours will vary a few minutes each day as the Sun varies in rising time. Always use the hours after Sunrise which equal your Destiny Number.

For best results in partnerships or friendships, their Destiny Number should be the same as yours. Those who have Destiny Numbers not similar to but harmonious with yours will make fairly good friends, companions, and partners. Those who have Destiny Numbers which clash with yours will not make satisfactory associates, and your relations with them will not be permanent or congenial.

Secure the Monthly Number of any month and year (By Monthly Number is meant the numerical figure for any month reduced to a single digit). Add it and your Destiny number together, which is your Monthly Number for that month. Then refer to the Gallery of Numbers for the general indications for the month. As an example we will see what the indications for Mary Smith are for the month of June 1968:

June 6

1968 added together 24

Destiny Number of Mary Smith 9
                                          _____
                              Total   39

3 plus 9 equals 12, 1 plus 2 equals 3, which is her Monthly Number for June 1968. To find Mary Smith's indications for June 1968, refer to Gallery of Monthly Numbers under 3.

Secure your own Monthly Number in the same way, using your Destiny Number instead of Mary Smith's. It will frequently happen that several months will respond to the same Monthly Number, but they will change from year to year.

GALLERY OF NAME NUMBERS

1. The number of Creation, of Beginning, of First Impulses, or the source of Energy. Persons whose name vibrates to this number are trail blazers. Most of all their lives they have been leaders and thinkers along pioneer lines, and they are usually popular in whatever sphere of society they choose to move. They are constructive in thought and like to be doing something new and out of the ordinary. They do not follow in the path of others and generally have the courage of their convictions. There is a lower level to this number, also. Those who respond to this lower plane are eccentric, egotistical, haughty, dominating, and selfconscious. If your name responds to this number, make every effort to overcome weak tendencies which might show up in your character.

2. The number of Beauty, Culture, Truth, Perception, and Consciousness. It is a decided feminine number and causes the person to respect and appreciate the refined and intellectual things in life. It is the number of cooperation,

attraction, affection, emotion, and enthusiasm. Those whose name responds to this number are warm friends, congenial companions, interesting entertainers, and good judges of human nature. The lower plane of this number causes the person to be hasty, sensitive, and inclined to be too particular. If your name responds to this number, strive to overcome any undignified tendencies that might show up in your character.

3. The number of Enlightenment, Thoroughness, and Refinement. This number causes a person to be tender, affectionate, sympathetic. Very cautious about details, prone to self-sacrifice for some idealistic principle and often willing to do without things to assist friends. It is the number of the Holy Trinity and causes the person to be highly religious and impressionable, intuitive and magnetic.

4. The number of Realization, Security, Protection, Stability, and Ambition. Those whose name responds to this vibration are true friends and good company. They possess brilliant and inventive minds and are inclined to reach the goal of their ambitions regardless of obstacles. They usually live a life of activity and variety and have many interesting experiences from which they learn much of the usefulness of life.

5. The number of Uncertainty, Hesitancy, Doubt, and Discouragement. Those whose name responds to this number will often become confused, restless, irritable, impatient, and moody. They find it hard to form congenial companionships and frequently disagree with the opinions of others. They sometimes feel that life has been unkind to them — as though they were living an existence against which their Nature rebels. If this is your name number and you feel you do not want to fight against this influence any longer, it might be a good idea to change your name slightly so it will respond to some other number. However, you can overcome it by exerting your will power if you keep on fighting.

6. The number of Dual Personality, Indecision, Temptation, and Excess. Those whose name responds to this number have a peculiar Nature. They are not always understood and very often are the cause of their own failures. If they will learn to gain from their experiences, they will make this a fortunate number, but drifting through life will never get them

anywhere. They like to follow the lines of least resistance and should overcome a tendency to indiscreet actions. Determination will help them conquer the uncertainties of this number.

7. The number of Spirituality, Mysticism, Wisdom, and Success. Those whose name responds to this number are receptive, studious, creative and intellectual. They possess a deep understanding and desire the finer things of life. If there are no other conflicting influences in their numbers, they make warm friends, valuable employees and ideal companions or partners. They have a magnetic personality, are very unselfish and possess a rare outlook on life.

8. The number of Justice, Evolution, Strength, Inspiration and Genius. Those whose name responds to this number have a strong personality. They are very magnetic, self-willed, independent, progressive, intuitive, and honest, candid, and straightforward in dealings. The number 8 vibration is an extremely strong one, difficult to overcome. It causes a person to be very active, seldom contented for a great length of time and eager for changes of events and scenery.

9. The number of Dominance, Efficiency, Psychic, Consciousness, Humanitarianism, and Renewed Energy. Those whose name responds to this number are clever, active, philosophical, and intuitive. They belong to the realm of prophets and possess an unusual telepathic Mind. They have a fertile imagination, high ideals, and are endowed with poetic or artistic abilities. They are usually very dignified and pleasant but odd and whimsical. They are refined, gentle, sympathetic and even-tempered. They make friends easily and are quick to solve the problems of others.

11. The number of Power, Courage, Success, Adventure, Impulse, and Energy. Those whose name responds to this number are merely an octave higher than those who respond to 2. They are deep thinkers and fond of exciting adventures. At times they are vague in their statements. Their mind grasps the general outcome of things, but they usually skip details. The number has such a powerful influence they often find themselves confused by many contradictions, likes, and dislikes. Clear thinking, determination, and concentration are qualities necessary to develop in order to control the restlessness this number creates.

22. The number of Rashness, Errors, Haste, Changeability. Those

whose name responds to this number should overcome a tendency to be critical, restless, and reckless. They often do not understand their own peculiarities. They say and do things on the spur of the moment and then wonder why they did it. They usually do not look before they leap. They are inclined to go to extremes, even against their own better judgment. They have a hard struggle with themselves, and it might be a good idea to change the name so as to respond to a better number vibration.

BIRTH PATH NUMBERS

(Secured from the Year, Month and Date of Birth)

1. If this is your Birth Path, you will have many strange experiences. You will go through life making your own conditions and carrying out your own ideas. You will lead a constructive life!

2. If this is your Birth Path, you will seem to go around in circles and have repetitions of certain experiences at regular intervals. If you cultivate self-control, you will have an interesting, useful life.

3. If this is your Birth Path, you will enjoy many of the better things of life. You will travel much and gain from the experiences of others. Yours will be a fortunate, contented life.

4. If this is your Birth Path, you will have many loyal friends. You will gain some prominence in the business or professional world. Yours will be a successful, pleasant life.

5. If this is your Birth Path, you will have many strange experiences, at times difficult to overcome; yet with your strong personality, you usually win out. Yours will be a long, contented life.

6. If this is your Birth Path, you are apt to be too careless of your actions and general health and welfare. Success will be attained only through firmness of purpose and stability. Yours is a changeable but useful life.

7. If this is your Birth Path, you will undertake and usually accomplish big things. New and interesting experiences will present themselves. You will be the master of your own destiny. Yours will be an unusually successful life.

8. If this is your Birth Path, you will lead an active life, but not necessarily a peaceful one. New ambitions will always spur

you onward. Frequent outbursts of temper alter your course
of life. Yours will be an adventurous career.

9. If this is your Birth Path, you will travel extensively, engage
in unusual affairs and odd professions. Literature, art, music,
and the stage will attract you. Yours will be an interesting
life.

11. If this is your Birth Path, you will engage in many risky
adventures. You will overcome obstacles by sheer force of
will power. You are captain of your Soul and master of your
destiny. Yours will be a progressive life.

12. If this is your Birth Path, you will create many of your own
difficulties. Losses may come through bad judgment or
unreliable associates. Learn to think constructively and act
with discretion. Cultivate self-control and you will succeed.

DESTINY NUMBERS

(Secured by Adding Name Number and Birth Path Number)

1. If this is your Destiny Number, you will achieve great success
through your constructive efforts. Some help will be given
you, but in the main you will be self-made.

2. If this is your Destiny Number, you will have many ups and
downs in life, but through the aid of friends and relatives you
eventually will be successful. You will have wealth if you
utilize all your faculties.

3. If this is your Destiny Number, you will experience many
successful ventures. The better things of life will assist you to
the goal of your ambitions.

4. If this is your Destiny Number, you will have a life of
usefulness, financial success, and honor. Choose your
profession carefully and forge ahead. Nothing can stop you if
you persist! You will likely acquire much property.

5. If this is your Destiny Number, you will stand in your own
way many times. Guard against accidents and do not trust
strangers. Your life is one of varied experiences, some
pleasant, others most discouraging.

6. If this is your Destiny Number, do not permit yourself to
drift. Control your emotions and make the best of your
opportunities. You are apt to overlook them! Success will
come to you if you are alert and industrious.

7. If this is your Destiny Number, you may expect to attain
prominence in life. Your light will shine far and you will

travel extensively. Friends will be attracted to you.

8.   If this is your Destiny Number, you will encounter financial difficulties often, but usually will overcome them with experience and shrewdness. Your life will be very active.

9.   If this is your Destiny Number, you will live a very useful, contented life. You possess many talents, are admired by friends, and enjoy an excellent reputation.

11. If this is your Destiny Number, you will lead a very active life, will succeed in big undertakings, and be prominent in your sphere of life. You will be master of your own destiny and creator of your fortune.

22. If this is your Destiny Number, the lower qualities of your Nature may control your life unless you strive to change them. Avoid schemes and questionable enterprises. Be deliberate in all projects. Overcome moods.

MONTHLY NUMBERS

(These are secured by adding the Destiny Number to Number of Month and Year of birth.)

1.   Any month which responds to this number is a month of new happenings. It is a good month to make and start things, to take trips, ask favors, start new business ventures and write letters. Anything you can manage to carry on without aid from others should succeed this month. It is a good time to buy, advertise, hire new help, look for new work, and make changes.

2.   Any month which responds to this number is a month of varied experiences, unexpected turns in events. If unmarried, there is possible wedlock; slight restlessness and danger through carelessness can occur. This month holds many arguments and broken friendships unless you make an effort to control things. Think much, but say little. Guard your health and avoid conflicts.

3.   Any month which responds to this number is ideal for carrying out plans, making changes, taking trips, handling finances, dealing with business and professional people. Important beneficial changes are apt to occur in your domestic or personal life. Make the most of your present opportunities.

4.   Any month which responds to this number is a good month to try to complete unfinished tasks, to make an effort to

realize your ambitions, secure the good will of others, deal in lands, property, and legal affairs. If you exercise a reasonable amount of determination and good judgment, you should succeed at this time. You should be able to now build a foundation for future activities.

5.   Any month which responds to this number is a month in which you should use caution in all you undertake. Guard against fires, accidents, losses, slander, scandal, extravagance, and outbursts of temper. Guard your health and take no risks or chances on anything. Distressing bits of news may come to you this month but refuse to be alarmed. Avoid litigation, general unrest, and loss of friends.

6.   Any month which responds to this number is a month in which much depends upon your own initiative. You can make it either a profitable or unprofitable month. You may experience some trouble in your domestic affairs and minor delays in carrying out your plans, but if you retain poise you will be able to straighten out everything satisfactorily. Guard your health and control your temper.

7.   Any month which responds to this number is a month of good results. Follow your hunches and impressions. A good time to read, study, or investigate; also favorable for visiting, planning, traveling, starting new enterprises, seeking new work, buying, selling, and investing. New friends and pleasant experiences should enrich your life now.

8.   Any month which responds to this number is a month of radical changes, new ambitions, and much progress. During this month's influence, you will be enthusiastic and courageous. Deal with prominent people, develop new propositions, advertise, travel, attend to important financial matters, and push all things of material importance. Avoid undue haste and too much force. Guard against accidents, fires, and minor injuries.

9.   Any month which responds to this number is a very important month. You will have opportunities to complete tasks which have been pending for a long time. Things you start now will be easier to accomplish. You will have renewed hopes and ambitions and new ideas should be carried out carefully. Develop your personality and energy.

11.   Any month which responds to this number is a month of intense activity. You will be busy, yet seem to lack time to finish your plans. However, the headway you gain will be

permanent. You will discover you have a stronger will power than you realized and you can conquer obstacles more easily at this time. It is a month of rise to power, new adventures, and a realization of ambitions, partial or complete.

22.   Any month which responds to this number is a month in which to be careful. You are apt to be influenced by others to your detriment. Avoid extravagance, rashness, temptations, losses, and controversy over legal matters. Control your emotions and temper. Guard your health and take no risks or chances. You are likely to be impulsive and hasty.

Most all technical students of Astrology as well as the professional practitioners use Numerology in conjunction with Astrology in making their forecasts. Because your Astrologer has found, after nearly a quarter century of practice and research, that it is usually advantageous to the client to know what Numerology holds in store for him as well as Astrology, you are given the opportunity to compare your Numerological outlook with that as shown by your Astrology forecast.

Ascertaining your own outlook for each year is relatively simple, easy to understand, and very interesting in its interpretation. You will find that when your Special Birthday Outline, Your Monthly Forecast, and your Numerological Forecast indicate practically the same thing, it is very likely that the conditions so indicated should occur. In some instances Numerology will show conditions with which you will meet in an entirely different vein than Astrology shows, thus opening new opportunities for you.

You will have observed that your own life runs in cycles. After a certain number of year, somewhat similar conditions will repeat themselves. The answer, or rather the cause of this, is explained by Numerologists as being due to the vibration of various numbers.

To make this one of the most complete and comprehensive Occult outlines you've ever read, your author has prepared this addition to your reading so you may have a firmer grasp on your own Life and perhaps enjoy greater success and prosperity. You will find one simple rule which unlocks the fundamental law in Numerology. Use it to the fullest extent and ultimately you will benefit from it.

To ascertain just what Numerological vibration you are to be ruled by during any year, past, present, or future, there is but one simple, easy to understand rule. Add together the number of your birth month, plus the number representing the day of birth, plus the final number or digit of the year you wish to forecast.

For example: If your birthday is April 26 and you wish to know what Numerological vibration is in force during the twelve months from April 26, 1968 to April 26, 1969, add the number of the month (April is the 4th month of the year) to your date of birth (26). The way Numerologists do this follows:

4 plus 2 plus 6 which equals 12. Now, in this branch of Numerology you must resolve any two figured number to ONE figure. Thus 12 is reduced to its final number 1 plus 2 (12) equals 3.

Since we wish to forecast for the year 1968, we add the 3 which already has been obtained by adding the month and date of birth to the year for which the forecast is desired, thus: 3 plus 1 plus 9 plus 6 plus 8 (1968). This equals 27, which must again be reduced (2 plus 7) or 9. On the pages which follow you'll find a forecast based on each number from 1 to 9. Remember, before going further you must reduce your numbers to a final digit or number from 1 to 9.

To simplify this matter still further, here is the final digit number of each month of the year:

January	No. 1	May	No. 5	September	No. 9
February	No. 2	June	No. 6	October	No. 1
March	No. 3	July	No. 7	November	No. 2
April	No. 4	August	No. 8	December	No. 3

Do you see why October is Number 1? As October is the 10th month, we add 1 plus 0 which equals No. 1. November is the 11th month, and we add 1 plus 1 or 2; December is the 12th month so we add 1 plus 2, which equals 3.

FORECAST FOR YEAR NUMBERS

1.   If your year vibrates to this number, many new opportunities are likely to come to you and events occur which will start you on a 'new leaf' or cycle. It seems better for you to discard the old and look forward to these new opportunities; new friendships, new work or business. You will feel like starting something new and should not hesitate in doing so, especially if your Birthday Outline and Monthly Transit Forecast also indicate a good period for you. Some old matters will have to be settled it seems, but this can be done and you will find the period from April or May around to October or November will be the time when these new opportunities may present themselves. If you have made mistakes in the past, forget them and start a new cycle now.

2.   If your year vibrates to Number 2, it shows you probably started something new during the twelve months prior to this period and you should not be discouraged if things have not shaped themselves as you at first thought they would. An opportunity to travel or change residence may now come, but it is well for you to consult the Astrological to see if this would be a good time to do those things. Health conditions should be good and you will start to benefit from this vibration by the time the Fall months arrive. The main point to remember when you are under a Number 2 vibration is that you must not become discouraged if things do not turn out as you desire immediately. Just give them a little more time, a little more patience, and you will be all right.

3.   If your year vibrates to Number 3, you are more certain to become publicly recognized for your accomplishments. If you have been trying to develop a new business and have not been quite as successful as you would desire, your ambitions are very likely to be gratified during the twelve months in which this Number 3 vibrates. This is a fine period in which to advertise anything, either your business, real estate, or to seek a position through a public notice. There seems to be quite some important social success for you in this period, and if single, possibility of courtship. This is a fine vibration for advancement and progress so make an effort to utilize every opportunity that may present itself.

4.   If your year vibrates to Number 4, you can depend upon it. This period is one in which you should not give too much

time to pleasure or social activity nor for travel and change. Primarily, it is time to make important plans, getting down to business as regards your immediate future. Between June 1st to the first of October seems to be the time when you will be in best harmony for the vibrations Number 4 set in force. Any disappointments which come to you would be the result of too much social activity, pleasure, travel, or change. Be sure to compare this yearly vibration with your Astrology forecast. But if a question exists between the two systems, you will always be doing right in deciding along Astrology lines.

5.   If your year vibrates to Number 5, it marks a time when you will desire and have opportunity to make changes, to travel, and to live in an entirely different environment. This is a good time to take chances, to speculate and try hazardous things which you would not, probably, at any other time undertake. This is a period which calls for courage and initiative, and you may find the opportunities to make changes will come between May or June and October and November. Not surprising if you entered some commercial pursuit or obtained a better office or clerical position at this time. Important letters are likely to be sent and received and some of these messages turn out very well. Important agreements or documents may also be signed during the Number 5 period. Push ahead vigorously.

6.   If your year vibrates to Number 6, you'll find many of your real-personal affairs that have been 'hanging fire' and could not heretofore be settled, will now be amenable to settlement. Especially this is so in your social, domestic, or matrimonial spheres. So this is the year for you to settle any old standing matters or differences and to make new friends. Young folks may now court or have offers of marriage, and in the domestic lives of many will occur happy, wholesome events. If there have been some important quarrels or disputes with friends and you feel this was unjustified, it is possible to become friends again under this Number 6 vibration.

7.   If your year vibrates to Number 7, you will find the period a fine time to rest, mentally and physically, and take an inventory of your affairs. It would be a good time to travel or

make important changes, but if you decide to buy some rather expensive article be sure to make a thorough examination of it. Another condition which number 7 brings about is the occurrence of very sudden and entirely unlooked for events. Things will seem to happen out of a clear sky, and many of those rather startling events may prove very helpful and create worth-while opportunities to be developed later on. To those engaged in professional work, Occult or mail order lines, and aviation, this should be a very prosperous year.

8. If your year vibrates to Number 8, it marks a time when you'll begin to see success coming to you through efforts along a certain cherished line during the past few years and which has been slow in coming up to this time. This is a time when one frequently buys real estate or sells it, deals with older folks, or obtains a promotion in some old, established company. If you must ask favors, now would be the time to do it, and confine your requests to people past 45 years of age. You now become more active and seek to advance yourself in a business and financial way. It is a very good time to do this, and if your Astrology forecast shows that Saturn is in good aspect to your Sun at any time during the coming months, then this number 8 vibration will be doubly effective. If Saturn is adverse or in inharmonious relation to your Sun, then this vibration will not be good.

9. If your year vibrates to Number 9, it marks a time when you may do some things that require great initiative and courage. Perhaps some of the things you do will be a little impulsive, so try to distinguish the border-line here between an impulsive act and one that is justified, but requires courage and initiative. Do not be too easily discouraged in your present work or job, as this is not exactly the right time to make sudden changes unless your Astrology forecast promises these things. If Jupiter is favorable to your Sun in your Astro-forecast, you may make considerable money through speculation or games of chance during the period over which this Number 9 governs. It is not best for you to change your residence, although you will strongly feel the urge to do so. When you are under a 9 Numerological vibration, it is always better still more carefully to study your

Astro-forecast as that will hold the 'key' to your own situation.

DEFINITIONS

Name and Number: The number secured by transferring the letters in a person's name to numbers. This shows the general characteristics the person has developed from the use of his name through life.

Birth Path Number: The number secured by transforming the month, date, and year of birth into numbers. This shows the general trend of the person's life and the outstanding events to be experienced.

Destiny Number: The number secured by adding the Name Number and Birth Path Number together. This shows whether your name adds or subtracts to your Birth Path indications. If it hinders you, the name should be changed for the future.

Monthly Number: The number secured by adding your Destiny Number to the digit of any month and year. This shows the general indications for any month of any year for you. Monthly numbers must be figured out each year, as they change from year to year.

7
The Tarot

It is known to many persons who are not Occult students that the Tarot is a method of divination by means of seventy-eight symbolical picture cards, to which great Antiquity and high importance are attributed by several expositors. Their literary history is also fairly well known. They were mentioned first by the French archaeologist Court de Gebelin at the close of the eighteenth century, and were attributed by him to Egyptian origin. About the same time the subject was taken up by a professed Cartomancer named Alliette, who wrote a great deal about them in several tracts. He endeavored to trace their connection with Egypt through the Jewish Kabbalah. The inquiry then fell into neglect, except as far as the Continental fortune-tellers were concerned, until the year 1855, when Eliphas Levi made his first contribution to Occult subjects and science.

Eliphas Levi says the Tarot cards are a key to the Esoteric Tradition of the Jews and "the primitive source of Divine and human Tradition." He institutes an analogy between the symbols of its four suits and the four letters of the Divine Name *Tetragrammaton* and between the ten *Sephiroth* and the ten small cards belonging to each sequence. He gives also the correspondences between the twenty-two Trump Cards and the letters of the Hebrew Alphabet, for which he quotes the authority of Kabbalistic Jews. The Tarot is actually, as it is claimed to be, of considerable importance symbolically, and it has Kabbalistic connections.

The Hebrew symbolism of the Tarot is laboriously elaborated, yet becomes disorganized if there is any doubt as to the attribution of its Trump Cards to the Hebrew Alphabet. Now, there is one card which bears no number and is allocated, therefore, according to the discretion of the interpreter. It has been placed in all cases wrongly by the uninstructed because they had nothing but their private judgment to guide them.

The true nature of Tarot symbolism is, perhaps, a secret in the hands of a very few persons, and outside that circle, all operators and writers may combine the cards as they like and attribute them as they like, but they will never find the right way. The symbolism is, however, so rich it will give meanings of a kind in whatever manner it may be disposed, and some of these may be suggestive, though illusory none the less. The purpose of this chapter is to show that published Tarots and the methods of using them are serviceable for divination and fortune telling. They are the key of the Kabbalah.

No calculation or scientific observation is necessary for the Tarot. Its entire theory rests upon Nature; there is no accident. Every happening in the Universe is caused by preestablished laws.

The event is subject to this fundamental rule: cards mixed at random do not yield haphazard results but a suit of figures is bound magically to the diviner and to the inquirer.

The practice of the Tarot is based upon a Prophetic gift of man which manifests itself through Clairvoyance. No doubt this state arises more frequently than we care to admit. Who has not, even if only once in his life, had that sensation called foreknowledge? Some future event is witnessed so clearly, so plastically, its beholder knows immediately and with absolute certainty this will happen. And it does!

The suits are four: Wands, Cups, Swords and Pentacles, answering to Diamonds; Pentacles answering to Hearts; Cups, or Spades; Swords and Wands answering to clubs. Each suit consists of fourteen cards, the ace and nine others, and four court cards, king, queen, knight, and knave. The four aces form the keys of their respective suits.

Older authorities differ as to the names, figures, and meanings of the various keys:

Court de Gebelin	Mathers	Falconnier	Hebrew Alphabet	Alphabet des Mages
Bataleur, of Pagad	Juggler	Magician	Aleph	Athoim
High-Priestess	High-Priestess Female Pope	Sanctuary	Beth	Beinthin
Queen	Empress	Nature	Gimel	Gomor
King	Emperor	Conqueror	Daleth	Dinain
High-Priest	Hierophant or	Hierophant	He	Eni
Marriage	Love Pope	Trial	Vau	Ur
Osiris	Charlot	Victory	Zain	Zain
Justice	Justice	Justice	Cheth	Heleta
Wise Man	Hermit	Sage	Teth	Thela
Wheel of Fortune	Wheel of Fortune	Sphinx	Yod	Joithi
Strength	Strength	Strength	Kaph	Caita
Prudence	Hanged Man	Sacrifice	Lamed	Luzara
Death	Death	Death	Mem	Mataloth
Temperance	Temperance	Sun	Nun	Nain
Typhon	Devil	Typhon	Samech	Xirou
Maison Dieu	Lightning-Struck Tower	Pyramid	Ayin	Olelath
Dog Star	Star	Star	Pe	Pilon
Moon	Moon	Love	Tzaddi	Tsadi
Sun	Sun	Awakening	Qoph	Quitolath
Last Judgment	Last Judgment	Crown	Resh	Rosith
Fool, or Mat	Fool	Atheist	Shin	Sicben
World	Universe	Night	Tau	Toth

There are people specially gifted with such prescience or premonition. They stimulate their abnormal sensibility in many ways. Gazing at the Crystal produces an autohypnotic condition. In fact, any glistening or colorful object when stared at for a time may become equally stimulating to the imagination. Some Clairvoyant people are able to tell where the stone which they press against their foreheads was found. They can describe the landscape on which the stone lay, as well as the person who picked it up.

The primary function of the Tarot cards seems to be such stimulation. In scrutinizing the vividly colored images, the diviner will provoke a kind of autohypnosis, or if he is less gifted, a concentration of the Mind resulting in a profound mental absorption. The Tarot's virtue is to induce that Psychic or mental state favorable to divination.

The striking Tarot figures, especially the trumps or Major Arcana, appeal mysteriously and waken in us the images of our subconscious.

Many of the Tarot figures are medieval allegories. The allegory of Force of trump eleven is no mystery to the iconologist. The wheel of Fortune, Trump ten, is a theme used in Romanesque rose-windows. Similar affiliations can be detected without too much difficulty. Most, but not all, of these figures now belong to the orb of the Christian civilization. Yet, actually, the original trump cards and pip cards are of a more venerable age. Thoth-Hermes invented the first Tarot leaves and the Holy Kabbalah holds the true key to the Tarot, just as the Tarot holds the key to the Kabbalah.

The experts of the Tarot connect the game with the divinatory art of Antiquity. Such noble antecedents make the Tarot more venerable. To us, such preoccupation seems unnecessary; the Tarot cards with or without this famous ancestry have attracted many and still fascinate.

The twenty-two Major Arcana cards were called *Man*, and with him they are concerned — with his desires and fears, his wisdom and activities, his goodness and badness, and his physical constitution. The whole world simmers down to Man; in two cards only is the human element missing: in the

Wheel of Fortune, number X, where animals caricature the human, and in figure XVIII, the Moon, in which two stargazers of the sixteenth century have been replaced by a dog and a wolf barking at the Moon. They, too, are caricatures of Man.

"As it is above, it is below." The Tarot thus represents the microcosm of Man, or the state of things below.

The Tarot is both the generator and the battery. It gives birth to one's thoughts and also nurses them. In studying the cards, one is stimulated to visualize images of intellectual and Psychic experiences. Returning again to them later, we will recall these images which would have "fallen into the void" without this mnemonic help. The Tarot produces for us an independent and self-sufficient World, and our Psyche is made objective and detached for contemplation.

The Tarot figures are stereotypes, but what they suggest is in constant flux or evolution. They do not express or lead to an established doctrine. On the contrary, they liberate us from such bonds. This liberation may have a psychotherapeutic effect, but above all, they free faculties in us which are suppressed by conventions and daily routine. They stimulate a Creative power which appeals to the artist. They are the "poetry made by all" of the Occult postulate.

There is no key to the Tarot. There are as many interpretations as there are individuals who consult the cards. The cards, we repeat, are not manipulated by means of theories and doctrines; they are interpreted through a Natural gift, found among the learned and the profane. The nineteenth-century Magi sought to introduce into the game an esoteric doctrine, resembling Hermetism. Their ideals might be justified as a reaction against the shallowness and the extravagant optimism of their contemporaries. But their rigid self-assurance lacked the virtue found in some Tarot cards, namely humor and irony. What they believed to be the Truth they professed with a prophetic vigor which did not tolerate contradiction. They called "Sublime Secrets" inherited from the sages of Antiquity what we would describe as Occult human traits.

The desire to establish an infallible dogma of the Tarot is a mistake. It is also wrong to change or "correct" the figures of the games which are timeless prototypes. The beautiful Major Arcana have arisen from Antiquity, and this is precisely one of the attractions of the game. To reform them to fit dogmatic expressions is to deprive them of their constant Values. Such corrections are not sought by those who have accepted the images for centuries and still discover the marvels in them now.

Like Astrology, the Tarot proposes a method for predicting future events and Man's character. The future, the Cartomancers say, cannot be explored by mathematics. The stargazers wish to discover the world order by calculations and abstractions. The Tarot diviners, on the other hand, discover futurity by intuition, prophetic images drawn from the vaults of the subconscious.

Neither does their strife have much in common with Hermetism. Their social element is opposed to it. Hermetism isolates the adept. The Tarot is a means of communication. The Hermetic is concerned with his own felicity or improvement; the Cartomancer is preoccupied with his patients' disquietudes. The Hermetic Master grows more indifferent to the accidents of Life the higher he ascends the degrees of initiation. The Tarot diviner wants to know what will happen here below, how the Astral World will act upon Man.

THE MAJOR ARCANA

For this higher Arcane, we give the immediate meaning:

I.   The Magician . . . . The inquirer, all cards lying close to this card are important for the inquirer's destiny

II.   The High Priestess . . . The female inquirer, this card has the same qualities as the Magician, but for inquiring women

III. The Empress . . . . Initiative, Action

For minor inquiries, I recommend consulting only five cards of the twenty-two Major Arcana. These are mixed and the inquirer is asked by the Cartomancer to name a number lower than twenty-two. If he chooses seventeen, the seventeenth card is taken from the pack and set out. Its meaning is affirmative. The cards are shuffled again, and by the same process, another card is selected whose meaning is negative. In this way, five cards are exposed and arranged. One means affirmation, two negation, three discussion, four solution, and five determination or synthesis. Thus an inquiry is answered by the prophecy of the Tarot.

TAROT MINOR ARCANA

The fifty six Minor Arcana cards are divided into four groups, Pentacles, Swords, Wands, and Cups, numbered from one to ten. Each suit is ruled by four court cards, King, Queen, Knight, and Knave.

In their organization the Minor Arcana cards recall modern card games. They were originally separated from the Major Arcana which form an independent set. The two do not mingle well in prophecy.

The twenty-two Major Arcana depict the following figures (their meanings were given in the previous list).

I.   The Magician: executing some legerdemain behind his table.
II.   The High Priestess: a woman crowned with a tiara, enthroned.
III. The Empress: a woman with scepter and coat of arms.
IV.   The Emperor: a crowned and entrhroned man, seen in profile
V.   The Hierophant: blessing two kneeling people.
VI.   The Lovers: a youth between two women; above, Cupid with his bow.
VII. The Chariot: pulled by two horses carrying a king or hero.
VIII. Strength: its allegory, a woman with scales and word.
IX.   The Hermit: an old man with lantern and staff.
X.   The Wheel of Fortune: whirling around three animals.
XI.   Justice: a female figure forcing open a lion's mouth.
XII. The Hanged Man: a person suspended by one foot from a gibbet.
XIII. Death: cutting off with his scythe the heads and members of man.
XIV. Temperance: a female figure pouring a liquid from one jug into another.

XV. The Devil and two satellites.

XVI. The Tower: men precipitated from a tower struck by fire or lightening.

XVII. The Stars: a woman kneeling in the water, pouring out two liquids from two jugs. Above are eight stars.

XVIII. The Moon: two dogs bark at the Moon; in a pool is the Cancer of the zodiac, the Moon's house.

XIX. The Sun: two children in front of a wall, above, the luminary.

XX. The Judgment: an angel blowing the trumpet, which summons the resuscitated.

XXI. The World: a nude woman in the mandorla; at the four corners, the emblems of the four Apostles.

One Major Arcana is not numbered: the Fool. Dressed like a king's jester, carrying his bundle on a stick or spoon, he walks dreamily, unaware a dog is biting his thigh.

Here is the full list of the direct significance of the cards:

MINOR ARCANA CARDS:

WANDS

King: dark-haired man, married, having family; a friend.
Queen: dark lady, serious, good counselor, mother.
Knight: young man, dark-haired, a friend.
Knave: child, dark-haired, friendly, sent by near relation.
Ace: beginning of an enterprise.
Two: difficulty, obstacle to the enterprise, unforeseen.
Three: initial success, the base is laid out, encouragement.
Four: renewed difficulty.
Five: obstacle overcome by assiduity, victory.
Six: failure, the obstacles overcome the enterprise.
Seven: success, one part of enterprise achieved.
Eight: opposition to final achievement.
Nine: final success, the task is performed.
Ten: uncertainty in the conduct of the enterprise.

CUPS

King: blond man, friend, judge, clergyman, bachelor.
Queen: blond woman, friend, mistress, sweetheart, fiancee.

Knight: young man, blond, lover, beloved.
Knave: blond child, arrival, birth.
Ace: beginning of love.
Two: obstacles deriving from one of the couple.
Three: both have fallen in love.
Four: a third person provokes opposition.
Five: the obstacle is overcome.
Six: destroyed love, widowhood.
Seven: triumph of love.
Eight: deception.
Nine: pregnancy.
Ten: uncertainty.

SWORDS

King: dark-haired, evil man.
Queen: calumnious, dark-haired woman, evil action.
Knight: spy, young man, dark-haired enemy.
Knave: bad news, delay, bad child.
Ace: beginning of tense relation. (This and the
    following cards indicate that the opposition
    comes from the outside.)
Two: opposition which will not last.
Three: hatred.
Four: success against the enemy.
Five: having been overcome, the enemy is now triumphant.
Six: overcoming the opposition, the enemy is rendered harmless.
Seven: the enemy has been able to achieve his evil plans.
Eight: but he is only partly successful.
Nine: persistent hatred.
Ten: insecurity in matters of friendship.

PENTACLES

King: blond man, enemy or also indifferent.
Queen: blond woman, enemy or indifferent.
Knight: young man, foreigner, blond, arrival.
Knave: letter, envoy, blond child.
Ace: heritage, gifts, economy.

Two: difficulties concerning the establishment of wealth.

Three: moderate gain.

Four: loss.

Five: another transaction restores the equilibrium.

Six: heavy loss.

Seven: fortune.

Eight: the established wealth is again reduced by losses.

Nine: durable fortune.

Ten: changeable luck, gains and losses.

The Pentacle cards indicate things that come from uphill, the country, or the exterior.

The following method of using a full Tarot pack is taken from Mathers:

The full pack of 78 cards having been first duly shuffled and cut, deal the top card on a part of the table which we will call B, the second card on another place which we will call A. Then deal the third and fourth cards on B, and the fifth on A and so on, dealing two cards to B and one to A until the pack is finished. A will then consist of 26 cards, and B of 52. Now take the B pack. Deal the top card on a fresh place D, and the second on another place C, third and fourth on D, and fifth on C and so on. There will now be three heaps — A, 26 cards; C, 17; D, 35.

Take up the heap D and deal the top card on a fresh spot F, second card on another spot E, and proceed as before. There will now be four heaps — A, 26 cards; C, 17; E, 11; F, 24.

Put F on one side altogether; it is not used in the reading. Take A and arrange the 26 cards face upwards from right to left so that they come in the form of a horseshoe, the top card being at the lowest right-hand corner. Read their meaning from right to left. When this is done so as to make a connected answer, take the first and twenty-sixth and read their combined meaning, then the second and twenty-fifth, and so on. When finished, put A on one side and take C, and read it exactly the same way, then E last.

The synthesis of the prophecy is gained by the study of the whole "conjunction." The arrangement of the great game for the consultation of an important decision was indicated.

Minor cards and Major Arcana are mixed together and laid out in the order indicated. The cards lying in the upper part of the arrangement, i.e., the farthest away from the Cartomancer express the present, the cards to the left, the future; and the cards to the right, the past. One leading card is always placed in the middle.

It is clear that the more cards are chosen, the more difficult it is to bring their meaning to a synthesis, and greater lucidity is demanded from the diviner. It is advisable to begin with a small game and not to unfold the cards too often. A moment of concentration should be expected, or a feeling that "it will work."

According to most Tarot experts, the Major Arcana change their meanings when they are turned upside down. An ill-boding image like the Tower may be interpreted as ambivalent in this case. It should be remembered that the Major Arcana numbers are interpreted prophetically. If the inquirer wishes to know when the prediction will come true, numbers may be counted as days, months, years, according to the diviner's premonitions. The numbers of the cards are also interpreted Kabbalistically by some experts.

8

Using the
Magic Mirror

To bring to you a better understanding of life's great possibilities and a full realization of some of your powers is the purpose of this chapter on Crystal Gazing and Clairvoyancy. You have been blessed with certain qualities which, if wisely directed, cannot fail to strengthen you in mind and body and bring greater happiness not only to you, but through you, to all with whom you come in contact. To get the most out of life, you must know how to think through constructively and calmly.

Success is attained only through honest, earnest effort in everything you do. If you make this a rule and abide by it in your business affairs as well as in your social activities, the reward will be great, for you will achieve not only in channels heretofore undreamed of but you will have a radiant personality which will attract people to you. Contentment and good health will also be counted among the gifts for which you will be grateful also.

If you will put yourself heart and Soul into the experiments on Crystal gazing suggested in the pages which follow and devote only a short period each day to them, you will be amazed at the beneficial results you will obtain. Some people are Natural Clairvoyants. They readily see with the

Mind's eye impressions received as a picture in the Crystal, not merely on its surface but through its center, and can easily concentrate on the thought the vision or forms conjure up.

It may be you are one of the fortunate ones endowed with this Clairvoyant faculty and so without much effort are able to use it constructively to benefit yourself and others, thus adding materially to the happiness and contentment of this troubled world. Perhaps you may possess this Clairvoyant Power but are not aware you have it. It lies dormant within you and needs only to be brought to your consciousness to enable you to find your real place as well as your mission in life.

There is also a third possibility! Nature may not have endowed you with any Psychic Power at all, and you could gaze into the Crystal until your eyes water without seeing anything in its depth. In the latter case, neither the Crystal nor the experiments connected with it explained in the text need lose their advantages to you. From them you can learn how to concentrate properly, how to gain mental control, and how to be a positive, constructive thinker instead of one whose thoughts scatter at every disturbing or distracting change or mood. With the physical poise and mental control thus acquired, you will attract only the best influences and conditions to you and because of them others will seek you out for guidance in their problems.

Many prominent men and women of our day have a knowledge of Psychic subjects. Most of us have read about the Psychic experiences of the late Sir Arthur Conan Doyle and Sir Oliver Lodge. Many of the world's greatest thinkers and teachers possessed Psychic gifts or knowledge. Just to mention a few: Mohammed, Buddha, Plato, and Martin Luther. Socrates was Clairvoyant, and throughout his life he received messages and help from "a still, small voice." This also indicates he was Clairaudient (a Spiritual Hearer), which is referred to later in this chapter.

Napoleon was a student of the Occult Sciences. George

Fox, English religious leader and founder of the Quakers, had Psychic experiences, as did also John Wesley, founder of Methodism; Emanuel Swedenberg, Swedish scientist and Mystic, recognized only the Spirit World as a Reality. The world of sense — our material world — was real to him only as it reflected the world invisible, the Soul. It was quite by accident that George Sand, the French novelist, discovered when a child her ability to see pictures in the Crystal. In later years, when writing, she formed a habit of concentrating on the Crystal for inspiration. It has been said that the idea of "Paradise Lost" was suggested to John Milton by his guardian angel in a dream.

The Bible contains many incidents which allude to Clairvoyancy, and in the Scripture Clairvoyants and Clairaudients were known as Seers or Prophets. Jacob clairvoyantly saw angels ascending and descending the ladder. Christ possessed Clairvoyant power, for character and Mind of men were like an open book to him.

Thus the great and small alike have been given this gift by our Creator — Omnipotent and Omnipresent, All Powerful and All Seeing. Whether you are a natural Clairvoyant or whether your latent Clairvoyant faculties are undeveloped and with instruction and personal practice may be brought to your consciousness, or whether you possess no Clairvoyant power at all — you can find much of help and interest in the pages which follow. They will point out how to develop concentration, self-control, and other qualities you may not have realized were yours. If you follow their suggestions you cannot fail to be stronger mentally and physically, and you will be better equipped to help yourself and others, meet life's problems and hurdle many difficulties and obstacles. Such was the thought underlying the author's purpose in preparing this chapter. If you benefit from it and will continue to profit by its lessons, the labor of love will have rich reward for both of us.

The word Clairvoyance comes from the French meaning "clear seeing." The physical eye perceives only material things. To see that which is Spiritual, we must vision with Spiritual sight. Clairvoyance helps us to do this; in fact, it frequently has been referred to as "second sight." Crystal gazing is a branch of Clairvoyance. All Crystal readers are Clairvoyants, but not all Clairvoyants are Crystal readers.

Clairvoyance is always constructive even though it may foretell a great catastrophe or accident. The source of Clairvoyant vision is not known, but those who have made a deep study of it are confident that it comes as a result of Natural Law and is not the visual hallucinations of a distorted brain. The ability to see Clairvoyantly comes when the Mind's eye forms visions of certain scenes, events, and personages. Spiritual pictures project themselves through the physical eye. Not all people possess this faculty.

You often have visions of friends and later learn they were thinking of you at that very moment. This, you say, is mental telepathy. Then, again, while walking alone, quite suddenly you have seen something or somebody beside you when you knew no one or nothing possibly could be there. You also may have visioned the form of a loved one or devoted friend at a distance at the very moment of death, or you may have visualized certain signs or symbols which you could not understand. Such experiences show you have Natural Clairvoyant power, but it is dormant. You should learn how to develop it!

To the uninitiated, it is hard to believe you can see in a Crystal anything other than the fanciful pictures you are apt to imagine in clouds, in frost on windows, or stains on a damp wall. Such reflections could easily be conceived to be landscapes with rivers, hills, or mountains. A person either can induce pictures in the Crystal or he cannot. The pictures seen in the Crystal are not consciously selected or created. They come and go like figures in a dream to the surprise of the gazer without any conscious effort or choice on his or her part. In fact, Crystal gazing has been likened to a dream, except the vision is voluntarily brought about, although it is little, if at all, under the control of the gazer or Scryer.

HISTORY

Crystal gazing was once thought to be a branch of magic but now is generally accepted as an important phase of experimental psychology. History and romance, ancient and modern, contains many interesting legends and stories about magic mirrors and magic Crystals. Some of these date back to the Greece of the 4th century B.C.

The practice was traced among the natives of North and South America, Asia, Australia, and Africa. In all countries the Crystal was used for the purpose of divination and the process usually explained as the result of a Spirit, Angel, or Devil. Those who have visited India know of the use made of the round mass of rough-hewn, polished glass and the superstitious awe with which it is regarded.

In former days, the High Priest of the Buddhist or Hindu temples, when attired in the consecrated robes for festive ceremonies, wore one or more small crystals of dazzling brilliancy suspended from his neck on a chain of great value. It was believed that through their power he was able to commune with the Spirit or Spirits to whom he and his followers showed great reverence and to whom they interceded for solutions to their problems. The Crystal served much as the famous oracle of Apollo at Delphi, which is said to have given responses in answer to inquiries of worshippers.

Among the Ancients, the Seer muttered certain prayers over the Crystal and then gave it into the hands of a youth or virgin. They taught the importance of purity. When Crystal gazing or any Occult ceremony was performed, young boys and girls were employed in divination as no others were deemed pure enough for Spiritual revelations. In instances of Crystal gazing, particularly, it was they who read in the brilliant ball of glass the answers to questions asked, usually conveyed by means of written characters on the Crystal. Sometimes, the Spirits called upon were supposed to appear in the Crystal and respond to questions put to them. Many savage races gazed into the water's depth or any clear depth to foresee distant events for enlightenment on immediate problems.

In bygone days the ceremony of Crystal gazing for divination purposes was elaborate and spectacular, including the Lamen or Holy Table, the use of swords, wax candles in highly polished gilt or brass candle sticks, compasses, and many other accompaniments identified with magical functions. These rites were performed by priests or others personally trained by those who understood the invisible forces of the world unseen. They resorted to frequent washing and prayers three or four days prior to consulting the Crystal.

They sought its help, counsel or advice most generally when the Moon was in its increase — going toward the full. Every preparation for gazing was made when the Moon was increasing. The room and everything pertaining to the ceremony was immaculately clean and void of anything likely to disturb or detract attention. The object then was to bring the actual presence in the Crystal of certain Spirits and to evoke from them answers to questions presented to them. Nowadays, we use the Crystal, or any other medium for that matter, to develop the Clairvoyant power of the individual gazer. Through it he is brought into contact with the world unseen.

Before explaining the various experiments you should practice to awakened Clairvoyant powers, it might be interesting to tell you something about the Crystal itself and its care.

The word Crystal is from the Greek meaning "clear ice," or "frozen water." As early as the 4th century B.C., the Greeks supposed it to be a hard substance from frozen water. This belief persisted until the end of the sixteenth century, when the name Crystal was applied only to ordinary quartz or rock crystal. Later, it was more generally applied to "any symmetrically formed mineral, solid, transparent, or opaque, contained or bounded by plane surfaces." Its smooth, even surfaces were noted by the ancients but were regarded as accidents or as "pleasing to the gods." Even to this day this colorless, transparent variety of quartz often is called rock crystal.

Crystals are distinguished from other bodies by the sameness of internal structure. Their physical properties are the same in parallel directions and are generally different in direction not parallel. Globes or eggs for crystal gazing purposes can be made of beryl, rock crystal or glass.

There is no such thing as a genuine "rock crystal," although quartz glass is frequently referred to as "rock crystal." The few specimens of real rock crystal in the world are priceless. An irregular mass of some three inches in diameter is valued at twenty-five thousand dollars, and the only piece in existence of that size is in a museum. Real rock crystal means a piece of glass formed by volcanic action. Commercially there is the term "rock crystal" applied to exceptionally clear glass. But it is still artificial glass, no more or less.

The average "solid glass ball" as sold in stores which carry Occult merchandise is all right so long as it is reasonably clear looking. A few bubbles or pin heads do not matter, although it should be as round a sphere as possible with no surface ridges. It is impossible for the makers to have a three or four inch glass ball perfectly clear. Plate glass less than an inch thick is frequently not perfectly clear, so you can see how difficult it is to have several inches of clear glass.

For the student, the three-inch Crystal is suggested. The Bohemian Crystal is recommended, as it is the clearest and most flawless obtainable. Of course, the advanced medium will use the size he or she finds best suited to his or her special power of divination. The medium or large sized Crystals (4 to 5 inches) are those generally used because they give greater range of vision and are not so tiring to the muscles of the eyes. However, the point the student must early learn in his study is that the size is of much less importance than the perseverance and patience he brings to his daily experiments while mastering the art of Crystal gazing.

Your crystal always must be immaculately clean. Should

it become very dirty or discolored, it can be restored to its brilliancy by mixing six parts of water with one of alcohol and boiling the Crystal in this solution for almost fifteen minutes. Remove and rub carefully with a brush dipped in the liquid. Rub dry with a chamois. Should only the surface of the Crystal become dirty or soiled, wash with soap suds, rinse well, immerse in alcohol or vinegar and water, then polish with a piece of velvet or chamois.

Moonlight is beneficial to the crystal. The chemical and active rays or influence of direct sunlight are harmful because they tend to destroy its magnetism. Extremes of heat and cold are also injurious. After you have used your Crystal, put it away carefully in its case. Keep it in a dark place and permit no one to handle it, as handling by others spoils the magnetism and destroys its sensitiveness.

The Ancients sought to use the Crystal only when the Moon was on its increase, so it seems logical to conclude that a strong link between the Crystal and the Spirit World is magnetism. This magnetism is attracted to and is in the Crystal because of its iron properties. Many authorities have advanced the theory that the greater the increase of the Moon, the greater the supply of the Moon's magnetism in the Crystal. In Astrology, Crystals are said to be influenced by the Moon as are the intuitive powers of the Mind and brain.

It cannot be too strongly emphasized that you alone should handle your Crystal because of its sensitiveness and the likelihood of mixing magnetisms. You may permit others to gaze into your Crystal but not to touch it. The person for whom you are going to look, of course, should be allowed to hold it in his hands for a few hands for a few moments prior to its use. But none other! They might draw your magnetism and so prevent you from achieving good results.

The magnetism with which your Crystal is charged comes from your eyes and from your eyes and from the ether. The Crystal seems to be the medium between the brain and the universe. Your Crystal may be magnetized by making passes with the right hand, about five minutes at a time, which will help to give it strength and power. Passes for a similar length of time made with the left hand help to increase its sensitiveness.

Brunettes and all dark-eyed, brown-skinned people are more magnetic and charge the Crystal quicker than do their opposites. This darkness is due to the excess of the protoxide of iron in the blood. However, the magnetism of the brunette is no more effective than that of the blonde.

If you would adhere strictly to the methods of the Ancients, your Crystal should be enclosed in a frame of ebony or box wood and be highly polished. But most mediums now prefer placing it on a table. If held in the hand, it was made to lean away from the gazer and be held so that no reflections or shadows were visible in it. If you should stand your Crystal on a table, drape folds of black velvet around it to shut out all reflections. The back of the Crystal should be held toward the light. Never turn its face to the light.

It is best to have the Crystal several inches below your eyes and at such a distance from you that your eye may be bent upon it without effort or strain. Unless you are very far sighted, it is seldom placed more than eighteen or twenty inches away. The average distance is about ten to fourteen inches. There is no set rule! Comfort is the prime essential! Should you find you get better results and it relieves your eyes and rests your body to have your Crystal higher or lower, adjust it to your personal comfort.

As in the case of proper adjustment of the Crystal to your vision, there is no general rule as to time for readings or gazing. However, it is generally conceded that the best time for its use are at sunrise, at midday, and at sunset. From ten p.m. to two a.m. is considered the worst time. As stated, the Ancients considered it of greatest importance in their reading to have the Moon in its increase.

RIGHT MENTAL ATTITUDE

There are three qualities absolutely essential to success in crystal gazing — *calmness, patience,* and *perseverance.* You must also have the right mental attitude and be able to concentrate constructively, not intensely, and without apparent effort. Never use the Crystal directly after a meal, and, of course, you realize the necessity of watching your diet, abstaining from indigestible foods, and avoiding all alcoholic drinks.

You should live simply, take plenty of outdoor exercise and try to be calm and poised at all times. These are great aids not only to your ultimate success in Crystal gazing, but also in everything you do. Mental restlessness, anxiety, or ill health are not conducive to progress. Another important consideration is deep breathing. Cultivate this habit, for all brain power is very dependent upon lung capacity. Clairvoyance needs light, air, sleep, and proper diet as much as it does the magnetism produced through mechanical or artificial mediums.

In exercising your Clairvoyant faculty or in bringing it to your consciousness, you will have to rely solely upon yourself for best results. However, there are some simple rules in sitting for development which should be observed. You also will be greatly benefited if you undertake the experiments which we shall describe slowly and consciously. If these are followed, they will bring you amazing results. Crystal gazing makes possible great opportunities for investigating and experimenting in things Psychical. But you will have to persevere daily for many short periods until you have mastered the art.

Select a medium-sized room, one in which you are not likely to be interrupted or disturbed by sounds or outside noises. The room should be comfortably warm or about 60 degrees, depending, of course, upon the season of the year and your own reaction to temperature or that of the person for whom you may be sitting. If possible, mirrors, ornaments, pictures, or anything of a glaring color which might have a tendency to attract notice should be removed. Should a fire be necessary, see that it is well screened off to prevent its light rays from reflecting in or coming in direct contact with your Crystal.

This also applies to any artificial light in the room,

which should be subdued, not dark but dimly lighted, so as to prevent clear reflections from falling upon the ball. Incandescent light is best because of its softness. Some Crystal readers prefer a dim red light, others a yellow or blue. Whatever the choice, they place a piece of tissue paper of the same shade around it to soften it more. You may experiment with any soft shade you desire.

As already indicated, the Crystal or any other medium in Clairvoyancy is merely the vehicle to promote concentration. Whether you prefer to place it on a table, pedestal, or rest it on a cushion of dark velvet or cloth, it should be partially covered with a black cloth arranged so as to shut out any reflection. The shade of velvet also is optional — black, dark blue, or green may be used, whichever is more restful to your tired or perhaps Occult sensitive eyes.

In the early stages of your study, solitude is advisable. If you sit alone for development, you conserve your magnetism. Others in the room draw this magnetism and so retard your results. From the very first, make it a practice to select the same time, the same place, and the same position. This repetition should be adhered to until you have developed an almost automatic ability to get results. Then it no longer will be necessary because you will have mastered concentration. Sit facing the North! If you live in a southern country, face the South.

Should any person or persons be in the room while you are experimenting, they must be cautioned to remain absolutely quiet and be seated at a distance from you. Your back should be to the light, and the Crystal should be at a proper focus. Of course, later whwn you have become proficient in the art of reading, questions will be put to you by others. But this should be done always in a soft, low tone, never loudly nor abruptly.

For the first sittings, ten minutes — never more than fifteen — are ample! Those fortunate persons gifted with Natural Psychic powers and those whose dormant Clairvoyant powers are easily brought to consciousness may obtain results quickly. But do not be disturbed during these first sittings if you perceive nothing in the Crystal after many attempts. Be calm, patient, and continue trying daily.

Results in crystal gazing in most instances are slow! The following experiments will have to be repeated many, many times before any one of them will be mastered. You will not be wasting one moment's time, for you will be developing qualities and characteristics which will be of value in any future venture. After each experiment, put your Crystal away carefully in its case and keep it in a dark place.

Now for the first experiment which is to teach you how to find comfort in sitting. The position itself does not matter, just so you are comfortable and learn to overcome restlessness. If at first you feel nervous and want to change your position, do so. But try to concentrate on the thought which is your wish to conquer this restlessness. As you progress you will unconsciously take a natural, comfortable position and resume it at each subsequent sitting. Then what you are to do with your hands and legs will be of less interest and command less attention. You will be able to devote your energy to calm, relaxed concentration upon your experiment.

During the first sittings, you will also learn just the number of inches below your eyes and the right distance from you to place the Crystal. Like your body and Mind, your eyes must be relaxed. If you master the art of comfortable sitting and placing of the Crystal to best advantage to your eyes, you already will have taken an important step toward ultimate success as a Crystal reader.

Remember that your progress will probably be slow and gradual. If from the first you try to rush results you will get a wrong start. You will lose the sense of consistency and the value of proper practice. So do not try to hurry! Haste makes waste!

Now for the second step or the teaching of Mind control. This is of essential importance in every undertaking. Without it there can be no worthwhile achievement, no realization of ambition, no development of character, no great happiness, nor fulfillment of one's cherished desires.

When at first you try to direct your attention to the

Crystal, your thoughts will naturally wander. You will perhaps think of things of importance and unimportance, of something you should not do. You will be disturbed by noises in the house or outside and decide they must be stopped if you are to get anywhere.

Let your thoughts stray, if you find it difficult to concentrate. Do not permit this to annoy you or make you tense. Later you will learn how to control those thoughts. It will take time and effort to shut them out. Give your attention entirely to the Crystal. But if you have the patience and continue to persevere, you can and will succeed. Do not hurry!

If you are making headway in switching your thoughts, and your eyes seem to tire from gazing into your Crystal so steadily, this, too, is perfectly natural. Close your eyes for a few moments, relaxing them completely or look elsewhere about the room. While you are so relaxing, you can assure yourself that at the next sitting, when you again resume this second experiment, you are going to have better control of your senses. Your eyes and ears will obey, as well as your thoughts. By these attempts to fix attention solely upon the Crystal, your Mind will soon automatically react toward it, and as you continue the practice (never more than ten or fifteen minutes at each sitting) other thoughts will cease to project themselves unless you will them to come. Then you will have achieved the second all-important step in crystal gazing — how to think constructively and to expel from your Mind all thoughts other than those of immediate interest or concern.

Henceforth, you will think only what you will! Think and hear only what you wish to hear by proper direction and concentration. You will not make many of the mistakes you have made in the past. You will have gained renewed faith, courage, and confidence in yourself. Your vision for and purpose of the future will be clearly defined.

Keep practicing the second experiment until you attain a good degree of mastery. Forget the number of times you attempt it! It may be ten, but it may also be a hundred! But is anything worth while in life arrived at through a short cut? Would there have been any achievement or success in the world if our artists or scientists gave up easily?

Do not be discouraged over seeming failure. You are learning many things in the second experiment which will prove of great value later. No longer will you be a creature of impulse. You will think things over from now on and act only when calm, relaxed, and poised. With the reawakening of your latent power of intuition, you will advance yourself in any station of life.

Above all, you are learning how to think things over and think things through constructively. It is worth the effort to practice conscientiously daily, if the pot of gold at the rainbow's end brings to you a better and happier existence. Success and achievement never came through lax methods. It is stick-to-itiveness that brings results! In Crystal gazing, this second experiment is the most difficult. Once mastered, the rest of the work and study is comparatively easy.

With success of the second experiment assured, we are not going to close the eyes for a moment or two. Let us select as our subject for visualization the trip you are planning. Think of the means of transportation you may take — auto, train, bus, or boat. Picture them in your Mind's eye, also scenes enroute or some interesting experience you may have. Pleasant surprises at your journey's end and any circumstances which might develop during your stay may all be visualized. Or you may develop some interesting facts around your Crystal. Recall instances which led to your possession of it. In your Mind's eye see the interesting ceremonies of the Ancients in their use of it. Think of ots interesting background and, if necessary, read up on the subject! Try to remember the name of the chemical substance of which it is composed, the manner in which it was brought to its present state of brilliancy, or the various types of men employed in its making. You first became attracted to it and the study of Crystal gazing are excellent thoughts. You might also try to forecast the future by reenacting in your mind's eye possible scenes of things to come.

These are only sample subjects! If you learn to think of everything in like manner, it will not be long before you will be able to recall or bring to immediate command details and to analyze them readily. Try this test for awhile daily, not only with your Crystal, but with other subjects or objects.

.Your thinking powers will be greatly improved by following this exercise and you will be amazed when you discover how your Mind automatically records incidents of which you were not consciously aware. This will train you to analyze and concentrate on any one subject without permitting your Mind to wander off on any other tangent.

You have learned several important phases of Crystal gazing: how to be seated comfortably, where to place your Crystal to suit your vision, how to get best results, how to control your thoughts and actions during the short periods you give to each sitting, and how to visualize or bring to your mind's eye places. By this time, the lessons will be carried out by you unconsciously, just as you perhaps learned how to control unconsciously and automatically the various mechanisms of an automobile.

You are now ready for the third experiment or to learn how to direct your attention to the Crystal itself. To put your eye through its surface to its center depths! At no time should this be a forced effort!

Do it naturally, without strain to your eyes. Do it slowly and let your gaze be calm and steady. Of course, your mental attitude will be in tune with your effort and your body will be relaxed. As with the other experiments, do not prolong this one over fifteen minutes. As you progress and results become apparent, the time may be increased gradually. But under no circumstances should you give more than one hour to any one sitting.

It is a good idea at all sittings to give a few seconds to thoughts of improving your health, to the affirmation of greater daily progress in your study, and the assurance to yourself of ultimate success in Crystal gazing.

You have now reached the point where you will know how much Clairvoyant power you possess. It will not be long before you notice your Crystal becomes hazy or appears to be a milky ball. In this cloudy state small pinpoints may glitter through it like tiny stars, caused, no doubt, by the iron and magnetism diffused through it.

At times the Crystal will seem alternately to appear and disappear and give way to a dense blackness. When you reach this stage of Crystal gazing, you know you have what you were so desirous of knowing. You really are endowed with crystalline visions and may proceed with confidence.

As you continue with this advanced experiment, you will discover it does not take so very long before the Crystal appears to turn into a mist or for a moment seems to disappear from your sight. Then, later, you will be able to reach this stage in less time than it takes to tell it. It is advisable not to try to see visions, scenes, or objects in the Crystal the first time you have this experience.

You are anxious to carry the experiment further, it is true, but it is best to proceed slowly as you did with the other two experiments, and be sure. You will likely be a little tense because of your initial success and will want to regain composure.

Your Clairvoyant powers will reveal themselves now in the fourth experiment when the visions, pictures, and scenes, will appear to form in the mist or the place where the crystal seemed to vanish. These, at first, may or may not have any significance to you. The vision or forms may be faces, they may represent a series of events, or be merely pictures. Presently they may dissolve and disappear when a second picture may take its place, or you may get several pictures, visions, and scenes at the same time. Do not be alarmed over what you may see in the Crystal. In later trials and experiments you will learn to analyze these visions or forms when they appear.

If you require to see events which are taking place at a great distance, look through the Crystal. It is generally conceded visions appearing in the extreme background indicate a time more remote from those seen nearer, whether of the past or future. Those coming in the foreground or close to the gazer denote the present or immediate future.

Visions have been classified in two groups: the symbolic, indicated by the appearance of symbols, such as a house, boat, airplane, furniture, etc.

The other group comes under the heading of actual scenes or persons in action or otherwise. People of an active, positive Nature — the more excitable yet determined type — usually perceive symbolically or allegorically. Those of a more passive temperament generally receive direct, or what is know as literal, interpretations.

When you find you are fairly well on the road to proficiency in Crystal gazing, you can give readings to others. Just how much you will be able to see and interpret will depend largely upon yourself and conditions, the degree to which your Clairvoyant faculty has been developed, by your surroundings or the influences about you, and your mental attitude and that of the person for whom you may be sitting. Always try to create a positive and favorable outlook. For the most satisfactory results, a kindly, sympathetic feeling on the part of the reader and the person for whom he is reading is necessary.

Note carefully everything you see in the Crystal. If gazing for another, describe all you see. What at first may seem to you to be too trivial to mention, may later develop into something of utmost value and importance. When a person gazes into the Crystal with evil intent, it will react upon him with disastrous results. Evil Spirits are not identified with the good, and vice versa. If we try to be good and helpful, we will be guided by the good. Like attracts like! As it is below, so it is above!

However, to comparatively few is real Clairvoyant sight given. Some arrive at seeing the ball grow milky or misty and can go no farther. Others see pictures of persons or landscapes which are motionless and in black and white only. Others see in the Crystal figures of persons or animals in color. Some people with strong powers of visualization, or the ability to see things in the mind's eye, cannot visualize forms in the crystal; others are only moderately successful. But a great many never see anything at all in the ball. If you are one of the latter, it means that you do not possess the particular gift which gives this Clairvoyant sight.

It has been estimated that 75 out of every 100 people can become partially Clairvoyant; 63 in 100 become sensitive; 45 in 100 can reach the second degree of clairvoyance; 32 in 100, the third degree; 14 in 100, the fourth degree; 5 in 100, the fifth degree; and 2 in 100, the 6th degree of Clairvoyance. It is generally conceded that 56 men in 100 can become Seers and of 200 women, 180 become Seeresses.

Visions may be classified as follows:

1. Images of something unconsciously observed. New reproduction, voluntary or spontaneous, and bringing no fresh knowledge to the mind.
2. Images of ideas unconsciously acquired from others by telepathy or otherwise. Some memory or imaginative effect which does not come from the gazer's ordinary self. Revivals of memory. Illustrations of thought.
3. Images, clairvoyant or prophetic. Pictures bringing information as to something past, present or future which the gazer has no other chance of knowing.

TABLE OF INTERPRETATIONS

To give a complete list of interpretations of things seen clairvoyantly would be impossible. Besides, there is no hard and fast rule to their interpretation. The following are a few of the more common views seen and an explanation of their meaning. Of course, they may relate to the past, present or future:

Accident: an accident

Ambulance: an accident

Bed with adult or child in it: sickness

Birds: news from a distance. Black birds, bad news; white birds, good news.

Coffin: death. If large, an adult; if small, a child.

Explosion: catastrophe or explosion.

Faces: smiling, a good sign; haggard and worried, a bad sign.

Fire: a building on fire or a a fire engine: fire.

Flowers: a lucky sign

Funeral: death, a funeral.

Gloves: present of a pair of gloves to be received.

Gold: much good fortune.

Judge and Jury: legal matters pending.

Letter: Letter on the way.

Marriage scene, with budding trees and flowers: marriage in the spring of the year; if wintry scene, denotes marriage to take place in winter.

Money: favorable sign. Copper, fair prosperity; silver, more favorable condition in sight; gold, much prosperity.

Ring: a gift of a ring to be received.

Sailors with crossed swords: fighting on sea.

Serpents: enemies; warning to be cautious

Soldiers with crossed swords: fighting on land.

Stars or Lights: if bright or silvery, indicate that spirit forms are hovering near.

Surgical operation: with coffin, deaths; without coffin, recovery.

Train: a journey on land.

Watch: gift of a watch to be received.

Water, Body of: with ships — voyage on water.

Wreck, railroad or ship: railroad catastrophe or shipwreck.

The gazer is able to foretell much from the appearance of the Crystal. The following are some of the indications to which most Mediums adhere:

Bright and silvery Crystal, good sign; denotes prosperity.

If milky color, general unsettled condition.

If very dark, cloudy, and gloomy, trouble, sickness enemies, or death.

White clouds are very favorable indications.

Black clouds are unfavorable.

Violet, green, or blue clouds denote happiness and joys in prospect.

Red, crimson, orange, or yellow clouds portend trouble, danger ahead, or illness; unexpected, disappointing surprises; slander, loss, grief.

> Ascending clouds mean "Yes," in answer to
> question put to gazer.
> Descending clouds mean "No," to questions asked.
> Clouds or shadows moving toward the gazer's right
> hand indicate that spirits are present which
> are friendly as well as interested.
> Clouds or shadows moving toward his left hand
> denote that the seance has come to an end.

Visions in the extreme background indicate a time more remote from those visions seen nearer, whether of the past or future. Those appearing in the foreground or closer to the gazer indicate the present or immediate future.

That which appears on the left-hand side of the gazer is real or a form of an actual thing. The vision appearing on the right-hand side is symbolical. As already stated, visions are classified in two groups: the symbolical, such as those of a boat, house, flag, or building; the other group comes under the heading of actual scenes or persons in action or quiet.

CLAIRAUDIENCY

Clairaudiency is defined as "the act of hearing, or the ability to hear sounds not normally audible; claimed as a special faculty in connection with Spiritual Mediumship." If you possess Clairaudient powers, the Crystal will help to bring them to your consciousness. The same experiments as suggested for Crystal gazing may be carried out, except, of course, instead of visions or pictures in the Crystal, the Psychic Phonomena will become apparent in sound, as though the words were actually spoken.

In Clairaudiency the thought vibrations manifest themselves on the auditory system instead of sight. As in the case of Crystal gazing, if unable to see anything in the Crystal, your Mind lacks the particular development that makes possible this sense of sight, so in Clairaudiency, if you do not hear, it shows your sense of hearing is not affected by your thought. In each instance, it is the application of the Mind and its powers to your thoughts whereby results are attained.

But if you possess neither Crystal gazing nor Clairaudient power, you can profit immeasurably by the use of the Crystal. This powerful medium for concentration, with proper application, will teach you how to think constructively, how to gain mental control, and how to use to best advantage your intuitive power.

Your life will be richer and finer because you have learned to persevere with calmness and patience, have gained poise, courage, and confidence. Disappointments and obstacles will not so easily again swerve you from any purpose or goal if its purpose be worthy and noble. Unconsciously, you will apply these attributes to your everyday affairs, to your mental, physical and financial advantage.

Because of a better and broader understanding of life, you will be able to help yourself as well as others and so increase your own happiness and of all persons with whom you come in contact.

9

The Other
Psychic Sciences

On the one hand, the history of Kabbalism is so imbedded in
Occultism that it is scarcely known or admitted in any
distinct connection. On the other hand, to the pure Mystic
there is so much in the Kabbalistic system which is extrinsic
to the subject of Mysticism that there is a temptation to
underrate its influence. A few preliminary considerations are
presented, based on the fact that Western Mysticism was the
channel of a great Tradition in Christian times.

The correspondence and difference may, perhaps be
brought into harmony if one regards Mysticism in two
ways — as a philosophical doctrine, or rather body of
doctrine (an ordered metaphysics), but also as a mode of
conduct practiced with a defined purpose (as mystical
doctrine and mystical life). It should be understood that the
doctrine is rooted in first-hand experience derived from the
course of Life. The practical Mystic is the Saint on the path
of ascent into the mystery of Eternal Union.

I conceive the Kabbalah, like other metaphysics, as
having useful and reassuring lights. It is a source of
intellectual consolation that one of the most barren of all the
ways pursued by the huamn Mind has its own strange flowers
and fruit. The ZOHAR at least has the power of stirring those

depths in the human heart which are beyond the senses. It seems occasionally to "strike beyond all time, and backward sweep through all intelligence." To say this is to confess that it is of the eternal Soul speaking here under the common influence of right reason. Now the speech of the human Soul is not without a message to the Mystic, be it even in certain cases a word of warning only.

Between Occult arts and Mystical science there is the common point of union. Beneath this fantastic resemblance there is the more important fact that they both deal with inner and otherwise uninvestigated capacities of the human Soul. There is no person really mystic other than the Occultist conventionally understood as the Mystic on the path of attainment in Life while exploring the world of Psychic power.

Every dream is regarded as an admixture of truth and falsehood, but the thesis is a dream realized according to the interpretation placed upon it. Should this be favorable, favors will overwhelm the man, but in the contrary case, he will be weighed down by adversity. The reason is that the word governs, and it follows that no dream must be disclosed to anyone by whom the dreamer is not loved. There are in all three degrees dream, vision, and prophecy, and the greatest of these is Prophecy.

Now it so happens that the Doctrine of Signatures, of which we seem to hear first in Paracelsus — so far as Latin writing in Europe is concerned — and which was derived from him into the Theosophical system of Jacob Bohme, is a doctrine of Kabbalism. The Zoharic allusions are few and far between in respect of actual definition; they enable us — with the aid of their developments — to conclude the mental environment of Paracelsus included some reflections from Zoharic sources.

According to the sage of Hohenheim, there are elements and signatures of elements; a science of the signatures exists, and it teaches how Heaven produces man at its conception, how also he is constellated thereby. Stones, herbs, seeds, roots, and all things whatsoever are known by their signatures, that which lies within them being discovered thereby. In respect of man, signature has three species, which are Chiromancy, Physiognomy and Proportion. Such things were part of the decried Occult sciences and they were matters of observation arising from that doctrine of correspondences.

There are seven considerations regarding hair in the *ZOHAR* and the dispositions indicated:

1. Hair which is crisp or frizzy and inclined to stand up signifies a choleric temper; the heart is tortuous like the hair, and such a person should be shunned.

2. Straight and silky hair is usually that of a good companion, one who succeeds in business—if not undertaken alone. He is prudent respecting Supreme Mysteries, but cannot hold his tongue about matters of daily life.

3. Hair that is coarse and straight signifies one who does not fear God, but works evil knowingly. He will become better, however, if he reaches an advanced age.

4. A man having black and glossy hair will succeed in material things, but he must work alone.

5. The success of a black and dull-haired man is rather of an intermittent kind, and he may quarrel with his business associates; should he take to the study of the Holy Law, he will make progress therein.

6. A prematurely bald man will do well in business; but he will be crafty, avaricious, hypocritical and one who makes a pretense of religion.

7. A man who grows bald in the natural course of years will undergo great changes otherwise; if he has been of good conduct previously, he will now be bad, but he will turn into paths of virtue if he has been so far an evil liver.

Some of the conclusions are a little hard and arbitrary — under the reserve of Sacred letters, and certain alternative readings at a later stage do not endorse them entirely. But from this secondary account comes a ruling in respect to auburn hair. On the understanding that it is curly, the head which wears it will fear sin, will feel compassion for all in misfortune, and will have the welfare of others as much at heart as his own.

Physiognomy is a larger subject and is treated at some length. Here a few typical examples:

The man whose forehead is low and flat acts without thinking, is fickle in notions, believes himself wise, and understands nothing. His tongue is like a biting serpent.

The man who has deep wrinkles on his forehead which are not in parallel lines and which are replaced when he speaks by parallel and less deep wrinkles is to be shunned under most circumstances, as he seeks nothing but personal interests and will keep no secrets.

A large and full forehead denotes the best kind of personality, capable of acquiring knowledge with the least pains and successful in all search after spiritual felicity. In money questions he may succeed at one time and fail at another, but he is not solicitous regarding material things.

The man with blue eyes has a tender heart and one that is free from wickedness, but he follows his own ends and is careless proportionally about wrong done to others. He seeks pleasure but not of an unlawful kind, yet if he should fall into evil ways, he would remain therein.

A man with green, shining eyes is touched with madness, believes himself superior to others, and lets them know it; he will not prevail against enemies, and he is inept for the Mysteries of the Law.

A man with clear but yellowish eyes is passionate, though often sympathetic towards the sufferings of others, yet is he cruel in his anger, and he also cannot keep secrets.

A man with dark grey eyes will succeed in the Mysteries of the Law, and if he perseveres in its study he will make steady progress therein. He will also prevail over enemies.

The distinctive marks of the countenance are modified by conduct, and differ from general inherited types, which correspond broadly to the four living creatures of Ezekiel's vision. There are those which are distinctively human, those which are leonine, bovine, and in aspect like that of the eagle. There are also four types which are said in *ZOHAR* to be imprinted by the Soul.

1. That of the virtuous man, who is distinguished by a small horizontal vein on either temple, the one on the left being bifurcated and crossed by another small, vertical vein.

2. That of a man who returns to his Master after leading a bad life. He is repulsive at first, but others are finally drawn towards him; he does not care to be looked straight in the face because he thinks that his past may be legible. He is alternately pale and yellow. He has one vein descending from right temple to cheek, another under the nose and this joins with two veins on the left cheek. These last are united by another vein, but the last will disappear when the man is habituated to a virtuous life.

3. That of a person who has fallen off completely from the good way. He has three red pimples on either cheek and some faint red veins beneath them. Should he be converted the pimples would remain but the veinlets vanish.

4. That of a man who has been incarnated a second time to repair the imperfections of his first sojurn on earth. He has a vertical line on the right cheek near the mouth, and two deep lines on the left cheek, also vertical. His eyes are never bright, his health is poor, and the cutting of his hair and beard changes his appearance completely. Thick lips are those of the evil speaking. If a medium lower lip is cleft, the person will be of violent temper, but he will succeed in business. Unusually large ears are a sign of stupidity and even of tendencies to mania; persons with very small and well-shaped ears are awakened in mind and yearn for knowledge.

PALMISTRY

The hand, more than the other parts of the body, reflects the forces from above. Since the world is a hierarchy, the miniature world (man) must necessarily be organized similarly. In the system of man, the hand fulfills a unique function, that of the mediator between the above and the below, between the intellectual microcosm, residing in the head, and the material microcosm which dwells in the body.

If the brain is comparable to the unmoved mover, the Magi say, then the hand may be called the active force through which the mover manifests himself. Thus, the hand occupies the second rank in the Microcosmic hierarchy and is, after the head, the most worthy of investigation.

Chiromancy gathers from the heavenly imprints upon the hand two virtues: character and destiny, a conclusion which all divinatory methods share. This is deductive as well as prophetic, rational and irrational. When reading his patient's hand, the Chiromancer uses his reason and his divinatory gift. The lines whose significance were established by tradition are the scaffold upon which the Magus sets his imagination. Imagination is the force which performs the marvel, as Agrippa, Paracelsus, and others have taught us.

It is useful to compare these early schemes with modern palmistry. Far more importance is given to the fingers today. They confirm the marks in the palm and add many interesting details to the more general information gathered from the palm. The upper phalanx of the thumb expresses will, the lower, logic. In the three phalanxes of the index finger reside religion, ambition, and sensuality. The middle finger contains prudence, the tendency to experiment, and concentration.

The ring finger informs us of the individual's artistic gifts, his critical sense, and his successes. The little finger belongs to sociability; it is marked with the signs of study, speculation, and shrewdness. All the upper phalanxes give information concerning the subject's intellect; the middle phalanxes, of his intelligence; and the lowest phalanxes, of his instincts.

The most important lines of the palm are those of Life, of Destiny, of the Heart, of the Head, and of Intuition. A shorter line that descends from the art or ring finger reveals artistic talents, and several parallel lines upon the wrist give supplementary information about the length of Life.

Besides the lines of the hand, its "mounts" are

important to the Palmist. The hump of the thumb, called the mount of Venus, informs us about the individual's love; the mount of Jupiter, below the index finger, is marked by ambition; the mount of Saturn, below the middle finger, reveals man's independence; the mount of the Sun, below the ring finger, is that of Apollo, or art.

And below the little finger, the mount of Mercury reveals commercial aptitudes. At the edge of the palm, opposed to the thumb, are the mounts of Mars, denoting steadiness and resistance, and of the Moon containing the marks of imagination and melancholy.

Close by are the lines of travel and above, in the mount of Mercury, those of union. Distant from the mount of Venus in the realm of shrewdness (lowest phalanx of the little finger), is marked the number of children the person will have.

It has been accepted that the left hand, which does not work as much as the right, holds the Signs preserved better and not distorted. On the left is inscribed the primitive destiny given by the Stars at man's birth. On the right hand are those changes which man causes daily by his will and work. If man's Will is free, why should one inspect his left hand? If he modifies his destiny, the Stars' original marks offer no valuable information. But if the Stars are omnipotent, then there is no point in inspecting the right hand. Will, labor, and intelligence cannot overcome that which has been decided by the Horoscope. This strife as to whether man is free or not cannot be ended by the Chiromancer. One may recognize whether the subject is living according to his inclinations and if his activities are in accord with the gifts bestowed upon him at birth. Accepting this, we can say the Stars influence, but do not irretrievably decide our destiny.

It is usual to divide the science of palmistry into two principal sections: Cheirognomy, or the science of interpreting the characters and instincts of men from the outward formations and aspects of their hands; and Cheiromancy, or the science of reading the characters and instincts of men, their actions and habits, and the events of their past, present, and future lives, in the lines and formations of the palms of their hands.

The first of these branches is the modern and more scientific one. It is really the easiest to master and to practice, and though less interesting than the second, is absolutely indispensable to a proper study of the lines of the palm. Master the subject of the general formation of hands and you are well on the way to a mastery of the art of reading palms.

> The index finger is named for Jupiter.
> The middle finger for Saturn.
> The ring finger for Apollo.
> The little finger for Mercury.

METHOD OF READING

First, with the eye, or better, by means of a ruler, measure the length of the fingers at the back, from the center of the knuckle of the longest finger to its tip, then measure the palm from the highest opening between any two fingers, and the first line running around the wrist, or the point wherein your judgment the palm ends and the wrist begins.

The length of the fingers should be greater in all cases than the length of the palm, or at any rate about the same. In the lower animals and the lower orders of men the palm is longer than the fingers, till the fingers become little more than toes and the nails grow over the ends of the fingers like claws.

The Elementary hand has short fingers, the skin is coarse and often hard, though not always, and the palm thick and chubby. The thumb is short, thick, and usually square at the end. Persons with such a hand have no control over their passions and have little mind or capacity for education.

They are brutes, and like brutes may commit murder in a drunken passion. Like brutes, too, they may be amiable, though never very appreciative of another, and may grow rich through their activity in the lower planes of life. The pure type of Elementary hand is rarely found in civilized countries though something approaching it is common.

Everyone has noticed how differently are shaped the fingertips of all persons of education and intellectual power. These differences have caused Cheirologists to divide hands into classes which represent corresponding types of character. The Ancient teachers considered that there were seven of these classes because they also reckoned seven planets and seven temperaments.

The modern palmists teach that there are three Natural divisions, the Conical, Spatulate and Square, and two smaller classes contained within the three principal types but with peculiarities of their own, the Extreme Pointed and the Mixed type.

"Pure types," that is, fingers entirely conic, spatulate, or square are seldom met with. We must master the simple types, however, and learn to combine their qualities when we find the types themselves combined in any particular hand:

1.   The Conic Type represents Ideality.
2.   The Spatulate represents Action.
3.   The Square represents Reason.

The Conic hand has long elliptical nails, not very large but delicate, and the whole hand corresponds. The fingers are long and tapering, the palm by no means thick, and the skin is usually smooth and clear.

Subjects with conical-shaped tips to their fingers dream rather than act, especially if the hand generally be soft. "People with the Conic hand are often, in fact, designated 'the children of impulse.' There is a great variety in connection with this type, but it is more usually found as a full, soft hand with pointed fingers and rather long nails. Such a formation denotes an artistic, impulsive nature, but one in which love of luxury and indolence predominate."

Persons possessing this type of hand are usually brilliant, clever, and gifted as musicians or artistis, especially if the ring finger, the finger of Apollo, is proportionately long. They often fail, however, because of lack of application or willingness for hard work.

The Spatulate hand has fingertips like a druggist's spatula, or ladle. The ends of their fingers seem abnormally developed by constant work on details. Persons possessing this type are the workers of the world. They carry out the ideas of the Conical type. The thumb must always be large. "The great pronounced characteristics of this type are: action, movement, energy, and, of course, the harder or firmer the hand the more pronounced will these characteristics be.

"A man of this type is resolute, self-confident, and desirous of abundance rather than of sufficiency. In love he will be more constant and faithful than the conic or pointed-handed subject by reason of his want of inclination toward things romantic and poetic. With a small thumb the Spatulate subject will try to do much, but will fail through want of inclination toward things romantic and poetic. With a small thumb the Spatulate subject will try to do much, but will fail through want of perseverance and uncertainty in his course of action."

Persons of this class are fond of order and regularity and are always doing something. They are strict and even tyrranical, but always just. If the palm be hard, they will work themselves; if soft, they make others do the work. But action of some sort is a necessity and they are restless when forced to be idle.

The Square hand has nails more or less square at the ends, and the fingertips are nearly square. The hand itself is broad, and the palm is nearly square, especially at the wrist and at the base of the fingers. Usually the joints are rather large, especially the joints nearest the palm, the thumb with the root well developed, the palm itself of medium thickness, hollow, and rather firm. The whole hand is usually a very large one.

Such a hand is often known as the useful hand since it is so common in the useful walks of life; carpenters and mechanics of all kinds, inventors, architects (especially builders of useful buildings). In fact, everyone engaged in a strictly useful occupation which also requires intelligence and reasoning judgment possess this hand.

Possessors of Square hands (as may be seen by the knotted joints) are thinkers; they must have a reason for everything. They do not work so hard as those with spatulate fingertips, but they will probably accomplish more. They have very little sympathy with the beautiful in any form, especially when it is not also useful, and despise persons with conic fingers.

They are preeminently the world's artists and poets. "They are sincere and true in promise, staunch in friendship, strong in principle, and honest in business. Their greatest fault is that they are inclined to reason by a twelve-inch rule and disbelieve all they cannot understand."

The best musicians (composers and theorists) have always delicately squared fingers with slightly developed joints and small thumbs. Singers and performers on violin and piano are more likely to have conic hands with enough of the square type to give them perseverance in practice.

The Mixed hand as a type is so called because it has distinct characteristics of several of the three elementary types we have just been considering. The nail on one finger may be square, that on another may be Conic, and that on a third, Spatulate. There may be square nails and fingertips on long, tapering fingers, or conic nails and tapering fingers on square palms. The Mixed hand must be judged first of all by the prevailing type.

If two or more of the fingers are Spatulate, the type is Mixed Spatulate; if two or more are Conical, it is Mixed Conical; if two or more are Square, it is Mixed Square. Each finger should be read separately and then the balance carefully adjusted.

A pointed or Conic Jupiter always gives the love of reading and perception and modifies the sterner qualities of the other fingers. Thus, the argumentativeness of the square fingers may be modified by the tact of a long-pointed

Mercury, while a pointed hand with a square Saturn has the saving grace of prudence to correct its vagaries.

All palmists agree that the Mixed hand is the most difficult to read, and at the same time it is the most common. It is the hand of ideas, of versatility, and generally of changeability of purpose. A man with such a hand is adaptable to both people and circumstances, clever, but erratic in the application of his talents. He will be brilliant in conversation, and be the subject of science, art, or gossip. Such hands find their greatest scope in work requiring diplomacy and tact.

The only chance that people with mixed hands have of becoming really distinguished is to take the best talent they have and cultivate it to the exclusion of the others. But they seldom have the strength of purpose to effect this.

The old palmists describe two other types, the Philosophic and the Psychic, spoken of as the Exaggerated Conic.

The Philosophic are divided into two classes or sections; one of the materialists, whose ideas are derived from external influences, and the other of the idealists, whose ideas are evolved from their inner consciousness.

The distinguishing characteristics of these hands are the knotted joints of the fingers. The first joint, or that nearest the fingertips, if well developed gives the idealistic class, or those whose reasoning and philosophy is concentrated on mental subjects; the second joint, or that nearest the palm, if well developed gives the materialistic class, or those whose reasoning and philosophy is concentrated on physical and material matters.

The hand with knotted joints (in English countries) usually belongs to the college professor or scientists. Persons with such a hand glean wisdom, but seldom gather gold. They are students rather than workers. The knotted joints may belong to the Conic, the Square, or the Spatulate type of hand, and so this is not properly a separate type. Moreover, in common life it is a type peculiar to Oriental nations, especially to India.

In character they are silent and secretive; they are deep thinkers, careful over little matters, even in the use of little words; they are proud with the pride of being different from others; they rarely forget an injury, but they are patient with the patience of power.

The Psychic or Exaggerated Conic hand is still more rarely found. It is the most beautiful and delicate, but, alas! the most useless and impractical type of hand. This type of hand is very small and delicate, having a think palm and fine fingers which are long and delicately pointed, or with joints only just indicated by a very slight swelling. It has generally a pretty little thumb.

To these subjects belong the domains of the beautiful ideal, the land of dreams, of Utopian ideas, and of artistic fervor; they have the delicacy and true instinct of art of the conic hand, but without its sensualism, its egotism, and its worldliness. The luxurious dreaming Orientals are almost exclusively of this type. Among them we find Spiritualists, Mediums, and many persons who prove the easy prey of impostors. In countries where such hands predominate and hold the reins of government, we find that rule is maintained by superstition, by priests, and by fetishism.

Such subjects are ruled by heart and by Soul; their feelings are acute, their nerves highly strung, and they are easily fired with a wondrous enthusiasm. Theirs are the talents which produce the most inspired poetry. But in our material Western world, the possessors of such hands are invariably classed as failures. To their own hearts, however, their lives are anything but failures in spite of the fact that suicide is common among them.

We have considered the types of nails and fingertips under the head of Types of Hands. There are, however, many special points to be considered in connection with the fingers and the hand in general.

If the fingers looked at from the front (not measured from the back as previously described) appear to be short, the subject will be found to be impulsive, hasty, quick in thought and action, and inclined to regard the whole of a subject rather than trouble about details.

Long fingers love detail and are constantly inclined to curiosity, worry, and fidgetiness.

A well-balanced character will have the fingers and palm of equal length (or they will appear to be in good proportion). Such a person will appreciate the wide sweep of the horizon and yet note lovingly the daisies 'neath our feet.

A finger is said to be "good" when it is straight, well-developed, and in proportion to the other fingers; "bad" when it is too long or too short, twisted, crooked, or bent.

When the hand is held palm upward, and one finger appears to stand up, that is, said to be the dominant finger and will give the keynote of the character. The qualities indicated by the different fingers will vary in degree with the power of that finger and must be judged accordingly.

Fingers set evenly on a line above the mounts are said to indicate success.

Any finger set below the others loses some of its power. Mercury low-set shows that circumstances are against the subject and that life will be a struggle. If Apollo is set lower than Saturn, the artistic faculties will not receive their full cultivation. Saturn is seldom displaced.

A large hand indicates a love and appreciation of details and minutiae; a medium-sized hand denotes comprehension of details and power of grasping a whole; while very small hands betray always the instincts and appreciation of synthesis. The large-handed subject will have things small in themselves, but exquisitely finished, while the small-handed subject desires the massive, the grandiose, and the colossal.

Artists in Horology have always large hands, while the designers and builders of pyramids and colossal temples always have small hands. In Egyptian papyri and hieroglyphic inscriptions, the smallness of the hands of the persons represented always strikes one at first sight. In like manner, persons with small hands always write large, while people with large hands always write (naturally) small.

A hand that is hairy on the back betokens inconstancy, while a quite hairless and smooth hand denotes folly and presumption. A slight hairiness gives prudence and a love of

FINGERS

JUPITER (index finger)

Good	Too Long	Too Short	Crooked
Love of Rule	Tyranny	Dislike of Responsibility	Lack of Honor

SATURN (middle finger)

Prudence	Morbidity	Frivolity	Hysteria

APOLLO (ring finger)

Love of the Beautiful	Love of speculation (gambling)	No artistic sense	False ideas of art

MERCURY (little finger)

General capacity	Craft	No executive ability	Wanting in business tact

luxury to a man, but a hairy hand on a woman always denotes cruelty.

Hair upon the thumb denotes ingenuity; on the third and lower phalanges of the fingers only, it betrays affectation, and on all the phalanges a quick temper and choleric disposition. Complete absence of hair upon the hands betokens effeminacy and cowardice.

If the hands are continually white, never changing color (or only very slightly) under the influences of heat and cold, they denote egotism, selfishness, and a want of sympathy with the joys and sorrows of others.

Redness of the skin denotes sanguinity and hopefulness of temperament! Yellowness denotes biliousness of disposition; blackness, melancholy, and pallor, a phlegmatic spirit. Darkness of tint is always preferable to paleness, which betrays effeminacy, the best color being a decided and wholesome rosiness, which betokens a bright and just disposition.

The color of the nails shows whether the circulation is good or not. If they are dark, the circulation is bad. Sometimes they will be fairly purple. This is an indication of temporary ill-health.

Bright red nails indicate a hot temper, pink nails a hasty temper, and white nails a calm temper. If the color lies in bands of pink and white, the temper is intermittent and depends on the nerves and the state of health.

Large nails feel more lasting anger than small ones. Short nails show mockery and criticism. "Almond" or "filbert" nails, if pink, are often peevish; if white, indifferent.

Flat nails show some tendency to paralysis.

Fluted nails (those with small ridges running from top to bottom) show backache and spinal trouble.

Ridges across the nails show an illness.

White specks show nervousness or a temporary condition of nervous exhaustion or slight illness.

Round nails are said to show a tendency to consumption. (This means roundness from side to side the whole length of the nail.)

A square base indicates a desire for revenge.

Soft rounded base indicates amiability.

Wedge-shaped base indicates quickness to take offense and feel slights.

Very long nails much curved in any direction show a

weak physical constitution and tendency to throat and lung trouble.

Short nails curved and fluted would show merely throat trouble.

Short and small nails in general show tendency toward heart disease. Large moons indicate a good circulation, small moons heart disease. Short nails inclined to lift or curve up at the edges because they are so flat indicate serious nerve disease and paralysis, especially if they are patched with white and are brittle.

Long nails indicate calmness and resignation and their owners take things easily. Long nails show an artistic nature and great ideality and a tendency to be visionary. Short-nailed persons, on the contrary, are extremely critical, inclined to logic, reason and facts. They are quicker, sharper, and keener in judgment than the long-nailed people and have a keener sense of humor and of the ridiculous. If nails are broader than they are long, they show a pugnacious disposition and a tendency to worry and meddle with other people's business.

If the fingers are thick they show love of ease and luxury.

If when the fingers are held together and the hand is looked at toward the light, spaces sufficient to let the light pass can be seen between the bases of the fingers, generosity is indicated. If the fingers fit tightly together, avarice and extreme selfishness are to be read.

Twisted and badly formed fingers with few lines in the palms show a tyrannical and cruel, if not a murderous, disposition.

Hands which open and close very stiffly betray stubbornness.

People whose fingers have a tendency to turn back, being supple and elastic, are generally sagacious and clever though inclined to extravagance. They are always curious and inquisitive.

If the little fleshy ball or pad be found on the face of the first phalanx it is a sign of sensitiveness and sensibility toward other people and, consequently, tact (due to a fear of giving pain) and taste (the natural possession of sensitive people).

The thumb is perhaps the most important single member of the many-fold hand. It gives the keynote of the whole character, and therefore, merits discussion by itself.

The three phalanges show respectively:

First (nail), will.
Second (middle), logic.
Third (part of palm), love.

If the first phalanx is long, and firm to the touch, and spatulate, the Will will be constant and little affected by the opinions of others. If the point is soft and tapering, even if very long, the power of the Will is unused and the subject is swayed by others. If heavy, almost clubbed, we find unreasoning obstinacy.

If the thumb is very supple and turns far back we read generosity that in extreme cases goes to extravagance, even to complete lack of honor in the matter of spending money. Suppleness of the whole thumb is said to be a sign of dramatic talent. A depression in the center of the first phalanx shows susceptibility to flattery.

If the second phalanx is long, strong and proportionately developed it shows the power of abstract reasoning, of seeing all sides of an argument. It checks enthusiasm and, with a small first phalanx, gives indecision. Such people give good advice but do not follow it themselves. "Waisted," that is, cut away at the sides, there is the power to see only one side of the question, and it reduces all argument to a personal matter.

The finer formation of the thumb is the indication of the greater development of the intellectual will, and the coarse formation is that of the nature that will use more brute force in the accomplishment of an object. It follows, therefore, that the waist-like appearance, which is a portion of the finer development, indicates the tact born of mental power, whereas the fuller, coarser development indicates force in the carrying out of a purpose, in keeping with the characteristics of each Nature.

The part of the third phalanx lying outside of the mount of Venus shows the power of the emotions. If combined with a heavy mount of Venus, we get sensuality. If this phalanx is long and clear, the passions are more ideal; if short and thick, they are earthly. If the outer angle of the second joint is acute, a good ear for music is said to be indicated. The second joint is associated especially with time, the third with tune.

If the thumb is set very high and straight, it shows lack of adaptability and care for money to the verge of meanness. If it is high set and the first phalanx turns back, the subject spends money on himself.

When all the phalanges of the thumb are well balanced, strong and long, constancy of purpose is shown. A good, well-developed thumb can entirely redeem an otherwise bad hand by bringing the modifying power of personal will to bear upon the inherited tendencies, making the idle energetic from conviction that labor brings the highest good, the self-indulgent temperate because reason shows the healthful result of abstinence.

On the other hand, a weak, illogical thumb can render every talent otherwise shown in the hand useless. The small top phalanx and the small size of the whole member show the fickle, obstinate, yet weak-minded individual who lacks perseverance and is absolutely unreliable. Nothing is brought to perfection, and the mind, swayed by the opinion of the last speaker, is incapable of sustained effort.

The size of the palm must be judged by comparison with the fingers. No special measurements can be given, but a little practice will soon teach the right proportions. It should be measured from the base of the second finger to the first line of the bracelet.

A narrow palm belongs to the conventional hand, with fingers set closely together. Its narrowness generally consists in the small development of the mounts of Mercury, Mars, and the Moon. We find people with these narrow palms lack cheerfulness, pluck, and imagination. Sometimes the thumb is pressed closely toward the hand and makes it appear narrow. This limits the stretch and prevents spontaneous generosity.

A square palm gives love of fresh air and, if hard and flat, a tendency toward outdoor sports.

A wide palm shows a good development of all the mounts.

When the palm is flat and lies on a level with the surrounding mounts, it shows the Plain of Mars is developed; fighting and aggressive powers are used, and circumstances, however outwardly unfavorable, are forced in the end to yield.

Far different is the result of the hollow palm. With a lack of aggressiveness, drifting whither circumstances seem to lead, easily daunted, these characters need the sustaining moral force of a stronger nature to urge them to combat. Should a child's hand have this peculiarity, he should never be snubbed. Each effort should be encouraged and attempts made toward personal action should never be ridiculed. These hollow palms belong to sensitive Minds to whom a breath of ridicule is a poison wind stunting all growth and retarding every effort.

The consistency of the palm is also a very important factor in delineating a hand. When firm, even if in appearance it is soft, it will show energy, but not aggressive activity.

When hard, flat, and firm we have the fighting animal, never yielding, always doing.

When the palm is soft and flabby, we find indolence and laziness, which is accentuated and united with a love of luxury in food and life. When the back of the hand is also fat and the third phalanx much developed, these people will always like others to do their work for them; even thinking is frequently too much trouble.

When these fat hands and thick fingers have a palm which feels firm to the touch, then their energy will expend itself chiefly on the gratification of their own gastronomic faculties. "Dinner" will be the one thing to live for.

A thin palm, even when flat, denotes delicate health; a firm, not too large one, warm to the touch, hard, but not unduly so, good health; a thick, clumsy palm shows the preponderance of the animal instincts, brute force, and egotism.

A thick palm is the characteristic of those for whom the alphabet consists of one letter — the capital "I" — while the flexible palm will generally show an adaptable character, fond of variety and change.

The soft hand has more poetry in its composition than the hard. Thus, an artist with hard hands will paint things real and actual rather than ideal, and his pictures will be more active and manly than those of a softer-handed artist, who will paint the images of his fancy and whose works will show greater soul, greater diversity, and more fantasy.

A Spatulate subject with hard hands will engage in active exercise, athletics, and the like, while the similar but softer-handed subject prefers to watch others engaged in active occupations.

People with soft hands have always a love of the marvelous, being more nervous, more impressionable, more imaginative than those with hard hands. A very soft hand has a still greater degree of fascination for the strange and uncanny, being rendered additionally supersititious by bodily laziness. The tendency is still more pronounced if the fingers are pointed.

Soft hands are often more capable of tenderness and affection than True Love, but hard hands are generally the more capable of True Love, though less prone to demonstrative tenderness and affection.

To be perfect, a hand should be firm without hardness and elastic without being flabby; such a hand hardens only very slowly with age, whereas an already firm hand often becomes extremely hard. Smoothness and a gentle firmness of the hand in youth betoken delicacy of the Mind, while dryness and thinness betray rudeness and insensibility.

The wrinkles on the hand should also be noticed. A soft, wrinkled hand shows impressionability and uprightness of Soul, and a wrinkled hard hand is that of a person who is pugnacious, irritating, and teasing, especially if the nails be short.

The back of the hand lined and wrinkled always indicates benevolence of mind and sensitiveness of Soul.

The man with the firm, strong hands and the developed mount of Venus is the man who will exert himself to amuse others with feats of grace and agility, who will romp with children, and work hard to contribute his share to the general harmony.

The study of the mounts forms the connecting link between Cheirognomy, or the general study of the hand, and Cheiromancy, or the study of the lines on the palm. Some palmists class them under one division, others under the other.

There are seven mounts, which are in reality slightly raised portions of the palm. They are indicated as follows:

1. Mount of Jupiter, at base of index finger.
2. Mount of Saturn, at base of middle finger.
3. Mount of Apollo, at base of ring finger.
4. Mount of Mercury, at base of little finger.
5. Mount of Venus, at base of the thumb.
6. Mount of the Moon, on side of hand opposite thumb.
7. Mount of Mars, between Mount of Mercury and that of the Moon.
7a. Second Mount of Mars, influenced by Jupiter, under thumb, below Venus.

On a firm hand you will not see any marked rise when a mount is really very well developed. On the contrary, if it is wanting or badly developed, a hollow will be found. On a soft hand the mounts will be more prominent, but will have no more significance than the lesser development on a hard hand. It is manifest from the start that the type of hand must be taken into consideration in judging either mounts or lines. A hand may be callous, however, from hard work, and still the mounts will be unaffected.

The mounts will sometimes be found directly at the base of the fingers with which they are connected, but again

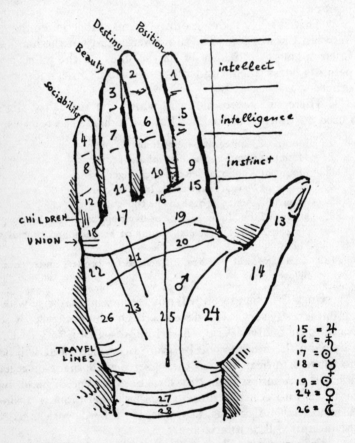

1 RELIGION
2 PRUDENCE
3 ART
4 STUDY
5 AMBITION
6 EXPERIMENT
7 CRITICISM
8 SPECULATION
9 SENSUALITY
10 CONCENTRATION
11 SUCCESS
12 SHREWDNESS
13 WILL
14 LOGIC

15 AMBITION
16 INDEPENDENCE
17 ART
18 COMMERCE
19 HEART
20 HEAD
21 TALENT
22 RESISTANCE
23 INTUITION
24 LOVE
25 DESTINY
26 IMAGINATION
27 } RESTRICTA
28 }

Beauty
Destiny
Position
Sociability

intellect
intelligence
instinct

CHILDREN
UNION →

TRAVEL
LINES

15 = ♃
16 = ♄
17 = ☉
18 = ♀☿
19 = ☉♀
24 = ♀☿
26 = ☾

The Major Lines of the Hand, According to Modern Palmistry

THE MOUNTS

MOUNT OF JUPITER

Good	Excess	Wanting
Pride and self-respect	Conceit	Lack of self-respect

MOUNT OF SATURN

Love of solitude and agriculture	Morbidness	Frivolity

MOUNT OF APOLLO

Mercy and talent	Mercy without justice gambling	Cruelty, dullness

MOUNT OF MERCURY

Buoyancy, cheerfulness, talkativeness	Chattering, indifference to feelings of others	No sense of humor

MOUNT OF MARS

Power of endurance	Stolidity	Cowardice

MOUNT OF THE MOON

Imagination and originality	Eccentricity	No imagination

MOUNT OF VENUS

Affection	Sensuality	Coldness

they may lean much toward some other mount. A mount is said to be "good" when it is evenly developed, well-placed, and firm when gently pressed. Then the quality belonging to it has been cultivated. It is said to be "unfavorable" when it encroaches or is overdeveloped and usurps another's position. Then the qualities indicated are either in excess, unused, or wanting.

The influence of the mount which is principally developed may be either good or bad. This may be arrived at by inspecting the formation of the tips of the fingers, the consistency of the hand, and the development of the thumb. Thus, pointed fingers reveal an intuition, a lofty idealism of the quality. Square fingers will look at the reasonable aspects of character, and Spatulate will cultivate the material qualities of the mount.

The following summary of qualities or characteristics and their signs will be found of great utility in answering questions easily and quickly.

Acquisitiveness: Fingers curved inward, and no stretch between first finger and thumb.

Adaptability: A flexible thumb, especially at first joint; flexible palm and fingers.

Anger: Red nails (square bases show revenge), low mounts of Mars (they give control when developed).

Art: For painting, long fingers for detail, short for effects; large hands; Mount of the Moon well-developed for imagination and originality; Mercury high for the imitative quality; first phalanx of Apollo long and wide for form and color; Mount of Apollo high for animal painting. For sculpture, rather small hands, long fingers (knots no objection), the first phalanx of all the fingers long for deftness in detail, Apollo finger dominant for distinction in form, and mounts of Luna and Mercury high for originality and imitativeness. For the drama, long fingers, Mercury dominant; turned back thumb; good mounts of Mercury and Luna; Saturn mount and finger dominant for tragedy; percussion (Mars and Mercury) developed for comedy.

Ambition: Long, strong and straight finger of Jupiter; high mount and cross on second phalanx for social ambition; first phalanx of Apollo finger wide and long in addition gives artistic ambition; a long and dominant Mercury finger; good thumb, the ambition to business; good first phalanx of Mercury turns the ambition to diplomacy.

Analysis: Long, knotted fingers for investigation; short nails for criticism; well-developed second phalanx of thumb for logic.

Benevolence: Mount of Venus for emotion; Luna for sympathy; thumb for constancy; stretch between first finger and thumb for generosity.

Bohemianism: Long, widely separated fingers, flexible palm, sloping Head Line, short, turned-back thumb, and well developed Luna.

Calculation: Long, knotted fingers, long finger of Mercury (squared).

Caprice: Short first phalanx of thumb, short fingers, soft hand.

Concentration: Long fingers, long and strong thumb.

Conventionality: Straight, stiff fingers, set close together, stiff palm, straight thumb.

Construction: Long first phalanges of all fingers, spatulated, and mounts of Mercury and Moon.

Courage: Both mounts of Mars high and hard, Plain of Mars high, Saturn low, and Luna not very high. This gives extreme courage of an almost brutal type. A good Mount of Mars on the percussion will alone give passive courage.

Courtesy: Medium palm and fingers flexible, Plain of Mars not too high, and mounts of Jupiter, Luna, and Mercury well developed.

Craft: Long finger of Mercury (dominant) and strong thumb.

Deceit: Long finger of Mercury and high Mount of Luna. Liars with poor memory and little imagination from low Luna are successful in their deceit.

Devotion: For religious devotion, subject should have long, pointed finger of Jupiter, pointed thumb, Luna developed toward wrist, and soft palm, high mounts of Saturn and Venus.

Eccentricity: Mount of Luna highly developed sometimes with excrescences.

Egotism: Thick, white, firm palm, high Mount of Jupiter, low Luna and Mercury.

Energy: Hard, firm palm, well developed Plain of Mars.

Enmity: Lines on Mars denote enemies; short nails square at base; high mounts on Saturn and Luna.

Economy: Stiff thumb, long knotted fingers.

Eloquence: Long fingers of Mercury and Jupiter, and high mounts of Luna and Mercury.

Fatalism: Heavy finger and mount of Saturn, soft, hollow, palm, and thumb turned outward.

Firmness: Long equally balanced thumb, knotted fingers that are fairly long.

Foolishness: Weak first phalanx of thumb, soft hand.

Gratitude: Good thumb, high mounts of Venus and Luna.

Heroism: High mounts of Mars, Luna, and Venus.

Honesty: Straight finger of Jupiter and good thumb.

Idiocy: Twisted fingers, turned-in thumb, and a hand altogether badly developed.

Idleness: Soft, fat palm, with no knuckles visible.

Impulse: Short fingers, small thumb.

Justice: Long, straight finger of Jupiter, long and strong thumb.

Love: Platonic love is given by a strong thumb and small lines running parallel. Friendship is given by high mounts of Luna and Venus. Passionate love is indicated by high mounts of Luna and Venus and many encroaching influence lines with a weak thumb (allowing the love to rule the Life).

Madness: Head line broken and drooping to Luna; high mounts of Saturn and Luna. If Mercury is absent and there are stars on Mars, the madness will be homicidal.

Melancholy: Long, heavy finger and mount of Saturn, no mount of Mercury, and a development of Luna toward the wrist (generally long, knotted fingers).

Method: Both knots, long fingers and thumb.

Narrow-mindedness: Quadrangle very narrow, fingers and thumb conventional.

Occultism: Long, smooth fingers, Luna developed toward wrist, Line of Intuition present, and the *croix mystique* in quadrangle.

Order: Long, knotted fingers; straight Head Line.

Perception: The first phalanx of all the fingers cushioned, and the mount of Luna developed.

Practicability: Hard hand, medium palm and fingers, good thumb.

Pride: Long finger of Jupiter, especially third phalanx, long and high mount of Jupiter. If mount of Jupiter leans toward Venus, we have family pride.

Prudence: Evenly developed and strong thumb, finger of Saturn well but not too well-developed.

Reason: Long second phalanx of thumb, medium palm and
   fingers.
Religion: Straight finger of Jupiter pointed, long first phalanx of
   Mercury finger giving eloquence, straight and well developed
   thumb. (This analysis applies to clergymen.)
Reverence: Long, smooth finger of Jupiter.
Sociability: Developed mount of Jupiter, mount of Mercury and
   medium palm and fingers.
Tact: Long, pointed first phalanx of Mercury.
Timidity: Depression at base of third phalanx, depression of Mars
   on percussion, hollow palm.
Vanity: High mount of Jupiter sloping toward the base of the
   finger.
Wit: Mount of Mercury and finger well developed, first phalanx
   long for repartee; Mars under Mercury well developed.

TEA LEAVES

Tea leaves were used for centuries as a means of foretelling
future events. Tea is most commonly used because it gives
better indications for the reader. Many people attribute
teacup reading, as it is called, to a Clairvoyant power
possessed by the reader, the teacup and grounds merely
acting as a point of concentration. However, teacup grounds
do form various images and pictures in the cup and can be
plainly seen by anyone. Some of the more complicated
pictures are more difficult to ascertain by the
less-experienced person, but with practice and patience, it is
easy to learn how to read fortunes from the teacup.

The person giving the reading is called the "Reader," and
the person to whom the reading is given is called the "Sitter."
The Sitter drinks the tea from the cup, leaving only a few
drops in the bottom of the cup. The cup should be turned
around three times by the hand with a swinging movement
from right to left. This distributes the leaves or grounds
about the bottom of the cup. Turn teacup upside down to
drain away the moisture. This procedure should be
conducted by the Sitter, under the Reader's direction.

Upon careful examination, you can discern various images

or pictures caused by the formation of the grounds. Study these carefully and from different positions. Various designs will be revealed, and each design has a meaning.

The meaning of these designs will be explained, and the reader should learn the meaning of each; however, you can easily refer to this chapter for the desired information. In some instances, the meanings of one design will contradict the meaning of another, so these interpretations must not be taken as a whole but taken as part of a general reading. Bad influences or indications will be balanced by good influences. The reading must be formulated from the general meaning of all designs shown in the cup.

Needless to say, it is necessary to exercise the imagination to see some of the designs, but if the grounds from any kind of a design, giving you some reason to interpret it as a certain object, then it should be considered.

The reading of fortunes in the teacup will be found an interesting pastime. You can read your own fortune, or read for your friends. Many people have great faith in this method of divination, and a careful record of interpretations reveals many instances where the future was foretold with unerring accuracy.

LIST OF SYMBOLS

Acorn: Success.

Aircraft: Unexpected journey, perhaps disappointment.

Anchor: Should grounds form a design of such nature as to cause you to believe it to resemble an anchor, and it is clearly shown, the meaning may be interpreted as love and constancy. However, if the anchor is cloudy and indistinct, the meaning is just the reverse. This design appearing at the bottom of the cup means great happiness.

Angel: Good news.

Arch: A journey, perhaps to another land.

Arrow: Bad news in a letter.

Axe: You will overcome the difficulty.

Bagpipe: Disappointment.

Ball: Represents someone who is connected with outdoor sports.

Balloon: Whatever is most in the mind will not last long.

Basket: If empty, it shows money trouble. If full, expect a present.

Bat: Disappointment.

Bayonet: Illness or accident.

Beans: Trouble about money.

Bear: A journey.

Beasts: If other than dogs, indicate misfortune. The figure of a dog shown at the top means faithful friends. The same figure in the middle means the reverse, and at the bottom means secret enemies. Thus, it will be noted throughout the interpretation of these signs that when the figure is revealed at the top and clearly favorable circumstances are indicated, and as the figure recedes in the cup and becomes less distinct, the conditions become adverse.

Beehive: Business success. If bees are flying around it the gain will be very considerable.

Beetle: Scandal.

Bell: Unexpected news. If more than one bell, a wedding.

Birds: Good news. If the birds are flying the news will come quickly.

Bird's Cage: Something stands in the way of happiness. If the cage door is open, the obstacle is passing.

Bird's Nest: Happiness in love and home.

Boat: A visit from a friend.

Book: If open it is a promise of success in some new direction or of a new lover. If closed, a sign of delay. Sometimes a book will represent one of studious habits or whose work is connected with books, if such a person is in the mind of the Inquirer.

Boomerang: Someone is plotting.

Boots: Success.

Bottle: One bottle stands for pleasure. A row of bottles indicates illness. Sometimes, however, the bottles stand for someone whose work is connected with them, a wine merchant, a chemist, doctor, or nurse. The sitter must decide whether such a person is in her thoughts.

Bouquet: Happy love.

Bow or Bow and Arrow: Scandal.

Box: If with the lid open, some trouble connected with a love-affair will soon be cleared up. If with lid closed, something that has been lost will be found.

Bridge: An opportunity that will lead to success.

Bugle: Hard work and great endeavor are required.

Building: A removal.

Butterfly: Inconstancy. This symbol depends on those near it.

Camel: Unexpected news.

Candle: Sickness.

Cannon: News of a soldier or of someone who serves the President in any capacity or who works in the Government.

Cap: There is a need of caution.

Car: Good Fortune.

Cart: There will be delay.

Cat: Quarrels.

Chain: An engagement or wedding.

Chair: Unexpected visitor.

Chimney: Take every care in what you are about to do.

Church: Unexpected money.

Cigar: New friend.

Circles: Are often shown in the cup and they represent financial affairs, the receipt of money for the Sitter. If the circle is cut or connected with lines, the money will be forthcoming, but a delay will first be experienced.

Clock: The Inquirer is thinking of the future. The surrounding symbols will give the answer.

Clover: Is an odd design, but not difficult to detect. If it appears at the top of the cup, good fortune is close at hand. If the clover is nearer the bottom, good fortune is more distant.

Coat: A parting.

Coffin: Is a sign of illness, or death. One hardly need seek an interpretation when a sign of this character appears, as it is self-explanatory.

Comb: A false friend.

Corkscrew: Trouble caused by curiosity.

Crab: An enemy.

Crescent: A railroad trip.

Crown: Such as worn by a king or queen, signifies honor and the the respect of friends.

Crown and Cross: A combination of both means welcome news or good fortune will reach you through the death of another.

Cross: Like the coffin, is a sign of death, not necessarily for the sitter, but does connect the sitter with the occurence.

Crutches: A friend will help.

Cup: Success is at hand.

Curtain: A secret has been kept. If the curtain seems drawn back the secret will not be of great importance.

Dagger: Be careful of what you say and do.

Dancer: A disappointment.

Deer: Disputes.

Desk: News in a letter.

Devil: Bad influences are around.

Diamond: Legacy coming very unexpectedly.

Dog: At the top, faithful friends; in the middle, they are untrustworthy. A dog at the bottom means secret enemies.

Dish: Quarrels at home.

Donkey: Be brave and patient and all will be well.

Doves: Everything good.

Dragon: Sudden change.

Drum: A journey about new work.

Duck: Luck in speculation

Eagle: A change for the better.

Ear: Unexpected news.

Earrings: Trouble through misunderstandings.

Eel: Distasteful duties to perform.

Eggs: New plans and hopes. Perhaps news of a birth.

Elephant: Your friend is to be trusted.

Engine: Hasty news.

Eye: You will conquer the difficulty.

Faces: Several faces are the sign of a party or some gathering of people. If a face resembles that of someone known to the Inquirer, it represents that person. An ugly face shows there is a secret enemy. A pretty face foretells happiness.

Fan: A flirtation is in progress.

Fangs: Beware of trouble.

Feet: It will be necessary to make an important decision.

Fence: Success is near.

Finger: This symbol has no meaning of its own, but special heed must be given to that at which it points.

Fish: Indicates good news will be received from over the water.

Flag: Danger, quarrels.

Flowers: A marriage of much interest.

Fly: Small annoyances.

Fork: A false friend.

Fountain: Great success.

Frog: Success through change or work or removal.

Fruit: Prosperity.

Gallows: You will conquer your enemies.

Gate: Go onwards. All is well.

Geese: Unexpected visitors. A good time.

Giraffe: Mischief caused by want of thought.

Goat: News of a sailor.

Gondola: Love affair at sea.

Grapes: Happiness.

Grasshopper: News of a friend, probably a soldier.

Gun: Quarrels.

Hammer: Some work that is not congenial.

Hand: A good friend or loyal lover. If clenched, it means a quarrel.

Handcuffs: Trouble.

Hare: The return of an absent friend.

Harp: Beginning of an affair of the heart.

Hat: A present.

Hawk: Someone is jealous.

Heart: Is a good omen, if surrounded with dots. The meaning may be interpreted as coming money and happiness. A ring or oval near the heart means an approaching marriage.

Heavenly Bodies: Sun, Moon, and Stars signify happiness and success.

Hen: Happiness at home.

Hoe: Plenty of work.

Horse: Prosperity.

Horseshoe: Great good luck.

Hourglass: Delays are dangerous.

House: All is well.

Human figures: Generally are good, and denote love and marriage.

Indian: News from afar.

Initials: When letters of the alphabet appear they are the initials of freinds. Should a triangle be near an initial the letter stands for one who is as yet unknown.

Interrogation: (mark of) It is very uncertain.

Jewelry: A present may be expected.

Jug: A gathering of old acquaintances.

Kettle: Illness.

Key: A change in occupation.

King: A splendid symbol. A powerful friend.

Kite: Scandal.

Knife: Broken friendship or parted lovers.

Ladder: A rise in life.

Lamp: Success in money matters.

Leaf: An encouraging sign for the future.

Leaves: Good fortune is coming.

Letter: Means the receipt of sudden news. If clearly shown, the news will be good; if the letter is surrounded with dots, it means money. However, if clouds surround the letter, bad news of loss of money may be expected.

Lily: If it appears at the top of the cup, indicates a happy marriage. At the bottom, reverse the interpretation.

Lion: You will win through.

Lock: Under a great strain.

Man: Signifies a speedy visitor. If the arm is held out, he brings a present. If figure is very clear, he is dark; if indistinct, he is of light complexion.

Medal: You will be rewarded.

Mice: Beware of thieves.

Monkey: Scandal.

Moon: A definite conclusion will soon be reached.

Mountains: Are frequent in the cup, and may mean good or bad fortune, and must be interpreted according to other designs also shown in the cup at the time of the reading.

Mushroom: An obstacle in your path of business.

Needle: Something you have done will be talked about.

Numbers: If the Inquirer's lucky number is amongst the symbols, it is the best possible signal. When a number appears near a symbol foretelling an event, it indicates the number of days which will pass before the event takes place.

Nut: You will attend a formal reception.

Oar: Safety from impending disaster.

Octopus: Danger signal. Someone is plotting your downfall.

Ostrich: A trip by air over land and sea.

Owl: Scandal.

Padlock: If open, a surprise. If closed, a warning.

Palm Tree: Happiness connected with love or marriage.

Parrot: Either travel or news from afar.

Pears: Good fortune.

Pickaxe: Worry connected with work.

Pig: A present.

Pigeons: If flying, important news. If sitting, improvement in trade.

Pillar: Friends will help.

Pine Tree: All will be well.

Pipe: This represents the thoughts of a man. The symbols near will give indications of his identity or the nature of his thoughts.

Pistol: Danger.

Pod: A small start, with increasing prosperity.

Prong: Necessity, the mother of invention, will help your cause.

Rat: A treacherous enemy.

Raven: Bad news.

Razor: Quarrels and partings.

Ring: A frequent figure, is a sign of marriage and if clearly shown, the marriage will be a happy, successful one. If clouds are near the ring, the marriage will prove a failure and dissatisfaction result. A second ring at the right of the cup means the wedding will not occur.

Rose: Friendship.

Scissors: A misunderstanding in which a tie will be broken.

Sheep: Always a good omen.

Shell: Good news.

Ship: A successful journey or the thoughts of someone on a ship.

Shoes: A change that will point to success. Probably new work.

Snakes: Are a bad omen, and if forewarned by such a sign, great caution should be exercised to avoid misfortune.

Squares: Mean satisfaction, comfort and happiness.

Squirrels: Happiness at home. Prosperity after a hard time.

Star: Good luck is coming.

Steamer: A journey or news from overseas. Or a person who is on board such a ship.

Steeple: A stroke of bad luck.

Straight Line: Usually indicates a journey, and the length of the journey may be measured correspondingly by the length of the line.

Table: Watch surrounding symbols.

Telephone: Trouble for which forgetfulness is to blame.

Tent: A love nest for two.

Thimble: Changes at home.

Tomahawk: Gains by determination.

Trees: If a single tree be revealed, recovery from ill health is denoted. If a group of trees are revealed and clearly shown, this means that impending trouble may be avoided. If several trees appear in the cup, and wide apart and plainly shown, it is a good indication.

Triangle: Signifies an unexpected receipt of money or legacy.

Unicorn: A secret marriage.

Vase: News of recovery from illness.

Vegetables: Present unhappiness will be followed by content.

Violin: Gaiety and much company.

Wagon: A wedding trip in foreign lands.

Wavy Lines: If long in length, signify losses and hardships. The importance of these lines depends on the length and clearness.

Wedding Cake: News of a wedding.

Wheel: Fulfillment of desire.

GETTING ALONG WITH OTHERS

To get along more harmoniously in a business or social way with your associates, you will find a little knowledge of the basic characteristics of those born under each of the twelve Zodiac Signs will be very helpful. Here is a brief outline for each sign.

ARIES: In dealing with people born between these dates you should be firm but courteous, not mince your words nor be effeminate. These folks are aggressive and hate to stall or delay, but you must use persuasion and not force if you would achieve better success with them. They are trustworthy and slightly susceptible to flattery, especially those having birthdays during the April part of this sign.

TAURUS: In dealing with people born between these dates you should not appear over-anxious to convince them of your friendship or of the merit of any proposition you are offering. Taurus natives will see your point long before you've fully explained or reached it. When contacting them in person, be sure your clothes are neat and conservative and let them talk all they wish. They are very susceptible to flattery.

GEMINI: In dealing with people born between these dates you should be cheerful and open your conversation as early as possible with some reference to a current news item or local event of mutual interest. Be sure you are quite thoroughly familiar with the subject on which you desire to converse because Gemini folks have a very keen intellect and are profound readers. They are extremely sensitive, so be on your guard not to offend them either by word or act. A little praise works well, but don't carry it to extremes.

CANCER: in dealing with people born between these dates you should quickly touch upon any domestic subject, and if you know of some family or business accomplishment of theirs don't delay mentioning it — make it a point to do so early in the conversation. They are very changeable folks, easily offended and any business deals should be closed "on the spot" as tomorrow would likely bring a change in their decision. Let them think, however, that they alone are making the decision. That will help.

LEO: In dealing with people born between these dates you must praise their good work, good cooking, or fine judgment or even their personal appearance (if you are sufficiently acquainted with them to permit this). Be "straight from the shoulder" in what you wish to say to them and don't be surprised if they are a little stern or "hard." These folks are great pioneers, know what hardships are, and it is, therefore, essential that you be concrete and businesslike in the presentation of your proposition, even in a conversation not on a business basis. They are extremely quick thinkers.

VIRGO: In dealing with people born between these dates you must be jovial, carefree, and happy. These folks are very generous, will buy most anything and will help nearly everyone as long as they are not offended. Once you offend them by word or deed, you are done. There will never be a reconciliation. Women born under this sign are excellent cooks and dieticians and like to have their work praised, which provides a suitable ground for the opening conversation.

LIBRA: In dealing with people born between these dates you must be very refined and gentle. Talk in a calm, dignified, low voice, and the more beautiful language you use in expressing yourself, so much more impressed will any native of this sign be. These folks are usually very grateful for any kindness shown them and seldom forget a "good turn." They are not, as a rule, susceptible to flattery, so you must depend on logic and diplomacy. They possess a keen sense of justice which should be "played up" in your conversation.

SCORPIO: In dealing with folks born between these dates you would do well to respect their blunt, aggressive manner, but not be too timid in approaching them and never attempt to tell them more about anything of which they seem to be thoroughly familiar. They'll monopolize the conversation, and you'll do well to be a good listener and coacher. Just ask them a question or two at infrequent intervals, and they'll carry on and enjoy it. They possess great courage and may talk of events that bear out some deeds of heroism, and this often provides a good "opener" in any conversation. Possessed of an extremely bitter and sharp temper, they should not be antagonized in any way, so be sure not to arouse their ire, but maintain your poise and self-control at all costs. They are very good buyers of merchandise, but may drive a hard bargain.

SAGITTARIUS: In dealing with folks born between these dates you should never attempt to hide the truth from them; if you do and they find it out, as they most certainly will, you are finished, completely and thoroughly. Relate some incident in your own life that was extremely embarrassing to you and don't minimize the particular situation that was the most ludicrous or serious. If it involves a gross blunder on your part — so much the better. They are great admirers of loyalty and sincerity at all costs. Animal life and nature appeals to them strongly and provide a suitable "break-in" for any conversation. They are very thrifty folk, hard to sell to but a bargain appeals to them. They are often quite extensively interested in the Occult or mystical.

CAPRICORN: In dealing with folks born between these dates you must proceed slowly and methodically; should be cheerful and buoyant and conservative in your views and expressions, especially if you're in quest of business. Crack a "pun" occasionally, as they'll enjoy it and the impression will be good. These folks are inclined to be quite melancholy or moody so try to pull them out of this rut. Once you are in their good graces, the ties of friendship will be very strong and hard to break, and well worth any effort you've made to create the good feeling. Show them how to make their lives a little more bearable and happy. They are inclined to be miserly and more apt to "open up" on a big proposition than a small one if such an opportunity is a worthy one and will stand the acid test which they often apply to any business venture.

AQUARIUS: In dealing with folks born between these dates there seems to be no "set rule" to follow. They may appear to agree with you at the moment, but in the end take an entirely different course or view. They act a great deal on impulse, so when talking business you should "close" them as soon as possible — the "next day" likely will be too late. A stall means the door will be closed to further overtures. They are pioneers in thought and deed, so give them something new and different if you'd win. Realize, when talking to them, that more notables are in the Hall of Fame that were born under this sign than any other in the zodiac. You must be honest and aboveboard in your dealings with them, even to the smallest detail. Live up to your promises no matter how minor or insignificant they may seem and you should obtain good results.

PISCES: In dealing with folks born between these dates you should agree with them in most of what they say, even if you must sacrifice a little of your own individuality. Never be harsh or endeavor to "drive" them as this would immediately put cold water on your association. Be kind, and above all, sympathetic over their troubles, as these folks often believe they have more physical and economic vicissitudes than others. They are deeply impressed by speech or writing that is inspirational in nature or well done in some particular, and they possess some mighty original ideas of their own which you would do well to respect — even coach them on. If you can get them to talk on a subject of their hobby or "sideline," you'll soon find yourself in the "inner sanctum."

"BE NOT THE FIRST TO QUARREL, NOR THE LAST TO MAKE UP"

THE DOCTRINE OF MOLES

In the *ZOHAR*, we read: "All happens here below as it does above. On the firmament which envelops the universe,

Moles and Signs of the Zodiac

we see many figures formed by the Stars and Planets. They reveal hidden things and profound mysteries. Similarly, upon our skin which encircles the human being there exist forms and traits that are the Stars of our bodies."

The Magi interpreted this saying and examined the skin in their search for Prophetic signs. They chose the legendary Melampus of Ancient Greece for their patron. His treatise interprets the moles according to their position in the anatomy:

"A mole on a man's forehead signifies wealth and happiness; on a woman's forehead, it denotes that she will be powerful, perhaps a ruler. Close to the eyebrow of a man, the mole predicts a happy marriage with a pretty and virtuous woman, and it foretells similar fortune to girls. Moles on the bridge of the nose mean lust and extravagance for both sexes. When appearing on the nostrils, the mole signifies constant travel. Moles upon the lips of men and women betray gluttony, and on the chin, that they will possess gold and silver.

"Moles in the ear and on the neck are lucky omens; they predict wealth and fame. When upon the nape of the neck, however, the beauty spot carries an ill omen, that of being beheaded! Moles upon the loins are unfortunate, signifying mendacity, and ill luck for the descendants. When appearing on the shoulders, they predict captivity and unhappiness; on the chest, poverty. Moles on the hands announce many children, and under the arm-pits, they bring luck as they promise a wealthy and handsome husband or wife. Ominous are moles when found upon the heart and bosom and belly, as they signify voracity. They are a good omen when seen on the upper leg, announcing wealth; when upon the lower part of the stomach, they presage intemperance for men but the contrary for women."

Melampus concludes by implying that a still more elaborate method of mole interpretation exists, adding one should observe whether the mole is on the right or the left side of the body, as left carries a sinister and morbid meaning, and right predicts general wealth and probity.

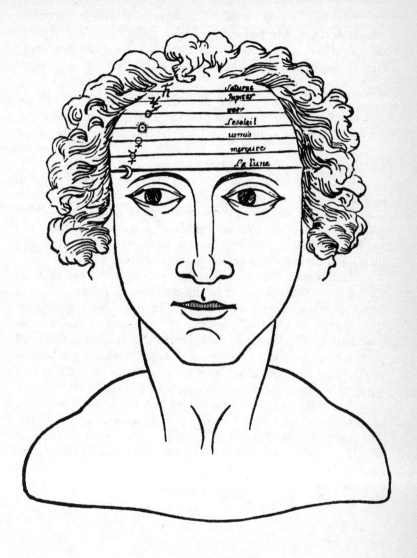

The Human Forehead and Planets

METOPOSCOPY

The doctrine of moles was overshadowed by another Occult Science, Metoposcopy, which judges man's character and his destiny from the lines engraved upon his forehead. The discovery of this Divinatory art was attributed to Jerome Cardan.

Metoposcopy is a mixture of Astrological calculation and empirically collected knowledge. Astrology teaches every part of the body is influenced by the Stars. The study of the lines in the forehead gains special importance since it is closer to Heaven than any other part of man.

Once this idea was accepted, it became necessary to control the results obtained through Astrological mathematics with observations gathered from Nature. Cardan searched and compared hundreds of human foreheads. His work is illustrated by some eight hundred woodcuts depicting heads and their frontal celestial demarcations.

The order of the planets corresponds to that in Astrology. Saturn is the "highest;" then follow in turn Jupiter, Mars, the Sun, Venus, Mercury, and the Moon. Having thus established the Planets' spheres of influence, the practicing Metoposcopits will mark the subject's forehead with seven equidistant and parallel strips, with the purpose of recognizing his subject's Planetary zones which are narrow or wide according to the measurements of the forehead.

A wrinkle in the zone of Jupiter is endowed with the characteristics attributed to the planet: magnamity, nobility, and pride. If the line crosses from one zone to another, it signifies the two Planets are in conjunction; their characteristics act upon and reinforce each other. Metoposcopy is nothing more than the Astrology of the Microcosm.

10

Methods of Winning

In every human mind is a spark of the gambling instinct or a desire to take chances that afford the thrill of gaining or losing in such a venture. Life itself is a speculation; a child is born — perhaps it will live and perhaps it will not — a merchant opens a business — perhaps he will succeed or perhaps he won't; an aviator takes a long flight — perhaps he will make a safe landing, or perhaps he will not. The desire to take chances is innate in all kinds of humanity, primitive or civilized.

Emerson said, "Astrology is Astronomy brought to Earth and applied to the affairs of men." Astrology, the oldest Science in the world, has outlined the proper courses for people to follow for many thousands of years. "There is a time and a place for all things," and no more practical Science in the world can be applied to mankind's daily affairs than the sciences of Astrology and Numerology.

Ptolemy, the greatest Astrologer and philosopher of Ancient times, said, "Judgment must be regulated by thyself, as well as by science . . . . it is advantageous to make choice of days and hours at a time constituted by the nativity."

While the author does not recommend nor encourage promiscuous gambling in any form, he is mindful of the fact that so long as human beings are constituted as they are at present they are going to indulge in some form of speculation. If people must speculate, this will show how to combine the laws that rule and regulate the universe with their own judgment. Accurate judgment is also necessary for the success of any enterprise, yet, by combining this with the fundamental laws of cause and effect outlined by the science of the universe, a greater measure of success may be attained.

We present this information for what it may be worth! It may appeal to you as a pastime flavored with the thrill of sport or a test of skill tempered by your judgment.

If we look at the life history of an individual as it stretches out from birth to death, it presents a remarkable record of events that appear to have no logical relationship to each other. In childhood, there may have been either great happiness or great sorrow and suffering regardless of character qualities, and there is nothing in the present life of the child to explain either. The child itself may be gentle and affectionate and yet it may be the recipient of gross abuse and cruel misunderstanding. In maturity we may find still greater mysteries.

Almost invariably there are mingled successes and failures, pleasures and pains, but when we come to analyze them we fail to find a satisfactory reason for them. We see that the successes often arrive when they are not warranted by anything that was done to win them, and for the want of any rational explanation we call it "good luck." We also observe that sometimes failure after failure comes when the man is not only doing his very best but when all of his plans will stand the test of sound business procedure. Baffled again, we throw logic to the winds and call it "bad luck."

"Luck" is a word we use to conceal our ignorance and our inability to trace the working of the Law. Suppose we were to ask a savage to explain how it is that a few minutes time with the morning paper enables one to know what happened yesterday in a city on the opposite side of the earth. He knows nothing of reports and cables and presses. He cannot explain it. He cannot even comprehend it. But if he is a vain savage and does not wish to admit his ignorance, he might solemnly assert that the reason we know is because we are lucky, and he would be using the work just as sensibly as we use it.

If by luck we mean chance, there is no such thing in this world. Chance necessarily means chaos and the absence of Law. From the magnificent, orderly procession of hundreds of millions of Suns and their world systems that wheel majestically through space down to the very atom with its mysterious electrons, the universe is a stupendous proclamation of the all-pervading presence of Law. It is a mighty panorama of cause and effect. There is no such thing as chance.

What, then, is good luck? We know people do receive benefits which they apparently have not earned, yet there cannot be result without a cause. They have earned it in other lives when the conditions did not permit immediate harvesting of the results of the good forces generated and Nature is paying the debt and making the balance of her books at this period. They have put themselves in harmony with evolutionary law — with the Divine Plan, and nothing which they need is withheld. With the insight of genius, Ella Wheeler Wilcox stated the Law:

> Luck is the tuning of our inmost thought
> To chord with God's great plan. That done, ah know
> Thy silent wishes to results shall grow,
> And day by day shall miracles be wrought!
> Once let they inner being selflessly be brought
> To chime with universal good, and lo!
> What music from the spheres shall through thee flow,
> What benefits shall come to thee unsought!

When we eliminate chance, we are forced to seek the cause of unexplained good or bad fortune beyond the boundaries of this Life because there is nothing else we can do. We have results to explain and we know they do not come from causes that belong to this incarnation. They must, of necessity, arise from causes belonging to a past Life.

This broader outlook on the life journey, extending over a very long series of incarnations, gives us a wholly different view of the difficulties with which we have to contend and of the limitations which afflict us. It at once shows us that in the midst of apparent injustice there is, in the long run, really nothing but Perfect Justice for everybody. All good fortune has been earned. All bad fortune is deserved, and each of us is, mentally and morally, what he has made himself. Masefield put it well when he wrote:

> *All that I rightly think or do,*
> *Or make or spoil or bless or blast,*
> *Is curse or blessing justly due*
> *For sloth or effort in the past.*
> *My life's a statement of the sum*
> *Of vice indulged or overcome.*
> *And as I journey on the roads*
> *I shall be helped and healed and blest.*
> *Dear words shall cheer, and be as goads*
> *To urge to heights as yet unguessed.*
> *My road shall be the road I made.*
> *All that I gave shall be repaid.*

Jupiter, the largest Planet in our Solar system, plays an important part in our lives, in fact, his size is three times as big as all the rest of the Planets put together. It takes twelve years for this planet to go through the twelve Signs of the Zodiac, and during this period it influences all human beings. Its cycle is, therefore, twelve years. In other words, every twelve years this planet is at the same place in the Heaven as at your birth and marks then the beginning of a new cycle for you. This law holds true for every man and woman, and thus it is possible to calculate the fortunate years for each one of us as well as to indicate those years when we are wasteful, extravagant, and careless and thus face losses.

King Solomon said, "To everything there is a season, and a time for every purpose under the Heaven." This means that human life should be planned in accordance with the Planetary influences operating at our birth and those influencing us now. But to each one of us is given the freedom to work in harmony with those great Natural Laws or to act contrary to them. It is up to us to plan our lives in such a way that we expand under favorable influences and that we hold back when the Planets are at critical angles.

Those who do not understand these laws go blindly ahead and blame destiny for their ill-luck. All of us, regardless of when born, have periods when we are fortunate and success smiles upon us, but from time to time we are under a cycle when our affairs go wrong and opportunities are few. Lucky for us, those cycles come at regular intervals and thus it is possible to indicate exactly the cycle you are under at a certain age of your life.

Regardless of other planetary influences operating in your life, the following cycles are fortunate for you and it is up to you to make use of them: at the age of 16, 20, 22, 26, 28, 32, 38, 40, 44, 46, 50, 56, 58, 62, 64, 68, 70, 74, 76, 80.

Of course, you may have some difficulties these years, but some good fortune will come your way, somebody will help you; an opportunity will present itself, and chances for making money are good.

Changes made will prove profitable and business will increase. It marks a fortunate time to expand in business, to take long journeys, for legal affairs, or to establish yourself securely. It is a time when things come our way, when we receive many gifts, when we win at games of chance, or when the opposite sex favors us. Your fortunate cycle last about nine months and starts about four months before your birth to four months afterward.

Next are the adverse cycles, also called cycles of restrictions. They mark periods in your life when you will not feel well, when your blood will be impure, and when you will be careless and extravagant. It is an adverse time to speculate or gamble and those in business should not expand or take on anything new without being sure it is not a wild scheme that will end up in a lawsuit. Others will refuse to cooperate, and some of us may even lose our jobs or have reversals in our business. In short, it is a time when you will not be lucky and it would be foolish for you to take chances. Thus, you will protect yourself against illusion and disappointments.

These cycles of restriction operate for nine months. In fact, you will feel them about four months before your birth-month and for four months afterwards: at the age of 15, 18, 21, 27, 30, 33, 39, 42, 51, 54, 57, 63, 69, 75, 78, 81.

History records many amazing predictions about the destiny of nations, rulers, and individuals all based on cycles, and this was the secret of the Egyptians as well as all past civilizations. It is up to every one of us to make use of these cycles in our affairs. Before any one makes a plan for the future, he should see if he is under a fortunate cycle or an adverse cycle. If it is a fortunate cycle, then he can go ahead with his plans, expand, take chances, and make radical changes in his affairs, yet if the cycle is adverse, it means that he must wait for at least one more year before launching new ventures or make any radical changes.

When your affairs are going smoothly and success is yours and you know it is a Fortunate cycle, you can time its end and thus do not expect your luck to last longer than it really will. If you are having success now and in a few months you will come under a critical cycle, then prepare yourself for it and do not live or act as though your good fortune would keep on going on for many more months. But if fate is unkind to you, when every hope is gone, you will want to know just when Luck, success, and happiness will be yours again. Consult these pages and see when your next favorable cycles will come and then go and prepare yourself for your ship to come in.

FORTUNATE NUMBERS

These methods, based on the Science of Numerology, are different for every person. The author has spent many years studying the Occult meanings of numbers, and while we do not guarantee results, many use them with great success.

Review

Name Number: The number secured by transferring the letters in a person's name to numbers. This shows the general characteristics the person has developed from the use of his name through life.

Birth Path Number: The number secured by transforming the Month, Date, and Year of the person's life and the outstanding events to be experienced.

Destiny Number: The number secured by adding the Name Number and Birth Path Number together. This shows whether your name adds or subtracts to your Birth Path indications. If it hinders you, the name should be changed for the future.

Monthly Number: The number secured by adding your Destiny Number to the number of any month and year. This shows the general indications for any month of the year for you. The Monthly Numbers change from year to year.

Name Numbers remain the same always, unless you change the spelling of your name. Birth Path Numbers never change; they always remain the same. Destiny Numbers remain the same unless you change the spelling of your name.

Any day which adds up to your Destiny Number is the best day for you. Mary Smith's lucky days in any month are 9th, 18th, and 27th. Her fairly good days are those which add to other odd numbers. The days which are neutral or slightly adverse are those which add up to even numbers. Work this out with your own Destiny Number and check off your good and adverse days on your calendar to guide you.

We wish to know if 1968 is a fortunate year for Mary Smith. Add 1968 thus: 1 plus 9 plus 6 plus 8 equals 24. Now add 2 and 4 which equals 6. This result is an even number, so it does not harmonize with Mary Smith's Destiny Number of 9; consequently, 1968 is not as fortunate for her as other years. The digit of the year must be the same or must be in harmony with your Destiny Number to be a Fortunate Year for you.

To find out your best hours of any day, find the time of Sunrise from your local daily paper. For example, suppose the Sun rises at 6:15 a.m. The first hour after Sunrise will be from 6:25 a.m. to 7:15 a.m. Mary Smith's best hours are the 9th hour after Sunrise and any other hour which adds up to 9, which would be the 18th hour after Sunrise. These hours will vary a few minutes each day as the Sun varies in rising time. Always use the hours after Sunrise which equal your Destiny Number.

For best results in partnerships or friendships their Destiny Number should be the same as yours. Those who have Destiny Numbers not similar to, but harmonious with yours will make fairly good friends, companions, and partners. Those who have Destiny Numbers which clash with yours will not make satisfactory associates and your relations with them will not be permanent nor congenial.

Secure the Monthly Number of any month and year (by Monthly Number is meant the numerical figure for any month reduced to a single digit). Add it and your Destiny Number together, which is your Monthly Number for that month. Then refer to the Gallery of Numbers for the general indications for the month.

It is not always necessary to work out the names of the months. Merely consider the number of the month: January, 1st month, therefore number 1; February, 2nd month, therefore, number 2 etc. October is the 10th month, therefore, 1 plus 0 equals 1. November is the 11th month, and you always leave 11 as it is. December is the 12th month, therefore, 1 plus 2 equals 3. Mary Smith's best month is the 9th month, which is September.

FOUR METHODS FOR USING YOUR FORTUNATE NUMBER

1. The Magic Hour: Use the number of the day of the week and the number of the hour at which you play or bet. Example: Suppose it is 4 p.m. on Friday (see clock) 4 p.m. is 1600; Friday is 5. Combine these to make 165 or 75. Then add 1

plus 6 plus 5 equals 12. Add again, 1 plus 2 equals 3. This gives four magic numbers: 165, 75, 12, 3, with the same strength. Use the one that suits you best.

2.   Strike the Keynote: Use the number of letters in your name and the hour of play. Suppose Jack Brown (9) wants a Lucky Number at 8 p.m. Combine 9 and 20 to make 92. And these: 9 plus 2 plus 0 equals 11. Add again, 1 plus 1 equals 2. This gives four magical numbers: 920, 29, 11, 2. Use the one that suits you best.

3.   Your Pinnacle of Success: Use the number of the day on which you were born and the number of the month. Suppose you were born on August 24th. Combine 24 and 8. This gives 248 or 68. Add 2 plus 4 plus 8 equals 14. Add again, 1 plus 4 equals 5. This gives you four Lucky Numbers of the same magic power: 248, 68, 14, 5.

4.   Lady Luck Method: Count the number of letters in your sweetheart's name and combine with the number of letters in your own name. Example: Maybelle Jones (13 letters) and Jack Brown (9 letters) makes 139 or 49. Add these: 1 plus 3 plus 9 equals 13. Add again, 1 plus 3 equals 4. This gives you four Lady Luck numbers: 139, 49, 13, 4. Use the one that suits the occasion best.

BUYING AND SELLING

It is believed by Astrologically minded people that this old science provides excellent rules for determining the proper times to buy and sell. The rules are based on the actual position of the Moon in the Zodiac.

Rule 1: Anything bought when the Moon is in Aries, Taurus, Gemini, Capricorn, Aquarius, or Pisces is said to be bought dearly and sold cheaply.

Rule 2: Anything bought to sell again is said to be bought cheaply and sold at a profit when the Moon is in Cancer, Leo, Virgo, Libra, Scorpio, or Sagittarius.

All almanacs and nearly all calendars give the four quarters of the Moon and its position in the Signs of the Zodiac.

DAYS OF THE WEEK

Sunday (Sun)
> Ask favors, deal with superiors or those in authority, seek work, buy, sell, write important letters, make new plans.

Monday (Moon)
> Do things that require quick results, travel, change, plant seeds, advertise, deal with women in a business way.

Tuesday (Mars)
> Impulsive influence; attend to law matters or anything requiring courage and initiative. Otherwise be cautious.

Wednesday (Mercury)
> Advertise, write letters, take short trips, sign legal papers, deal with brothers and sisters.

Thursday (Jupiter)
> Attend to all business or financial matters, ask favors, seek promotion or increased income. Usually one of the best week days.

Friday (Venus)
> Love, courtship, domestics.

Saturday (Saturn)
> Deal with elderly people.

SPECULATION AND WINNING

Astrology indicates the exact periods when you should speculate and when you should not do so. The Earth going through the twelve signs of the Zodiac forms certain configurations which indicate your prospects in any game of chance. Thus, you have regular periods every year when you will win or you may lose and it is up to you to make use of this information.

ARIES:

All Aries-born are inclined to take chances between July 22 and August 23. When you speculate in cooperation with others, it would be advisable that your partner is born under one of the following signs:

Aquarius   Sagittarius
Gemini   Libra
Leo

Miscellaneous Things to Observe

Those born between March 21st and March 28th will have better chances in speculation during the new moon.

Those born between March 29th and April 5th will have better chances in speculation during the second quarter of the moon.

Those born between April 6th and April 13th will have better chances in speculation during the full moon.

Those born between April 14th and April 10th will have better chances in speculation during the fourth quarter of the moon.

According to the Science of Numerology, the Celestial Number of Aries is 7. Mars, the ruling planet of this sign, has the Number of 6 for its numerical value. Combining these two numbers we have 7 plus 6 which equals 13. This number must now be reduced to a single digit; therefore, 1 plus 3 equals 4. The Number 4 is then the key number for all persons born in Aries. Bear this in mind on all occasions. When you buy a ticket of any sort, see that the Serial Number has 4 as the predominating number. Room Number 4 in a hotel, a street number containing a 4 or several 4's, horse number 4 in a race, player number 4 in a sport game, a card that totals 4 in a card game, a 4 rolled with dice, 4 on a spin wheel, etc. are considered fortunate for you.

Any day of the month that totals 4 is considered fortunate for you, thus, the 13th, the 22nd, and the 31st of a month because any of these dates reduced to a single digit make 4. The days of the month that are best for speculation are the 4th, 13th, 22nd, and 31st. However, you should engage in speculation only in your proper months or periods as explained below.

The proper hour for speculation is when your ruling Planet is governing. Refer to your daily paper, almanac, or calendar to find the time of Sunrise, then count the hours after Sunrise. These hours are the same every week, month, and year. Only the time of Sunrise changes.

Sunday: 7th, 14th, 21st hour after Sunrise. Monday: 4th, 11th, 18th hour after Sunrise. Tuesday: 1st, 8th, 15th, 22nd hour after Sunrise. Wednesday: 5th, 12th, 19th hour after Sunrise. Thursday: 2nd, 9th, 16th, 23rd hour after Sunrise. Friday: 6th, 13th, 20th hour after Sunrise. Saturday: 3rd, 10th, 17th, 24th hour after Sunrise.

TAURUS

All Taurus born are inclined to take chances between August 24 and September 23. When you speculate in cooperation with others, it would be advisable that your partner is born under one of the following signs:

Pisces	Virgo
Taurus	Scorpio
Cancer	Capricorn

Miscellaneous Things to Observe

Those born between April 21st and April 28th will have better chances in speculation during the new moon.

Those born between April 29th and May 5th will have better chances in speculation during the second quarter of the Moon.

Those born between May 6th and May 14th will have better chances in speculation during the full Moon.

Those born between May 15th and May 21st will have better chances in speculation during the fourth quarter of the Moon.

According to the Science of Numerology, the Celestial

Number of Taurus is 9. Venus, the ruling planet of this sign also has the number of 9. Combining these two numbers we have 9 plus 9 which equals 18. This number must now be reduced to a single digit; therefore, 1 plus 8 equals 9. The Number 9 is the key number for all persons born in Taurus. Bear this in mind on all occasions. When you buy a ticket of any sort see that the Serial Number has 9 as the predominating number. Room Number 9 in a hotel, a street number containing a 9 or several 9's, horse number 9 in a race. Player number 9 in a sport game, cards that total 9 in a card game, a 9 rolled with dice, 9 on a spin wheel, etc. are considered fortunate for you.

Any day of the month that totals 9 is considered fortunate for you, thus, the 18th and 27th because these dates reduce to a single digit making 9. The days of the month that are best for speculation are the 9th, 18th, and 27th. However, you should engage in speculation only in your proper months or periods as explained below.

The proper hour for speculation is when your ruling planet is governing. Refer to your daily paper, almanac, or calendar to find the time of Sunrise. Then count the hours after Sunrise. These hours are the same every week, month, and year. Only the time of Sunrise changes.

Sunday: 2nd, 10th, 16th hour after Sunrise. Monday: 6th, 13th, 20th hour after Sunrise. Tuesday: 3rd, 10th, 17th, 24th hour after Sunrise. Thursday: 4th, 11th, 18th hour after Sunrise. Friday: 1st, 8th, 15th, 22nd hour after Sunrise. Saturday: 5th, 12th, 19th hour after Sunrise.

GEMINI

All Gemini born are inclined to take chances between September 24 and October 23. When you speculate in cooperation with others, it would be advisable that your partner is born under one of the following signs:

Aquarius	Leo
Aries	Libra
Gemini	Sagittarius

Miscellaneous Things to Observe

Those born between May 22 and May 29 will have a better chance in speculation during the new Moon.

Those born between May 30 and June 6 will have better chance in speculation during the second quarter of the Moon.

Those born between June 7 and June 14 will have a better chance in speculation during the Moon.

Those born between June 15 and June 21 will have a better chance in speculation during the fourth quarter of the Moon.

According to the Science of Numerology, the Celestial Number of Gemini is 3. Mercury, the ruling planet of this Sign, has the numerical value of 4. Combining these two numbers we have 3 plus 4 which equals 7. The Number 7 is the key number for all persons born in Gemini. Bear this in mind on all occasions. When you buy a ticket of any sort see that the Serial Number has 7 as the predominating number. Room Number 7 in a hotel, a street number containing a 7 or several 7's. Horse number 7 in a race. Player number 7 in a sport game. Cards that total 7 in a card game. A 7 rolled with dice. 7 on a spin wheel, etc. are considered fortunate for you.

Any day of any month that totals 7 is considered fortunate for you, thus, the 18th and the 25th because these dates reduced to a single digit total 7. The days of the month that are best for speculation are the 7th, 16th, and 25th; however, you should engage in speculation only in your proper months or periods as explained below.

The proper hour for speculation is when your ruling planet is governing. Refer to your daily paper, almanac, or calendar to find the time of Sunrise, then count the hours after Sunrise. These hours are the same every week, month and year. Only the time of Sunrise changes.

Sunday: 3rd, 10th, 17th, 24th hour after Sunrise. Monday: 7th, 14th, 21st hour after Sunrise. Tuesday: 4th, 11th, 18th, hour after Sunrise. Wednesday: 1st, 8th, 15th, 22nd hour after Sunrise. Thursday: 5th, 12th, 19th hour after Sunrise. Friday: 2nd, 9th, 16th, 23rd hour after Sunrise. Saturday: 6th, 13th, 20th hour after Sunrise.

CANCER

All Cancer-born are inclined to take chances between October 24 and November 22. When you speculate in cooperation with others, it would be advisable that your partner is born under one of the following signs:

Pisces   Virgo
Taurus   Scorpio
Cancer   Capricorn

Miscellaneous Things to Observe

Those born between June 22 and June 29 will have better chances in speculation during the new Moon.

Those born between June 30 and July 7 will have better chances in speculation during the 2nd quarter of the Moon.

Those born between July 8 and July 17 will have better chances in speculation during the full Moon.

Those born between July 18 and July 23 will have better chances in speculation during the 4th quarter of the Moon.

According to the Science of Numberology, the Celestial Number of Cancer is 8. The Moon, the ruling planet of this sign, has the numerical value of 3. Combining these two numbers we have 8 plus 3, which equals 11. This must be reduced to a single digit; therefore, 1 plus 1 equals 2. The Number 2 is the key number for all persons born in Cancer. Bear this in mind on all occasions. When you buy a ticket of any sort, see that the serial number has the predominating number 2 in it. Room Number 2 in a hotel, a street number containing a 2 or several 2's, Horse number 2 in a race, player number 2 in a sport game, cards that total 2 in a card game, a 2 rolled with dice, 2 on a spin wheel, etc., are considered fortunate for you.

Any day of any month that totals 2 is considered fortunate for you, thus, 11th, 20th, 29th because these dates reduce to a single digit 2. Therefore, the days of the month that are best for speculation are 2nd, 11th, 20th, 29th. However, you should engage in speculation only in your proper months or periods as explained below.

The proper hour for speculation is when your ruling planet is governing. Refer to your daily paper, almanac or calendar to find the time of sunrise, then count the hours after sunrise. These hours are the same every week, month and year. Only the time of Sunrise changes.

Sunday: 4th, 11th, 18th hour after Sunrise. Monday: 1st, 8th, 15th, 22nd hour after Sunrise. Tuesday: 5th, 12th, 19th hour after Sunrise. Wednesday: 2nd, 9th, 16th, 23rd hour after Sunrise. Thursday: 6th, 13th, 20th hour after Sunrise. Friday: 3rd, 10th, 17th hour after Sunrise, also the 24th. Saturday: 7th, 14th, 21st hour after Sunrise.

LEO

All Leo born are inclined to take chances between November 23 and December 22. When you speculate in cooperation with others, it would be advisable that your partner be born under one of the following signs:

Aquarius	Leo
Aries	Libra
Gemini	Sagittarius

Miscellaneous Things to Observe

Those born between July 24 and July 31 will have better chances in speculation during the new Moon.

Those born between August 1 and August 7 will have better chances in speculation during the 2nd quarter of the Moon.

Those born between August 8 and August 16 will have better chances in speculation during the full Moon.

Those born between August 17 and August 23 will have better chances in speculation during the 4th quarter of the Moon.

According to the Science of Numerology, the Celestial Number of Leo is 5. The Sun, the ruling Planet of this sign has 9 as its numerical value. Combining these two numbers we have 5 plus 9, which equals 14. This must be reduced to a single digit; therefore, 1 plus 4 equals 5. The Number 5 is the key number for all persons born in Leo. Bear this in mind on all occasions. When you buy a ticket of any sort, see that 5 is the predominating number. Room number 5 in a hotel, a street number containing one or several 5's, horse number 5 in a race, player number 5 in a sport game, cards that total 5 in a card game, a 5 rolled with dice, 5 on a spin wheel, etc. are considered fortunate for you.

Any day of any month that totals 5 is considered fortunate for you, thus, the 14th or 23rd because these dates reduce to a single digit 5. Therefore, the days of the month that are best for speculation for you are the 5th, 14th, and 23rd. However, you should engage in speculation only in your proper periods as explained below.

The proper hour for speculation is when your ruling Planet is governing. Refer to your daily paper, almanac, or calendar to find the time of Sunrise, then count the hours after Sunrise. These hours are the same every week, month, and year. Only the time of Sunrise changes.

Sunday: 1st, 8th, 15th, 22nd hour after Sunrise. Monday: 5th, 12th, 19th hour after Sunrise. Tuesday: 2nd, 9th, 16th, 23rd hour after Sunrise. Wednesday: 6th, 13th, 20th hour after Sunrise. Thursday: 3rd, 10th, 17th, 24th hour after Sunrise. Friday: 7th, 14th, 21st hour after Sunrise. Saturday: 4th, 11th, 18th hour after Sunrise.

VIRGO

All Virgo-born are inclined to take chances from December 23 to January 20. When you speculate in cooperation with others, it would be advisable that your partner is born under one of the following signs:

Pisces	Virgo
Taurus	Scorpio
Cancer	Capricorn

Miscellaneous Things to Observe

Those born between August 24 and August 31 will have better chances in speculation during the new Moon.

Those born between September 1 and September 7 will have better chances in speculation during the 2nd quarter of the Moon.

Those born between September 8 and September 17 will have better chances in speculation during the full Moon.

Those born between September 18 and September 23 will have better chances in speculation during the 4th quarter of the Moon.

According to the Science of Numerology, the Celestial Number of Virgo is 8. Mercury, the ruling planet of this sign has the numerical value of 4. Combining these two numbers we have 8 plus 4 which equals 12. This number must be reduced to a single digit; therefore, 1 plus 2 equals 3. Number 3 is the key number for all persons born in Virgo. Bear this in mind for all occasions. When you buy a ticket of any sort, see that 3 is the predominating number if it contains a serial number. Room number 3 in a hotel, a street number containing a 3 or several 3's, horse number 3 in a race, player number 3 in a sport game, cards that total 3 in a card game, a 3 rolled with dice, 3 on a spin wheel, etc., are considered fortunate for you.

Any day of any month that totals 3 is considered fortunate for you, thus, 12th, 21st, 30th because these dates reduce to the single digit 3. Therefore, the days of the month that are best for speculation for you are 3rd, 12th, 21st, 30th. However, you should engage in speculation only in your proper periods as explained below.

The proper hour for speculation is when your ruling Planet is governing. Refer to your daily paper, almanac, or calendar to find the time of Sunriseq then count the hours after Sunrise. These hours are the same every week, month, and year. Only the time of Sunrise changes.

Sunday: 3rd, 10th, 17th, 24th hour after Sunrise. Monday: 7th, 14th, 21st hour after Sunrise. Tuesday: 4th, 11th, 18th hour after Sunrise. Wednesday: 1st, 8th, 15th, 22nd hour after Sunrise. Thursday: 5th, 12th, 19th, hour after Sunrise. Friday: 2nd, 9th, 16th, 23rd hour after Sunrise. Saturday: 6th, 13th, 20th hour after Sunrise.

LIBRA

All Libra-born are inclined to take chances between January 21 and February 19. When you speculate in cooperation with others, it would be advisable that your partner is born under one of the following Signs:

Aquarius   Leo
Aries   Libra
Gemini   Sagittarius

Miscellaneous Things to Observe

Those born between September 24 and September 30 will have better chances in speculation during the new Moon.

Those born between October 1 and October 7 will have better chances in speculation during the 2nd quarter of the Moon.

Those born between October 8 and October 17 will have better chances in speculation during the full Moon.

Those born between October 18 and October 23 will have better chances in speculation during the 4th quarter of the Moon.

According to the Science of Numerology, the Celestial Number of Libra is 6. Venus, the ruling planet of this Sign, has a numerical value of 9. Combining these two numbers we have 6 plus 9 which equals 15. This number must be reduced to a single digit; therefore, 1 plus 5 equals 6. The number 6 is the key number of all persons born under Libra. Bear this in mind at all times. When you buy a ticket of any sort see that the serial number has 6 as the predominating number. Room number 6 in a hotel, a street number containing a 6 or several 6's, horse number 6 in a race, player number 6 in a sport game, cards that total 6 in a card game, a 6 rolled with dice, 6 on a spin wheel, etc., are considered fortunate for you.

Any day of any month that totals 6 is considered fortunate for you, thus, 15th, 24th because these dates reduce to the single digit 6. Therefore, the days of the month that are best for speculation for you are 6th, 15th, 24th.

However, you should engage in speculation only in your proper periods as explained below.

The proper hour for speculation is when your ruling Planet is governing. Refer to your daily paper, almanac, or calendar to find the time of Sunrise, then count the hours after Sunrise. These hours are the same every week, month, and year. Only the time of Sunrise changes.

Sunday: 2nd, 9th, 16th, 23rd hour after Sunrise. Monday: 6th, 13th, 20th hour after Sunrise. Tuesday: 3rd, 10th, 17th, 24th hour after Sunrise. Wednesday: 7th, 14th, 21st hour after Sunrise. Thursday: 4th, 11th, 18th hour after Sunrise. Friday: 1st, 8th, 15th, 22nd hour after Sunrise. Saturday: 5th, 12th, 19th hour after Sunrise.

SCORPIO

All Scorpio-born are inclined to take chances from February 20 to March 20. When you speculate in cooperation with others, it would be advisable that your partner is born under one of the following Signs:

Capricorn	Cancer
Pisces	Virgo
Taurus	Scorpio

Miscellaneous Things to Observe:

Those born between October 24 and October 30 will have better chances in speculation during the new Moon.

Those born between October 31 and November 8 will have better chances in speculation during the 2nd quarter of the Moon.

Those born between November 9 and November 16 will have better chances in speculation during the full Moon.

Those born between November 17 and November 22 will have better chances in speculation during the fourth quarter of the Moon.

According to the Science of Numerology, the Celestial Number of Scorpio is 5. Pluto, the ruling planet of this Sign has the numerical value of 3. Combining these two numbers we have 5 plus 3 equals 8. Number 8 is the key number for all persons born in Scorpio. Bear this in mind on all occasions. When you buy a ticket of any sort, see that the serial number has 8 as the predominating number. Room number 8 in a hotel, a street number containing an 8 or several 8's, horse number 8 in a race, player number 8 in a sport game, cards that total 8 in a card game, an 8 rolled with dice, 8 on a spin wheel, etc. are considered fortunate for you.

Any day of the month that totals 8 is considered fortunate for you, thus, 17th and 26th, because these days reduce to the single digit 8. Therefore, the best days for speculation for you are 8th, 17th, and 26th. However, you should engage in speculation only in your proper periods as explained below.

The proper hour for speculation is when your ruling Planet is governing. Refer to your daily paper, almanac, or calendar to find the time of Sunrise, then count the hours after Sunrise. These hours are the same every week, month, and year. Only the time of Sunrise changes.

Sunday: 7th 14th, 21st hour after Sunrise. Monday: 4th, 11th, 18th hour after Sunrise. Tuesday: 1st, 8th, 15th 22nd hour after Sunrise. Wednesday: 5th 12th, 19th hour after Sunrise. Thursday: 2nd, 9th, 16th, 23rd hour after Sunrise. Friday: 6th, 13th, 20th hour after Sunrise. Saturday: 3rd, 10th, 17th, 24th hour after Sunrise.

SAGITTARIUS

All Sagittarius are inclined to take chances between March 21 and April 20. When you speculate in cooperation with others, it would be advisable that your partner is born under one of the following Signs:

Aquarius	Leo
Aries	Libra
Gemini	Sagittarius

Miscellaneous Things to Observe:

Those born between November 23 and November 29 will have better chances in speculation during the new Moon.

Those born between November 30 and December 7 will have better chances in speculation during the second quarter of the Moon.

Those born between December 8 and December 16 will have better chances in speculation during the full Moon.

Those born between December 17 and December 22 will have better chances in speculation during the 4th quarter of the Moon.

According to the Science of Numerology, the Celestial Number of Sagittarius is 8. Jupiter, the ruling planet of this Sign has the numerical value of 9. Combining these two numbers we have 8 plus 9 equals 17. Now this must be reduced to a single digit, thus 1 plus 7 equals 8. The key number for all persons born in Sagittarius is 8, the same as for Scorpio. There are only 9 digits, therefore some Zodiacal Signs have duplicate numbers since there are 12 Signs. Bear in mind at all times that 8 is your Celestial Number. When you buy a ticket of any sort, see that the serial number has a predominance of 8 in it. Room number 8 in a hotel, player number 8 in a sport game, horse number 8 in a race, a street number with an 8 or several 8's, cards that total 8 in a card game, an 8 rolled with dice, 8 on a spin wheel, etc. are considered fortunate for you.

Any day of any month that totals 8 is considered fortunate for you, thus, 17th and 26th, because these dates reduce to a single digit 8. Therefore, the best days for speculation for you are 8th, 17th, and 26th. However, you should speculate only in your proper periods as explained below.

The proper hour for speculation is when your ruling Planet is governing. Refer to your daily paper, almanac, or calendar to find the time of Sunrise, then count the hours after Sunrise. These hours are the same every week, month, and year. Only the time of Sunrise changes.

Sunday: 6th, 13th, 20th hour after Sunrise. Monday: 3rd, 10th, 17th, 24th hour after Sunrise. Tuesday: 7th, 14th, 21st hour after Sunrise. Wednesday: 4th, 11th, 18th hour after Sunrise. Thursday: 1st, 8th, 15th 22nd hour after

Sunrise. Friday: 5th, 12th, 19th hour after Sunrise. Saturday: 2nd, 9th, 16th, 23rd hour after Sunrise.

CAPRICORN

All Capricorn-born are inclined to take chances between April 21 to May 21. When you speculate in cooperation with others, it would be advisable that your partner is born under one of the following Signs:

Capricorn
Pisces
Taurus

Cancer
Virgo
Scorpio

Miscellaneous Things to Observe:

Those born between December 23 and December 30 will have better chances in speculation during the new Moon.

Those born between December 31 and January 6 will have better chances in speculation during the 2nd quarter of the Moon.

Those born between January 7 and January 14 will have better chances in speculation during the full Moon.

Those born between January 15 and January 20 will have better chances in speculation during the 4th quarter of the Moon.

According to the Science of Numerology, the Celestial Number of Capricorn 8, Saturn, the ruling planet of this Sign has the numerical value of 3. Combining these numbers we have: 8 plus 3 which equals 11. This must be reduced to a single digit, thus, 1 plus 1 equals 2. The key number for all persons born in Capricorn is 2, the same as for those born in Cancer. There are only nine digits; therefore, some Signs have duplicate numbers, since there are only twelve Signs. Bear in mind at all times that 2 is your Celestial Number. When you buy a ticket of any sort, see that the serial number has 2 predominating. Room number 2 in a hotel, player number 2 in a sport game, horse number 2 in a race, a street number with 2 or several 2's in it, cards that total 2 in a card game, a 2 rolled with dice, 2 on a spin wheel, etc. are considered fortunate for you.

Any day of any month that totals 2 is considered fortunate for you, thus, 11th, 29th, etc. because these reduce to the single digit 2. Therefore, the best days for speculation for you are 2nd, 11th, and 29th. However, you should speculate only in your proper periods as explained below.

The proper hour for speculation is when your ruling Planet is governing. Refer to your daily paper, almanac, or calendar to find the time of Sunrise, then count the hours after Sunrise. These hours are the same every week, month, and year. Only the time of Sunrise changes.

Sunday: 5th, 12th, 19th hour after Sunrise. Monday: 2nd, 9th, 23rd hour after Sunrise. Tuesday: 6th, 13th, 20th hour after Sunrise. Wednesday: 3rd, 10th, 17th, 24th hour after Sunrise. Thursday: 7th, 14th, 21st hour after Sunrise. Friday: 4th, 11th, 18th hour after Sunrise. Saturday: 1st, 10th, 17th, 22nd hour after Sunrise.

AQUARIUS

All Aquarius-born are inclined to take chances between May 22 and June 21. When you speculate in cooperation with others, it would be advisable that your partner is born under one of the following Signs:

Aquarius	Leo
Aries	Libra
Gemini	Sagittarius

Miscellaneous Things to Observe:

Those born between January 21 and January 28 will have better chances in speculation during the new Moon.

Those born between January 29 and February 6 will have better chances in speculation during the 2nd quarter of the Moon.

Those born between February 7 and February 14 will have better chances in speculation during the full Moon.

Those born between February 15 and February 19 will have better chances in speculation in the 4th quarter of the Moon.

According to the Science of Numerology, the Celestial Number of Aquarius is 8. Uranus, the ruling planet of this Sign has the numerical value of 4. Combining these two numbers we have 8 plus 4 which equals 12. This must be reduced to a single digit, thus 1 plus 2 equals 3. The key number for all persons born in Aquarius is 3, the same as Virgo. There are only 9 digits; therefore; some signs must have duplicate numbers, since there are twelve Signs. Bear in mind at all times that 3 is your Celestial Number. When you buy a ticket of any sort, see that the serial numbers have 3 as the predominating number. Room number 3 in a hotel, a street number containing a 3 or several 3's, horse number 3 in a race, player number 3 in a sport game, cards that total 3 in a card game, a 3 rolled with dice, 3 on a spin wheel, etc., are considered fortunate for you.

Any day of the month that totals 3 is considered fortunate for you thus, 12th, 21st, 30th, because these reduce to the single digit 3. Therefore, the best days for speculation for you are 3rd, 12th, 21st, and 30th. However, you should speculate only in your proper periods as explained below.

The proper hour for speculation is when your ruling Planet is governing. Refer to your daily paper, almanac, or calendar to find the time of Sunrise, then count the hours after Sunrise. These hours are the same every week, month, and year. Only the time of Sunrise changes.

Sunday: 3rd, 10th, 17th, 24th hour after Sunrise. Monday: 7th, 14th, 21st, hour after Sunrise. Tuesday: 4th, 11th, 18th hour after Sunrise. Wednesday: 5th, 12th, 19th hour after Sunrise. Thursday: 2nd, 9th, 16th, 23rd hour after Sunrise. Friday: 6th, 13th, 20th hour after Sunrise. Saturday: 1st, 8th, 15th, 22nd hour after Sunrise.

PISCES

All Pisces-born are inclined to take chances between June 22 and July 23. When you speculate in cooperation with others, it would be advisable that your partner is born under one of the following Signs:

Capricorn	Cancer
Pisces	Virgo
Taurus	Scorpio

Miscellaneous Things to Observe:

Those born between February 20 and February 26 will have better chances in speculation during the new Moon.

Those born between February 27 and March 5 will have better chances in speculation during the second quarter of the Moon.

Those born between March 6 and March 13 will have better chances in speculation during the full Moon.

Those born between March 14 and March 20 will have better chances in speculation during the 4th quarter of the Moon.

According to the Science of Numerology, the Celestial Number of Pisces is 8. Neptune, the ruling planet of this Sign has the numerical value of 5. Combining these two numbers we have, 8 plus 5 equals 13. This must be reduced to a single digit, thus, 1 plus 3 equals 4. Number 4 is the key number for all persons born in Pisces, the same as for those born in Aries. There are only nine digits; therefore, some Signs will have duplicate numbers since there are twelve Signs. Bear in mind that your key number is 4. When you buy a ticket of any sort, see that the serial number has 4 as the predominating number. Room number 4 in a hotel, a street number containing 4 or several 4's, horse number 4 in a race, player number 4 in a sport game, cards that total 4 in a card game, a 4 rolled with dice, 4 on a spin wheel, etc., are considered fortunate for you.

Any day of the month that totals 4 is considered fortunate for you, thus, 13th, 22nd, and the 31st of a month, because these days reduced to a single digit make 4. The days of the month that are best for speculation are 4th, 13th, 22nd, and 31st. However, you should engage in speculation only in your proper periods as explained below.

The proper hour for speculation is when your ruling Planet is governing. Refer to your daily paper, almanac, or calendar to find the time of Sunrise, then count the hours after Sunrise. These hours are the same every week, month, and year. Only the time of Sunrise changes.

Sunday: 2nd, 9th, 16th, 23rd hour after Sunrise. Monday: 5th, 12th, 19th hour after Sunrise. Tuesday: 6th, 13th, 20th hour after Sunrise. Wednesday: 3rd, 10th, 17th, 24th hour after Sunrise. Thursday: 7th, 14th, 21st hour after Sunrise. Friday: 1st, 8th, 15th, 22nd hour after Sunrise. Saturday: 4th, 11th, 18th hour after Sunrise.

Conclusions

You should look upon man as a part of Nature whose end lies in Heaven. In the Heavens you can see man, each part for itself, for man is made of Heaven. And the matter out of which man was created also indicates to you the pattern after which he was formed. External Nature molds the shape of internal Nature, and if external Nature vanishes, the inner Nature is also lost, for the outer is the mother of the inner. Thus, man is like the image of the four elements in a mirror, if the four elements fall apart, man is destroyed. If that which faces the mirror is at rest, then the image in the mirror is at rest, too. And so philosophy is nothing other than the knowledge and discovery of that which has its reflection in the mirror. And just as the image in the mirror gives no one any idea about his Nature and cannot be the object of cognition but is only a dead image, so is man, considered in himself; nothing can be learned from him alone.

For knowledge comes only from that outside being whose mirrored image he is.

Heaven is man, and man is Heaven, and all Men together are the one Heaven, and Heaven is nothing but one man. You must know this to understand why one place is this way and the other that way, why this is new and that is old, and why there are everywhere so many diverse things. But all this can be discovered by studying the Heavens.

Just as the firmament with all its constellations forms a whole in itself, so man in himself is a free and mighty firmament. And just as the firmament rests in itself and is not ruled by any creature, the firmament of man is not ruled by other creatures, but stands for itself and is free of all bonds. For there are two kinds of created things: Heaven and the Earth are one kind, man is of the other.

Everything that Astrological theory has profoundly fathomed by studying the Planetary Aspects and the Stars can also be applied to the firmament of the body.

The light of Nature in Man comes from the Stars, and his flesh and blood belong to the material elements. Thus two influences operate in man. One is that of the firmamental light, which includes wisdom, art, reason. The second influence emanates from matter, and it includes concupiescence, eating, drinking, and everything that relates to flesh and blood. Therefore, one must not ascribe to the Stars that which originates in the blood and flesh. For Heaven does not endow one with concupiscence or greed. From Heaven come only wisdom, art, and reason.

Nature emits a light, and by its radiance She can be known. But in man there is still another light apart from that which is innate in Nature. It is the light through which man experiences, learns, and fathoms the Supernatural. Those who seek in the light of Nature speak from knowledge of Nature, but those who seek in the light of man speak from knowledge of Super-Nature. Man is more than Nature; he is Nature, but he is also a Spirit; he is also a Soul, and he has the properties of all three. If he walks in Nature, he serves Nature; if he walks in the Spirit, he serves the Spirit; if he walks with the Soul, he serves the Soul. The first is given to the body, the others are given to the Mind and are its jewel.

Thus, Nature is subject to man; she belongs to him as to one of her blood; he is her child, her fruit, which was made of her in the body of the elements and the Ethereal body.

Where else can Heaven be rediscovered if not in Man?

Since it acts from us, it must also be in us. Therefore, it knows our prayer even before we have uttered it, for it is closer to our hearts than to our words.

Thoughts are free and are subject to no rule. On them rests the freedom of Man, and they tower above the light of Nature. For thoughts give birth to a creative force that is neither elemental nor sidereal. Thoughts create a new Heaven, a new firmament, a new source of energy, from which new arts flow. When a man undertakes to create something, he establishes a new Heaven, as it were, and from it the work that he desires to create flows into him.

Astrology is an indispensable art; it should rightly be held in high esteem and studied earnestly and thoroughly. For it teaches each man the condition and disposition of his soul, his heart, his thoughts; it teaches him whether they are false or righteous and good; whether they are malignant or not. And it teaches how the hour of conception affects the child's fate, although it is less important than the conjuncture of the Stars at the time of his birth.

The Astrologer should be able to find his bearings in the firmament with the help of his Natural reason in a Natural way, as a philosopher finds his way among the things of Nature which derive from the elements. The firmament lies imprisoned in the hands of the Supreme Mover. What this hand intends to do with it is not hidden to the Astrologer.

Know there are two kinds of Stars — the Heavenly and the Earthly, the Stars of folly and the Stars of wisdom. And just as there are two worlds, a Little World and a Great World, and just as the great one rules over the little one, so the Stars of the macrocosm rule over and govern Man.

In the Stars there dwells reason, wisdom, ruse, strife, and weapons, just as they do in us Men. For we originate in them; they are our parents, and from them we have received our reason, wisdom, and strife. We have received all these from the Stars, and, accordingly, these same things are in the Stars with the sole difference that in us Men they become material, corpeal, visible, while in the Stars they are invisible, subtle, Spiritual. But let no one fancy that the wisdom and reason, which we have received from Heaven, come directly from the Soul. They do not come directly from It, but exist in us Men as a reflection of the corresponding qualities of the macrocosm, the Great Creature. But the wisdom which comes to us from the Soul stands above the other and is stronger than the Heavens and the Stars.

Man's wisdom is in no way subjugated, and is no one's slave; it has not renounced or surrendered its freedom. Therefore, the Stars must obey man and be subject to him, and not he to the Stars. Even if he is a child of Saturn and if Saturn has overshadowed his birth, he can still escape Saturn's influence; he can master Saturn and become a child of the Sun.

The wise man is the man who lives by Divine Wisdom. The wise man rules over both bodies — the sidereal and the material. Man must serve both! He must go the ways of each in order to fulfill the Law and live in harmony with Nature and with the Divine Spirit. He must not prefer the mortal body and its reason to the eternal image, nor must he reject this image for the sake of the animal body. The wise man lives after the image of the Soul and is not guided by the ways of the world. And he who imitates the Soul will conquer the Stars.

452

APPENDIX

THE HEBREW ALPHABET

A

ALEPH. Man himself as a collective unity, a principal, the lord and master of the earth. The universal man, and the human genre. Esoterically, Unity, the central point, the abstract principle of a thing expresses its power, stability, and continuity; the superlative, a kind of an article, as a prefix rendering the meaning more serious and enhancing its significance.

Its numerical number is 1.

B

BETH. The mouth as man's organ of speech, his interior, and his habitation; it denotes virility, paternal protection, and interior action and movement. It is the integral and indicative article of the Hebrew language.

This letter in conjunction with the one preceding it — Aleph — forms all ideas of progress, of graduated advance, the passage from one state to another: locomotion.

Its numerical number is 2.

G

GIMEL. The throat and everything that is hollow. It denotes every kind of opening, outlet, canal, and manner of things concave, hollow, and profound. It expresses organic covering and serves to produce all derived ideas of the bodily organism and its actions.

Its numerical number is 3.

D

DALETH. Signifies breast, bosom. It is the emblem of the universal quaternary, that is, the origin of all physical existence. Symbolically, every nourishing substance, and abundance of possessions.

It expresses division and things divisible. Chaldaic: an article of a very distinctive nature.

Its numerical number is 4.

H

HAI. Everything that vitalizes, i.e., air, life, and being. It is the symbol of universal life, and represents the breath of man, the spirit, and the soul. Everything that vivifies. Life and the abstract idea of being. It is an article especially emphasizing and giving prominence to objects and persons.

Its numerical number is 5.

W

WAW. Signifies the eye of man and becomes the symbol of light; it also represents the ear and becomes the symbol of the sound of the air; the wind. In its quality as a consonant, it is the emblem of water and represents the taste and the appetite. As a grammatical sign is is considered to be the image of mystery most profound and most incomprehensible, the symbol of the knot that unites, and of the point which separates Being and Non-being.

Its numerical value is 6.

Z

ZAIN. Signifies whistling and applies to all piercing noises which penetrate the air and reflect themselves in it. As a symbol it is represented by a stroke, a dash, or an arrow. Everything that tends to a given point. As a grammatical sign it is the abstract image of a tie which connects things with one another.

Its numerical number is 7.

CH

CHETH. Signifies the principle of vital aspiration and is the symbol of elementary existence. It represents the field of man, his labor, and everything that requires an effort on his part; his care, his solicitude. As a grammatical sign of life absolute and the sign of relative life. It also is the image of equilibrium and of equality, and attaches itself to all ideas of effort and of normal action.

Its numerical number is 8.

T

TETH. Signifies an asylum, a refuge, which man provides for himself for his protection. As a grammatical sign it denotes resistance and shelter. Its esoteric meaning is that of a hiding wall erected to guard something precious and a watch over a dear object in the midst of danger.

Its numerical number is 9.

J

YOD. Signifies all manifested power. It represents the hand of man, his pointing finger. As a grammatical sign it denotes potential manifestation in contra-distinction to actual, and also intellectual duration and eternity. As a consonant it is of inferior value and means only material duration. Plato thought it designated everything tender or delicate.

Its numerical number is 10.

Q

KAAW. Signifies every subject that is hollow in general and the half-closed hand of man in particular. As a grammatical sign it is the symbol of reflection and assimilation and typifies the assimilative nature and the passing life.

It is a kind of mold, receiving and communicating indifferently all forms. The movement which it expresses is that of similitude and of analogy.

Its numerical number is 20.

L

LAMES. Signifies extension. As a symbolical image it represents the arm of man and the wing of a bird; everything that extends or elevates itself, displaying its proper nature. It denotes a movement of extension, of direction, expressing reunion, coincidence, dependence, and possession.

Its numerical number is 30.

M

MEM. Signifies woman. It is the symbolical image of man's mother and companion. Everything that is fruitful and formative. Employed as a grammatical sign it denotes maternity, external, and passive action. Placed at the beginning of words it expresses that which is local and plastic; while at the end, it becomes the collective sign. It develops a being in infinite space as much as its nature permits, or it unites through abstraction one or two of the same species. It is the extractive article and is used to designate an action divided in its essence, or something taken out from a number of similar things.

Its numerical number is 40.

N

MM. Signifies the son of man, every being that is individualized and distinctive. At the end of a work it denotes augmentation and extension. It has the double virtue of recoiling upon itself and of spreading out. At the commencement of a word it expresses the former while as a final it signifies the latter.

Its numerical number is 50.

S

SAMECH. Signifies to hiss. It is considered to be the type of a bow and esoterically represents the great cosmic bow, the string of which hisses in the hands of mankind. As a grammatical sign it is the circular movement having a definite relation to the limited circumference of every sphere.

Its numerical number is 60.

E

AIM. Signifies hearing. It represents the ear of man and its interior parts. It is the symbol of all noises and indistinguishable sounds. Everything that is devoid of harmony. It typifies the cavity of the chest.

As a grammatical sign it stands for the material sense, the image of emptiness and nothingness. It is used to describe everything crooked, low, and perverse.

Its numerical number is 70.

P

PEI. Signifies the open mouth. It is the symbol of expression through which man makes himself known in the outer world, hence the literal meaning, mouth. The Second Race of Man. The outlet. The outward and visible means for the Spirits manifestation.

Its numerical number is 80.

TZ

TZADDI. Signifies the dart or fish hook. Esoterically related to accomplished ends and the later Third Race. Also related to the double hermaphrodite Caduceus.

The sign of protection and signifies guidance from above. God's favor shown to the Disciple on the Path.

Its numerical number is 90.

Q

Q-OPH or COO-EPH. Signifies nature's submerged stratum. Literally, the APE. Related to the subliminal consciousness. The evolutionary stage which is behind us.

Its numerical number is 100.

R

REISCH. Signifies individual movement, determination, and progress. Literally, means head. It is the symbol of the Fifth Race. Indicates independence, self-help, self-initiated endeavor. Also, direction, a center of generating motion starting of its own accord.

Its numerical number is 200.

SH

SHEIN. Signifies light movement and sweet sounds. Esoterically it symbolizes that part of a bow from which the arrow darts hiss. It is the sign of relative duration and of the movement appertaining to it.

At the commencement of a verb it is given a double power of conjunction.

Its numerical number is 300.

TAU

TAW. Signifies reciprocity. The ancient Egyptians regarded

this letter as a symbol of the universal soul.

It stands for sympathy and for perfection, of which it is the emblem.

Its numerical number is 400.

The uses to which the science of the Hieroglyphical meaning of the Hebrew letters can be put are manifold. First and foremost, by its aid the student can re-interpret the Scriptures for himself by analyzing each word and then synthesizing the meanings of the letters entering into the composition of the word he wishes to understand esoterically.

The result which this process will yield to the really serious student will more than reward him for his initial trouble. It will open his eyes to see wondrous things in what hitherto have been meaningless Shiboleths and empty phrases. Every Hebrew word thus examined will reveal some truth of the inner life which will serve to guide the student in his quest for knowledge.

Final Letters.	Figure.	Names.	Corresponding Letters.	Numerical Power.
Mother	א 1	Aleph	- - -	1
Double	ב 2	Baith	B	2
		Vaith	V	- -
	ג 3	Gimmel	G	3
	ד 4	Daleth	D	4
	ה 5	Hay	H	5
	ו 6	Wav	W	6
Single	ז 7	Zayin	Z	7
	ח 8	Cheth	Ch	8
	ט 9	Teth	T	9
	י 10	Yood	Y	10
Double	כ 11	Caph	C	20
		Chaph	Ch	- -
Single	ל 12	Lamed	L	30
Mother	מ 13	Mem	M	40
	נ 14	Noon	N	50
Single	ס 15	Samech	S	60
	ע 16	Ayin	- - -	70
Double	פ 17	Pay	P	80
		Phay	Ph	- -
Single	צ 18	Tzadè	Tz	90
	ק 19	Koof	K	100
Double	ר 20	Raish	R	200
Mother	ש 21	Sheen	Sh	300
		Seen	S	- -
Double	ת 22	Tav	T	400
		Thav	Th	- -

The Hebrew Alphabet and numerical values.
Note the spelling is different from that listed
in the appendix. There are many acceptable
spellings of the Hebrew letters.

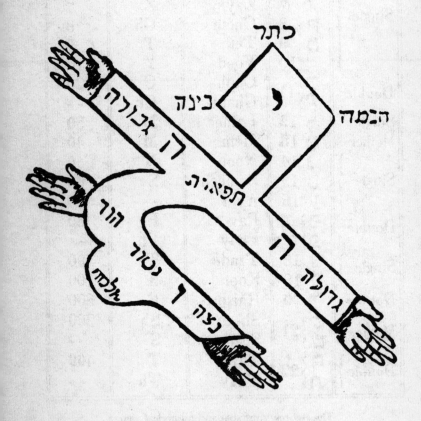

Kabbalistic Ideogram of the Letter Aleph.

METHODS OF PREDICTION

Classification	Basis	Characteristics	Applicability
Intuitive	Revelation	Transcendental inspiration and absolute faith in the validity of the prediction	Religious Prophecy
	Inspiration	Sudden realization of hidden connections	Many discoveries and inventions
Deductive	Verifiable laws	Deduction of particular predictions from a general principle	Science, Sociology
Inductive	Individual experience	Unsystematic deductions by false analogy	Work, particularly crafts
	Experiment	Generalization of systematized, individual investigations	Science, Technology
	Statistics	Conclusions from aggregates according to probability theory	Meteorology, medicine, public opinion polls, economic research, insurance, government
Activist	Individual action	Predictions of the results of voluntary behavior	Everyday life
Activist	Planning	Long-range and complex objectives, creation of new conditions	Industry, public finance, armament
Imaginary	Creative	Utopias, science fiction	Literature, Art
	Unconscious	Visions, generally based on wish fulfillment and past events	Dreams, Visions, Hallucinations

THE KABBALISTIC MANIFESTATIONS AND
THE ASTRAL WORLD (AFTER PAPUS)

1. Kether corresponds to the Empyrean.
2. Chokma corresponds to the Primum Mobile.
3. Binah corresponds to the Firmament.
4. Chesed corresponds to the Saturn.
5. Geburah corresponds to the Jupiter.
6. Tiphereth corresponds to the Mars.
7. Netzach corresponds to the Sun.
8. Hod corresponds to the Venus.
9. Jesod corresponds to the Mercury.
10. Malkuth corresponds to the Moon.

THE ANCIENT PSYCHIC AND OCCULT SCIENCES

AEROMANCY: The divination of the future from the Air and sky. This goes beyond the range of weather prognostications and concentrates upon cloud shapes, comets, spectral formations, and other phenomena not normally visible in the Heavens. Even in modern times such visions have caused much speculation and consternation among human viewers.

ALCHEMY: The science of transmuting the base metals into gold or silver with the aid of a mysterious Psychic substance terms the "Philosophers' Stone." Alchemists claim to prolong human life indefinitely by means of a secret life elixir.

ALECTRYOMANCY: A bird, a black hen or white gamecock, is allowed to pick grains of corn from a circle of letters, thus forming words with Prophetic significance. Another method is to recite the letters of the alphabet, making note of those at which the cock crows.

ALEUROMANCY: This requires slips with answers to questions which are rolled in balls of dough and baked. These are mixed up and one is chosen at random and presumably will be fulfilled. Our modern "fortune cookies" are a survival of this Ancient ritual.

ALOMANCY: The divination by salt, which accounts for some of our modern superstitions.

ALPHITOMANCY: A form which utilizes special cakes which are digestible by persons with a clear conscience, but are distasteful to all others.

ANTHROPOMANCY: An Ancient and long-outlawed form of human sacrifice.

APANTOMANCY: A method which forecasts from chance
   meetings with animals, birds, and other creatures. It
   may be said to include modern omens of the "black
   cat" variety. The classic was the founding of Mexico
   City on the spot where Ancient Aztec soothsayers saw
   an eagle flying from a cactus and carrying a live snake.
   This omen represents the Mexican coat-of-arms of
   today.

ARITHMANCY or ARITHMOMANCY: The Ancient form
   of Numerology that applies chiefly to divination
   through numbers and letter values, as discussed in the
   chapter on Numerology.

ASTRAGYROMANCY: This was divination with dice
   bearing letters and numbers. It has developed into the
   modern Fortune Telling by Dice.

ASTROLOGY: The Ancient Science of the Stars was
   basically a form of divination, as persons who could
   foretell changes in the heavens were capable of
   predicting the smaller affairs of mankind. Modern
   Astrology makes no extravagant claims, but has retained
   enough of the old tradition to become a fascinating
   subject and it is treated in this volume.

AUGURY: The general art of divination, covering many
   forms included in this list, and applying chiefly to
   interpretations of the future based on various signs and
   omens.

AUSTROMANCY: The divination by a study of the winds.

AXIOMANCY: This requires an ax or hatchet which answers
   questions by its quivers, or points out the direction
   taken by robbers or other miscreants.

BELOMANCY: One of the most Ancient types of divination
   and requires the tossing or balancing of arrows.

BIBLIOMANCY: This involves divination by books.

BOTANOMANCY: This requires the burning of tree branches and leaves to gain the desired answers.

BUMPOLOGY: A strictly modern term which is a popular nickname for Phrenology.

CAPNOMANCY: The study of the smoke rising from a fire and is performed in varied ways.

CARTOMANCY: Fortune telling with cards.

CATOPTROMANCY: An early form of crystal gazing, utilizing a mirror which was turned to the Moon to catch the lunar rays.

CAUSIMOMANCY: This involves divination from objects placed in a fire. If they fail to ignite, or burn slowly, it is a good omen.

CEPHALOMANCY: Divinatory procedures using the skull or head of a donkey or goat.

CERAUNOSCOPY: Draws omens from the study of thunder and lightning.

CEROSCOPY: A fascinating. form of divination in which melted wax is poured into cold water, forming bubbles which are interpreted.

CHIROMANCY: The divination from the lines of a person's hand.

CHIROGNOMY: The study of traits through general hand formation.

CLAIRAUDIENCE ("Clear hearing") and CLAIRVOYANCE ("clear seeing"): These are twin subjects which have come under intensive study in modern Parapsychology. This science regards them as forms of extrasensory perception.

CLEROMANCY: A form of lot casting, akin to divination with dice, but simply using pebbles or other odd objects, often of different colors instead of marked cubes.

CLIDOMANCY (CLEIDOMANCY): This is worked with a dangling key which answers questions.

COSCINOMANCY: This is similar, utilizing a hanging sieve.

CRITOMANCY: The study of barley cakes in hopes of drawing omens from them.

CROMNIOMANCY: This finds significance from onion sprouts.

CRYSTALLOMANCY: A term for Crystal gazing.

CYCLOMANCY: Pertains to divination from a turning wheel.

DACTYLOMANCY: The early form of Radiesthesia, where a dangling ring indicates words and numbers by its swings.

DAPHNOMANCY: This requires listening to the laurel branches crackling in an open fire; the louder the crackle, the better the omen.

DEMONOMANCY: Divination through the aid of demons.

DENDROMANCY: This is associated with both the oak and mistletoe.

GASTROMANCY: An Ancient form of ventriloquism, with the voice lowered to a sepulchral tone as though issuing from the ground. Prophetic utterances were delivered in a trance-like state.

GELOSCOPY: This was the art of divination from the tone of someone's laughter.

GENETHLIALOGY: This was the calculation of the future from the influence of the stars at birth.

GEOMANCY: Occult practice which began with tracing figures in the ground and later was extended to include random dots made with a pencil. These were interpreted according to accepted designs, a predecessor of our modern doodles.

GRAPHOLOGY: The analysis of character through one's handwriting, and it was studied in Ancient times and given a Psychic significance.

GYROMANCY: This was performed by persons walking in a circle marked with letters until they became dizzy and stumbled at different points, thus, they were "spelling out" a prophecy.

HALOMANCY: Another term for Alomancy, or divination by salt.

HARUSPICY, HIEROMANCY, HIEROSCOPY: These all had to do with observing objects of Ancient scarifice and drawing prophetic conclusions.

HIPPOMANCY: This was a form of divination from the stamping and neighing of horses.

HOROSCOPY: Pertains to the casting of an Astrological Horoscope.

HYDROMANCY: Divination by water and covers a wide range of lesser auguries, such as the color of water, its ebb and flow, or the ripples produced by pebbles dropped into a pool, an odd number being good, an even number, bad. Our modern "tea leaf" and "coffee ground" readings date from this.

ICHYOMANCY: This involved fish as factors in divination.

LAMPADOMANCY: This signified omens from lights or torches.

LECANOMANCY: This involved a basin of water in the divinatory process.

LIBRANOMANCY: Requires incense as a means of interpreting omens.

LITHOMANCY: Utilizes precious stones of various colors. In its more modern form of divination, these are scattered on a flat surface, and whichever reflects the light most fulfills the omen. Blue means good luck soon. Green means realization of a hope. Red means happiness in love or marriage. Yellow means disaster or betrayal. Purple means a period of sadness. Black or gray means misfortune. Colored beads may be used instead of jewels for this purpose.

MARGARITOMANCY: A procedure utilizing pearls which were supposed to bounce upward beneath an inverted pot if a guilty person approached.

METAGNOMY: A comparatively modern form of intuitive divination covering past or distant scenes and future events while viewed during a hypnotic trance.

METEOROMANCY: This lists the omens dependent on meteors and similar phenomena.

METOPOSCOPY: The reading of character from the lines of the forehead. It is based on Astrology and has factors akin to Palmistry. Yet, it belongs under the head of Physiognomy.

MOLYBDOMANCY: Draws mystic inferences from the varied hissings of molten lead.

MYOMANCY: Concerns rats and mice, the cries they give, and the destruction they cause, all as prophetic tokens.

NUMEROLOGY: This is of Ancient origins, but is a modern form for interpreting names and dates in terms of vital numbers. All of these are indicative of individual traits.

OCULOMANCY: A form of divination from the eyes.

OLINOMANCY: Utilizes wine in determining omens.

ONEIROMANCY: The interpretation of dreams.

ONOMANCY: Answers the question of "what's in a name" by giving meanings for names of persons and things. But it has comparatively little importance as a modern divinatory art.

ONOMANTICS: A development of Onomancy and is applied to personal names. Some of these names are obvious in meaning, as Hope, or Victor. Other names are easily translatable, as Sophia for wisdom, or Leo for lion-hearted. Others have been extended or elaborated, but their basic meanings may be found in many dictionaries or standard reference works.

ONYCHOMANCY: A study of the fingernails in the sunlight, looking for any significant symbols that can be traced. ONYOMANCY is similar and somewhat more practical, being an interpretation of personal characteristics from the nails as a minor phase of Palmistry.

OOMANTIA and OOSCOPY: These are terms applied to Ancient methods of divination by eggs.

OPHIOMANCY: This covers divination from serpents.

ORNISCOPY AND ORNITHOMANCY: These are concerned with omens gained by watching the flight of different birds.

OVOMANCY: Another form of egg divination.

PALMISTRY: One of the most interesting of the Psychic Sciences and has reached a high state of modern development. Long known as the "language of the hand," it interprets the lines and general formations of the hands according to well-accepted rules.

PEGOMANCY: Requires spring water or bubbling fountains for its divinations.

PESSOMANCY: This involves pebbles.

PHRENOLOGY: Deals in head formations and is a modern form of Psychic Science.

PHRENOPATHY: A similar subject incorporating hypnotism.

PHRENOLOGY: A similar subject incorporating hypnotism.

PHYLLORHODOMANCY: An intriguing type of divination dating from Ancient Greece. It consists of slapping rose petals against the hand and judging the success of a venture according to the loudness of the sound.

PHYSIOGNOMY: This is highly modern in its treatment and deals with character analysis through physical appearance of the features.

RECOGNITION: An inner knowledge of things to come, which may lead to Prediction, which is the announcement of such future events.

PREMONITION: This is a foreboding of the future.

PROGNOSTICATION: This goes into specific details or the greater art of Prophecy. It connotes inspired knowledge of important future events with their fulfillment certain.

PSYCHOGRAPHY: A form of mysterious writing, usually of a divinatory type.

PSYCHOMETRY: The faculty of gaining impressions from a physical object, either regarding its owner or the history of the object itself.

PYROMANCY and PYROSCOPY: Forms of divination by fire, wherein powdered substances are thrown on the flames; if these kindle quickly, it is a good omen.

RHABDOMANCY: Divination by means of a wand or stick. It is of Ancient origin; much of its history is obscure, but it was the forerunner of the divining rod.

RHAPSODOMANCY: Performed by opening a book of poetry and reading a passage at random, hoping it will prove to be an omen.

SCIOMANCY: A term for divination gained through Spirit aid.

SIDEROMANCY: The burning of straws on a hot iron and studying the figures thus formed, along with the flames and smoke.

SORILEGE: The casting of lots in hope of a good omen. It has many phases and variations dating from antiquity and is still practiced today.

SPODOMANCY: Provides omens from cinders or soot.

STICHOMANCY: Another form of opening a book, hoping a random passage will give inspiration. This is something many people follow today.

STOLISOMANCY: Draws omens from oddities in the way people dress.

SYCOMANCY: Performed by writing messages on tree leaves; the slower they dry, the better the omen. A more modern way is to write questions on slips of paper, roll them up, and hold them in a strainer above a steaming pot. Whichever paper unrolls first will be the one answered. A blank slip should always be included in the group.

TEPHRAMANCY: The seeking of messages in ashes. Tree bark is often burned for this purpose, and the diviner looks for symbols in the ashes as with tea leaves.

TIROMANCY: An odd form of divination utilizing cheese.

XYLOMANCY: Divination from pieces of wood. Some diviners pick them up at random, interpreting them according to their shape or formation. Others put pieces of wood upon a fire and note the order in which they burn, thus forming conclusions as to their omens, good or bad.